D1141760

Aspects of the Iron Age in Central Southern Britain

Edited by Barry Cunliffe and David Miles

CHESTER COLLEGE

ACC. No.	DEPT.
9115 5701	Q

CLASS No.

936.2202 CUN

LIBRARY

C

Copyright © Oxford University Committee for Archaeology and
individual authors 1984

Published by the Oxford University Committee for Archaeology
Institute of Archaeology
36 Beaumont Street
Oxford

ISBN 0 947816 02 X

Typesetting by Oxford Publishing Services, Oxford
Printed by Information Printing, Eynsham, Oxford

Contents

Contributors

Tim Allen. Oxford Archaeological Unit, 46 Hythe Bridge Street, Oxford.

Owen Bedwin. Archaeology Section, Essex County Council, Planning Department, Globe House, New Street, Chelmsford, CM1 1LF.

Barry Cunliffe. Institute of Archaeology, 36 Beaumont Street, Oxford, OX1 2PG.

Robert Ehrenreich. Institute of Archaeology, 36 Beaumont Street, Oxford, OX1 2PG.

Andrew P. Fitzpatrick. Department of Archaeology, University of Durham, 46 Saddler Street, Durham, DH1 3NU.

Annie Grant. 26 Beckwith Road, London, SE24.

Richard Hingley. 30 St. John Street, Oxford.

Martin Jones. Department of Archaeology, University of Durham, 46 Saddler Street, Durham, DH1 3NU.

George Lambrick. Oxford Archaeological Unit, 46 Hythe Bridge Street, Oxford.

David Miles. Oxford Archaeological Unit, 46 Hythe Bridge Street, Oxford.

Peter Northover. Department of Metallurgy and Science of Materials, Parks Road, Oxford.

Simon Palmer. Oxford Archaeological Unit, 46 Hythe Bridge Street, Oxford.

Mark Robinson. University Museum, Parks Road, Oxford.

Chris Salter. Department of Metallurgy and Science of Materials, Parks Road, Oxford.

Lyn Sellwood. Institute of Archaeology, 36 Beaumont Street, Oxford, OX1 2PG.

Foreword

by Barry Cunliffe and David Miles

On 26–27 March, 1983, the Department of External Studies of the University of Oxford organized a weekend conference entitled *Wessex and the Thames Valley in the Iron Age*, jointly with the Institute of Archaeology and the Oxford Archaeological Unit. The aim of the weekend was to present a range of new work most of which had been generated either directly or indirectly by two major research programmes concerned with Iron Age society and economy, the one undertaken by the Oxford Unit in the Upper Thames Valley, the other by the Institute of Archaeology in Wessex. To broaden the scope a little additional speakers were invited to contribute.

In the event the speakers offered a great deal that was new while discussion proved to be lively. The general view of the participants was that the conference formed a suitable basis around which to create a publication. The present volume contains all the major papers given, each of which has been extended and entirely rewritten, to which several new contributions have been added. It fairly reflects the current state of research in the various fields selected for treatment but it must be stressed that we are dealing here only with those aspects of the subject where, it seems to us, there have been significant advances in recent years, and where we have been able to persuade busy researchers to take the time to present their results.

Wessex and the Upper Thames Valley offer a range of interesting contrasts both in the actual nature of the Iron Age settlement and in the manner in which research has been organized over the last fifteen years or so. In the Upper Thames Valley virtually all the significant work has been in the hands of the Oxford Archaeological Unit. Sites have been very carefully selected for excavation, from among those threatened with destruction, according a structured research design. Emphasis has been placed on large-scale excavation and systematic sampling of a variety of well-preserved settlement types. Biological analysis has been particularly successful at revealing the relationships between settlements and their landscapes and between farming communities. The constraints of rescue archaeology mean that many of these sites are on the gravel terraces. However, fieldwork projects on the Thames Valley floodplain and the limestone uplands have gone some way to counteract the excavation bias and show some directions for future research. Wessex and Sussex together form a much larger area and it is only to be expected that research has been more fragmented. In Sussex, the Sussex Archaeological Unit has pursued a programme of examining the smaller enclosures, thought to be Iron Age, with a particular emphasis on the coastal plain which hitherto has been somewhat neglected. In Wessex there have been two relevant research designs. The Wessex Archaeological

Trust has pursued a programme of research and excavation into the industrial sites of the Isle of Purbeck — a project nearing completion which is soon to be published. Meanwhile the Institute of Archaeology at Oxford is engaged in a long-term programme concerned with social and economic change in Wessex. The project is currently focussed on the large-scale excavation of a hillfort (Danebury, Hants.) and two ports-of-trade (Hengistbury Head, Dorset and Mount Batten, Devon) and is generating data for several individual research topics. In addition to this Wessex has been fortunate to receive, in a more ad hoc manner, the attention of a number of other archaeologists working on Iron Age sites.

A wealth of new information has been generated: it is only to be regretted that so little has been published (with the notable exception of projects undertaken by the Central Excavation Unit).

Alongside these long-term research projects, instigated by various organizations, there has been much individual research focussed mainly on environmental and technical problems. Some of these themes are reflected among the papers presented here.

It is notoriously difficult for those closely involved in ongoing programmes of research to stand back and attempt to assess the future but a little crystal gazing, no matter how imperfect, may not be out of phase. Many of the questions we are now asking require large, well-collected data-sets to enable even the germs of answers to be formulated. In consequence the last 15 years has seen a major change of strategy away from small-scale excavations to far larger scale involvement often leading to the total or near total excavation of settlement units. Those carrying out such projects are only too well aware how time-consuming and costly this kind of work is particularly if all the data recovered are to be properly processed and published. Against the background of diminishing resources and rising costs it is doubtful if many new programmes of extensive area excavations will be possible in the foreseeable future. Nonetheless the absence of any significant work in hillforts in the Upper Thames region and the fact that no Cotswold settlement has been properly sampled, let alone excavated on a satisfactory scale, means that we must contemplate some carefully selected programmes of area excavation in the future if our understanding is to advance further in the Oxford–Cotswolds region. But what has been done has laid a valuable base on which to build and when the results of work completed have been fully published and assessed it ought to be possible to design a new generation of research, involving a suite of sampling strategies, far less expensive to pursue than our current work. Could it be, therefore, that our conference marks the end of one era and the beginning of another?

The conceit, so typical of conference organizers, may yet prove to be justified.

The editors have been helped in many ways by many friends and colleagues. In particular, they would like to thank Professor Sheppard Frere for his very careful reading of the texts, Nick Pollard for producing copy proofs of all the line illustrations and Lynda Smithson for acting as a sub-editor for the project.

Landscape and Environment of Central Southern Britain in the Iron Age

Mark Robinson

Introduction

The first millennium BC was a period of considerable and rapid environmental change in Britain. The impact of man on the landscape in the Neolithic was drastic, but it was not until the Iron Age that his effects became general over much of the British Isles, with an open man-made agricultural landscape replacing the formerly predominant vegetational cover of semi-natural woodland. The first millennium BC is also regarded as a period when the climate became colder and wetter than previously, with perhaps a greater climatic change than any which had occurred since the warming of the climate at the end of the last glaciation.

Most of the chapters in this book are concerned with the chalk and coastal areas of Hampshire, and/or the Upper Thames Valley, so the first section is a survey of the landscape and environment of these regions and their surrounds. In order to place the regional developments in a broader context, the second part of this chapter considers the major environmental changes occurring over much of the British Isles in the first millenium BC.

The Chalk and Coastal Areas of Hampshire

This region consists of the Tertiary sands and clays of the Hampshire Basin along the south coast rising northwards to the chalk of the Hampshire Uplands. To the east it is bounded by the anticline of the Weald: a SE continuation of the chalk to the coast (the South Downs) and a N–S belt of Upper Greensand. The northern boundary is the westernmost extension of the sands and clays of the London Basin, from which the chalk slope of the Berkshire Downs rises further to the north. In geological terms, the western boundary is arbitrary, the chalk continuing westwards into Dorset and Salisbury Plain.

Along the south coast is a series of estuaries formed from drowned valleys. Flowing into Southampton Water, the largest of these estuaries, are the rivers Test and Itchen, which together drain much of the chalk in the region. The chalk landscape is of undulating hills and valleys, often with steep scarps and dry valley-bottoms. The chalk mostly ranges in altitude between 50–110 m OD, with a few hilltops in the west of the region and a more general area in the east rising to 150 m or more.

There is an extensive covering of sands and gravels along the coast, extending about 5 km inland, but otherwise the drift geology is limited. The valley-bottoms of the Test and Itchen are narrow and do not have the wide gravel terraces and broad floodplains which characterise the Upper Thames Valley. Clay-with-flints occurs on the chalk hilltops, especially over the high ground in the east of the region, but the degree of cover is not as great as on the chalk of the Berkshire Downs and Chilterns. Poor acidic soils have tended to develop on some of the Tertiary and later sands and gravels, for example in the area of the New Forest. The chalk tends to have thin calcareous soils, sometimes with a loessic component, on the slopes and deeper loams in the valley bottoms, but the chalkland soils of today are very much the product of several thousand years of agriculture. Formerly, loess was probably much deeper and more extensive over the chalk (Catt 1978). The soils on the clay-with-flints are sometimes loamy if they have a high sand and loess content, but they can be intractable, acid, stony clays.

The Pre-Iron Age Background

Much of the evidence for the Iron Age and earlier environment comes from sites peripheral to the region. Evans (1972) has examined mollusca from soils associated with several Neolithic monuments on the chalk at the foot of the Marlborough Downs in the vicinity of Avebury. Typically, they show that after clearance the environment remained permanently open. For example, at South Street the upper sediments in the quarry-ditch of a long barrow showed that the general ground-surface remained short-turfed grassland throughout the Bronze Age (Evans 1972, 328–332).

A substantial beetle assemblage has been examined from a Bronze Age shaft, dated to about 1380 bc, on the Wiltshire chalk at Wilsford, 13 km south of Avebury (Osborne 1969). The fauna indicated a very open grassland landscape, and was dominated by scarabaeoid dung beetles.

Important evidence for the vegetation has come from recent work on localised polleniferous deposits adjacent to the Wessex chalk (Waton 1982). The most valuable site was a fen on the Itchen floodplain near Winchester which was so situated that most of the pollen was likely to have been derived from plant communities on the surrounding chalk. The Winchester pollen sequence began in the Boreal and confirmed the picture from the other Winchester sites of early permanent clearance. The elm decline clearance was dated to 3680 ± 90 bc, with arboreal and shrub pollen dropping to 10% of the total dry-land pollen. Thereafter, tree and shrub pollen fluctuated between values of 10 to 30%, showing the persistence of limited woodland and/or scrub. During the early and middle Bronze Age, the representation of cereal-type pollen was poor, suggesting the importance of grassland, but from about 1000 bc onwards cereal

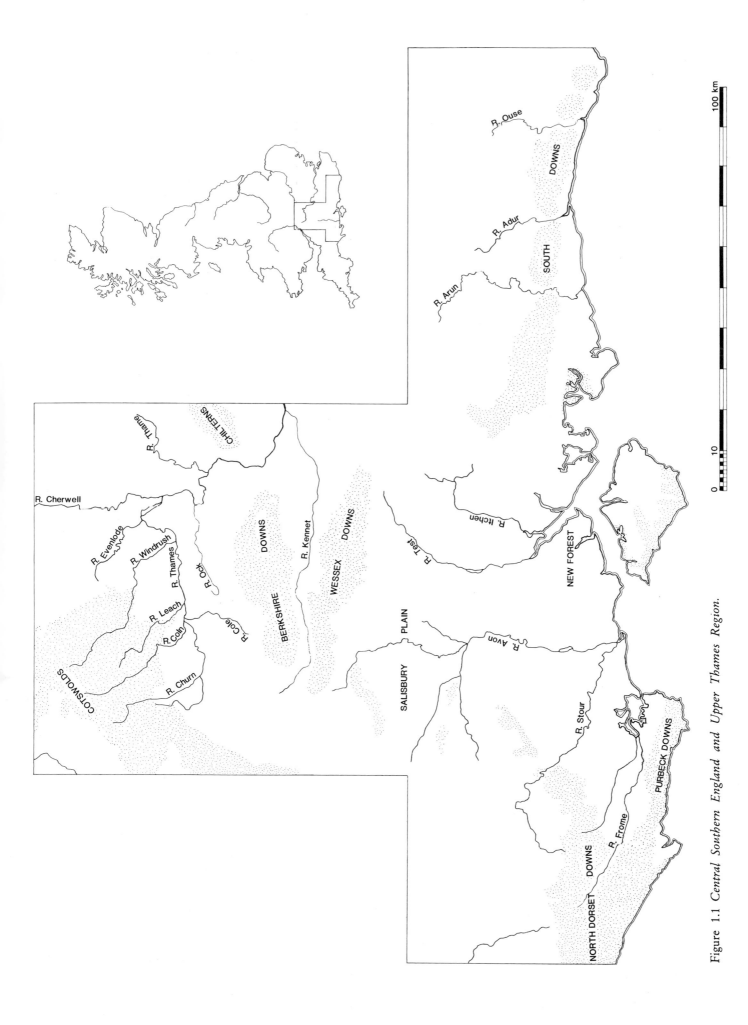

Figure 1.1 *Central Southern England and Upper Thames Region.*

2

pollen rose to what, for cereal pollen, are relatively high values of 1–4%, suggesting considerable arable.

It is not intended to give the results of field survey in any great detail, but they confirm the presence of large cleared areas on the chalk before the Iron Age. Blocks of Celtic fields, rectangular arable plots generally between about 0.1 and 0.4 ha, levelled by subsequent ploughing, are extensive on the chalk (Bowen 1978). Some of these systems date back to the middle Bronze Age. From the late Bronze Age onwards, the construction of linear ditch-systems shows the organisation of the landscape on a very large scale. They sometimes slighted Celtic fields (Bowen 1975, 51–54; 1978). It has been suggested that these ditches were associated with pastoral management, but some could have been territorial boundaries (Bradley 1978, 47). Intensive fieldwork on the chalk around Chalton showed that there was a proliferation of settlements and a spread of field-systems throughout the first millennium BC.

In contrast, pollen analysis of a valley mire at Snelsmore, near Newbury, in an area where the chalk is overlaid by base-deficient clay-with-flints and plateau gravels, showed little disturbance of forest cover until the end of the Bronze Age (Waton 1982).

A Bronze Age barrow on Tertiary sands in the New Forest at Burley sealed a developing podzol on which a *Calluna* heath with much *Pteridium* grew (Dimbleby 1962, 53–56). At Moorgreen, near Botley, there was an immature podzol beneath a Bronze Age barrow on sand (Dimbleby 1965, 357). Pollen analysis showed that the site had not even been completely cleared when the barrow was built; thus the soil must have been very susceptible to damage. Further evidence for conditions on the Tertiary deposits near the coast comes from the Dorset heathlands west of the region, near Poole. Pollen analysis from a very small peat bog on the Reading Beds at Rimsmoor suggested that the first major clearance lasted from about 1050 bc to 900 bc but much woodland remained present (Waton 1982). After that period, some tree regeneration occurred, but it was incomplete. Soil and pollen analysis of the turf sealed by early and middle Bronze Age barrows at three sites on the Dorset heathlands showed that extensive clearance had already taken place around them and that heathland conditions, with podzolisation, were developing or fully developed (Ashbee and Dimbleby 1958, 154–159; Dimbleby in Case 1952, 158–159; Piggott and Dimbleby 1953).

Similar conditions existed on the Tertiary sands to the NE of the region. A round barrow at Ascot sealed a *Calluna* heath on a well-developed podzol (Bradley and Keith-Lucas 1975). On the gravels of the River Kennet at Burghfield, near Reading, pollen analyses of some late Bronze Age ponds suggested a largely open landscape but with some woodland (Bradley *et al.* 1980, 277–282).

By the start of the Iron Age in the 7th/6th centuries BC, the natural forested Hampshire landscape had been altered out of all recognition. Much of the chalk had perhaps remained open and had been continuously farmed since the Neolithic. During the late Bronze Age there was probably an intensification of agriculture on the chalk. The linear ditch systems slighting arable fields need imply no more than the ordering of the pastoral aspect of the landscape into larger units. Some woodland survived on the clay-with-flints, but the settlement-density of the chalk would imply that in many areas it had become a managed resource. Along the coast, however, some of the vulnerable soils on the sands and gravels had already suffered much damage following clearance and over-exploitation by the middle of the Bronze Age. By the Iron Age, they would either have supported rough heathland grazing or it is possible that woodland regeneration had taken place; for example podzols beneath oak woodland at several sites in the New Forest had formed during an undated heathland phase (Dimbleby and Gill 1955). Some of the soils in the Tertiary basin, however, would probably have proved more resilient and still have been available for Iron Age agriculture.

The Iron Age Environment

Molluscs from the later fills of Neolithic monuments on the Wiltshire chalk indicated open conditions throughout the Iron Age. The short-turfed grassland persisted at South Street until, perhaps in the Roman period, it was ploughed (Evans 1972, 328–332). The Iron Age part of the pollen sequence from Winchester suggested a continuation of the open agricultural conditions which prevailed in the late Bronze Age (Waton 1982).

During the Iron Age there was an increase in settlement density on the chalk. The building of hillforts provided foci around which large tracts of the landscape were divided into pastoral areas, defined by linear ditches, and blocks of arable fields, as, for example, at Woolbury (Cunliffe 1974, 177). The gradual expansion of the linear ditch systems shows that the landscape did not become fossilised during the Iron Age. Grain-storage pits became very abundant in the hillforts as the Iron Age progressed, and substantial quantities of charred grain can commonly be found on Iron Age sites (Jones, this volume).

A consequence of the arable intensification was an increase in soil-erosion. The dry valley bottoms on the chalk often contain colluvium. The careful excavation by hand of a trench through a minor dry valley bottom at Chalton, recording three dimensionally all the artifacts discovered, revealed colluvial sediments up to 1.8 m thick. Pottery suggested that colluviation began at some time in the Bronze Age/early Iron Age (Bell 1981, 79–81; 1982, 135–6). Little pre-Roman colluvium was present in the bottom of a neighbouring major dry valley, and it was suggested that sediments had been removed by a seasonal stream.

The polleniferous deposit on the clay-with-flints at Snelsmore gave evidence of moderate clearance around 620 bc, herb and grass pollen rising to 40% of the total dry-land pollen, which lasted throughout the Iron Age (Waton 1982).

The pollen sequence from Rimsmoor, on the Tertiary deposits near Poole, continued throughout the Iron Age and showed a second major clearance phase between about 350–150 bc. Again it was followed by incomplete tree regeneration (Waton 1982). Pollen analysis of a buried soil beneath the bank of a late Iron Age enclosure at Longslade Bottom, in the New Forest, showed clearance to be taking place at this date (Eide 1981). Pollen analytical investigations are taking place on several peat bogs in the New Forest (Barber 1975; Barber 1980). At two sites in the central part of the forest oak-alder-hazel woodland apparently remained undisturbed until historical times. At a third nearby site, peat growth was only initiated around 500 bc (extrapolating from a radiocarbon date of 495 ± 70 ad further up the profile) and it was suggested that this had been caused by climatic change or increased run-off caused by deforestation.

All the evidence suggests that the Wessex chalklands were being fully exploited to support a rising population in the Iron Age. The arable and pastoral aspects of the landscape were highly organised on a large scale. It is possible that soil erosion was responsible for some areas on the chalk being put down to pasture, and intensive land-use seems to have gone on longest after the Iron Age in areas like Chalton, where some superficial loess cover survives (Bell 1981, 85). However, there was much arable on the chalk throughout the Iron Age and any loss of arable land may in part have been compensated for by an expansion onto the heavier soils, which is perhaps what was occurring with the clearance at Snelsmore. Agricultural stress on the chalklands may also have been the reason for the clearance of secondary woodland on what seems to have been marginal land at Rimsmoor. It was noted that this clearance coincided with the increased fortification taking place in Wessex during the middle of the Iron Age (Waton 1982, 85).

As in the late Bronze Age, much of the woodland which the pollen record shows surviving on the chalkland throughout the Iron Age was probably retained for the supply of wood and timber rather than representing unused land. It is possible that under-exploited woodland was only present on the Tertiary clays, from which little information is available, and on some of the sands and gravels to the south, including parts of the New Forest.

The Upper Thames Valley

At its fullest extent, the Upper Thames Valley consists of the entire drainage basin of the River Thames above the Goring Gap. The landscape of the region has resulted largely from the erosion of Jurassic and Cretaceous sedimentary rocks which gently slope SE. Running in a band along the NW side of the region in Gloucestershire and NW Oxfordshire is the limestone of the Cotswolds; much of it around 200 m OD, but rising considerably higher. At the foot of the Cotswold dip-slope is the broad expanse of the Oxford clay vale, drained from the west by the Thames, which collects various tributaries from the Cotswolds and the eastern end of the vale. The sandstones and limestones of the

Oxford Heights, mostly up to 100 m OD, comprise the next range of hills. The Thames finds its way through them at Oxford. Beyond these hills is a second clay vale which the Thames crosses. Running along the south and east sides of the region is another range of hills, the Downs to the west and the Chilterns to the NE. From the clay rises a bench of Upper Greensand then the scarp of the chalk, with a crest at around 200 m OD or more. The Thames drops from about 70 m OD in the Oxford clay vale above Lechlade to about 40 m OD at the Goring Gap, where it flows between the Downs and the Chilterns.

Flanking the Thames in the clay vales are extensive terraces of limestone gravel, in places 5 km or more wide. The most important are the first terrace, rising to 2–3 m above the present river-level, and the second terrace at 8.5 m above river-level. There is a broad alluvium-covered floodplain to the Thames and its tributaries. On top of some hills in the region and at the foot of the Cotswolds in the Wychwood area are boulder clays or glacial sands and gravels with a high quartzite content. Clay-with-flints occurs on the dip slope of parts of the Downs and is more extensive on the Chilterns.

Most of the region now has calcareous to circum-neutral soils. Only on the sands and on the non-calcareous glacial drift are more acidic soils now present. As in Wessex, however, the modern soils are very much the product of agriculture, and non-calcareous stone-free loams or silt loams were formerly widespread on the Cotswolds and the gravel terraces.

The Pre-Iron Age Background

Extensive Neolithic and early Bronze Age ritual complexes in the Dorchester and Abingdon areas, and large clusters of ring ditches, show that the Thames gravels have had a long history of use.

Detailed biological investigations of a late Bronze Age pond on the second or third Thames terrace at Mount Farm, near Dorchester, indicate that at least some parts of the gravel terrace were very open indeed (J. Greig and M. Robinson, unpublished). Tree and shrub pollen averaged only 4% of the total pollen. The pollen gave just a hint of some insect-pollinated shrubs, but their pollen tends to be greatly under-represented in deposits, so that the presence of seeds of such species as *Thelycrania sanguinea* and *Crataegus* cf. *monogyna* suggests that scrub may have been a little more abundant. Grassland seems to have predominated, with *Plantago lanceolata* pollen at 23% of the total and Gramineae at 37%. There was a little cereal pollen and chaff, but no evidence of a major arable component to the landscape. Radiocarbon dates of 1050 ± 80 bc and 900 ± 70 bc were obtained from the pond. There is little sign of pre-Iron Age field-systems on the gravel terraces, although a possible example exists at Long Wittenham (Thomas 1980).

An 8th/7th-century bc occupation-surface overlying a silted river channel on the Thames bank at Wallingford produced a molluscan fauna characteristic of open, relatively dry grassland, *Vallonia excentrica* and *Pupilla muscorum* being abundant (Robinson, unpublished). In the lower Windrush Valley, however, woodland clearance was still taking place on the floodplain during the late Bronze Age. A radiocarbon date of 850 ± 90 bc was obtained from alder charcoal in the bottom of a tree-clearance pit at Mingies Ditch, Hardwick, although it is possible that regeneration subsequently occurred on this site (Robinson, unpublished).

The evidence from several sites on the Thames floodplain, where ancient ground-surfaces survived beneath earthworks, suggests that, before the Iron Age, there had been little Holocene alluviation (Robinson and Lambrick 1984). The lack of preserved organic remains or much gleying in deeper Bronze Age features on the floodplain, for example at Port Meadow, Oxford, and Mingies Ditch, in contrast to Iron Age ditches on these sites provides evidence of at least a seasonally low water-table. It seems that little, if any, flooding was taking place.

Just beyond the Upper Thames Basin, on the chalk of the dip slope of the Berkshire Downs, Celtic fields were organised on a large scale from the middle Bronze Age onwards and, from the late Bronze Age onwards, linear ditches cut some of the arable fields (Bradley and Richards 1978). On the crest of the Downs at Ram's Hill molluscan analysis has shown that this fortified hilltop was cleared and then reverted to scrub or woodland several times in the Bronze Age (Evans in Bradley and Ellison 1975, 139–149). At perhaps 900–800 bc the site was cleared for the final time, and, after an episode of ploughing, a turf line developed over the Bronze Age enclosure ditch, containing an open-country molluscan fauna indicative of short, grazed, grassland. Nearby, at the long barrow of Wayland's Smithy, woodland which had colonised the site in the Neolithic was cleared towards the very end of the Bronze Age and ploughing took place (Kerney and Bradley and Ellison 1975, 121,200). Further to the east, several sections through the Berkshire Grims Ditch, a late Bronze Age or possibly earliest Iron Age linear boundary, produced open-country molluscan faunas from the primary silts (Bowden in Ford 1982, 32–35).

There seems to have been relatively limited activity in the Cotswolds until the latest Bronze Age and most barrow cemeteries are small compared with those on the Thames gravels (Lambrick 1983, 51), although, for example, the Rollright Stones were adjacent to an area of grassland (Robinson, unpublished).

The Thames gravels became the focus of agricultural activity in the region during the later Neolithic and remained so throughout most of the Bronze Age. The floodplain of the River Thames itself was probably cleared permanently at an early date, but woodland remained up some of its tributaries. On the other geologies there seems to have been under-exploited land, and it is possible that the clays had remained thickly wooded. On the Berkshire Downs, however, the degree of Bronze Age activity on the dip slope suggests that only on the crest itself was there much abandoned land

(R. Bradley, pers. comm.). The late Bronze Age clearance in the region marked the beginning of a general agricultural intensification and expansion.

The Iron Age Environment

There was a much greater density of occupation-sites on the Thames gravels in the Iron Age than previously (Benson and Miles 1974). Some, especially on the second and higher terraces, have numerous grain-storage pits and large quantities of charred cereal remains can be recovered from them, as for example at Ashville, Abingdon (Jones in Parrington 1978). Small sub-rectangular ditched fields adjacent to house-enclosures proliferated on the gravel terraces during the Iron Age. A re-organisation may have occurred in the late Iron Age with the appearance of small fields laid out alongside droveways, but their dating is uncertain and it is possible that they represent a Roman development. However, the main areas of arable and grassland on the gravels remained unenclosed.

Waterlogged deposits were obtained from several middle Iron Age hut circles with small attached compounds at Farmoor, on the floodplain and the edge of the first Thames terrace (Lambrick and Robinson 1979). The site probably dated from about 250–100 bc. The landscape was very open indeed; less than 0.1% of the Coleoptera were from species which attack woody plants and only about 3% of the total pollen was from trees and shrubs. Macroscopic remains of woody species were almost absent. The pollen suggested that the landscape had been predominantly grassland, while the importance of pasture was confirmed by the abundance of dung beetles such as *Aphodius* spp. Waterlogged seeds and insects from an Iron Age site towards the upper reaches of the Thames Valley, at Claydon Pike near Lechlade, suggested an environment of wet grassland (Robinson, unpublished). The site consisted of many hut circles and enclosures upon islands of first-terrace gravel, separated by hollows of floodplain.

Grassland predominated on the floodplain of the lower Windrush at Mingies Ditch, Hardwick, around what was perhaps a pioneering settlement bringing an area of rough grassland or scrub into more intensive use (Robinson 1981, 256–259). A radiocarbon date of 220 ± 90 bc was obtained from wood preserved in the bottom of one of the pair of ditches which enclosed the site. Tree pollen made up 4% of the total pollen in samples of peat from these ditches, while shrub pollen, mostly *Salix*, comprised another 13% of the total. Macroscopic remains of a wide range of shrubs were abundant in the ditches, but in contrast only 1.7% of the total terrestrial Coleoptera fed on woody species. Perhaps the macroscopic shrub remains had been derived from species-rich hedges adjacent to the ditches. The abundance of beetles from the super-family Scarabaeoidea, both chafers, which have larvae that feed on roots in permanent grassland, and dung beetles, which are restricted to dung of large herbivores in the field, emphasise the pastoral nature of the site.

The preservation of organic remains in Iron Age

ditches at Mingies Ditch and Port Meadow suggests that the water-table had risen on the floodplain after the Bronze Age activity ceased at these sites. The water table continued to rise at Mingies Ditch during the Iron Age, for there was a 'recurrence surface' for peat preservation in the enclosure ditches, although there was no evidence of flooding. However, the presence of riverine aquatic mollusca, including *Bithynia tentacula* with their periostraca intact, in some of the small, isolated, gullies of the Farmoor settlement provides evidence that the floodplain there was inundated contemporaneously with presumably seasonal occupation (Lambrick and Robinson 1979, 109–110, 125). This perhaps represents the onset of regular seasonal flooding over much of the Thames floodplain. Alluviation, which sealed many of the Pleistocene sites on the floodplain including Farmoor, may have begun in the late Iron Age.

On the crest of the Downs at Ram's Hill, the short turfed grassland persisted throughout most of the Iron Age until the site was ploughed in about 50 BC (Evans in Bradley and Ellison 1975, 139–149). Open conditions were likewise indicated by mollusca from the silts of the Berkshire Grims Ditch (Bowden in Ford 1982, 32–35). Three sites have given evidence for Iron Age arable on the Chilterns escarpment. At the western end, two sections through the South Oxfordshire Grims Ditch revealed a thin ploughsoil covering the chalk beneath the bank (Case and Sturdy 1959; Robinson in Hinchliffe 1975, 129–132). Near the watershed between the Upper Thames and Ouse basins at Pitstone a ploughwash with early Iron Age pottery at its base truncated a Neolithic ditch (Evans 1966, 355–357).

At the foot of the Cotswolds, some woodland survived into the Iron Age on the acid soil of the glacial drift in the Wychwood area. Pollen analysis of the soil buried beneath the rampart of Eynsham Hall Camp showed the site to have been oak woodland before its fortification (G.W. Dimbleby, pers. comm.). Many hillforts were constructed in the Cotswolds themselves during the Iron Age, implying that this part of the region was well populated (Lambrick 1983, 53–54). Grain-storage pits do not seem to have been numerous within these forts, for example Rainsborough (Avery *et al.* 1967), in complete contrast to the Hampshire hillforts such as Danebury (Cunliffe, this volume). Perhaps the Cotswolds were predominantly grassland during the Iron Age and they did not become a major grain-producing area until the Roman period.

The Thames gravels probably continued as the most densely populated and intensively farmed part of the region throughout the Iron Age. It is now becoming clear that each occupation-site on the gravels was not a self-sufficient mixed farming settlement, but that the whole valley bottom was organised on a larger scale. This is illustrated well by work now in progress in the Stanton Harcourt area, although unfortunately it is unlikely that all the sites were contemporary. On the dry second gravel terrace at Gravelly Guy, a large middle Iron Age settlement has many grain-storage pits which contain much charred cereal remains, suggesting the importance of arable. Nearby, waterlogged remains from an isolated Iron Age ditch on gravelly clay at the edge of the truncated third terrace gave evidence of localised hazel woodland set against a background of an open landscape on the slope between terraces. At Mingies Ditch, on the floodplain, and a similar site on the first terrace at Northmoor, pastureland was predominant. Such a system would have put the various soils to their best uses: grassland on the floodplain and wetter parts of the first gravel terrace, much arable on the second and higher terraces and perhaps coppices on the clay between terraces. However, it must be assumed that settlements on the gravel terraces also directly exploited parts of the valley sides or had interdependent relationships with sites on the clay slopes and limestone hills.

The chalk of the Downs and Chilterns was important agriculturally during the Iron Age and shared many developments with the Hampshire chalklands such as Celtic fields, linear ditch systems and colluviation, although much of the clay-with-flints on the dip slope of the Chilterns may have remained wooded. Much of the Cotswolds was probably cleared before the end of the Iron Age, on present evidence mainly for grassland. Relatively undisturbed woodland possibly survived on large tracts of the claylands.

The rise in water-table of the Thames floodplain followed by the onset of seasonal inundation was possibly a consequence of the deforestation of a large part of the Thames catchment, causing increased run-off. Flooding would have forced a change in the way in which the floodplain was managed: Mingies Ditch seems to have been a permanent settlement with repeated rebuildings, perhaps spanning several generations; molluscan and botanical evidence suggests that the Farmoor settlements were only occupied seasonally and for a relatively few years (Lambrick and Robinson 1979, 125). However, it is possible that the loss of winter pasture through flooding would have been more than offset by an increase in grass growth during the summer. Until post-Iron Age alluviation, much of the floodplain had a very thin covering of soil over the gravel and must have been very susceptible to drought stress.

Comparison between Wessex and the Thames Valley

It is not easy to make a direct comparison between the two regions because much of the Hampshire evidence is based on pollen and molluscan sequences from deposits which were forming throughout the entire first millennium BC and in places distant from human habitation. The Thames Valley evidence has tended to be a diversity of plant and invertebrate remains which accumulated rapidly in man-made features on occupation sites, and no long sequences are available.

Both regions, however, are characterised by 'core areas', the Thames gravels and the Hampshire chalk, which possess resilient soils, able to maintain their agricultural productivity even though they were cleared and continuously exploited long before the Iron Age.

(On the chalk, the ease with which soil-depth and nutrient-supply can in part be maintained by ploughing into the bedrock would have been an important factor on slopes suffering soil-erosion). During the Iron Age, intensive arable production in the core areas supported the dense settlements on the chalk and the gravels, filling their numerous grain-storage pits and producing a surplus for exchange with other areas.

The differences in geomorphology and soil-distribution between the two regions, however, is likely to have resulted in dissimilar landscapes in the Iron Age. The Hamshire chalkland perhaps presented a mosaic of arable in the form of blocks of Celtic fields and grassland, with use in part dependent upon localised soil-depth and the degree of slope, while woods or coppices covered the more intractable patches of clay-with-flints. The landscape of the Upper Thames Valley was probably stratified into different agricultural zones stepping up the valley sides: grassland on the floodplain flanking the river, much open arable on the gravel terraces, then woodland or grassland on the clay and more open conditions on the limestone and sandstone above. The absence of Celtic fields from the Thames gravels was probably because the terraces were too flat to need measures to prevent slope-erosion.

In both Hampshire and the Upper Thames Valley there was expansion into other parts of the region during the Iron Age. In the Thames Valley, this was probably largely a result of population-growth as there is no evidence for serious soil-deterioration on the gravels; but in Hampshire, loss through colluviation of loessic soils on the chalk may have caused additional pressure. While it is possible that there was some degree of environmental stress in parts of the regions as the Iron Age progressed (and Jones, this volume, provides good evidence for declining levels of soil nitrogen in the arable fields), it did not result in a catastrophe. Both regions possessed large areas of productive agricultural landscapes which retained their importance into the Roman period.

Aspects of the Environment of Britain During the First Millennium BC

Unlike on the Wessex chalk and the Upper Thames gravels, large-scale clearance only took place over much of Britain after the end of the Bronze Age. Yet the climatic deterioration of the early first millennium BC, from which there has never been a complete recovery, creates an apparent paradox of increasing arable activity in a climate becoming less suitable for agriculture.

Climate

The generally accepted sequence for climatic deterioration (that is, the climate becoming cooler and wetter) in the first millennium BC is as follows: a slight deterioration may have begun as early as about 1250 bc, then deterioration occurred more rapidly after about 850 bc with the climate reaching its wettest by about 650 bc; after about 400 bc there seems to have been a partial recovery, with a somewhat warmer climate until about ad 450 (Turner 1981, 251–261). Lamb (1981, 54–55) estimated that there was a fall of nearly 2°C in overall mean temperature in England between about 1000 and 750 bc, and he regards the amelioration of c. 400 bc as slight, with a return to colder conditions by c. 200 bc. Barber (1981), using NW European as well as British evidence, suggests that there was a climatic deterioration c. 1500–1400 bc, a catastrophic decline to a cooler and/or wetter climate around 900–600 bc and possibly a further decline around 100 bc. He leaves open the degree of recovery to warmer and/or drier episodes between deteriorations.

The estimated fall in temperature would have shortened the growing season by five weeks (Lamb 1981, 55) and upon this climatic deterioration have been based various theories of an environmental 'catastrophe' towards the end of the Bronze Age. It has been suggested that the linear ditches, probably bounding grassland, which slight some Celtic field-systems in Wessex might have been linked with climatic deterioration (Bowen 1978, 122; Evans 1975, 149). Various authors have noted field-systems in upland Britain abandoned to become covered by peat in the late Bronze Age, and many of the extreme views are summarized in (although not necessarily held by) Mercer (1981, xviii–xix). It has been postulated that 1000–500 bc was a period of agricultural contraction and re-adjustment in Britain. There was a massive population diminution consequent upon an agricultural debacle. In the lowlands, large areas once arable became rich grassland with wetter conditions, although prime agricultural land such as on the Thames gravels remained arable. One response was the cultivation in southern England of new crops better suited to the wet climate, especially spelt wheat, and a greater tendency for winter sowing.

Not all archaeologists share the view of an environmental catastrophe. Whittle (1982) argues that while the climate change would have posed problems for many pastoral communities, they could, for the most part, have been overcome. Bradley (1978, 27, 51–53) regards the late Bronze Age and early Iron Age as a period of expanding clearance and increasing arable.

It is worth considering the evidence for climatic deterioration. As pointed out by M. Jones during questions on this paper, direct evidence for past change in temperature, for example oxygen isotope ratios, tends to be reliable, whereas indirect evidence based upon changes in wetness is often ambiguous.

Ratios of O^{18}/O^{16} from an ice core in North Greenland (Dansgaard et al. 1969) and from algal lime sediment in a lake on the island of Gotland in the Baltic (Morner and Wallin 1977) do indeed suggest a general cooling in the first millennium BC. The results from Gotland are very interesting: they show a fall in average summer lake-temperature during the Sub-Boreal to Sub-Atlantic transition, starting around 700 bc and continuing until the end of the millennium, by which date the temperature had fallen by 2°C, to 0.5°C below the present-day temperature. The degree to which such results are

7

relevant to Britain is uncertain (Turner 1981, 251).

The British evidence for climatic change during this period, reviewed in detail by Turner (1981, 251–261), is from peat stratigraphy:

1. Flooding of raised bogs on the Somerset levels with calcareous waters from the surrounding hills. This resulted in wooden trackways being laid across the bog surfaces, as a response by the local inhabitants to the increasing wetness, and the replacement of acid raised-bog peat formation with topogenous fen-peat growth, covering both raised-bog surfaces and trackways. The onset of flooding was in about the late 9th century bc, but there is evidence of *increasing* inundation up to at least 450 bc, possibly even 250 bc.
2. The late Bronze Age date for the onset or an increase in the rate of peat growth on upland sites, including the spread of blanket peat over abandoned field-systems.
3. Recurrence surfaces for peat growth on raised bogs and an increase in the rate of peat growth. Both are largely dependent on the ratio between rainfall and evaporation on the bog surface. The classic piece of work was by Turner (1964, 74–76; 1965, 343–344) on the SE raised bog at Tregaron, where well-humified peat just below a recurrence surface gave a radiocarbon date of 1004 bc and weakly humified peat immediately above was dated to 696 bc, showing that the bog had stopped growing for about 300 years. From 696 bc to 404 bc the rate of peat growth was 1 cm in three or four years; thereafter, only 1 cm in c. 50 years.

There has been too great a tendency to adopt a simple climatic explanation for some of these events, which might in fact have been due to the complex interaction of many factors on the hydrological regime, of which climate was only one.

By the early first millennium bc, extensive clearance was taking place on the hills which form the main catchment area for the Somerset Levels (Coles 1978, 88). Ignoring any additional complications caused by sea-level changes, increased and more rapid run-off consequent upon clearance is just as likely a cause of flooding as an increase in rainfall, and it has already been noted that the late first-millennium BC rise in water-table and onset of flooding in the Upper Thames Valley was possibly related to clearance in the drainage basin (p. 9). This analogy can be taken further: clay alluvium was being deposited at Meare Village on the Somerset Levels during the Iron Age (Evans in Coles 1981, 44–45; Coles 1981, 67), while alluviation was well underway on the Upper Thames floodplain in the Roman period. In both cases, the sources of alluvium are likely to have been agricultural activity on the surrounding slopes.

Climatic change, soil maturation and human activity can all induce blanket peat formation (Moore 1975). Clearance, nutrient-loss from grazing or cropping (and even the abandonment of well-managed agricultural land or pasture) can all initiate the process of upland soil-deterioration which ultimately favours blanket peat (Limbrey 1975, 152–172). There is quite a wide range of

dates for the onset of blanket peat growth, but this in itself does not invalidate a climatic argument. Each site would have its own threshold for peat initiation, and once some peat is present, conditions then become more favourable for further peat formation. Circumstantial evidence from many sites, however, suggests that human land-use often effected the crossing of the hydrological threshold for peat-formation (Moore 1975).

The Bronze Age was a period of expansion into fragile ecosystems, and the soil-deterioration on some sites was certainly unrelated to climatic change. The development of heathland before the middle of the second millennium BC in Dorset and elsewhere has already been mentioned (p. 3), similarly, podzolisation brought about by man on the eastern edge of the North Yorkshire Moors by c. 1500 bc is also well known (Dimbleby 1962). Turner gives the example of Leash Fen, an upland topogenous bog in Derbyshire where the rate of peat-growth contrasted with Tregaron (Hicks 1971). A twentyfold increase in the growth rate after 340 bc was coincident with large-scale clearance of the catchment for pasture. A wetter environment produced by clearance resulted in peat-formation being less humified in a valley mire at Cefn Graenog, North Wales (Chambers 1983, 116–18).

Raised bogs probably provide the best evidence for climatic change in Britain during the first millennium BC, especial increased wetness causing the crossing of the threshold for renewed peat-growth of a bog. Human influence can have some effect on raised bogs, although not nearly as much as for topogenous bogs/fens.

On balance, it is probable that there was a climatic deterioration in the first millennium BC. However, the ambiguity of much of the evidence and the large scale of environmental changes brough about by man from this period onwards mean that it is very difficult to provide constants against which the path of climate can be followed. For instance, it is possible that the wetter and/or cooler climate between c. 850–650 bc was part of a cyclical oscillation, and that recovery was almost complete. It is also possible that the deterioration was not much more severe than other Holocene climatic oscillations, but that on this occasion the effects of man had left many sites more vulnerable than before.

Many of the postulated archaeological consequences of the climatic change are contentious in their own right. Even at its most severe, the climate in the first millennium BC is not thought to have been much cooler or wetter than at present. Yet it is drought, not waterlogging, which is sometimes a problem to modern farmers on the chalk of southern England; nor is the growing season too short. Soil-erosion or the rearrangement of territorial boundaries are more likely than climatic change to have caused a shift from arable to pasture on some areas of the chalk. Emmer (*Triticum dicoccum*), the main Bronze Age wheat, is just as tolerant of heavy and waterlogged soils as spelt wheat (*T. spelta*), which largely replaced emmer in southern England during the late Bronze Age/early Iron Age (information from G. Hillman and my own cultivation experiments). At present there is no evidence that autumn sowing was an Iron Age innovation, although it is plausible that it became more widespread with the intensification of arable farming in the Iron Age. Again, emmer is well suited as a winter cereal in England and more than sufficiently cold-hardy (Hillman 1981, 146–8).

Agricultural Intensification

An open agricultural landscape covered large areas in SE England, especially on light soil, by the end of the second millennium BC and some upland areas had been permanently deforested (Tinsley 1981; Turner 1981). Elsewhere, there were a few other large cleared areas. There had been a gradual increase in clearance throughout the Bronze Age, but much of Britain still remained wooded and many minor clearances only lasted a century or so before woodland regeneration took place. In the Iron Age there was much extensive and permanent clearance.

> England, Wales, parts of central and NE England were cleared and both uplands and lowlands subsequently used for settled agriculture or permanent grazing for the very first time. Mixed farming appears to have been practised in a surprisingly wide range of habitats.
>
> (Turner 1981, 275)

Settlement spread onto heavier soils (Bradley 1978, 123), especially in areas with substantial pre-Iron Age clearance.

Even though this wave of intensified clearance was at its peak during the Iron Age, its origins can perhaps be traced back to the late Bronze Age in parts of southern England, during the same period when some upland sites in other regions were being abandoned. For example, a radiocarbon-dated pollen sequence from Hockam Mere, Norfolk, showed the landscape to have been partly open from the later Neolithic onwards, but around 800 bc there was a major increase in the pollen of the Gramineae and ruderals consequent upon a much larger scale of clearance (Sims 1978, 57–58). Similar but undated sequences have been obtained from Seamere (Sims 1978, 58–9) and Old Buckenham Mere (Godwin 1968, 101–4). At Frogholt, Kent, there had already been some clearance before the end of the second millennium BC but in the late Bronze Age there was a phase of greatly accelerated clearance dated to 690 bc (Godwin 1962). There is evidence for agricultural expansion from the late Bronze Age onwards in Wessex and the Upper Thames Valley.

There seems to have been much greater emphasis on arable in southern England and the Midlands during the Iron Age than in earlier periods, although again this development perhaps had its origins in the late Bronze Age. Pollen results from Winchester suggest a shift in a predominantly pastoral landscape to more arable from about 1000 bc onwards (Waton 1982, 82). Carbonised cereal remains seem ubiquitous on Iron Age sites in this part of England, and substantial finds are commonly made. In contrast, carbonised grain is generally sparse on pre-first-millennium BC sites, even though arable played a part in the economy throughout the Bronze Age. Secondary products from domestic animals were perhaps as important as meat production in the Iron Age

(Grant, this volume; R. Wilson, pers. comm.) and it is possible that cereal comprised a greater proportion of the human diet than previously.

Bell (1981, 84; 1982, 136–8) has shown that colluviation in dry valley bottoms consequent upon ploughing was not just a process of later prehistory, but this phenomenon does seem to have been particularly prevalent during the Iron Age. The first millennium BC was the period when the number of sites shown by Bell (1982, 137), which may have been experiencing colluviation, reaches its maximum.

All these trends agree with the substantial rise in human population which has been postulated as occurring throughout the first millennium BC (Cunliffe 1978).

The reasons for the agricultural intensification are somewhat unclear. Iron tools would undoubtedly have been an important asset for clearance and cultivation, but they were not available in the earliest part of the period. No other obvious technological changes occurred and the adoption of new crops during the first half of the first millennium BC (Jones 1981, 104–10; Jones, this volume), while presumably representing an improvement related to expanding arable, does not provide sufficient explanation for the cause.

A peculiarity of the Bronze Age is that even by the end of the second millennium BC, much of the English landscape was still not being used to its full potential. Agricultural man had already been present in Britain for two and a half thousand years, more than sufficient time to allow for the necessary population-expansion to carrying-capacity. There were many lowland areas remaining uncleared which, given the available technology, could have provided a sustained agricultural yield. Possibly there were various social constraints on land-use and population-growth during the Bronze Age. The landscape of parts of Britain underwent a considerable transformation between about 1300 and 700 bc, from being organised around ceremonial areas and religious monuments to being organised principally for agricultural purposes (Bradley 1978, 121–2). Perhaps amassing large herds of domestic animals as an expression of status took precedence over agricultural expansion to feed a growing population, just as in some periods of the Bronze Age much metalworking effort was diverted towards making prestige rather than functional items.

Conclusions

The environmental changes during the Iron Age in Hampshire and the Upper Thames Valley were the result of the proliferation of settlements and an arable intensification in regions which already possessed much open landscape. The Hampshire chalk and the Thames gravels, with their resilient soils which had largely been cleared of woodland and were permanently farmed long before the Iron Age, remained the focus of activity, but the expansion also encompassed previously uncleared and abandoned areas. Increased soil-erosion on the chalk and the onset of flooding on the Thames floodplain were unintentional consequences of the pressure being put on the landscape. The developments in Hampshire and the Upper Thames Valley during the Iron Age were part of a general trend which swept over much of Britain and probably had its origins in the final Bronze Age. The entire first millennium BC ought to be seen as a period of agricultural expansion, and only in parts of the Highland Zone is it at all likely that the climatic deterioration early in this period caused any serious reversal, perhaps accelerating the abandonment of over-exploited land. Indeed, some of the evidence used to indicate climatic deterioration requires reexamination. For much of

Britain, the Iron Age represents the period of heaviest impact of prehistoric man on the environment (Simmons 1981, 290). It is as important to consider whether social factors inhibited agricultural intensification in earlier periods as it is to look for innovations and environmental changes in the first millennium BC which might have caused agricultural expansion. Hampshire and the Upper Thames Valley are of particular interest because it was probably in regions such as these that the agricultural expansion of the first millennium BC had its origins and where, during the Iron Age, the landscape was most productively organised.

References

ASHBEE, P. and DIMBLEBY, G.W. 1958: The excavation of a round barrow on Clicks Hill, East Stoke Parish, Dorset. *Proc. Dorset Nat. Hist. and Archaeol. Soc.* 80, 146–159.

AVERY, M., SUTTON, J.E.G. and BANKS, J.W. 1967: Rainsborough, Northants, England: excavations 1961–5. *Proc. Prehist. Soc.* 33, 207–306.

BARBER, K.E. 1975: Vegetational history of the New Forest: a preliminary note. *Proc. Hants. Field Club and Archaeol. Soc.* 30, 5–8.

BARBER, K.E. 1981: Pollen analytical palaeoecology in Hampshire: problems and potential. In Shennan, S.J. and Schadla Hall, R.T. (editors), *The archaeology of Hampshire* (Hants. Field Club and Archaeol. Soc. Monograph 1), 91–94.

BARBER, K.E. 1982: Peat-bog stratigraphy as a proxy climate record. In Harding, A.F. (editor). *Climatic change in later prehistory* (Edinburgh), 103–113.

BELL, M. 1981: Valley sediments and environmental change. In Jones, M. and Dimbleby, G.W. (editors), *The environment of man: the Iron Age to the Anglo-Saxon period* (Oxford, BAR 87), 75–91.

BELL, M. 1982: The effects of land-use and climate on valley sedimentation. In Harding, A.F. (editor), *Climatic change in later prehistory* (Edinburgh), 127–142.

BENSON, D. and MILES, D. 1974: *The Upper Thames Valley: an archaeological survey of the river gravels* (Oxford, Oxford Archaeol. Unit Survey 2).

BOWEN, H.C. 1975: Pattern and interpretation: a view of the Wessex landscape. In Fowler, P.J. (editor), *Recent work in rural archaeology* (Bradford on Avon), 51–54.

BOWEN, H.C. 1978: 'Celtic' fields and 'ranch' boundaries in Wessex. In Limbrey, S. and Evans, J.G. (editors), *The effect of man on the landscape: the lowland zone* (London, CBA Res. Rep. 21), 115–123.

BRADLEY, R. 1978: *The prehistoric settlement of Britain* (London).

BRADLEY, R. and ELLISON, A. 1975: *Rams Hill: a Bronze Age defended enclosure and its landscape* (Oxford, BAR 19).

BRADLEY, R. and KEITH-LUCAS, M. 1975: Excavations and pollen analysis on a bell barrow at Ascot, Berkshire. *Journ. Archaeol. Science* 2, 95–108.

BRADLEY, R., LOBB, S., RICHARDS, J. and ROBINSON, M. 1980: Two late Bronze Age settlements on the Kennet gravels: excavations at Aldermaston Wharf and Knight's Farm, Burghfield, Berkshire. *Proc. Prehist. Soc.* 46, 217–295.

BRADLEY, R. and RICHARDS, J. 1978: Prehistoric fields and boundaries on the Berkshire Downs. In Bowen, H.C. and Fowler, P.J. (editors), *Early land allotment in the British Isles* (Oxford, BAR 48), 53–60.

CASE, H.J. 1952: The excavation of two round barrows at Poole, Dorset. *Proc. Prehist. Soc.* 18, 148–159.

CASE, H.J. and STURDY, D. 1959: Crowmarsh Gifford, Oxon. *Oxoniensia* 24, 99.

CATT, J.A. 1978: The contribution of loess to soils in lowland Britain. In Limbrey, S. and Evans, J.G. (editors), *The effect of man on the landscape: the lowland zone* (London, CBA Res. Rep. 21), 12–20.

CHAMBERS, F. 1983: New applications of palaeoecological techniques: integrating evidence of arable activity in pollen peat and soil stratigraphies Cefn Graeanog, North Wales. In Jones, M. (editor), *Integrating the subsistence economy* (Oxf. BAR S181), 107–122.

COLES, J.M. 1978: Man and landscape in the Somerset Levels. In Limbrey, S. and Evans, J.G. (editors), *The effect of man on the landscape: the lowland zone* (London, CBA Res. Rep. 21), 86–89.

COLES, J.M. 1981 (editor): *Somerset Levels Papers 7*.

CUNLIFFE, B.W. 1974: *Iron Age Communities in Britain* (London).

CUNLIFFE, B.W. 1978: Settlement and Population in the British Iron Age: some facts, figures and fantasies. In Cunliffe, B.W. and Rowley, R.T. (editors), *Lowland Iron Age Communities in Europe* (Oxford, BAR S48), 3–24.

DANSGAARD, W., JOHNSEN, S.J., MØLLER, J. and LANGWAY, C.C. 1969: One thousand centuries of climate record from Camp Century on the Greenland ice sheet. *Science* 166, 377–381.

DIMBLEBY, G.W. 1962: *The development of British heathlands and their soils* (Oxford Forestry Memoirs 23).

DIMBLEBY, G.W. 1965: Post-Glacial changes in soil profiles. *Proc. Royal Soc. London* (B) 161, 355–362.

DIMBLEBY, G.W. and GILL, J.M. 1955: The occurrence of podzols under deciduous woodland in the New Forest. *Forestry* 28, 95–106.

EIDE, K. 1981: Pollen and soil studies in the New Forest. In *Archaeological aspects of woodland ecology* (Summary of papers given at autumn conference of Association for Environmental Archaeology), 5.

EVANS, J.G. 1966: Late-Glacial and Post-Glacial sub aerial deposits at Pitstone, Buckinghamshire. *Proc. Geological Assoc.* 77, 347–364.

EVANS, J.G. 1972: *Land snails in archaeology* (London).

EVANS, J.G. 1975: *The environment of early man in the British Isles* (London).

FORD, S. 1982: Fieldwork and excavation on the Berkshire Grims Ditch. *Oxoniensia* 47, 13–36.

GODWIN, H. 1962: Vegetational history of the Kentish Chalk Downs as seen at Wingham and Frogholt. In Lünd, R. von W. and Lange, O.L. (editors), *Festschrift Franz Firbas* (Zurich, Geobotanischen Institut), 83–99.

GODWIN, H. 1968: Studies of the Post-Glacial history of British vegetation XV. Organic deposits of old Buckenham Mere, Norfolk. *New Phytologist* 67, 95–107.

HICKS, S.P. 1971: Pollen-analytical evidence for the effect of prehistoric agriculture on the vegetation of North Derbyshire. *New Phytologist* 70, 647–668.

HILLMAN, G. 1981: Reconstructing crop husbandry practices from charred remains of crops. In Mercer, R. (editor), *Farming practice in British prehistory* (Edinburgh), 146–148.

HINCHLIFFE, J. 1975: Excavations at Grim's Ditch, Mongewell, 1974. *Oxoniensia* 40, 122–135.

JONES, M. 1981: The development of crop husbandry. In Jones, M. and Dimbleby, G.W. (editors), *The environment of man: the Iron Age to the Anglo-Saxon period* (Oxford, BAR 87), 95–127.

LAMB, H.H. 1981: Climate from 1000 BC to AD 100. In Jones, M. and Dimbleby, G.W. (editors), *The environment of man: the Iron Age to the Anglo-Saxon period* (Oxford, BAR 87), 53–65.

LAMBRICK, G.H. 1983: *The Rollright Stones* (Oxford).

LAMBRICK, G.H. and ROBINSON, M.A. 1979: *Iron Age and Roman settlements at Farmoor, Oxfordshire* (London, CBA Res. Rep. 32).

LIMBREY, S. 1975: *Soil science and archaeology* (London).

MERCER, R. 1981: *Farming practice in British prehistory* (Edinburgh).

MOORE, P.D. 1975: The origin of blanket mires. *Nature* 256, 267–269.

MÖRNER, N.A. and WALLIN, B. 1977: A 10,000 year temperature record from Gotland, Sweden. *Palaeogeography, Palaeoclimatology, Palaeoecology* 21, 113–138.

OSBORNE, P.J. 1969: An insect fauna of late Bronze Age date from Wilsford, Wiltshire. *Journ. Animal Ecology* 38, 555–566.

PARRINGTON, M. 1978: *The excavation of an Iron Age settlement, Bronze Age ring-ditches and Roman features at Ashville Trading Estate, Abingdon (Oxfordshire) 1974–76* (London, CBA Res. Rep. 28).

PIGGOTT, S. and DIMBLEBY, G.W. 1953: A Bronze Age barrow at Turners Puddle Heath. *Proc. Dorset Nat. Hist. and Archaeol. Soc.* 75, 34–35.

ROBINSON, M.A. 1981: The Iron Age to early Saxon environment of the Upper Thames terraces. In Jones, M. and Dimbleby, G.W. (editors), *The environment of man: the Iron Age to the Anglo Saxon period* (Oxford, BAR 87), 251–286.

ROBINSON, M.A. and LAMBRICK, G.H. 1984: Holocene alluviation and hydrology in the Upper Thames basin. *Nature* 308, 809–14.

SIMMONS, I.G. 1981: Culture and environment. In Simmons, I.G. and Tooley, M.J. (editors), *The environment in British prehistory* (London), 282–291.

SIMS, R.E. 1978: Man and vegetation in Norfolk. In Limbrey, S. and Evans, J.G. (editors), *The effect of man on the landscape: the lowland zone* (London, CBA Res. Rep. 21), 57–62.

THOMAS, R. 1980: A Bronze Age field system at Northfield Farm? *Oxoniensia* 45, 310–311.

TINSLEY, H.M. 1981: The Bronze Age. In Simmons, I.G. and Tooley, M.J. (editors), *The environment in British prehistory* (London), 210–249.

TURNER, J. 1964: The anthropogenic factor in vegetational history I Tregaron and Wixall Mosses. *New Phytologist* 63, 73–90.

TURNER, J. 1965: A contribution to the history of forest clearance. *Proc. Royal Soc. London* B 161, 343–354.

TURNER, J. 1981: The Iron age. In Simmons, I.G. and Tooley, M.J. (editors), *The environment in British prehistory* (London), 250–281.

WATON, P.V. 1982: Man's impact on the chalklands: some new pollen evidence. In Bell, M. and Limbrey, S. (editors), *Archaeological aspects of woodland ecology* (Oxford, BAR SI46), 75–91.

WHITTLE, A. 1982: Climate, grazing and man: notes towards the definition of a relationship. In Harding, A.F. (editor), *Climatic change in later prehistory* (Edinburgh), 192–200.

Iron Age Wessex: Continuity and Change

Barry Cunliffe

Introduction

Until comparatively recently it would have been true to say that Wessex was the most intensively studied area of Iron Age Britain, and indeed this may still be so in spite of the rapid, and often spectacular, advances being made elsewhere, for example in the Upper Thames Valley and in Northamptonshire. But intensive study does not necessarily mean a clear understanding. This century may have seen a prodigious expenditure of effort on excavation, particularly in the 1920s and 1930s when well thought-out research designs were pursued with energy, but much of the work was small-scale. While providing spots on distribution maps, comparative sections through ramparts, and small assemblages of pottery and animal bones, it has offered little to the elucidation of the social and economic systems at work in the Iron Age community. This is no criticism of pre-war archaeology. The research programmes of that period were designed to answer specific questions which differ from those that now concern us, inevitably so in a rapidly-developing discipline like prehistory; but it is worth emphasising that necessary though it is to have a collection of broadly trawled data, and impressive though our Wessex distribution-maps may look, there are severe limitations to the usefulness of a rag-bag accumulation of this kind. We cannot expect data collected to satisfy one set of questions to be immediately usable in approaching a different and more sophisticated set.

The post-war era in Wessex has seen a continued spate of excavations motivated more by rescue needs than by clearly thought-out research aims (though there are notable exceptions). Much of the work has been on a larger scale than before, producing data sets susceptible to statistical analysis and thus more relevant to our present aspirations. Sadly, however, an unacceptably large proportion of the work completed in the 50s, 60s and early 70s still remains unpublished more than a decade later and is therefore unavailable for detailed study.

These paragraphs are not a cry of despair but simply a warning that alluring though the Wessex data may superficially appear to be, they must be used with circumspection. Before seeking to impose elaborate social models upon them we must become fully aware of the limitations (and strengths) and seek first to recognise the simple inherent patterning. Only then can the dynamics of the systems be sketched out in a coherent form. Once this groundwork has been done, however, we will be in a position to proceed to more complex model-building in order to provide explanations for social change on the one hand and a framework within which to design new, and perhaps more revealing, research-programmes on the other. It is the purpose of this paper to consider the present state of the data, to offer a preliminary ordering of them, and to identify, insofar as the evidence allows, continuity and discontinuity in the social and economic system. Where possible tentative explanations will be offered.

Some of the matters discussed here have been explored in varying degrees of detail in a succession of broadly-related papers (Cunliffe 1971; 1976a; 1976b; 1978a; 1981; 1982a; 1982b; 1982c; 1984a; 1984b; 1984c) in which full bibliographies are given. This paper is best considered to be a mid-term review.

Sequence and Chronology

Of prime importance to the study of any social system over time is the facility not only to define sequential development but also to provide a chronology, for without this the all-important factor of *rate of change* will be impossible to assess. The statement may be self-evident, but all too often in the recent literature the problem has been glossed over to the detriment of the arguments presented. In Wessex we are now in a relatively fortunate position. It has long been realised that over much of the area pottery was not only comparatively prolific but changed quite rapidly in style and technology. A ceramic sequence beginning with All Cannings Cross pottery and ending with 'Belgic' wares formed the basis of pre-war chronologies (Hawkes 1931; Wheeler 1943) and is still, with modifications, useful today. Some years ago the writer (Cunliffe 1966; 1974(8)) put forward a scheme of successive style-zones for the Wessex Iron Age, based on the then-available assemblages, and sought to attach to it rough dates, albeit often based on very little evidence. More recent work has offered the possibility for refinement both of the sequence and of its absolute dating.

The improved scheme developed from a detailed consideration of the very considerable collection of well-stratified pottery recovered from the current programme of excavations at Danebury (Cunliffe 1984a, 231–331). In summary nine successive *ceramic phases* (cp's) were defined. The first two, not present at Danebury, were based on an assessment of scattered material found elsewhere in Wessex principally from All Cannings Cross and certain Dorset sites, while knowledge of the last two (cp 8 and 9), thinly represented at Danebury, was much enhanced by the stratified sequence recovered from the recent excavations at Hengistbury Head. At the time of writing current work at the remarkable site of Potterne in Wiltshire offers the strong likelihood that cps 1 and 2 will soon be much further refined.

The Danebury assemblages, covering cp 3–7, were

subjected to a programme of radiocarbon dating. From the 70 assessments obtained it was possible to offer broad confirmation of the validity of the phases and to present a range of 'best-fit' absolute dates, the detailed arguments for which are presented elsewhere (Cunliffe and Orton 1984). A few, largely isolated, radiocarbon dates from other sites provide broad brackets for cps 1 and 2, while the appearance of amphorae and Gallo–Roman imports allow approximate dates to be offered for cps 8 and 9. The overall scheme is set out in Fig. 2.1 and is the best that can be offered on present evidence, though further refinement will soon be possible (see for example Lock 1984). For ease of discussion we group the ceramic phases into *earliest, early, middle, late* and *latest*, and it is under these generalised chronological headings that the Wessex Iron Age will here be considered.

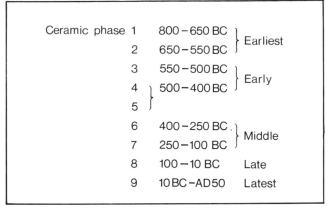

Figure 2.1 *Correlation of ceramic phases (cps) with absolute dates and phases.*

The Earliest Iron Age: *c.* 800–550 BC

For the purpose of this discussion the period from about the beginning of the eighth century until the middle of the sixth century — a period of 250 years or so — will be considered as the earliest phase of the Iron Age even though the quantity of iron in use was small and most of the tools and weapons current at the time were bronze, made in the traditions of the Late Bronze Age (Thomas forthcoming).

The pottery evidence, insofar as it is at present available, suggests a recognisable chronological development from an early phase (dominated by large S-profiled jars and jars with flaring rims, often highly decorated with stamped and incised geometric motifs, and by small bipartite bowls sometimes haematite-coated and sometimes furrowed around the shoulder and neck) to a late phase in which the large decorated jars became uncommon and the furrowed bowls, now with flaring rims, are more frequently found (Cunliffe 1966, 34–9). The division is not well demonstrated in the literature and should be regarded as little more than an approximation, pending further work at Potterne, where far more precise definition will be possible.

Two points in particular deserve emphasis: a) the earliest IA pottery in Wessex marks a distinct break with the last stages of the Deverel–Rimbury tradition which preceded it; b) the earliest pottery styles are very widely distributed across Wessex from the Berkshire Downs in the north to the Dorset coast in the south and from the eastern fringes of Somerset to the Test Valley (Fig. 2.2). A wide variation in fabric shows that similar styles of pottery were being made in a number of different areas. How these observations should be interpreted is less clear. One possibility is that the high degree of decoration and the widespread allegiance to a limited range of motifs may be part of a reflection of the desire on the part of the Wessex community to demonstrate a common ethnicity to distinguish themselves from neighbouring groups (cf. Hodder 1981). That the larger assemblages of decorated pottery tend to concentrate on the northern, north-western and southern fringes of the area might be thought to add support to such a suggestion, for in frontier zones the need to identify is all the greater. This is a theme to which we shall return.

The period seems to be one of intense resource-exploitation and quite possibly of manufacturing specialisation. Extraction of salt is attested in the vicinity of Kimmeridge on the Dorset coast (Davies 1936) and from the same area shale was quarried to be extensively worked on neighbouring Purbeck sites into armlets and other trinkets which were widely distributed across Wessex and beyond (Cunliffe and Phillipson 1968; Cunliffe 1982b, fig. 15). It was in this period that an extensive settlement developed on Hengistbury Head (Cunliffe 1978b) quite possibly attracted by the readily-available supplies of high-grade iron ore. Further north in Wiltshire the community occupying All Cannings Cross was engaged in producing unusually large quantities of bone tools (Cunnington 1923), while the recent work at Potterne has yielded evidence of bronze-working on a considerable scale (C. Gingell, pers. comm.). To this may be added a still flourishing bronze 'trade' with the adjacent coasts of Armorica witnessed by the extensive distribution of Breton axes concentrating on the Wessex coastal zone (Thomas forthcoming) and the single Sicilian axe from Southbourne, near Hengistbury, which adds a more exotic flavour. Although the data are very incomplete and largely unquantifiable the distinct impression given is of an intensification in production and exchange distinguishing the earliest IA of Wessex from the preceding period.

The harbours of the Dorset coast and the immediate hinterland appear to have served as a contact zone linked by the sea to Armorica and by the river-system, traversing a wide tract of heath, to the heartland of Wessex — a zone the importance of which was further enhanced by rare local commodities such as salt, shale and iron (Cunliffe 1982b). All the while that the Wessex communities were bound in systems of exchange to Armorica the contact zone would have flourished, and in this may lie the reason for its unusually dense settlement-pattern in the eighth to sixth centuries (Fig. 2.3).

The concept of a contact zone could be extended to explain the apparent richness of the settlements fringing

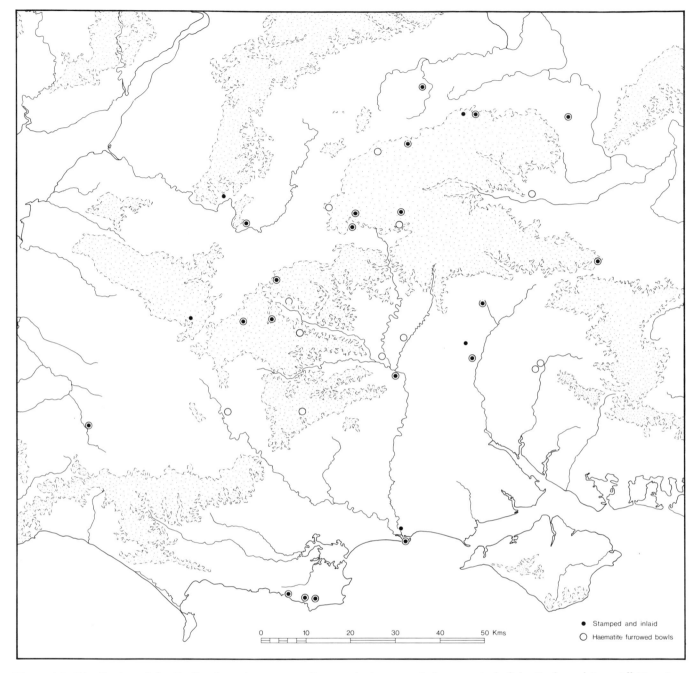

Figure 2.2 *Distribution of the Earliest Iron Age pottery. Sites producing ceramic forms typical of the Early and Late All Cannings Cross style are plotted. The types considered are large jars with stab-filled motifs, small bipartite furrowed bowls and flared furrowed bowls. The sites plotted are listed with references in Appendix 1. Source: Cunliffe 1984a with amendments.*

the western side of Wessex, along the interface between the chalk downland environment and the more varied geologies of the western counties. Through this region a range of rare commodities is likely to have passed. If such an hypothesis bears a semblance of truth one might expect to be able to detect evidence of the exchange-patterns in the material remains from settlements such as Potterne, All Cannings Cross, Longbridge Deverill Cow Down, etc. Herein lies the potential for testing.

The simple model which is offered, then, is one of a vigorous Wessex society displaying its ethnic unity through ceramic decoration. During this time the communities of the fringes, particularly the west and the south, developed socio-economic systems, sometimes involving specialist production, which allowed them to

serve as intermediaries in the exchange of goods between the Wessex chalkland massif and the south-west of Britain to the west and Armorica to the south (Fig. 2.4).

Settlement evidence for the period is comparatively plentiful. The largest sites at present known are *hilltop enclosures* of which three have been sampled on a reasonable scale (Fig. 2.5): Harting Beacon in Sussex (Bedwin 1978; 1979) and Balksbury I and Winklebury I both in Hampshire (Wainwright 1970 and forthcoming; Smith 1977; Robertson–MacKay 1977). All three share common characteristics; they are large (10.5, 18.0 and 6.8 ha respectively in area); defended by a comparatively slight rampart and ditch (timber-structured at Harting Beacon and Winklebury); and the interior is not densely occupied. An area-excavation of 1.9 ha at Winklebury

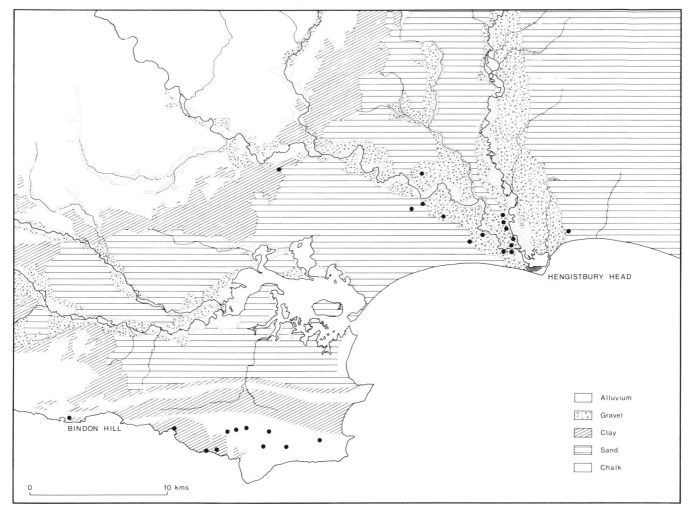

Figure 2.3 *The Wessex contact zone in the Earliest Iron Age.*

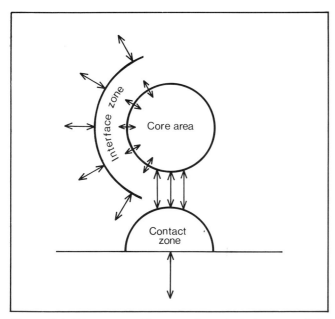

Figure 2.4 *Diagram to illustrate the principal zones of the Earliest Iron Age in Wessex and their relationships.*

has produced evidence of six circular post-built houses, 42 four-post 'granaries' and only three certain pits; Balksbury has yielded houses and four-post structures

while the smaller area-excavation in Harting Beacon has offered only four four-posters. A number of other 'hillforts' in Wessex appear to belong to this same general category, at least on superficial topographical grounds, in that they are large with slight defences and, where limited excavation or surface sherd-collection has added some detail, can usually be shown to belong to the earliest IA period. Some are shown in plan on Fig. 2.6 and a general distribution of possible sites is given on Fig. 2.22, but without further large-scale excavation it is difficult to say if those plotted all conform to the same general type as Winklebury, Harting and Balksbury.

Large hilltop enclosures are also known outside Wessex, for example in the Cotswolds, where sites like Norbury and Nottingham Hill quite possibly belong to the same category. Limited excavation in Norbury (Saville 1983) has shown that the site contained rows of four-posters though no dating evidence was recovered. In the Chilterns Ivinghoe Beacon has been demonstrated by excavation to be very similar (Cotton and Frere 1968) and can probably be dated to the eighth century on the basis of bronzes found in stratified contexts. Elsewhere, in north Northamptonshire, Nadbury Camp and the early phase of Borough Hill have superficial characteristics which link them to the same group. In other words the large, occupied hilltop enclosures of the earliest IA

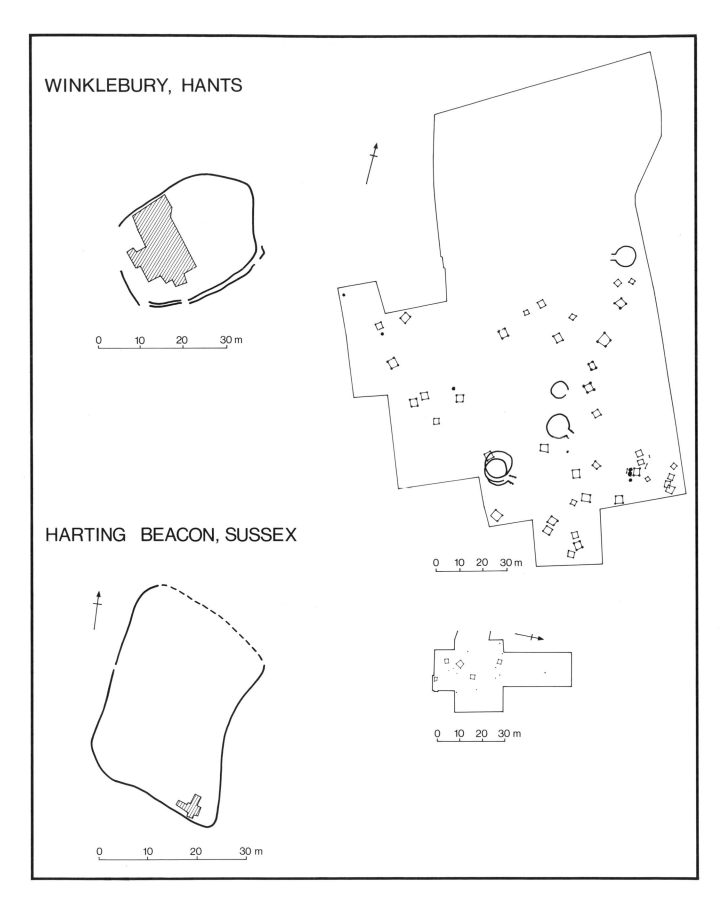

WINKLEBURY, HANTS

0   10   20   30 m

HARTING BEACON, SUSSEX

0   10   20   30 m

0 10 20 30 m

0 10 20 30 m

Figure 2.5 *Two well excavated Early hilltop enclosures of the Earliest Iron Age.*

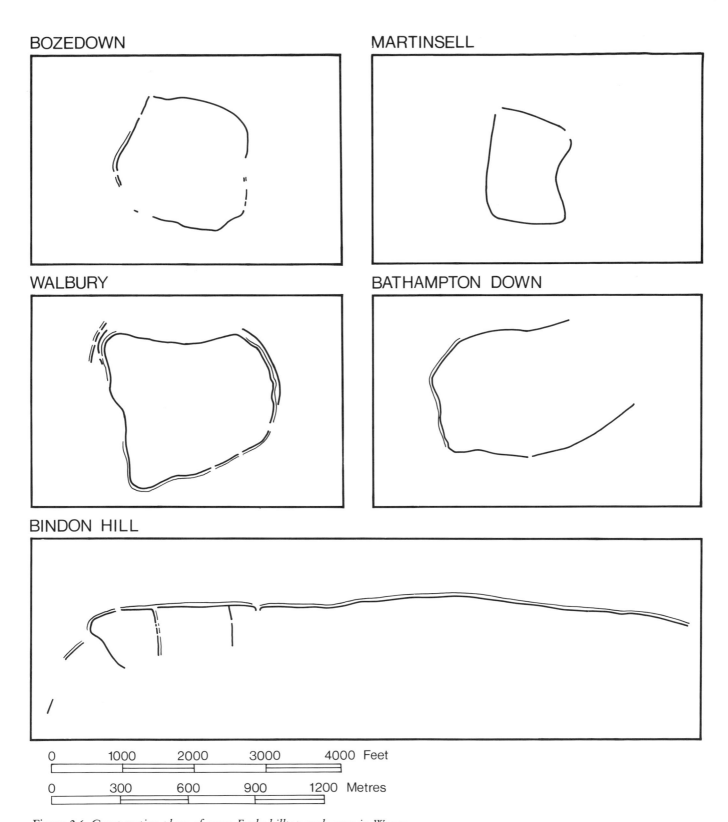

Figure 2.6 *Comparative plans of some Early hilltop enclosures in Wessex.*

appear to be a phenomenon which extends well beyond the bounds of Wessex.

The interpretation of these sites raises problems since, even in total, the quantity of artefactual, faunal and floral data is disappointingly small. That they do, however, represent the communal effort of a social group of some size is suggested by the considerable effort which must have gone into constructing the defensive circuit, not only the shifting of earth but the cutting and carting of timber and, where it was used, of stone. The presence of well-built houses at Balksbury and Winklebury, and the fact that at Winklebury houses were several times rebuilt, proves occupation but not necessarily continuous occupation.

Common to all hilltop enclosures so far excavated on any scale are rows of four-post structures usually referred to as granaries. This is not the place to enter into a detailed consideration of their many possible interpretations (e.g. Ellison and Drewett 1971), but simply to emphasise that since we do not (and possibly cannot) know the function of these structures, speculation will inevitably lead us into danger. If indeed they are granaries then the potential storage-capacity of these sites is considerable, and it could be that their prime function was to serve as communal grain-stores (Cunliffe 1976b, 347). On the other hand if they were the bases of fodder ricks (a distinct possibility) then the interpretation would change dramatically and it might be suggested that the hilltop enclosures were, in fact, the autumn/winter corrals for the community's livestock, guarded by some segment of the social group. The presence of barley grains around the structures is not particularly relevant to the argument, because barley cut green in the stalk makes excellent fodder.

If we take the evidence from the hilltop enclosures alone, interpretation is at something of an impasse; but one way forward is to compare them with broadly-contemporary settlements of other kinds. Of these the most useful are All Cannings Cross, Longbridge Deverill Cow Down, Potterne and Old Down Farm. Since work at Potterne has only just begun, Longbridge is still unpublished except in interim note and All Cannings is an old excavation not published to modern standards, the available data-base is somewhat thin: nonetheless various general points can be made.

In the first place several of the settlements of this period were enclosed with a ditch, and possibly with a bank and hedge, defining an occupation-area of 1–3 ha: this form of settlement continued throughout much of the *early* and *middle* IA. A second point of some relevance is that storage pits were found on most of the sites of this period. Of these the best known, Old Down Farm near Andover, Hants., produced clear evidence of a single large circular house together with 26 storage pits within a ditched enclosure just over a hectare in extent: the potential grain-storage capacity was considerable, and the range of artefacts recovered suggests an extended period of intensive occupation. The contrast between the 'farmsteads' and the hilltop enclosures is striking, and must surely imply differences in function. Without more evidence it is unwise to go further; but one quite plausible model would be to suggest that the 'farmsteads' were single- or extended-family units — the home base and the centre of the agricultural regime — while the hilltop enclosures reflected the common pastoral activities of the larger community. The vast upland enclosures would be well suited to pastoral functions, and in such a system would also serve as both a visible sign of society's cohesion and a location for communal meetings of a social, religious and political nature: they would serve to focus and to symbolise the larger social group.

A division into two 'settlement' elements is an over-simplification, and there are hints of this in the archaeological record. At Budbury, for example, a rectangular enclosure of about 3 ha, strongly defended with a double ditch-system, occupied the end of a steep promontory: from material found in a comparatively limited ex-cavation it was clearly intensively occupied (Wainwright 1970). Lidbury is another small but well-defended promontory site of this period: it produced 11 storage pits in a limited trial excavation (Cunnington 1917). The even less well-known Olivers Camp (Cunnington 1908) has similar characteristics and, further afield, Highdown in Sussex (Wilson 1940; 1950) belongs to the same category: it was strongly defended and intensively occupied. Sites like these (Fig. 2.7) could well be the settlements of a more aristocratic element displaying their power by choice of position and strength of defences. The possibilities for building complex social models are intriguing but we need to know far more about these sites before we can begin.

The early Iron Age: *c.* 550–400 BC

In central Wessex the *early Iron Age* can be characterised by the appearance of a highly distinctive range of fine pottery — tightly-made bowls coated with haematite and ornamented with horizontal cordons and with scratched geometric decoration inlaid with white paste. These 'scratched-cordoned bowls' (SCBs) when analysed prove to be made of brickearth, the nearest source of which is to be found just north of Salisbury (Williams and Wandibba 1984). The high degree of technical competence required in their manufacture and the close similarity in decorative style strongly suggests that they are a specialist product widely distributed among the Wessex communities which were otherwise using a more locally-produced range of ceramic products (Cunliffe 1984a, 254).

The distribution-pattern of these SCBs is interesting (Fig. 2.8). They are found at both hillforts and 'farmsteads' in such numbers as to suggest that the status of the site did not influence the quantity of fine pottery imported (or so it would seem on present evidence). There does, however, appear to be a marked fall-off in quantity along the line of the River Test. To the west considerable numbers of vessels have been found at the hillforts of Danebury and Quarley and at the farmstead of Meon Hill; but very little has come from the territory to the east of the river, even though a number of contemporary sites have been excavated. While this could, still, be an accident of survival and recovery it is tempting to suggest that the Test may have been a social boundary at this time across which specialised ceramics, symbolising the ethnic unity of the central Wessex community, did not pass. Insufficient is known of sites to the north and to the west to allow similar observations to be made with any assurance, except that the distribution appears to be confined to the chalklands.

In the southern part of Wessex, in Dorset, contemporary fine wares occur; but they are quite different in style, consisting of simple wall-sided, haematite-coated bowls usually without decoration. The two distribution-patterns are mutually exclusive, the boundary lying somewhere in the vicinity of the Stour valley (Fig. 2.8). To some extent this divide is the one already identified between the core area and contact zone of Wessex in the

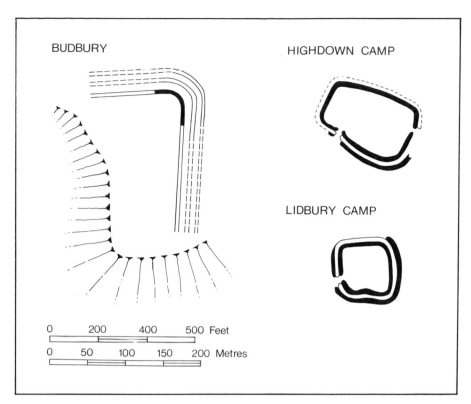

BUDBURY

HIGHDOWN CAMP

LIDBURY CAMP

0   200   400   500 Feet

0   50   100   150   200 Metres

Figure 2.7 *Comparative plans of fortified sites of the Earliest Iron Age.*

earliest IA, and it is a boundary which was to be maintained throughout the rest of the pre-Roman IA. Could it be that we are observing here the emergence of tribal boundaries which were to remain largely unaltered for more than half a millennium? The problem will be considered again after more evidence has been presented.

Using the SCB horizon as a broad chronological indicator (which, by considering associated coarse wares, can be extended beyond the narrow confines of its distribution) it is possible to define significant changes in the settlement-pattern at this time. Simply stated, there is no good evidence as yet to suggest that any of the early hilltop enclosures continued in use; instead, a new type of smaller and more strongly-defended hillfort was built in many parts of the region. These *early hillforts* were usually constructed as contour works, averaging 5 ha in extent. They were defended by a rampart, faced inside and out with timber, stone or a combination of the two, fronted by a berm and ditch, and were usually provided with two entrances facing each other on either side of the fort. A selection of the better-known examples is illustrated in Fig. 2.9 together with a distribution-map (Fig. 2.23). It should, however, be stressed that the known distribution is only a pale reflection of what must once have been a very much denser packing. Many, if not most, of the Wessex forts about which nothing is yet known may well have begun life in this period. The block of downland between the Test and Bourne provides a well-studied example, since all five forts have been sampled by excavation. One, Balksbury, appears not to have been used as a fort at this time, while the other four, Figsbury, Bury Hill, Quarley Hill and Danebury all provide evidence (admittedly of varying quality) to suggest that they were built at

roughly the same time in the early period. This pattern is probably typical of the rest of Wessex.

Four forts built at this time have been subjected to different degrees of area-excavation: South Cadbury (Alcock 1972), Chalbury (Whitley 1943), Maiden Castle (Wheeler 1943) and Danebury (Cunliffe 1984a). Of these the results of the South Cadbury excavation have not yet been published in detail; at Maiden Castle the areas exposed were comparatively small, and so confused by later structures that little could be said of the early internal arrangements except that the contemporary plan included post-built structures (at least one a four-poster) and a number of cylindrical pits. At Chalbury, on the other hand, although excavation was limited, the fact that the site was abandoned at the end of the early period strongly suggests that many of the 30 or so large circular depressions visible in the interior, like the three sampled by excavation, are likely to be huts belonging to the early fort. About an equivalent number of smaller depressions probably represent pits, of which one has been excavated. The plan of surface features (Fig. 2.10) shows a degree of internal zonation: huts for the most part lie around the periphery of the site, leaving an open space in the southern part of the central area; while pits concentrate in the northern zone. However, without large-scale excavation it would be unsafe to base much on the plan alone.

The idea that the interiors of the early hillforts were organised in functionally distinct zones is to some extent borne out by the excavation of Danebury (Fig. 2.10), where it is possible to distinguish a road running between the gates, with one or more side roads branching from it. The central part of the site was densely packed with pits, while the houses cluster in the

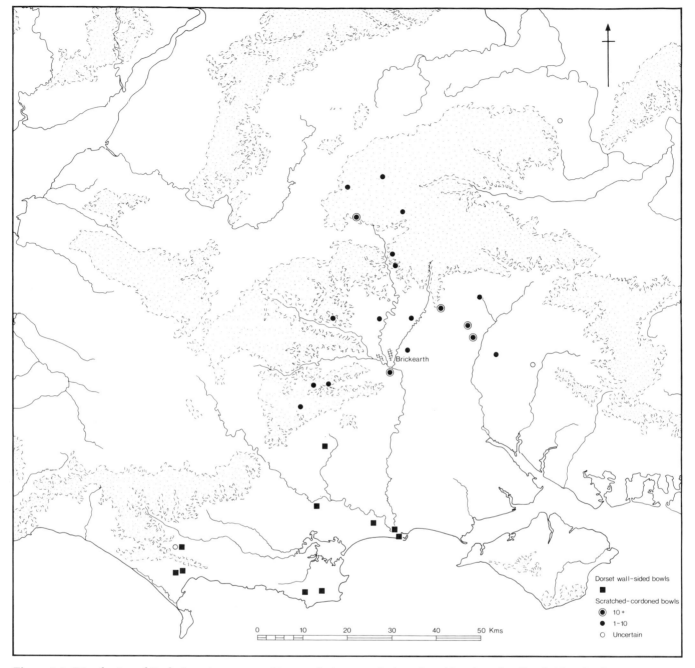

Figure 2.8 *Distribution of Early Iron Age pottery. Sites producing scratched-cordoned bowls and wall-sided bowls of Dorset type are plotted. The sites, with references, are listed in Appendix 1.*

southern part of the enclosure and in the zone immediately behind the rampart. In the centre, close to the summit of the hill, were found two small rectangular buildings which may have been shrines (Cunliffe 1984a *passim*).

Sufficient, then, survives from the interior of these early hillforts to show that they were quite densely settled with houses, pits and four-post structures, and that a degree of organised arrangement seems to have been maintained. It should be added that a wide range of domestic debris has also been recovered from them, implying an intensity of occupation quite unlike that experienced by the early hilltop enclosures.

As well as in size and the nature of the internal occupation, the two types of enclosure also differ in the strength and complexity of the enclosing earthworks.

While it is true to say that the early hilltop enclosures had defensive capabilities, it is equally true that, by comparison, the early hillforts were massively defended. Not only were the ramparts more substantial but there is ample evidence to show that several of the forts underwent successive rebuildings (e.g. Danebury, Chalbury, Figsbury and possibly St. Catherine's Hill). Add to this the presence of caches of slingstones within, and the fact that at least two (Danebury and Maiden Castle) can be shown to have had quite complex outworks at one of their gates in this period, and the grandiose defended nature of these early hillforts becomes apparent. It is for this reason that the distinction has been made between early hilltop *enclosures* and early *hillforts*. It could, of course, be argued that the scale of the defences and the entrance works reflect the desire of the

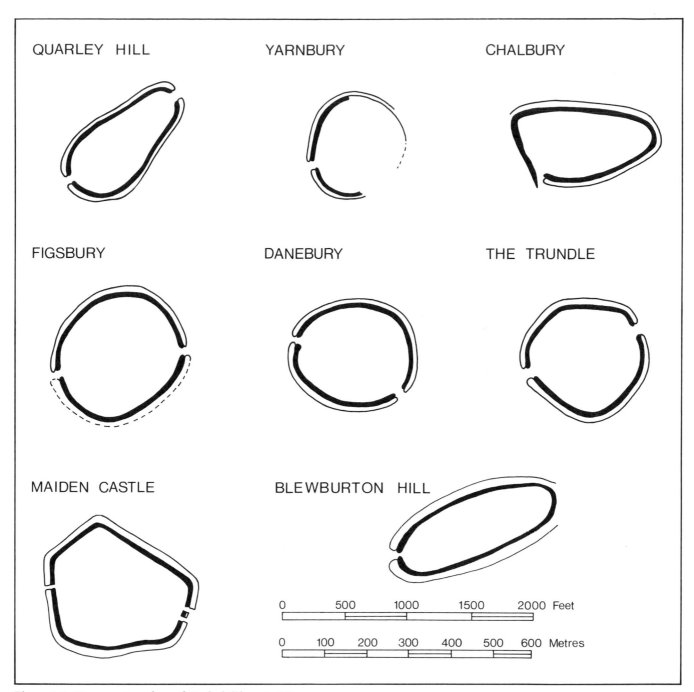

Figure 2.9 *Comparative plans of Early hillforts in Wessex.*

occupants to present an impressive face to others. This may be, but the slingstones and evidence for the partial burning of the defences at St. Catherine's Hill and Danebury during this period hint at a more bellicose situation.

Before general comment is offered on these observations the contemporary farmstead settlements must be considered. A substantial body of evidence is now available to suggest that many farmsteads remained in use over a considerable period of time (Fig. 2.11 offers a summary of the data, showing the duration of occupation of published sites in terms of the ceramic-phase scheme outlined above). In many cases the boundaries, once established, delimited the occupied area for the duration; but at Little Woodbury and Meon Hill early palisade-fences were later replaced with ditches quite

possibly backed by hedges growing on low banks. There is nothing about the farmsteads of the early period to distinguish them, in any significant respect, from what little is known of those of the earliest period and from the much better evidence for the middle IA phase. The continuity of use and the presence of the same range of structures and occupation-debris imply little change in this sector of the socio-economic system.

In summary, the evidence for the early IA period outlined above indicates that at one level in the social hierarchy there was rapid and quite dramatic development, with the appearance of a rash of strongly-defended hillforts; while at another, the family or extended-family level, little change can be discerned. There is nothing incongruous in this dichotomy, but possible explanations are best left until the situation in

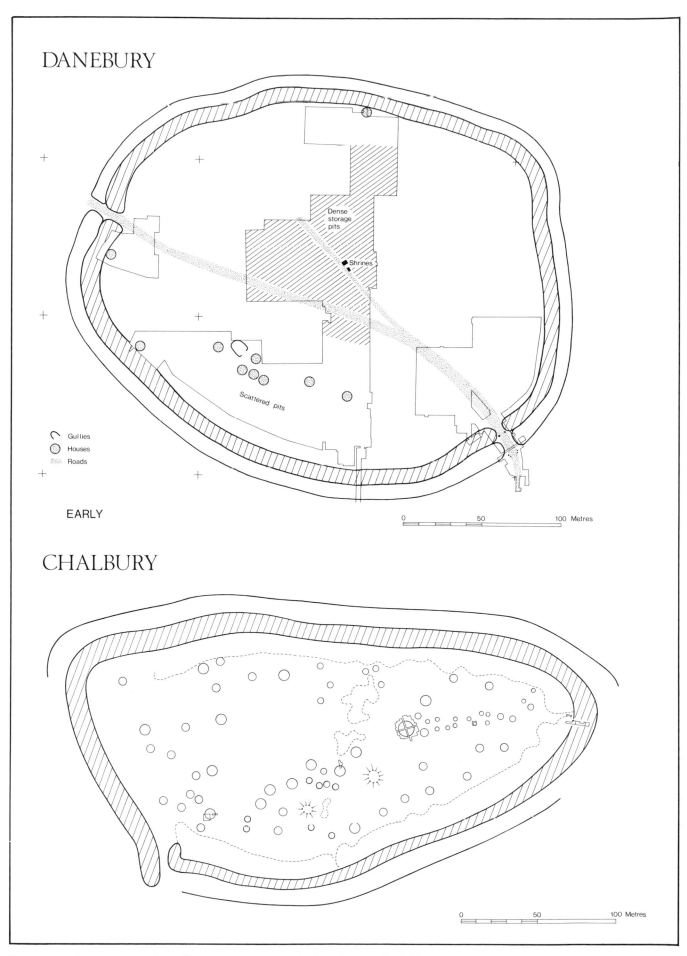

DANEBURY

Dense
storage
pits

Shrines

Scattered pits

Gullies
Houses
Roads

EARLY

0   50   100 Metres

CHALBURY

0   50   100 Metres

Figure 2.10 *Interior occupation of Early Iron Age date in Danebury and Chalbury.*

22

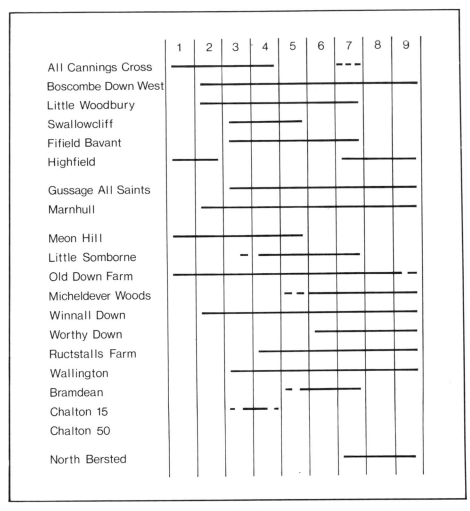

Figure 2.11 *The duration of occupation in selected farmsteads in terms of the ceramic phase scheme.*

the middle IA has been considered, to provide a broader perspective against which to view the problem.

The middle Iron Age: *c.* 400–100 BC

The ceramic development of Wessex in the middle IA is now comparatively well understood. The period begins with an assemblage of plain simple forms, usually fired in a reducing atmosphere, which develop without break from the earlier traditions. As the period proceeds, linear tooled decoration becomes increasingly common (Cunliffe 1984a, 254–6; Lock 1984a, 242–4) and a range of regional styles emerges (Cunliffe 1984a, Figs. 6.23, 6.24). Against this general background it is possible to discern a number of potentially interesting patterns.

Perhaps most evident is the continuing divide in ceramic tradition between southern Wessex (broadly Dorset south of the Stour) and the rest of Wessex. For convenience the ceramics of the southern zone are referred to as the *Maiden Castle–Marnhull style* and the rest as the *saucepan-pot continuum*. As the map (Fig. 2.13) will show, the saucepan-pot continuum covers a considerable area, stretching from the Severn estuary eastwards to a line joining the River Mole to Beachy Head and from the south coast northwards to the southern edge of the Thames Valley. The ceramics of the

Cotswold–Severn zone are in the same general tradition (Cunliffe 1984c); but these, and the south-western decorated wares of Somerset, present significant differences to the rest of the area and are best excluded from the present discussion.

The core of the saucepan-pot zone (Wiltshire, Hampshire, Berkshire, Surrey and Sussex) presents a remarkable degree of unity in ceramic form, technology and decoration; but when individual decorative motifs are considered it is possible to define at least four zones, three of which overlap while the fourth, based on Wiltshire, remains largely discrete (Fig. 2.14). The Wiltshire style-zone is defined not only by a restricted assemblage of motifs but also by at least one petrologically-distinct fabric. Significantly the distribution of these types coincides almost exactly with the distribution of the SCB of the early period. It may also be of interest that it is in precisely the same territory that the distinctive Wessex-style La Tène I fibula is distributed (Cunliffe 1974(8), 14–8).

If we accept that elaborate ceramic decoration may have been adopted by communities to define their ethnic unity, then the conclusion must be that south Wessex and central Wessex (roughly Dorset and Wiltshire), which had already distinguished themselves by the middle of the sixth century, maintained and even

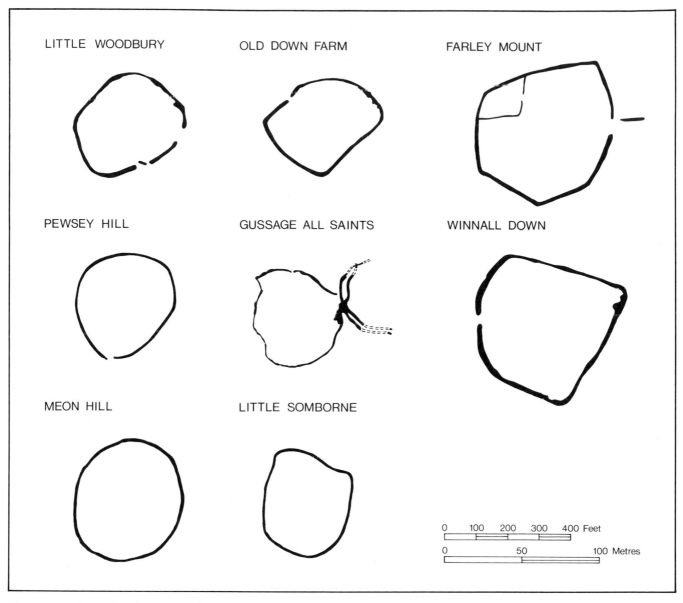

LITTLE WOODBURY   OLD DOWN FARM   FARLEY MOUNT

PEWSEY HILL   GUSSAGE ALL SAINTS   WINNALL DOWN

MEON HILL   LITTLE SOMBORNE

| 0 | 100 | 200 | 300 | 400 Feet |

| 0 | 50 | 100 Metres |

Figure 2.12 *Plans of Early and Middle Iron Age farmstead enclosures.*

intensified their separateness throughout the middle Iron Age. The rest of the saucepan-pot territory, eastwards of the Hampshire/Wiltshire border, although ceramically distinct from surrounding areas, does not, on present evidence, appear to be internally divided; but quantitative analysis of the overlap zones (when larger samples are available) may eventually show there to be rather more distinct boundaries. There is already some evidence to suggest that the Arun/Adur zone may have been the significant divide at this time that it clearly became later (Green 1981).

It has been suggested that the early period was a time when hillforts (*early hillforts*) were being built and maintained on an extensive scale throughout Wessex. During the middle period many of the early hillforts went out of use, while those that continued to be maintained were usually more massively defended: these we call *developed hillforts*. The general pattern is well represented in the Test–Bourne zone, where all the hillforts have been sampled. Of the four early forts three seem to have been abandoned by the end of the early

period, the fourth, Danebury, being greatly strengthened. The situation at Danebury is quite clear: the early defensive circuit was remodelled to create a massive rampart with a sloping external face continuous with the side of a deep V-shaped ditch. At the same time one of the entrances was blocked and the remaining one was totally reconstructed. To create sufficient material for the heightening of the rampart a substantial internal quarry-ditch was dug. Similar rebuilding-programmes are evident at a number of sites in southern Britain (in Wessex notably at South Cadbury and Blewburton).

Other patterns of refurbishment can also be recognised. At Yarnbury (Cunnington 1933) the old defences were totally abandoned and a new defensive circuit constructed beyond them greatly increasing the enclosed area, while at Torberry (Cunliffe 1976c) and Maiden Castle the old circuits were used in part but the enclosures were considerably enlarged. The same was probably true of many others such as Hambledon Hill (RCHM(E) Dorset 1970a, 92–3) and Flowers Barrow (RCHM(E) Dorset 1970b, 489–92), where detailed

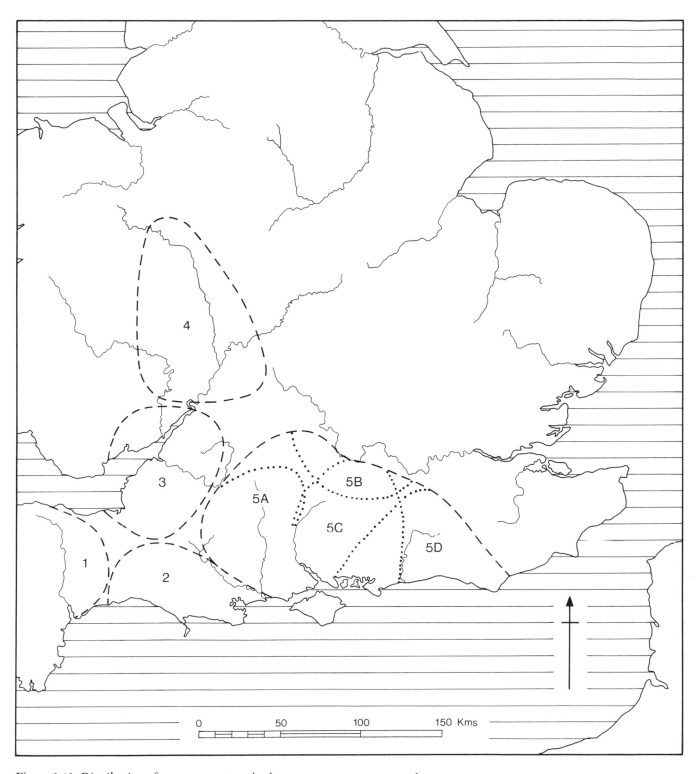

Figure 2.13 *Distribution of saucepan pots and other contemporary pottery styles.*

surface surveys allow the growth of the forts to be traced. Elsewhere hilltop enclosures of the earliest period were brought back into use, for instance Winklebury (Smith 1977), and possibly Hod Hill (Richmond 1968) (but here the surviving archaeological evidence is, at best, ambiguous). In addition, some new forts were founded on virgin sites: this can be demonstrated at several in Surrey and Kent (Cunliffe 1982a). The picture, then, is complex and may be summed up in simple diagram form (Fig. 2.15).

The same phenomenon is recognisable in other parts of southern Britain (e.g. Wilbury, Herts.; Hunsbury, Northants.; Breedon-on-the-Hill, Leics.; Wandlebury, Cambs.; and Bredon, Glos., to list only the better-known sites). To date the emergence of developed hillforts precisely is difficult. At Danebury the change took place at the beginning of cp 6, which can be dated on the basis of radiocarbon assessments to *c.* 400 BC. This is consistent with the scattered radiocarbon dates available in Surrey and the Weald (Cunliffe 1982a, 42–4). Elsewhere, wherever the evidence is recorded, rebuilding seems to have taken place during the currency

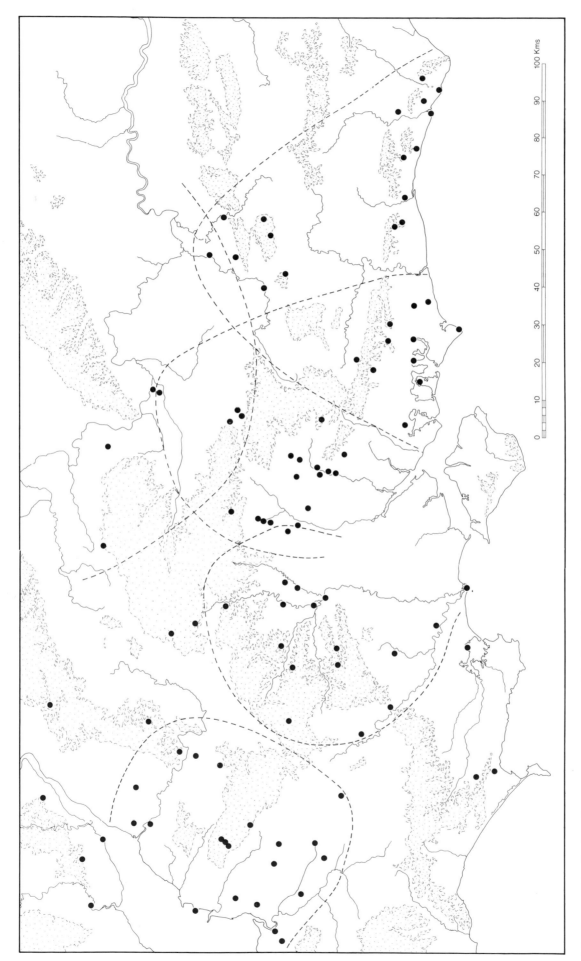

Figure 2.14 Distribution of saucepan pots in Wessex. The broken lines indicate the approximate boundaries of the distribution of distinctive stylistic motifs. (For details see Cunliffe 1984a, fiche 8D4).

100 Kms

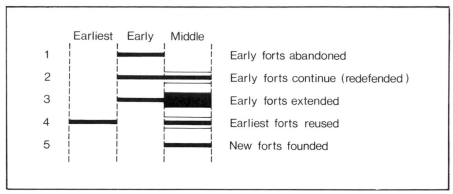

Figure 2.15 *Diagram to illustrate the reuse of hillforts.*

of pottery styles of, or equivalent to, cp 6 or 7. All that can safely be said, then, is that the developed hillforts are a phenomenon of the middle Iron Age, and that many of them probably originated in the period 400–300 BC.

The principal characteristic of the developed hillfort is its strongly-constructed defensive circuit, adopting the *glacis* principle (continuous slope from bank-crest to ditch-bottom) and an entrance approached by a long corridor usually (but not invariably) created by turning the rampart-ends inwards and siting the gate at the inner end. Some forts were, however, more elaborate, with multiple lines of defence and complex entrance earthworks and, as Fig. 2.16 shows, there was also a considerable variation in size. Complexity of plan must also reflect the different development histories of the individual forts. In other words the developed hillforts are likely to have varied in status one with another, and throughout the three centuries of the middle period there must have been changes in the fortunes of individual sites. The complex dynamics of the socio-political system is, therefore, fossilised in these forts; but without further large-scale excavation it will remain largely unreachable, except at a very general and incomplete level.

One general observation is worth making. When all sites possessing characteristics typical of developed hillforts are plotted, they exhibit a remarkable regularity in their spacing, each fort dominating a distinct block of territory often defined by natural landscape features (Fig. 2.24). Although the map is unavoidably a crude approximation to the true situation, and cannot reflect changes taking place within the three-hundred-year span of the middle period, it nonetheless strongly suggests that by this stage the Wessex landscape was divided into distinct territories each dominated by a single fort which, in all probability, represented a focus of socio-political power.

The interior organisation of developed hillforts is hardly known. Work at Maiden Castle was on too limited a scale to do more than show the enclosed area to be densely occupied with post-structures and many pits, the space in the lee of the ramparts being particularly favoured for houses. The same appears to have been true at South Cadbury. Trial excavations in the centre of Yarnbury (Cunnington 1933) also showed pits to be particularly common. For details, however, we have to rely on the excavations at Winklebury and Danebury which at first sight appear to offer contrasting pictures.

At Winklebury occupation of the middle IA occupied a restricted but quite extensive area in the centre of a much larger enclosure originating some centuries earlier. Post-structures, curved lengths of gullies probably belonging to huts and a number of pits were recovered (Fig. 2.17). At Danebury, on the other hand, the occupied area filled the enclosure and exhibited a high degree of planning, with rows of four- and six-post structures arranged along metalled streets in the southern half of the site, while houses, rebuilt many times over, occupied the peripheral zone just inside the rampart. The central and northern part of the site was occupied by pits and by gullies of circular plan (Fig. 2.17).

While the differences between the two sites are notable, they are quantitative rather than qualitative and could in part be explained simply by suggesting that Winklebury was occupied for only a brief period, while Danebury was in use throughout the entire middle period. The greater space available within the defences of Winklebury may also have been a factor, imposing less constraint on the layout, and thus the planning, of the settlement. Yet even if these suggestions are true the contrast between the two sites emphasises the complexity of the problem.

Analysis of the finds from Danebury suggests that the hillfort may have served a central-place function within its territory, raw materials, such as iron, bronze, shale and salt, being brought in for redistribution, while local commodities such as grain, wool and other animal products were accumulated and temporarily stored within the protection of the defences during the process of exchange. The details and arguments for this have been set out elsewhere (Cunliffe 1984a, 556–9). The presence of shrines represents another service which the fort was offering.

What emerges from this brief survey of the hillfort evidence is that the middle IA in Wessex saw the crystallising out of a few heavily-defended forts dominating clearly-defined territories within which they probably served as focal points. Here were articulated the social, economic, political and possibly religious systems of the community. Variation in defensive strength and difference in duration or intensity of

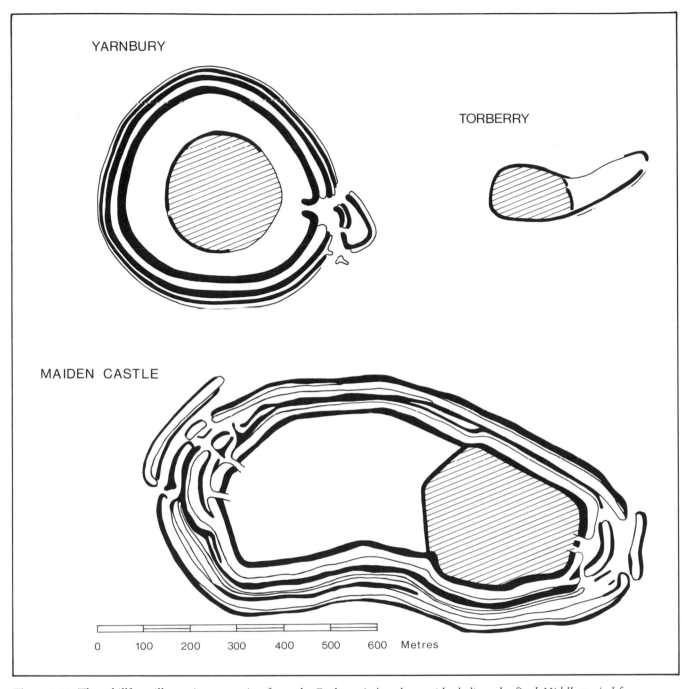

YARNBURY

TORBERRY

MAIDEN CASTLE

0   100   200   300   400   500   600   Metres

Figure 2.16 *Three hillforts illustrating expansion from the Early period enclosure (shaded) to the final Middle period form.*

occupation between forts is a reminder that the systems were dynamic.

The non-hillfort settlements of the middle IA are more numerous than those of succeeding periods (Cunliffe 1978a) and more varied. Roughly circular enclosures of traditional type such as Little Woodbury, Old Down Farm and Gussage All Saints continued to be occupied throughout the period; but additional, apparently unenclosed, settlements now appear: Battlesbury (Chadwick and Thompson 1956); Worthy Down (Dunning, Hooley and Tildesley 1929); and Winnall Down (Monk and Fasham 1980). The vast open settlement of Boscombe Down West (Richardson 1951) was already established by this time. It is in the middle period, too, that a new type of smaller enclosed settlement, the so-called 'banjo'-type, begins to appear (Perry 1970).

Recently-excavated examples at Bramdean (Perry 1974; 1982) and Micheldever Wood (Mond and Fasham 1980) show that, contrary to previous opinion, these enclosures were occupied even though the intensity (or duration) of occupation was not great.

Wherever detailed field-survey has been carried out on the Wessex downland, the impression given by the results (and without extensive excavation it can only be an impression) is that the landscape was densely packed with settlements, sometimes as close as 1–2 km apart. The extent of 'Celtic' field-systems, results of pollen analysis (Robinson, this volume) and the consideration of food-processing debris (Grant, this volume; Jones, this volume) leave little doubt that the economic base was mixed agriculture which, even by the early IA, had reached a degree of equilibrium and changed little

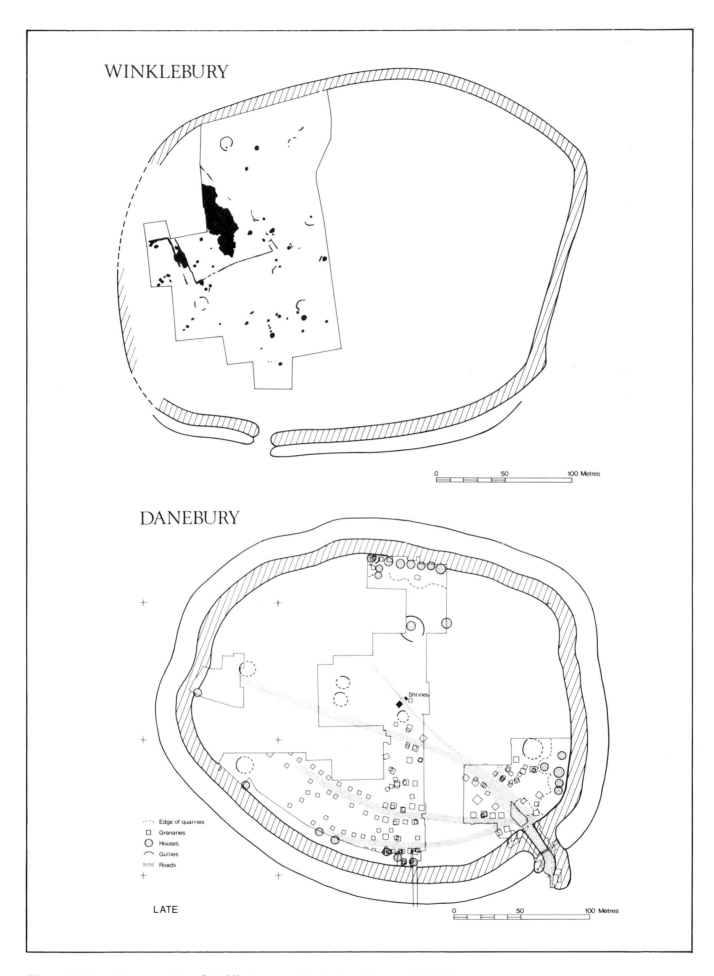

WINKLEBURY

DANEBURY

- - - - Edge of quarries
□ Granaries
◎ Houses
⌒ Gullies
▨▨ Roads
+

LATE

0   50   100 Metres

0   50   100 Metres

Figure 2.17 *Interior occupation of Middle Iron Age date in Danebury and Winklebury.*

throughout the early and middle periods. The relationship between the agricultural regimes of the farmsteads and hillforts is only dimly visible at the moment and is based entirely upon the analysis of the Danebury data; but Annie Grant's work has suggested that the fort was used as a centre for calving and lambing (Grant 1984, and this volume), while Martin Jones has been able to show that at least some of the grain brought to Danebury for storage originated in environmental zones far removed from the fort (Jones 1984). The implication would seem to be that a degree of interdependence existed between hillforts and farmsteads.

I good point to conclude with

Social change in Wessex: 800–100 BC

In this paper so far we have presented a body of data arranged in three broad chronological groups. Although it has necessarily been selective, the presentation has been as objective as possible with a minimum of interposed interpretation. We must now stand back and view the whole, in an attempt to see the broad development-trends and to offer some explanation for them. Sufficient will have been said above to demonstrate the limitations of the available data, in particular the lack of chronological precision, the incomplete nature of the evidence and the absence of a sufficient body of material to allow statistical testing. Given these constraints, any form of model-building will inevitably be far removed from reality. The exercise is, however, worthwhile so long as it focusses attention firmly on the questions which need to be asked, and can be asked. In other words, Iron Age studies (and indeed prehistory in general) is at a stage when creative model-building becomes an appropriate procedure, if by *creative* we mean the structuring of hypotheses containing the available data within a construct — an approximation — in which predictive value is inherent. The more useful of these models will offer predictions that are testable.

In this section four themes will be examined: hierarchy, production, population and ethnicity.

Much has been said of settlement, especially the strongly-defended enclosures generally classed as hillforts, partly because much care and attention has been lavished on them, but largely because by their very nature they represent the concerted efforts of a large sector of the community working under some kind of coercive or social control. The overall picture which emerges is of the construction, in the eighth to sixth centuries, of large hilltop enclosures, lightly occupied, and serving, it is suggested, as essentially pastoral enclosures for large social groups. If this is so, then they are likely also to have been centres for social gatherings held at fixed points during the farming year. Contemporary with these sites are the small strongly-defended fortlets producing a varied range of domestic debris: these may have been the home bases of an elite.

Some time in the sixth century it would seem that a major reorientation took place: earlier fortified sites were abandoned and a new range of intermediate-size hillforts were built, densely scattered across the landscape. Some of them suffered attack and periodic renovation and many have produced quantities of slingstones — evidence which together suggests a period of stress. The phase was brief, and by the beginning of the fourth century a pattern of wider-spaced and more strongly-defended 'developed hillforts' had emerged. Many of these seem to have remained in use, often in increasingly aggrandised form, for three centuries or more.

The picture may best be characterised by suggesting an *initial* socio-economic system passing through a period of change and emerging in a *re-ordered* form. The period of change was brief (c. 550–400) but was accompanied by stress.

Let us attempt to describe the two systems in a little more detail: the *initial* system (i.e. the earliest IA) involved:

a) the communal ordering of livestock, as witnessed by large hilltop enclosures and systems of ranch boundaries. This might well imply that land, or at least pasture, was communally and not individually owned

b) social organisation focussing on the rhythm inherent in stock management

c) the existence of an elite resident in defended fortlets and possibly maintaining control over the redistribution of rare commodities

d) the presence of non-elite living in a variety of settlements, some of them enclosed, of extended-family or single-family size.

The *re-ordered* system saw:

a) the creation of hillforts with a corn-storage potential well in excess of that required by the estimated resident community (Cunliffe 1984a, 555–6) and serving as focal points for calving and lambing (Grant 1984, 506–9, 513–4)

b) hillforts developing 'defensive' characteristics for display, beyond the reasonable needs of defence

c) hillforts becoming centres for manufacture and exchange

d) farmsteads of varying kinds remaining in use, optimally sited so as to utilise a range of farming resources.

If the selection and interpretation of these characteristics is to some extent subjective, further comment by way of explanation is even more so; but nonetheless it must be attempted. The simplest explanation of the change from one system to the other would be in terms of the elite taking over the ownership of land (and possibly of livestock) and creating hillforts where all the functions previously carried out at hilltop enclosures and at their own residential fortlets were performed. The creation of these new central locations, and the total abandonment of the old, could then be seen as a symbolic act establishing the new order. One could even go so far as to suggest that the siting of Quarley Hill and quite probably of Sidbury and others, which were actually once focal points in the old ranch-boundary system, was a deliberate act legitimising the right of the elite over land they had now appropriated.

Why such a change should have taken place in the sixth–fifth century is open to debate. There may have been instabilities inherent in the initial system beyond the reach of archaeological recognition; but one point is worth considering as a possible cause. It was at this time that the systems of cross-Channel 'trade', which linked Wessex with Armorica and beyond, broke down: bronze, and no doubt other commodities, which had passed into Wessex through the southern contact zone ceased to arrive. The reasons for the breakdown were European-wide and not controlled by the Wessex community. Thus a range of products manipulated by the elite, and quite probably used by them to maintain authority, ceased to be available. New methods of control would have been called for if the social system was to maintain its hierarchic structure. This may have led to the appropriation of land and thus to the control of its productive capacity. The hypothesis is not at variance with the data and has the added, if doubtful, benefit of being plausible.

A dramatic change of the type suggested would undoubtedly have caused stress, and it would have taken some time for a new socio-political equilibrium to be established. The rapid emergence of early hillforts, the evidence for renovation and in some cases for burning, and the abandonment of a number of them with fewer emerging to positions of dominance by about 400 BC, give some indication of the process and duration of this phase of re-ordering. By the fourth century the new social order had firmly established itself and the developed hillforts, redolent of power, were now a dominant feature of the landscape.

At this point it is necessary to introduce the two linked themes of production and population. One of the most interesting observations to be made of the Danebury data is that both crop-production and animal husbandry showed no significant change over nearly 500 years of the settlement's active existence (Grant 1984; Jones 1984). In other words, the food-producing regime, once established in the phase of re-ordering (the early IA) remained stable. This appears to have been true for much of Wessex (Grant, this volume) and would be consistent with the view that the new socio-economic system had attained a degree of equilibrium from the beginning.

There are few data available for the earlier system (the earliest IA), but the bone-reports from Budbury and Old Down Farm (period 3) both suggest that cattle were almost as common as sheep. This is in marked contrast to the early and middle IA sites of Wessex, where sheep are three or four times more common than cattle. The general point was noted many years ago (Clark 1947) and was then explained in terms of the decline in woodland, which provided a suitable habitat for cows and pigs, at the expense of expanding arable. This may in part be true, but the system was probably more complex. Cattle are most conveniently reared within 1–2 km of a water-supply to obviate the need for excessive droving, while sheep can be left for long periods in upland areas well away from permanent water. Now, since the manuring of the fields, particularly the thin upland soils, was a crucial part of the agricultural regime, sheep were clearly vital to the economy. Any expansion of arable into unwatered downland areas must have been accompanied by a corresponding increase in the number and size of flocks. Without such an expansion it is difficult to see why such large numbers of sheep need have been reared.

But there is another complexity that needs to be considered: thin downland soils constantly ploughed and cropped would decline both in mineral content and texture. This decline, manifesting itself most obviously in crop yield, would be slow at first, particularly if a minimal manuring regime was maintained, but would eventually accelerate to the level to which it became detectable. An obvious response would have been to crop less and/or increase intensity of manuring. It is an interesting question whether soil-deterioration, once started, could be halted by such methods. At any event the system had within itself an instability which might have led to a situation of recurring crisis.

There are hints at Danebury that the threshold of instability might have been reached towards the end of the third century, for at about this time the percentage of sheep increases to 66% of the total, compared with an average of 57% for the preceding three hundred years, while the flocks show a marked increase in peridontal disease (Grant 1984, 506). Neither observation need imply stress, but together they are the kind of evidence one might expect to find if the agricultural regime was beginning to experience difficulties.

Soil-deterioration, bringing with it a decline in crop-yield and an increase in livestock disease would significantly lower the holding-capacity of the land. As mentioned above, there is some evidence to suggest an increase in the number of settlements in the middle IA, and this might well reflect an increase in population. Together these two trends could begin to force society into a situation of stress, or at the very least could threaten its state of equilibrium. It would be wrong, of course, to visualise a situation in which there was permanent and deepening food shortage; but given technological constraints, taboos and social customs requiring conspicuous consumption and the destruction of wealth, the closer the population-level and the real (ultimate) holding-capacity approached each other the more the buffer zone between the social holding-capacity and the real holding-capacity would be impinged upon, and the more society would be required to adapt its behaviour. Pressure for adaptation would cause stress.

It could be that in the increasingly massive defences of the developed hillforts, the quantities of slingstones found in many of them and the periodic evidence of burning and slaughter, we are seeing some of the manifestations of this stress. It has also been suggested that the increase in the number of propitiatory burials at Danebury reflects developing social tension (Walker 1984, 462–3). The collapse of the social system which supported the hillforts in central southern Britain, sometime about 100 BC, may well (at least in part) have been caused by factors of this kind. These are problems to which we will return.

Little has yet been said of productivity and the exchange of goods, largely because the data required for considerations of this kind are not yet available; but analysis of the finds lost, discarded and deposited at Danebury shows that the vast bulk of the material could have been produced within the territory of the fort, and a high percentage of the rest was obtainable from one of the adjacent territories: very little was actually derived from any distance. Thus it would seem that exchange of goods over long distances was not widely practised in the early and middle IA (Cunliffe 1984a, 556–7), or if it was the system is archaeologically undetectable.

Internally within Wessex two commodities seem to have been produced in bulk: grain and wool. Since grain was the main staple (Grant, this volume) this is hardly surprising, and the very considerable storage capacities recorded are likely to reflect community needs; but wool is a different matter. The artefacts of woollen cloth-production — spindle-whorls, loom-weights and 'weaving' combs — are extremely numerous on the majority of Wessex sites, and there is some suggestion that a distinction can be made between farmsteads, where spinning was more common, and hillforts, where artefacts of weaving are found in greater quantity (Sellwood 1984, 438–9). While it is impossible to convert artefact-counts to actual quantities of cloth made the impression given is of massive production. In view of what has been said of the need to increase flocks to multiply the output of manure, wool-production is best seen as a by-product of the agrarian system. Nonetheless woollen fabrics, made up into convenient units such as cloaks or blankets could have played a significant part in the exchange-systems of the community, and may have taken on a social rather than a purely economic role (Freedman and Rowlands 1977).

Finally we must return to the problems of ethnicity which have been raised several times above. The appearance of the highly distinctive scratched-cordoned bowls of the early IA in the core area of Wessex and the presence in exactly the same area of the distinctive Wessex La Tène I fibula and, later, the Wiltshire style of decorated saucepan-pot assemblage, strongly suggests that this region, broadly modern Wiltshire, recognised itself as an ethnically distinct territory throughout the early and middle IA (550–100 BC), the first signs of this distinctiveness coming at just the moment when the initial socio-economic system had broken down and the period of reorganisation had begun. Exactly the same exclusiveness was maintained in Dorset south of the Stour. In eastern Wessex, that is in Hampshire and into West Sussex, the first assemblage of decorated ceramics makes its appearance some time towards the end of the third century BC, implying the possibility of a somewhat different socio-political development. All three regions, once established, maintained their differences throughout the late IA and well into the Roman period. Surely

here we are seeing the appearance of tribes.

One further point is worth exploring. There were two periods when decorated ceramics were widely used in Wessex: the early IA (550–400) and the later part of the middle IA (c. 200–100), with a span of two centuries or more between when pottery was largely undecorated. The first of these corresponds with the time of stress occasioned by a re-ordering of the socio-economic system, the second with the time when, it is suggested, the system was undergoing another phase of stress brought about by declining productivity and increasing population. The need to display allegiances in some easily recognisable manner would have been particularly strong at these times. The coincidence is notable.

The late and latest Iron Age: c. 100 BC–AD 43

The starting point for any discussion of the changes evident in the last century and a half of the pre-Roman IA in southern Britain must be two famous passages in Caesar's commentaries on his Gallic War and the one insight provided by Frontinus:

> The coastal areas [of Britain] are inhabited by invaders who crossed from Belgium for the sake of plunder and war and then, when the fighting was over, settled there and began to work the land; these people have almost all kept the names of the tribes from which they originated (BG V, 12).
>
> Within living memory their king [i.e. of the Suessiones] had been one Diviciacus, the most powerful ruler in the whole of Gaul, who had given control over a large area not only of this region, but also in Britain as well (BG II, 4).
>
> Commius, the Atrebatan, when defeated by the deified Julius fled from Gaul to Britain.   (Frontinus, *Strategemeta* ii, 13, 11)

Herein lie a series of historical assertions directly relevant to the questions of social and political change in southern Britain which, however, one views the reliability of Caesar's writing, cannot be ignored.

It is not the purpose of this paper to offer a detailed discussion of the historiography of thought on the question, but a brief outline must be given if the present state of the subject is to be understood. The discovery and excavation of the urnfield cemetery at Aylesford, Kent, in 1886 led Sir Arthur Evans to propose that the fine wheel-made pottery, north Italian imported bronze vessels and the rite of cremation-burial, found together at Aylesford, represented the intrusive 'Belgae' who, he suggested, arrived in Britain c. 150 BC (Evans 1890). The argument was taken further with the publication of another Kentish cemetery, Swarling, in the report on which Bushe-Fox suggested that it was possible to distinguish between the primary Belgic settlement in Kent, the Thames Valley and Essex, and the settlement of Commius and his followers in central southern Britain (Bushe-Fox 1925). This theme was taken up and given archaeological flesh in the seminal paper 'The Belgae of Gaul and Britain' published in 1931 by Hawkes and Dunning.

Subsequent archaeological response has been twofold. On the one hand the idea of a second Belgic invasion into central southern Britain has fallen from favour following an early attack by Maud Cunnington (Cunnington 1932a); on the other much attention, numismatic and archaeological, has been focussed on the problem of the Aylesford–Swarling settlement (Allen 1961; Birchell 1965; Hawkes 1968; Harding 1974; Hachmann 1976; Rodwell 1976; Stead 1976; Scheers 1977; Kent 1978; 1981; Tyers 1980).

By the early 1980s the state of the debate may be summed up by saying that:

a) most writers accept, usually implicitly, the validity of Caesar's statements and begin with the premise of a major folk-movement from Belgic Gaul into the region of Kent, Essex and the Thames Valley

b) most numismatists incline to the view that the majority of the Gallo-Belgic coins found in Britain arrived as 'payments' made at the time of Caesar's Gallic and British campaigns and should not be related to the earlier movements of people

c) most archaeologists, studying the pottery and associated metalwork agree that it is impossible to isolate with any degree of certainty a pre-Caesarian Belgic horizon in Britain. Much of the datable metalwork is of Augustan and Tiberian date.

In an attempt to refocus on the problem the present writer has offered the suggestion that the Aylesford–Swarling phenomenon is entirely a post-Caesarian development and reflects a particular socio-economic system which developed in response to the need to articulate a greatly-increased level of trade and exchange between Britain and Gaul in the early stages of the Romanisation of Gaul and therefore has little to do with pre-Caesarian events. The argument is further extended by suggesting that, had there been an incursion of some segment of a Continental Belgic population, the simplest explanation of all the available evidence, sparse though it may be, is that the initial settlement focussed on the Solent and its hinterland (Cunliffe 1984b). It is this second aspect of the problem which will be further examined here.

That there was a significant change in material culture in central southern Britain in the first century BC is widely recognised. Elsewhere, in a series of papers originating from the excavation at Hengistbury Head, the writer has sought to demonstrate that in about 100 BC, or perhaps a little earlier, long-established 'trade' routes along the Atlantic seaways were invigorated by the activities of Roman entrepreneurs who had settled in the newly-founded province of Gallia Transalpina and were attempting to exploit native markets beyond the provincial boundaries. This trade brought the old Wessex contact zone into prominence again, and there developed at Hengistbury a major port-of-trade where Continental products such as Italian wine (in Dressel 1 amphorae), purple glass and north-western French wheel-turned pottery were imported, and from where redistribution to the Wessex hinterland was organised. As a reciprocal measure, metals from the south west, shale from Kimmeridge and no doubt other less tangible products such as hides, grain and slaves, were collected for export.

The details of the archaeological data and their broad historical context are discussed elsewhere and need not further concern us here (Cunliffe 1978b; 1982b; 1984b). Suffice it to say that the *floruit* of this trading-axis seems to have been 100–50 BC, though there is now evidence that trade continued along the western seaways, on a much-reduced scale, for another century. A simple model to explain these phenomena is that the Roman annexation of Gaul enabled the Roman consumer-market to begin to exploit the productive capacity of the British Isles. All the while that direct Roman influence was restricted to southern Gaul (c. 120-c. 60 BC) the easiest way to obtain British raw materials was by using the long-established western sea-routes (the Hengistbury axis); but as soon as Gaul was conquered (c. 50 BC) a more direct route (the Aylesford–Swarling axis) could be established. In both cases exchange was articulated through native middle men — that is, it took place largely within existing social systems. However, as soon as the Rhine frontier had been firmly established, during the Tiberian period, direct economic contact could be developed between the Roman system and the communities of Essex and Hertfordshire (Cunliffe 1984b).

The main problem facing those who wish to study the social and economic development of southern Britain in the last century and a half before the Roman conquest is to distinguish between the effects of commercial relations established at the instigation of the Roman economy and the impact of any folk-movement which may have occurred. The answers (if indeed they are discernible) lie in the archaeological evidence, to which we must now turn.

One of the most noticeable changes to take place in the material culture of central southern Britain towards the beginning of the first century BC, was a dramatic improvement in potting technique. Over most of the region hand-made vessels heavily gritted with crushed stone (usually flint) gave way to harder-fired sandy fabrics, the majority of the vessels now being made, or at least finished, on the wheel. As might be expected most of the forms derive directly from native traditions, the only difference being that the wheel imposed a tighter control of the medium, leading to more-precisely moulded profiles. In this way the widely distributed bead-rimmed bowls and jars emerged. But beside these types were more exotic forms: necked-cordoned bowls, tazze and pedestal-based jars. The first two are types well-known in Armorica, and it is clear from the Hengistbury evidence that, in the first half of the first century BC, large numbers of these Armorican products were being imported to the Hengistbury region where they were copied in local fabrics, the copies being widely distributed inland. It seems quite probable, therefore, that the advance in ceramic technology was first introduced to the Wessex contact zone from Armorica, and disseminated thence to central Wessex and Dorset. In this context it may be relevant to point out that it was at precisely this time that the shale armlet industry of Purbeck changed from hand-cutting techniques to lathe-turning.

The pedestal-based jars, however, pose interesting

problems. They appear with the 'contact phase' pottery assemblage at Hengistbury in the period tentatively dated 100–50 BC, though in small numbers. The fabrics are totally unlike those of the north-western French imports and, as far as can be judged from preliminary XRF analysis, do not conform to local clays. Add to this the supporting observation that the type is largely unknown in Armorica but is common in the Seine valley and Upper Normandy, and it becomes reasonable to suggest that their appearance at Hengistbury in pre-Caesarian times, and elsewhere in the Solent region in less surely dated contexts, may be the result of a Seine–Solent axis of contact (Cunliffe 1984b). The point is one of considerable potential interest but requires more detailed analytical work before it can be pursued further.

A key question in the discussion is that of dating. Can we recognise a series of far-reaching changes in central southern Britain in the pre-Caesarian period? If one accepts that the Hengistbury axis flourished in the first half of the first century BC, and converging threads of argument (particularly the coin evidence) would seem to indicate that it did, then a useful horizon is established, the most obvious elements being Dressel 1a amphorae, wheel-turning, and close copies of Armorican imports. At present assemblages of this kind are not widely recognised (or at least published) in Wessex except at Danebury, where a distinct horizon can be isolated (late IA = cp 8) in contexts immediately above late saucepan-pot assemblages of cp 7. Here the horizon marks a dramatic change in the use of the hillfort: occupation was now restricted to a small area of the interior, much of the rest of which was given over to the corralling of animals (Cunliffe 1984a, 550), pits were no longer used and the entrance fortifications, burnt at the end of cp 7, were not rebuilt. In other words the socio-political function of the site underwent a major upheaval some time about, or soon after, 100 BC.

Evidence of this kind is not widely available, but abandonment at about this time has been suggested for St. Catherine's Hill, Hants. (Hawkes *et al.* 1930), Torberry, Sussex (Cunliffe 1976c) and South Cadbury, Somerset (Alcock 1980), and on less sure indications appears to be true for the majority of hillforts which have been excavated in Wessex. Two possible exceptions to the rule, Maiden Castle and Hod Hill, should be noted, but in both cases there are hints in the excavation reports that the 'Durotrigan' phase of re-defence and occupation (equivalent to our late and latest IA) may have come very late and may, indeed, have been a brief phase of reuse immediately before and after the conquest of AD 43. These are questions requiring careful re-examination, particularly in the light of the South Cadbury results where the excavation suggests a long period of abandonment before a very late phase of reuse and re-defence. At present it is fair to say that the general pattern over the whole of Wessex is of widespread abandonment of hillforts as heavily occupied and strongly defended settlements at the beginning of the first century BC. Occupation on a much reduced scale

continued in some, while others show signs of re-defence and reuse at about the time of the Roman conquest.

The first century BC also saw changes in the organisation of rural settlement. For the most part single large ditched enclosures of 'Little Woodbury' type were abandoned and instead settlements comprising a series of smaller ditched units emerged, sometimes on previously-occupied sites (e.g. Gussage All Saints (Wainwright 1979); Old Down Farm (Davies 1981); Worthy Down (Dunning, Hooley and Tildesley 1929); Winnall Down (Monk and Fasham 1980)) and sometimes at new locations, for instance at Tollard Royal (Wainwright 1968) and Rotherly (Pitt Rivers 1887) (Fig. 2.18). Elsewhere some of the 'banjo enclosures' established in the middle IA continued in use and may, in the late period, have taken on the more complex forms known to us at present only from aerial photography (Perry 1966; 1970). The break with the traditional settlement-pattern, established half a millennium earlier, is notable and must raise the question of there being a major reorganisation within the socio-economic system.

At the 'farmstead' level, where evidence exists (e.g. Tollard Royal, Rotherly, Gussage All Saints, Old Down Farm), the basic unit appears to be the enclosed settlement of single- or extended-family size about 30–50 m across, beyond which exist a number of ditched paddocks used for a variety of farming operations. Insufficient data are yet published for any general assessment to be made of the economy and the changes which it may have experienced at this time. Thus, although the form of the settlement has changed, there is nothing in the archaeological record to suggest any major dislocation in social structure; and until better data are published we are unable to assess the nature of the economic base.

The abandonment of the hillforts, previously centres of elite residence, production and exchange (if the arguments offered above are accepted) does, however, imply a major socio-political dislocation. The only substantially-defended sites which might be thought to have replaced them are the double-ditched enclosures at Bilbury (*Wilts. Archaeol. Mag.* 58, 32–4, 243–4; 59, 186–7), Boscombe Down West (Richardson 1951), Chisbury (Cunnington 1932b) and possibly Bury Hill (Hawkes 1940); but these may well date to the Roman conquest period or even after. Thus we are forced to the conclusion that the political structure of the early and middle periods was for some reason overthrown in the early years of the first century BC.

In the east of England, at this time, it is possible to recognise the emergence of a rather different kind of fortified enclosure usually sited so as to command route nodes. These we have called oppida, distinguishing between the earlier *enclosed oppida* and the later *territorial oppida* (Cunliffe 1976a). There is little yet to be said of this phenomenon in Wessex. The defences beneath Winchester (Biddle 1966; 1967; 1968) may be relevant to the discussion, but in the absence of published detail this question must remain open. How-

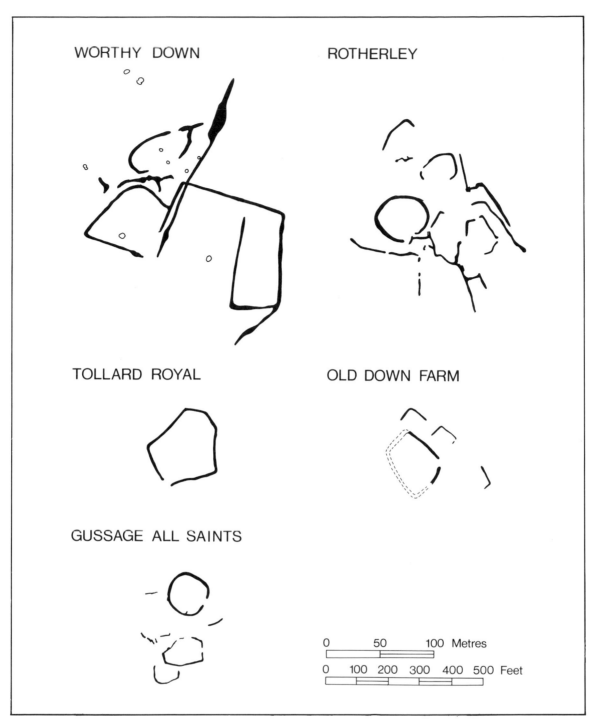

WORTHY DOWN   ROTHERLEY

TOLLARD ROYAL   OLD DOWN FARM

GUSSAGE ALL SAINTS

0   50   100 Metres

0   100 200 300 400 500 Feet

Figure 2.18 *Comparative plans of Late and Latest Iron Age farmsteads.*

ever, the dyke systems around Silchester and Chichester certainly conform to the general model of the *territorial oppidum*, and both sites, on this and other evidence, may reasonably be seen as urban or proto-urban agglomerations emerging in the decades before the Conquest in response to the political, economic and social changes brought about by the proximity of the Roman system, now firmly established in Gaul. Another change, dimly recognisable in the archaeological record of the late/ latest IA, is the appearance of cremation burial in central Wessex, an area in which previously the burial rite had involved excarnation followed by the limited interment of parts of the rotted corpse. Rich burials accompanied

by bronze-mounted buckets are recorded at Hurst-bourne Tarrant (Hawkes and Dunning 1932) and Marlborough (Hoare 1819; Fox 1958, 68–70) though the former is late, probably dating to the decade of the Roman conquest. It is difficult to judge how far back this rite can be traced in Wessex; but the earliest cremations at Owslebury (Collis 1968) could belong to the first half of the first century BC though we must await full publication before the point can be considered in any detail.

In south Wessex, broadly Dorset, a totally different burial rite is adopted in the late/latest IA — extended inhumations sometimes in small cemeteries. The difference between the two areas is a further reminder of the ethnic distinction we have already noted in the previous periods.

Ethnic differences are much more apparent in the late/latest IA. Not only are ceramic distinctions maintained but there are now, as we have just seen, considerable variations in burial rite. Even more impressive is the evidence provided by the locally minted pre-Roman coinages, which demonstrates a clear divide between the Durotriges of southern Wessex and the Atrebatic groups of central Wessex and west Sussex. The problems of boundaries are considered elsewhere in this volume (Sellwood, pp. 194–201); suffice it to say that the northern divide between the Atrebates and Durotriges would seem to lie in the vicinity of the Wylye or Nadder, with the lower reaches of the Salisbury Avon possibly marking the eastward extension of the Durotriges. The north-western limit of the Atrebates is difficult to discern with any precision, but may well coincide with the western edge of the chalk and greensand uplands (Fig. 2.19).

Social change in Wessex: c. 100 BC–AD 43

That there was significant social and political change in Wessex in the first century BC is beyond dispute. It remains now to consider possible causes and possible directions.

In outlining the evidence for the middle period of the IA it has been suggested that in the second century BC the socio-economic system, already in a state of unstable equilibrium, became subject to internal stresses which may have generated a momentum difficult to deflect. Whether or not the collapse of the elite system represented by the hillforts was entirely due to this it is impossible to say; but a system in a state of stress is highly vulnerable to external stimulus.

The most evident of the external events to impinge upon Wessex in the late second or early first century BC was the effects of reinvigorated trading-systems linking, via Armorica, ultimately to the Roman consumer-market of the Mediterranean. The Roman world required of the barbarian fringe raw materials, such as metals, hides and corn, together with manpower in the form of slaves. These were to be had in Britain in plenty. In return the Mediterranean offered a range of luxury goods of which wine is the easiest to recognise archaeologically and may, indeed, have been the most acceptable in Celtic society.

The trading connections with the ports of the Wessex contact zone brought in their wake new technologies, but they also brought the stimulus for social change. To expose a society, which had developed in isolation for centuries, to an unlimited external market for commodities which had not previously been produced in surplus, and to offer in return a totally new range of prestige goods such as wine, cannot have failed to have a dramatic and dislocating effect on traditional systems. One could even go so far as to suggest that for an already unstable society, the pressures were too much, and the elite system, with its hillforts, collapsed. The hypothesis is at least plausible, especially in the light of what happened to the west African kingdoms in the wake of European and American exploitation.

But the position may be even more complicated. If one accepts Caesar's assertion that a folk movement of Belgae actually took place, and a population of unknown size settled in a 'maritime region' of Britain, then allowance must be made for the impact of such a movement on Wessex society. If, then, one goes further and accepts that there is no archaeological evidence at all that the migration was to Kent and Essex (though of course it could have been), then any coastal area of south-eastern Britain within comparatively easy reach of the north-eastern French coast is eligible to be the landfall. On present evidence, slight though it is, the only area where north-eastern French pottery-styles are found in possible pre-Caesarian contexts is in the Solent region. It is in the Wessex hinterland behind that the alien burial rite of cremation takes hold at an early date, and it is here that the old social order based on hillforts collapses. The evidence is *very* tenuous and it must be admitted that without Caesar's reference few would have thought to explain the changes observed in terms of folk-movement. Nonetheless the possibility exists and is of interest.

A few further observations may be thrown into the balance. When, in 50 BC, Commius fled to Britain (Frontinus ii, 13, 11), he appears to have established himself in the north of Wessex very probably based at Calleva (Silchester). If the distribution of his coinage is an indication of his territorial domination, or of the acceptance of his authority, then the upper Thames Valley would seem to have been under his sway (Fig. 2.19). A possible historical scenario might well envisage Commius and his followers arriving in the Solent estuary, already controlled by the 'Belgae' who had arrived earlier, passing through the zone of primary Belgic settlement, to establish himself in an 'uncolonised' area to the north.

In this context the distribution of British Q coins is of some relevance since they are the prototypes from which the dynastic coinage of Commius and his house developed. British Q concentrates in a large territory which is almost exactly coincident with the distribution of the Wessex group of saucepan-pot styles prevalent in the second century BC. The simplest explanation for this is that the indigenous ethnic group (a tribe?) occupying this area was still a discrete entity in the 40s when British Q was being minted. British Q are closely derived from a Gaulish coinage (Gallo Belgic F), and there is now a possibility that some of the series may indeed have been imported. At any event Allen was surely correct in linking the origin of the type to the historical movement of Commius (Allen 1961, 116–8). The question which now arises is whether among the many and varied Gaulish coins found in the Solent area, and at present so little studied, can any be related to a pre-Caesarian movement into the region?

One final point deserves mention. When Ptolemy was

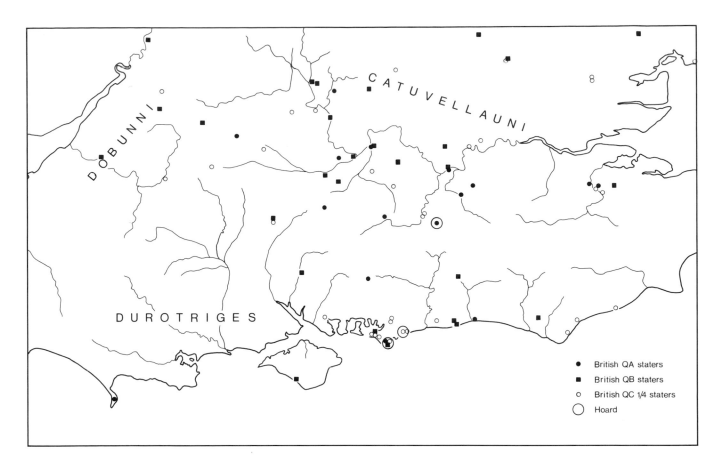

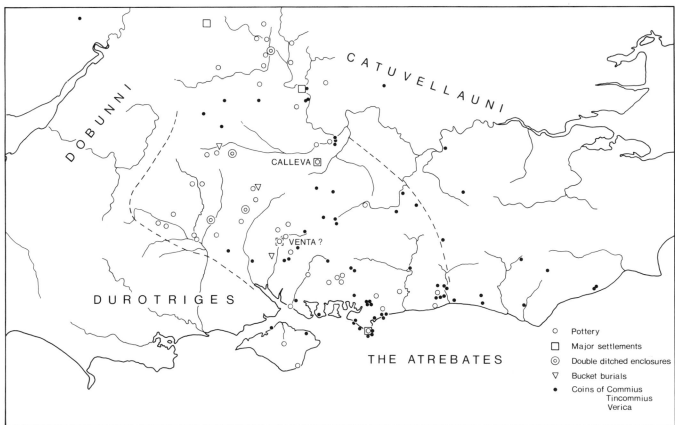

Figure 2.19 *Aspects of Atrebatic distribution. Source: Cunliffe 1984b.*

completing his Geography in the second century AD he (or more correctly his sources) had little doubt where the Belgae had settled. They were firmly located in Wessex with their capital at Winchester (*Venta Belgarum*). Taken together these disparate threads make a reasonable *a priori* case for suggesting that the pre-

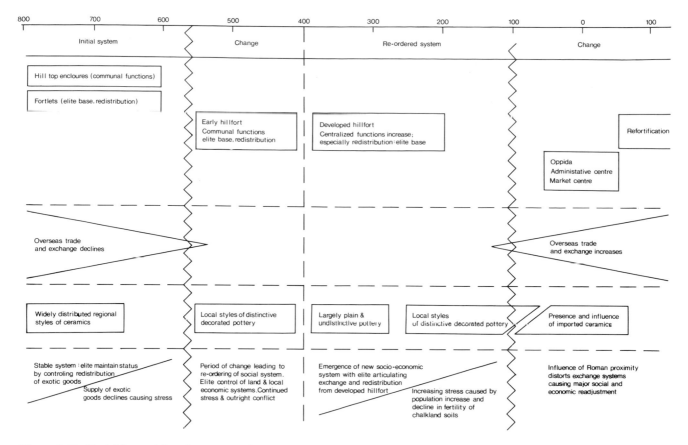

Figure 2.20 *Model for social and economic change in Iron Age Wessex.*

Caesarian immigrants may indeed have established themselves in one of the long-established Wessex tribal territories.

The digression on Belgae has been long, but necessarily so in order to explore a heresy of the kind offered here. Returning to the main theme, we have demonstrated widespread socio-political change beginning about 100 BC and have suggested three possible causes for it: increasing instability and stress in the social system; the dislocating effects caused by a sudden upsurge in trade with the Roman world; and the possibility of a folk-movement from Belgic Gaul. The three are not mutually exclusive.

The nature of the socio-political system which emerged is by no means clear. Where authority lay and how it was maintained are problems which cannot yet be approached; but when more attention has been paid to settlement-excavation and the greatly increased body of coin evidence has been reassessed further advances will surely be possible. The general impression given by what little data are available is that change was very rapid in the period 100 BC–AD 43; but before a new stable system could emerge the Roman Army had arrived.

Concluding remarks

The general model offered here is, of necessity, a simple one since the presently available data-set is too ill-focussed to support anything more complex. In summary we suggest an *initial system* dating from the eighth to the mid sixth century followed by a brief period of rapid change leading, in about 400 BC, to a new or *re-ordered system*. The re-ordered system lasted for three centuries until about 100 BC, when central southern Britain entered once more a phase of rapid change culminating in the Roman invasion of AD 43. It would be quite wrong, however, to give the impression that there were long periods of stability and stagnation: change was continuous; but what we are suggesting is that pace and intensity of change varied, and it is this that the coarse archaeological data are allowing us to detect.

The causes of the major shifts from each system to a period of rapid change have been considered briefly. The initial system came to an end, we suggest, largely because of the European-wide breakdown in the bronze trade, removing one of the staples that enabled the elite system to maintain itself. The collapse of the re-ordered system was brought about by dislocation caused by Roman entrepreneurs beginning directly to manipulate the exchange-networks in the period following 120 BC. The ever-approaching Roman frontier ensured constant stimulus for change in the next 120 years.

Against this background we have attempted to investigate rhythms evident in the constituent systems. At the socio-economic level it is suggested that two linked trends can be recognised, a rise in population and a decline in the fertility of the thin downland soils, together creating a situation of increasing stress. Political systems are more difficult to approach, but we suggest that the problem can be viewed on two levels: the unremitting emergence of territorially distinct tribal groups, against which the rise and subsequent collapse of centres of authority based on hillforts (?chiefdoms) is enacted, and imposed upon which there may have been a limited folk-movement from the Continent.

All this is, of course, over simple, but it is a beginning. Within the loosely-structured models offered here there are many possibilities for testing and even more for modification! What is needed, above all, is an improved data-set which will allow numerical comparisons statistically supported. The full publication of a score or so important unpublished excavations would be a useful beginning; but in the end only by carefully-planned research designs undertaken on an appropriate scale will we be able to advance from the anecdotal to the systematic.

Appendix 1: selected pottery distributions

Distribution of the Earliest Iron Age pottery shown on figure 2.2

The sites plotted are:

Avon

Little Solsbury	Falconer & Adams 1935; Dowden 1957, 1962

Berks.

Blewburton	Bradford 1942; Collins 1947, 1953, 1959
Boxford Common	Peake, Coghlan & Hawkes 1932
Rams Hill	Piggott & Piggott 1940
Wayland's Smithy	Atkinson 1965

Dorset

Eldons Seat	Cunliffe & Phillipson 1968
Hengistbury Head	Bushe-Fox 1915
Hill Brow	Calkin 1951
Kimmeridge	Calkin 1949; Davies 1936
Langton Matravers	Calkin 1949; Calkin & Piggott 1959
Marnhull	Williams 1951

Hants.

Danebury	Cunliffe 1984a
Meon Hill	Liddell 1933, 1935
Old Down Farm	Davies 1981
Stanmore	Hooley 1927
Winchester	Cunliffe 1964
Winklebury	Smith 1977

Somerset

Ham Hill	Taunton Mus: unpublished
Shepton Mallett	Shepton Mallet Mus: unpublished

Wilts.

All Cannings Cross	Cunnington 1923
Barbury	Meyrick
Battlesbury	Chadwick & Thompson 1956
Boscombe Down West	Richardson 1951
Budbury	Wainwright 1970
Cold Kitchen Hill	Unpublished and Cunnington & Goddard 1934
Cow Down	Information from Sonia Hawkes
Highfield	Stevens 1934
Highworth	Devizes Mus. (*WAM* 63, 118)
Lidbury	Cunnington 1917
Liddington Castle	Passmore 1914
Little Woodbury	Brailsford 1948
Martinsell	Meyrick 1946: *WAM* 69, 185
Oliver's Camp	Cunnington 1908
Pewsey	Devizes Mus. (*WAM* 68, 130; 67, 172)
Potterne	Devizes Mus. (*WAM* 67, 172)
Stockton Earthworks	Devizes Mus: unpublished
Upton Scudamore	Information from John Musty
Wedhampton	Devizes Mus: unpublished
Winklebury	Pitt Rivers 1888.

Distribution of scratched-cordoned bowls and Dorset wall-sided bowls shown on figure 2.8

Scratched cordoned bowls

Berks.

Blewburton (atypical)	Bradford 1942; Collins 1947, 1953, 1959

Dorset

Maiden Castle (atypical)	Wheeler 1943

Hants.

Danebury	Cunliffe 1984a
Little Sombourne	Neal 1980
Meon Hill	Liddell 1933, 1935
Old Down Farm	Davies 1981
Quarley Hill	Hawkes 1939
Winchester (atypical)	Cunliffe 1964

Wilts

All Cannings Cross	Cunnington 1923
Boscombe Down West	Richardson 1951
Chisenbury Trendle	Cunnington 1932c
Fifield Bavant	Clay 1924
Figsbury	Cunnington 1925
Fyfield Down	Meyrick 1946
Lidbury	Cunnington 1917
Little Woodbury	Brailsford 1948
Martinsell	Meyrick 1946
Oldbury	Cunnington 1871
Swallowcliffe	Clay 1925, 1927
Wilsford	Cunnington & Goddard 1934
Winklebury	Pitt Rivers 1888
Yarnbury	Cunnington 1933.

Dorset wall-sided bowls

Hants

Christchurch	Jarvis 1983

Dorset

Chalbury	Whitley 1943
Corfe Mullen	Calkin 1965
Eldons Seat	Cunliffe & Phillipson 1968
Ensbury Park	Calkin 1965
Gussage All Saints	Wainwright 1979
Hengistbury Head	Cunliffe 1978b

Langton Matravers	Calkin & Piggott 1939; Calkin 1949
Maiden Castle	Wheeler 1943
Quarry Lodden	Bailey & Flatters 1972

Appendix 2: selected hillfort distributions

Hillforts: the available data (figure 2.21)

Comparatively few hillforts in central southern Britain have been subjected to any degree of area excavation. Those that have include:

Balksbury, Hants.	Wainwright 1970
Chalbury, Dorset	Whitley 1943
Danebury, Hants.	Cunliffe 1984a
Harting Beacon, Sussex	Bedwin 1978, 1979
Hengistbury, Dorset	Cunliffe 1978 and un-published
Hod Hill, Dorset	Richmond 1968
Maiden Castle, Dorset	Wheeler 1943
Pilsdon Pen, Dorset	Gelling 1977
South Cadbury, Somerset	Alcock 1977, 1980
Winklebury, Hants.	Smith 1977; Mackay 1977.

A large number of other forts have been examined by trial excavations. These are shown on the figure and can be identified using the Ordnance Survey Map of Southern Britain in the Iron Age. Reference to Hogg 1979 will provide major references.

Distribution of Early hilltop enclosures (figure 2.22)

The sites plotted include:

Avon	Bathampton
Berks.	Bozedown?
	Rams Hill
	Membury?
Dorset	Hengistbury
	Hod Hill?
	Lulworth
Hants.	Balksbury
	Caesars Camp?
	Walbury
	Winklebury
Somerset	Ham Hill
Sussex	Harting Beacon
Wilts	Cley Hill?
	Martinsell Hill
	Ogbury

Distribution of known Early hillforts (figure 2.23)

The sites plotted include:

| Avon | Solsbury Hill |

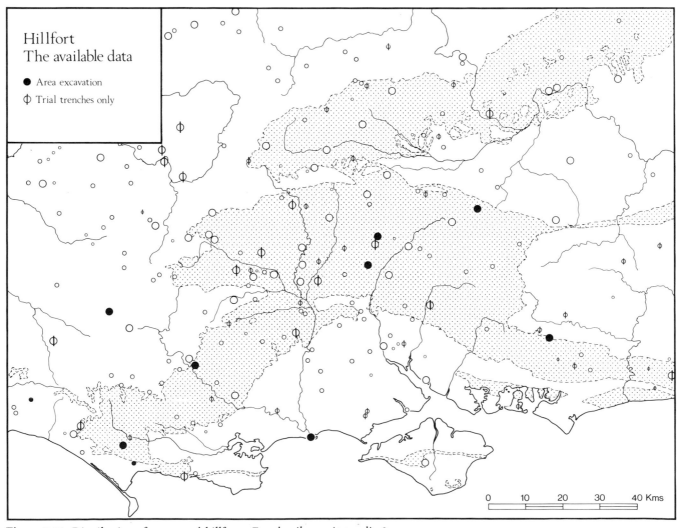

Figure 2.21 *Distribution of excavated hillforts. For details see Appendix 2.*

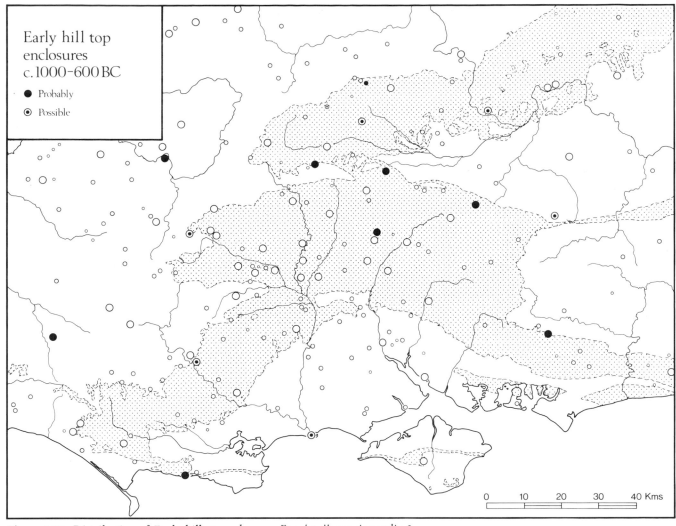

Distribution of developed hillforts (figure 2.24)

The sites plotted include:

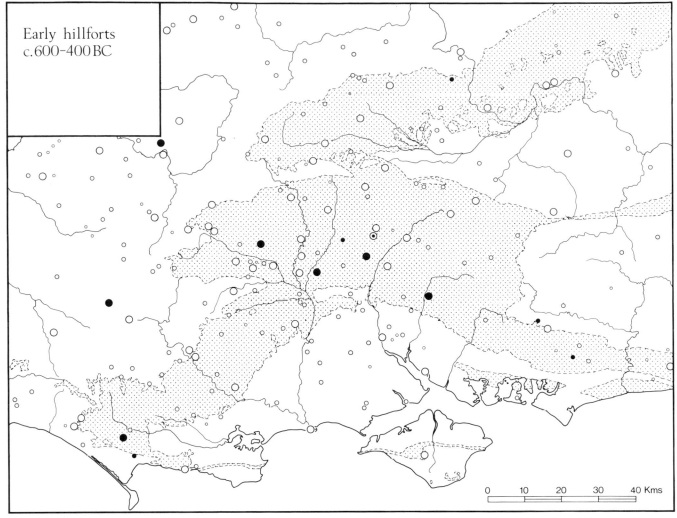

Figure 2.23 *Distribution of Early hillforts. For details see Appendix 2.*

References

ALCOCK, L. 1972: *By South Cadbury is that Camelot* (London).

ALCOCK, L. 1980: The Cadbury Castle sequence in the first millennium BC. *Bull. Board Celtic Studies* 28, 656–718.

ALLEN, D.F. 1961: The origins of coinage in Britain: a reappraisal. In Frere, S.S. (editor), *Problems of the Iron Age in Southern Britain* (London), 93–308.

ATKINSON, R.J.C. 1965: Wayland's Smithy. *Antiquity* 39, 126–33.

BAILEY, C.J. and FLATTERS, E. 1972: Trial excavation of an Iron Age and Romano-British site at Quarry Lodden, Bincombe, Dorset. *Proc. Dorset Nat. Hist. and Archaeol. Soc.* 93, 135–43.

BEDWIN, O. 1978: Excavations inside Harting Beacon Hill-fort, 1976. *Sussex Archaeol. Coll.* 116, 225–40.

BEDWIN, O. 1979: Excavations at Harting Beacon, West Sussex: second season. *Sussex Archaeol. Coll.* 117, 21–36.

BIDDLE, M. 1966: Excavations at Winchester 1965. *Antiq. Journ.* 46, 308–32.

BIDDLE, M. 1967: Excavations at Winchester 1966. *Antiq. Journ.* 47, 251–79.

BIDDLE, M. 1968: Excavations at Winchester 1967. *Antiq. Journ.* 48, 250–84.

BIRCHALL, A. 1965: The Aylesford–Swarling Culture: the problem of the Belgae reconsidered. *Proc. Prehist. Soc.* 21, 241–367.

BRADFORD, J.S.P., 1942: An Early Iron Age site on Blewburton Hill, Berks. *Berkshire Archaeol. Journ.* 46, 97–104.

BRAILSFORD, J.W. 1948: Excavations at Little Woodbury. Part II. *Proc. Prehist. Soc.* 14, 1–23.

BUSHE-FOX, J.P. 1915: *Excavations at Hengistbury Head, Hampshire in 1911–12* (Oxford, Soc. of Antiq. Res. Rep. 3).

BUSHE-FOX, J.P. 1925: *Excavation of the Late-Celtic Urn-field at Swarling, Kent* (Oxford, Soc. of Antiq. Res. Rep. 5).

CALKIN, J.B. 1949: The Isle of Purbeck in the Iron Age. *Proc. Dorset Nat. Hist. and Archaeol. Soc.* 70, 29–59.

CALKIN, J.B. 1951: Prehistoric Pokesdown. *Proc. Bournemouth Nat. Sci. Soc.* 40, 79–88.

CALKIN, J.B. 1965: Some Early Iron Age Sites in the Bournemouth Area. *Proc. Dorset Nat. Hist. and Archaeol. Soc.* 86, 120–30.

CALKIN, J.B. and PIGGOTT, C.M. 1939: Iron Age 'A' habitation sites at Langton Matravers. *Proc. Dorset Nat. Hist. and Archaeol. Soc.* 60, 66–72.

CHADWICK, S.E. and THOMPSON, M.W. 1956: Note on an Iron Age Habitation site near Battlesbury Camp, Warminster. *Wilts. Archaeol. Mag.* 56, 262–4.

CLARK, J.G.D. 1947: Sheep and Swine in the Husbandry of Prehistoric Europe. *Antiquity* 21, 122–136.

CLAY, R.C.C. 1925: An inhabited site of La Tène I date on Swallowcliffe Down. *Wilts. Archaeol. Mag.* 43, 59–93.

CLAY, R.C.C. 1927: Supplementary report on the Early Iron Age village on Swallowcliffe Down. *Wilts. Archaeol. Mag.* 46, 540–7.

COLLINS, A.E.P. 1947: Excavations on Blewburton Hill, 1947. *Berkshire Archaeol. Journ.* 50, 4–29.

COLLINS, A.E.P. 1953: Excavations on Blewburton Hill, 1948 and 1949. *Berkshire Archaeol. Journ.* 53, 21–64.

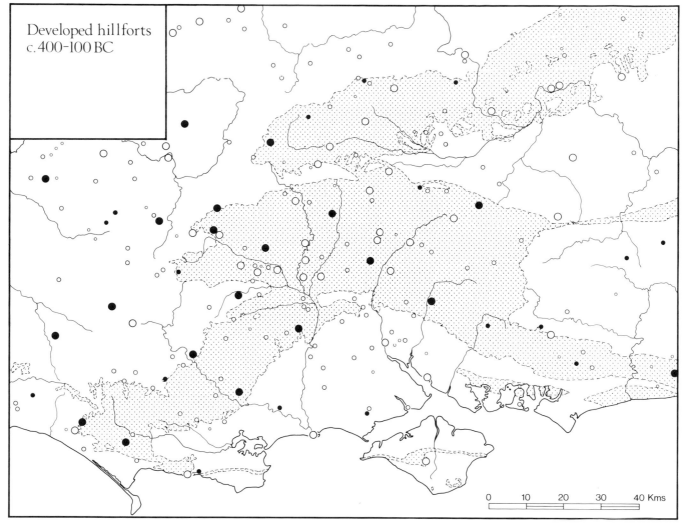

Figure 2.24 *Distribution of developed hillforts. For details see Appendix 2.*

COLLINS, A.E.P. and COLLINS, F.J. 1959: Excavations on Blewburton Hill, 1953. *Berkshire Archaeol. Journ.* 57, 52–73.

COLLIS, J.R. 1968: Excavations at Owslebury, Hants. *Antiq. Journ.* 48, 18–31.

COTTON, M.A. and FRERE, S.S. 1968: Ivinghoe Beacon, excavations 1963–5. *Rec. of Bucks.* 18, 187–260.

CUNLIFFE, B.W. 1964: *Winchester excavations, 1949–1960*, 1 (Winchester).

CUNLIFFE, B.W. 1966: *Regional Groupings within the Iron Age of Southern Britain* (Cambridge Ph.D. thesis).

CUNLIFFE, B.W. 1971: Some aspects of Hill-forts and their cultural environments. In Jesson, M. and Hill, D. (editors), *The Iron Age and its Hill-forts* (Southampton), 53–71.

CUNLIFFE, B.W. 1974(8): *Iron Age Communities in Britain* (London).

CUNLIFFE, B.W. 1976a: The Origins of urbanisation in Britain. In Cunliffe, B.W. and Rowley, T. (editors), *Oppida: the beginnings of Urbanisation in Barbarian Europe* (Oxford, BAR S11), 135–61.

CUNLIFFE, B.W. 1976b: Hill-forts and oppida in Britain. In Sieveking, G. de G., Longworth, I.H. and Wilson, K.E. (editors), *Problems in Economic and Social Archaeology* (London), 343–58.

CUNLIFFE, B.W. 1976c: *Iron Age Sites in Central Southern England* (London, CBA Res. Rep. 16).

CUNLIFFE, B.W. 1978a: Settlement and population in the British Iron Age: some facts, figures and fantasies. In Cunliffe, B.W. and Rowley, T. (editors), *Lowland Iron Age Communities in Europe* (Oxford, BAR S48), 3–24.

CUNLIFFE, B.W. 1978b: *Hengistbury Head* (London).

CUNLIFFE, B.W. 1981: Money and Society in pre-Roman Britain. In Cunliffe, B.W. (editor), *Coinage and Society in Britain and Gaul* (London, CBA Res. Rep. 38), 29–39.

CUNLIFFE, B.W. 1982a: Social and economic development in Kent in the pre-Roman Iron Age. In Leach, P.E. (editor), *Archaeology in Kent to AD 1500* (London, CBA Res. Rep. 48), 40–50.

CUNLIFFE, B.W. 1982b: Britain, the Veneti and beyond. *Oxford Journ. Archaeol.* 1(1), 39–68.

CUNLIFFE, B.W. 1982c: Iron Age settlements and pottery 650 BC–AD 60. In Aston, M. and Burrow, I. (editors), *The Archaeology of Somerset* (Taunton), 53–61.

CUNLIFFE, B.W. 1984a: *Danebury: an Iron Age hillfort in Hampshire*. Vols 1 and 2, The excavation 1969–1978 (London, CBA Res. Rep. 52).

CUNLIFFE, B.W. 1984b: Relations between Britain and Gaul in the first century BC and early first century AD. In Thompson, F.H. (editor), *Cross-Channel Trade between Gaul and Britain in the pre-Roman Iron Age* (London, Soc. of Antiq. Occ. Paper 4).

CUNLIFFE, B.W. 1984c: Settlement, hierarchy and social change in southern Britain in the Iron Age. *Analecta Praehistorica Leidensia* 15, 161–187.

CUNLIFFE, B.W. and ORTON, C. 1984: Radiocarbon age assessment (at Danebury). In Cunliffe 1984a, 190–8.

CUNLIFFE, B.W. and PHILLIPSON, D.W. 1968: Excavations at Eldon's Seat, Encombe, Dorset. *Proc. Prehist. Soc.* 34, 191–237.

CUNNINGTON, H. 1871: Oldbury Camp, Wilts. *Wilts. Archaeol. Mag.* 28, 277.

CUNNINGTON, M.E. 1908: Oliver's Camp, Devizes. *Wilts. Archaeol. Mag.* 35, 408–44.

CUNNINGTON, M.E. 1917: Lidbury Camp. *Wilts. Archaeol. Mag.* 40, 12–36.

CUNNINGTON, M.E. 1923: *The Early Iron Age inhabited site at All Cannings Cross* (Devizes).

CUNNINGTON, M.E. 1925: Figsbury Rings: an account of excavations in 1924. *Wilts. Archaeol. Mag.* 43, 48–58.

CUNNINGTON, M.E. 1932a: Was there a second Belgic invasion represented by bead-rim pottery? *Antiq. Journ.* 12, 27–34.

CUNNINGTON, M.E. 1932b: Chisbury Camp. *Wilts. Archaeol. Mag.* 46, 4–7.

CUNNINGTON, M.E. 1932c: The demolition of Chisenbury Trendle. *Wilts. Archaeol. Mag.* 46, 1–3.

CUNNINGTON, M.E. 1933: Excavations at Yarnbury Castle Camp 1932. *Wilts. Archaeol. Mag.* 46, 198–213.

CUNNINGTON, M.E. and GODDARD, E.H. 1934: *The Devizes Museum Catalogue*, Part 2.

DAVIES, H. 1936: The shale industries at Kimmeridge, Dorset. *Archaeol. Journ.* 93, 200–19.

DAVIES, S.M. 1981: Excavations at Old Down Farm, Andover. Part II: Prehistoric and Roman. *Proc. Hants. Field Club and Archaeol. Soc.* 37, 81–163.

DOWDEN, W.A. 1957: Little Solsbury Hill Camp. *Proc. Bristol Univ. Spelaeol. Soc.* 8, 18–29.

DOWDEN, W.A. 1962: Little Solsbury Hill Camp. *Proc. Bristol Univ. Spelaeol. Soc.* 9, 177–82.

DUNNING, G.C., HOOLEY, W. and TILDESLEY, M.L. 1929: Excavation of an Early Iron Age village on Worthy Down, Winchester. *Proc. Hants. Field Club and Archaeol. Soc.* 10, 178–92.

ELLISON, A. and DREWELL, P. 1971: Pits and post-holes in the British Early Iron Age: some alternative explanations. *Proc. Prehist. Soc.* 37, 183–94.

EVANS, A.J. 1890: On a Late-Celtic Urn-field at Aylesford, Kent. *Archaeologia* 52, 315–88.

FALCONER, J.P.E. and ADAMS, S.B. 1935: Recent finds at Solsbury Hill Camp near Bath. *Proc. Bristol Univ. Spelaeol. Soc.* 4, 133–222.

FOX, C. 1958: *Pattern and Purpose* (Cardiff).

FREIDMAN, J. and ROWLANDS, M.J. 1977: Notes towards an epigenetic model of the evolution of 'civilisation'. In Freidman, J. and Rowlands, M.J. (editors), *The Evolution of Social Systems* (London), 201–76.

GELLING, P.S. 1977: Excavations on Pilsdon Pen, Dorset, 1964–71. *Proc. Prehist. Soc.* 43, 263–86.

GRANT, A. 1984: Animal Husbandry (at Danebury). In Cunliffe 1984a, 496–548.

GREEN, C. 1981: Handmade pottery and society in Late Iron Age and Roman East Sussex. *Sussex Archaeol. Coll.* 118, 69–86.

HACHMANN, R. 1976: The problem of the Belgae seen from the Continent. *Bull. Inst. of Arch. Lond.* 13, 117–37.

HARDING, D. 1974: *The Iron Age in Lowland Britain* (London).

HAWKES, C.F.C. 1931: Hill Forts. *Antiquity* 5, 60–111.

HAWKES, C.F.C. 1939: The excavations at Quarley Hill, 1938. *Proc. Hants. Field Club and Archaeol. Soc.* 14, 136–94.

HAWKES, C.F.C. 1940: Excavations at Bury Hill 1939. *Proc. Hants. Field Club and Archaeol. Soc.* 14, 291–337.

HAWKES, C.F.C. 1968: New thoughts on the Belgae. *Antiquity* 42, 6–19.

HAWKES, C.F.C. and DUNNING, G. 1931: The Belgae of Gaul and Britain. *Archaeol. Journ.* 87, 150–335.

HAWKES, C.F.C., MYERS, J.N.L. and STEVENS, G.C. 1930: *St. Catherine's Hill, Winchester* (Winchester: reprinted from *Proc. Hants. Field Club and Archaeol. Soc.* 11).

HOARE, R.R. 1819: *The Ancient History of North Wiltshire* (London).

HODDER, I. 1981: *Symbols in Action* (Cambridge).

HOGG, A.H.A. 1979: *British Hill-forts: an Index* (Oxford, BAR 62).

HOOLEY, W. 1927: Hallstatt pottery from Winchester. *Proc. Hants. Field Club and Archaeol. Soc.* 10, 63–8.

JARVIS, K.S. 1983: *Excavations in Christchurch 1969–1980* (Monograph 5, Dorset Nat. Hist. and Archaeol. Soc.).

JONES, M. 1984: The plant remains (from Danebury). In Cunliffe 1984a, 483–95.

KENT, J.P.C. 1978: The origins and development of Celtic gold coinage in Britain. *Actes du Congrés International d'Archéologie: Rouen 3, 4, 5 juillet 1965*, 313–24.

KENT, J.P.C. 1981: The origins of coinage in Britain. In Cunliffe, B.W. (editor), *Coinage and Society in Britain and Gaul* (London, CBA Res. Rep. 38), 40–2.

LIDDELL, D.M. 1933: Excavations at Meon Hill. *Proc. Hants. Field Club and Archaeol. Soc.* 12, 127–62.

LIDDELL, D.M. 1935: Report on the Hampshire Field Club's excavation at Meon Hill. *Proc. Hants. Field Club and Archaeol. Soc.* 13, 7–54.

LOCK, G. 1984: Test 9: fine phasing by seriation within cp 7–8 (at Danebury). In Cunliffe 1984a, 242–4.

MEYRICK, O. 1946: Notes on some Early Iron Age sites in the Marlborough district. *Wilts. Archaeol. Mag.* 51, 256–63.

MONK, M.A. and FASHAM, P.J. 1980: Carbonised plant remains from two Iron Age sites in central Hampshire. *Proc. Prehist. Soc.* 46, 321–44.

NEAL, D.S. 1980: Bronze Age, Iron Age and Roman settlements at Little Somborne and Ashley, Hampshire. *Proc. Hants. Field Club and Archaeol. Soc.* 36, 91–144.

PASSMORE, A.D. 1914: Liddington Castle Camp. *Wilts. Archaeol. Mag.* 38, 576–84.

PEAKE, H., COGHLAN, H. and HAWKES, C.F.C. 1932: Early Iron Age remains in Boxford Common, Berks. *Trans. Newbury Dist. Field Club* 6, 136–50.

PERRY, B.T. 1966: Some recent discoveries in Hampshire. In Thomas, A.C. (editor), *Rural settlement in Roman Britain* (London, CBA Res. Rep. 7), 39–42.

PERRY, B.T. 1970: Iron Age enclosures and settlements on Hampshire chalklands. *Archaeol. Journ.* 126, 29–43.

PERRY, B.T. 1974: Excavations at Bramdean, Hampshire, 1965 and 1966, and a discussion of similar sites in Southern England. *Proc. Hants. Field Club and Archaeol. Soc.* 29, 41–77.

PERRY, B.T. 1982: Excavations at Bramdean, Hampshire, 1973 to 1977. *Proc. Hants. Field Club and Archaeol. Soc.* 38, 57–74.

PIGGOTT, S. and PIGGOTT, C.M. 1940: Excavations at Rams Hill, Uffington, Berks. *Antiq. Journ.* 20, 465–80.

PITT RIVERS, A.H.L.F. 1887: *Excavations in Cranborne Chase* Vol. 1 (London).

RICHARDSON, K.M. 1951: The excavation of an Iron Age village on Boscombe Down West. *Wilts. Archaeol. Mag.* 54, 123–68.

RICHMOND, I.A. 1968: *Hod Hill*, Vol. 2: *Excavations carried out between 1951 and 1958* (London).

ROBERTSON-MACKAY, R. 1977: The defences of the Iron Age hill-fort at Winklebury, Basingstoke, Hampshire. *Proc. Prehist. Soc.* 43, 131–54.

RCHM(E) Dorset 1970a: *An Inventory of Historical Monuments in the County of Dorset*. Vol. 3: *Central Dorset* (London).

RCHM(E) Dorset 1970b: *An Inventory of Historical Monuments in the County of Dorset*. Vol. 2: *South East* (London).

SAVILLE, A. 1983: *Uley Bury and Norbury Hillforts* (Bristol, Western Archaeol. Trust, exc. monog. 5).

SCHEERS, S. 1977: *Traité de numismatique Celtique II: La Gaule Belgique* (Paris).

SELLWOOD, L. 1984: Textile manufacture (at Danebury). In Cunliffe 1984a, 438–9.

SMITH, K. 1977: The excavation of Winklebury camp, Basingstoke, Hampshire. *Proc. Prehist. Soc.* 43, 31–130.

STEAD, I.M. 1976: The earliest burials of the Aylesford culture. In Sieveking, G. de G., Longworth, I.H. and Wilson, K.E. (editors), *Problems in Economic and Social Archaeology* (London), 401–16.

STEVENS, F. 1934: The Highfield pit dwellings, Fisherton, Salisbury. *Wilts. Archaeol. Mag.* 46, 579–624.

THOMAS, R. forthcoming: The Bronze-Iron Transition in Southern England.

TYERS, P.A. 1980: Correspondances entre la céramique commune La Tène III du Sud-est de l'Angleterre et du Nord de la France. *Septentrion* 10, 61–70.

WAINWRIGHT, G.J. 1968: The excavation of a Durotrigan farmstead near Tollard Royal in Cranborne Chase, southern England. *Proc. Prehist. Soc.* 34, 102–47.

WAINWRIGHT, G.J. 1970a: The excavation of Balksbury Camp, Andover, Hants. *Proc. Hants. Field Club and Archaeol. Soc.* 26, 21–55.

WAINWRIGHT, G.J. 1970b: An Iron Age promontory fort at Budbury, Bradford-on-Avon, Wiltshire. *Wilts. Archaeol. Mag.* 65, 108–166.

WAINWRIGHT, G.J. 1979: *Gussage All Saints. An Iron Age settlement in Dorset* (London, DOE Archaeol. Rep. 10).

WALKER, L. 1984: The deposition of the human remains (at Danebury). In Cunliffe 1984a, 442–63.

WHEELER, R.E.M. 1943: *Maiden Castle, Dorset* (Oxford, Soc. of Antiq. Res. Rep. 12).

WHITLEY, M. 1943: Excavations at Chalbury Camp, Dorset, 1939. *Antiq. Journ.* 23, 98–121.

WILLIAMS, A. 1951: Excavations at Allard's Quarry, Marnhull, Dorset. *Proc. Dorset Nat. Hist. and Archaeol. Soc.* 72, 20–75.

WILLIAMS, D.F. and WANDIBBA, S. 1984: Appendix 2 The fabrics: petrological examination (of Danebury pottery). In Cunliffe 1984a, fiche 8, frames D13–E3.

WILSON, A.C. 1940: Report on the excavation at Highdown Hill, Sussex, August 1939. *Sussex Archaeol. Coll.* 81, 173–204.

WILSON, A.C. 1950: Excavations on Highdown Hill, 1947. *Sussex Archaeol. Coll.* 89, 163–178.

Aspects of Iron Age Settlement in Sussex

Owen Bedwin

The Downs

Introduction (Fig. 3.1)

In broad outline, the pattern of Iron Age settlement on the South Downs has been known for some time. The preferred location for farmsteads is a ridge or spur of chalk, usually south-facing, and where the settlement is adjacent to, or surrounded by, arable fields. The observation that some of the area in the vicinity of each farm settlement is always free of surviving fields suggests land set aside for permanent pasture (e.g. Bishopstone, with lynchets on two sides of the rectangular enclosure). There is at present no evidence to suggest the existence of Iron Age settlements covered by later hillwash in dry valleys.

Settlement density is harder to estimate. On Bullock Down, an area of the chalk downs was intensively examined over a 5-year period (Drewett 1982). Only a single Iron Age settlement (the 6th/5th-century site at Heathy Brow) was found in an area of c. 5 km², though this was admittedly on the extreme north edge of the Downs, the most marginal farmland of all within that geographical zone. As part of the Bishopstone project (Bell 1977), fieldwalking of the block of downland between the Ouse and the Cuckmere located only eight other sites (in addition to the already known hillforts). Clearly, settlement density does not appear to reach the levels indicated for Wessex by the distribution of Iron Age material found at Chalton, Hants (Cunliffe 1976a).

There is considerable variation in the form of farm settlements. Many are 'open' settlements, though some of these, for instance Charleston Brow, are effectively delimited by the innermost edges of surrounding fields. Among enclosure sites, some of which are shown in Fig.

2, there is little obvious pattern. Consequently, even a preliminary enclosure-typology, such as that proposed for Hampshire (Champion and Champion 1981), is not yet possible. Certainly, there are no enclosures with antennae ditches, like Gussage All Saints or Little Woodbury in central Wessex. Nor are any D-shaped enclosures known, like the Hampshire examples at Winnall Down and Old Down Farm. Two banjo enclosures are known, however, both at the western end of West Sussex. One is at Selhurstpark Farm (shown in Fig. 3.2); the other, seen only fleetingly during the drought of 1976 but never again since, is at Denge Bottom, just to the west of Halnaker Hill. Neither of these banjos has been dated, but by analogy with the better-known Hampshire examples they should belong to the late Iron Age. Other enclosures, where dated, belong to the early Iron Age, e.g. Bishopstone, Binderton (F.G. Aldsworth, pers. comm.) and Glynde Quarry (Burstow 1961–2).

How enclosures or open sites vary in function or status is little understood. Given that no unploughed Iron Age settlement survives on the Sussex Downs (with the exception of the partly-excavated Muntham Court), it is arguable whether even large-scale excavation would provide many answers. Apart from this practical difficulty, there is in addition the conceptual problem of how wealth and status are likely to be reflected in the archaeological record. Status is always an elusive notion, but even the apparently more tangible one of wealth may be virtually invisible if wealth in the Iron Age was measured, not so much in terms of the size of houses or in the amount of personal jewellery, as in terms of the number of animals owned (see, for example, Wainwright

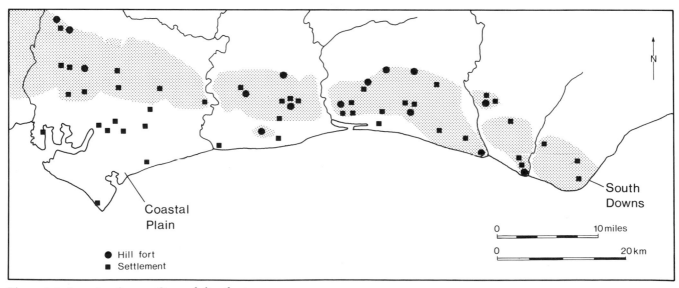

Figure 3.1 *Iron Age Sussex. General distribution map.*

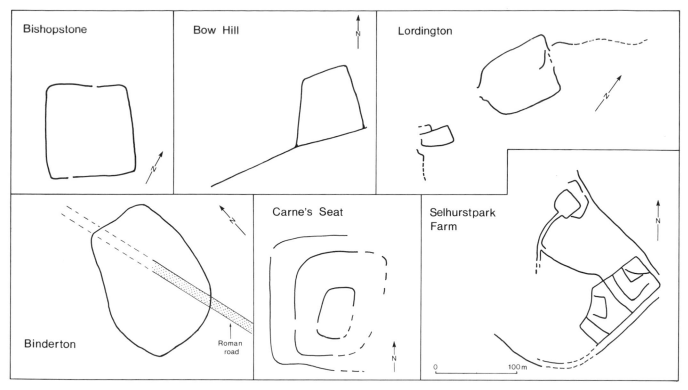

Figure 3.2 *Iron Age Sussex. Examples of enclosures on the South Downs (to the same scale).*

1979). The establishment of any kind of hierarchy of settlement-sites in Sussex would still appear to be a long way off.

Hillforts

Apart from farm settlements, the major type of Iron Age site is, of course, the hillfort. The 20 sites classified as hillforts are a remarkably heterogeneous group in terms of size, date and function (where known). Cunliffe's (1976b) division into *early* and *developed* hillforts is a useful one; three of the larger sites, Cissbury, Torberry and the Trundle, fall neatly into the coherent group of developed hillforts, of which Danebury in Hampshire is the best-studied example. But what of the remainder, for which the blanket term 'hillfort', is probably more of a hindrance than a help?

At least three do not seem to belong to the Iron Age tradition; these are the feebly-defended sites at Court Hill, Halnaker Hill and Belle Tout. Court Hill, excavated in 1982, has an early Neolithic carbon-14 date (Bedwin, forthcoming), and therefore probably belongs to the same class of monument as Bury Hill, West Sussex (Bedwin 1981). Halnaker Hill, excavated in 1981 and 1983, is similar in surface appearance to Court Hill, though unfortunately the dating evidence is equivocal; it may belong to the early Neolithic, but a late Bronze Age date cannot be ruled out (Bedwin 1982 and 1984a). Finally, the large (25 ha) enclosure at Belle Tout, which has been investigated on a number of occasions, still evades close dating. The most recent excavations (Bedwin 1982, 90–96) resulted in impasse; the artefactual evidence pointed to a Bronze Age or late Neolithic date, but the snail fauna from the ditch contained a species thought to have been introduced into this country during the Roman period. Either way, an Iron Age date looks unlikely.

Most of the remainder of the hillforts are securely dated to the early Iron Age, with the exception of the Devil's Dyke, which has never been excavated, and Castle Hill, Newhaven, now totally destroyed. High-down and the Caburn originated as small hill-top settlements, which only later were strongly fortified. In some ways, these two sites would be equally well classified as farm settlements, which for one reason or another, became strongly defended.

There are two more oddities, namely Ranscombe Hill and Wolstonbury. Quite why the former was ever regarded as a hillfort is hard to understand; it is far better interpreted, in terms of shape and siting, as a cross dyke, albeit rather better-built than most, since its bank is timber-laced. Then there is Wolstonbury, which is unusual in having the ditch *inside* the bank, an arrangement more typical of a henge monument. Curwen's (1930) trial excavations did produce a sherd of early Bronze Age pottery low down in the ditch, but numerous Iron Age sherds in the upper silts persuaded him that the early Bronze Age sherd was residual and that the earthwork belonged to the Iron Age. However, it remains at least possible that Wolstonbury is Sussex's only henge, and that it belongs, together with Rybury, Wiltshire (another inside-out 'hillfort') and the inner ditch at Figsbury Rings, Wiltshire, to a class of henge monument situated, not on a broad chalk plain, like Avebury and Stonehenge, but on steep hilltops instead.

As for the rest of the hillforts (Hollingbury, Harting Beacon, Seaford Head, Harrow Hill, Chanctonbury, Goosehill, Thundersbarrow, and ?Ditchling Beacon), their broadly similar early Iron Age dates should not be

47

allowed to conceal a fairly wide range of archaeological features from their interiors. Harrow Hill, the smallest hillfort in Sussex at 0.4 ha, contained a very large number of cattle skulls but little else (Holleyman 1937), and has, not unreasonably, been interpreted as an enclosure for slaughter. Hollingbury contained several round huts (Bedwin 1978; Holmes, forthcoming), whereas Chanctonbury appears to have been virtually empty (Bedwin 1980). If there is a common interpretation linking at least some of these sites it would be that they were primarily stock enclosures, perhaps used only seasonally. It was interesting to note that during the 1983 excavations at Seaford Head (in a wet March/April) parts of the hillfort interior, half of which is on clay-with-flints, became water-logged for several days. Thus, in a normal year, it is likely that this site at any rate would have been unusable as a stock enclosure from October to April.

House-types and internal organisation

Well-defined house-types are rare, but this is largely because most excavation has been carried out on plough-damaged sites. Nothing resembling the substantial post-built round house from Little Woodbury has yet been found. Where traces of houses have survived, there is evidence of both round and rectangular houses. Round houses are known from Hollingbury, where five circular structures of diameters from 5.5 m to 13 m were defined by shallow ring gullies (Bedwin 1978). At Heathy Brow, a hut-site was defined by a feature consisting of a compact layer of calcined flint, charcoal, pottery and sandstone fragments, the whole measuring 5.5 m across, though there was no ring gully or associated post holes. If these two sites are typical, it would suggest that the standard round house in Sussex may often have been stake-built, sometimes with its stakes bedded in a gully. Inevitably, all traces would be rapidly removed by ploughing.

The evidence for rectangular houses is equally convincing. At Heathy Brow, only 15 m from the round house mentioned above, and contemporary with it, was another feature characterised by calcined flint, charcoal, pottery and sandstone fragments. This was interpreted as a rectangular hut, 8 m by 5 m. At Charleston Brow in East Sussex and Park Brow in West Sussex, rectangular surface depressions rich in domestic debris have been found. At the latter site, a rectangular structure, 10 m by 3 m, was identified, consisting of two parallel rows of post holes (Wolseley and Smith 1924). A similar configuration was found at Bishopstone (Bell 1977). Clearly, a structure 10 m by 3 m would be rather narrow for a hut, but if the postholes represent uprights providing support halfway up each side of a sloping roof, then the ground area of such a hut could be quite considerable. As yet, there is no indication of any distinction between round and rectangular huts in terms of date, function or status.

As for internal organisation within farm settlements or hillforts, relatively little can be said. This again derives from the fact that so much excavation has been done on heavily ploughed sites where huts and other shallow features have been destroyed. (All this is in remarkable contrast to the situation which exists for the middle Bronze Age; here settlement-excavations in Sussex have revealed small earthwork-enclosures, with internal divisions provided by fences, within which are round huts, to which, in favourable circumstances, functions can be assigned). Thus, in spite of large-scale excavations at a number of sites, our knowledge of the spatial organisation of activities within them remains limited. Only at Heathy Brow (Bedwin 1982) has any kind of organisational unit been identified, namely a hut site, working-hollow and posthole cluster, and that with some diffidence. Where enclosures and hillforts are concerned, there is a fairly consistent pattern of structures clustering just inside the boundaries, for instance the four-posthole structures at Harting Beacon (Bedwin 1979) and at Bishopstone (Bell 1977), and the huts inside Hollingbury.

Programmes of flotation, which on sites outside Sussex have successfully identified particular areas associated with crop-processing, have been unproductive. This may be partly connected with the much lower numbers of pits on Sussex sites compared with central Wessex.

Economy and environment

The general picture of Iron Age subsistence based on mixed farming needs little revision or updating since the last review (Bedwin 1978). This is not, however, a matter for complacency. In particular, information about crops is still scarce. Bishopstone has provided the most complete record: in the early Iron Age, c. 90% of the seeds recovered were spelt, with a few percent barley. Other species, but only represented by a single identification, were oats and peas. For the late Iron Age (a single sample from one context) the only crop was barley. Spelt was also identified in an Iron Age posthole at Slonk Hill (Arthur 1978, 131).

As regards animal husbandry, the four most important species were cattle, sheep/goat, pig and horse. At Slonk Hill, sheep was the predominant species, increasing from 51% to 61% from the 6th/4th to the 3rd/1st centuries BC. At Bishopstone, sheep and cattle are both recorded at 34% for the Iron Age as a whole, though the bone-specialist has reported that there was a general tendency for sheep to become more numerous in the later Iron Age (Gebbels 1977, 280).

There is little evidence from any site of a significant contribution from hunting or fowling. A few finds of red deer bones from Harting Beacon, Torberry, Slonk Hill and Bishopstone indicate a consistent, but low, level of hunting, though Harcourt's warning that hunted species may be under-represented in the bone record should be remembered (Harcourt 1979). Bird bones have been noted in only very small numbers.

More important is the contribution from the collecting of shellfish, notably at sites on the south side of the Downs. At Bishopstone, mussel was the commonest species followed by oyster, with cockles, limpets and periwinkles also present. A crab claw, probably from the edible species *Cancer pagarus L*, was also found. At Slonk Hill, mussel was the commonest type, followed by oyster, this order being reversed during the Roman period. By contrast, Harting Beacon, on the north edge of the Downs, yielded no shellfish. Fish, either freshwater or marine, are little represented: there are four unidentified vertebrae from Bishopstone.

Evidence about the environment comes from the analysis of snail assemblages. The evidence from Bishopstone pointed, not surprisingly, to an open environment, indicative of continuing agriculture. From the two early Iron Age hillforts on the north edge of the Downs, Harting Beacon and Chanctonbury, the picture is rather one of damp overgrown grassland, which would argue against heavily-grazed short turf, such as might be expected if they were stock enclosures. Finally, there is the possibility of complementary information in the form of an early Iron Age pollen sequence from excavations at the hillfort on Seaford Head (Bedwin 1984b). Although on the South Downs, a section through the eastern defences of the hillfort revealed a profile (including a ditch 1.6 m deep) entirely in clay-with-flints. Beneath a substantial bank was a well-defined old land surface, in which it is hoped that pollen has survived.

The Coastal Plain

The settlement pattern

The evidence for the development of permanent settlement on the West Sussex Coastal Plain during the Neolithic, Bronze Age and Iron Age has been recently reviewed (Bedwin 1983). At the moment, there appears to be no evidence of settlement during the Neolithic; colonisation begins during the Bronze Age, though perhaps only on a limited scale. During the Iron Age, however, and especially from the 4th/3rd centuries BC, there is considerable evidence of a new type of settlement, namely square or rectangular enclosures, linked by trackways and with adjacent field-systems. All these features are defined by ditches, some of them substantial. The first of these to be found was at North Bersted (Bedwin and Pitts 1978) on a brickearth subsoil at 4 m OD. There was an extensive network of drainage ditches, acting as the boundaries of rectangular or trapezoidal fields. One of the enclosures defined by the ditches was a settlement focus, with a small round hut (ring gully), 6 m across. Domestic debris was plentiful, and the settlement was dated to the 3rd/1st centuries BC.

At Copse Farm, Oving (15 m OD), an extensive series of crop-marks has been identified by F.G. Aldsworth from aerial photographs (Fig. 3.3). These all correspond

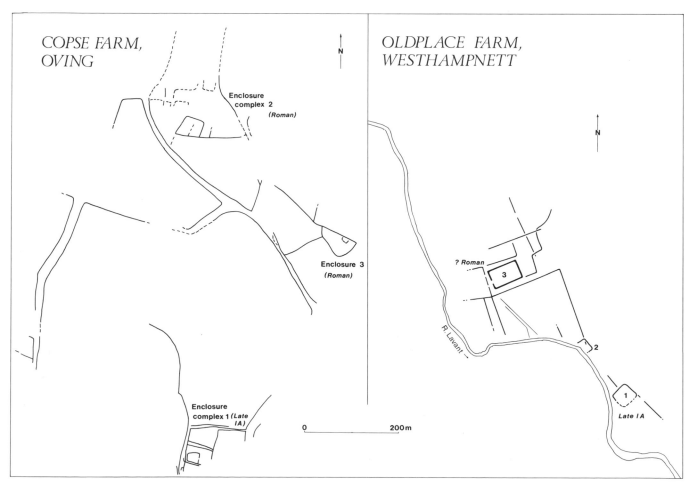

Figure 3.3 *Iron Age Sussex. Examples of enclosures on the Coastal Plain.*

49

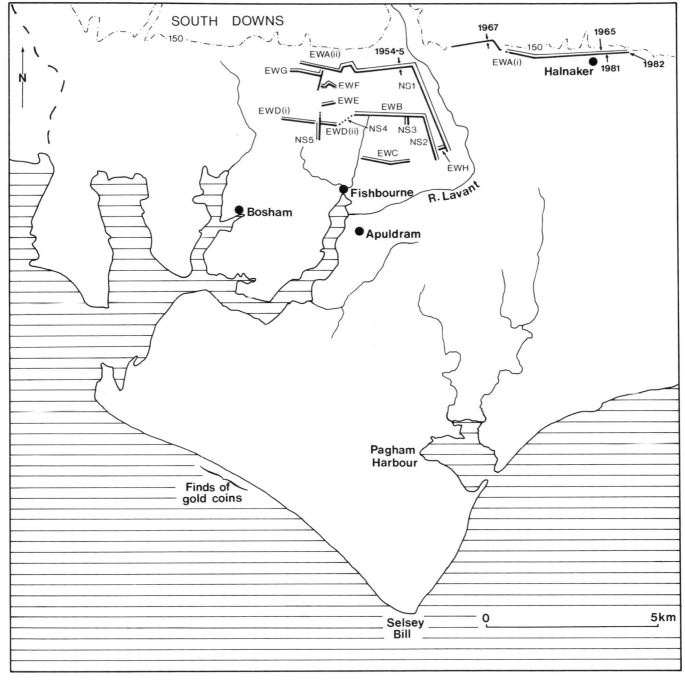

Figure 3.4 *Iron Age Sussex. The Chichester dykes.*

to ditches and represent a series of enclosures and linking trackways. Excavations here in 1980, 1982 and 1983 have dated Enclosure complex 1 to the late Iron Age (1st century BC until shortly before the Roman invasion). Part of a single round house, 9 m across, was found. Enclosure complexes 2 and 3, plus associated trackways, are Roman. Interestingly, this site seems from the crop-mark evidence to be simply settlement-enclosures and trackways without any extensive field-system of the North Bersted type.

At Oldplace Farm, Westhampnett, there is another crop-mark site (Fig. 3.3). Again, there are enclosures, trackways, and, to the north of Enclosure 3, which is probably Roman, a series of what may be rectangular

fields. Trial excavation in 1981 of Enclosure 1 dated it to the 3rd/1st centuries BC.

It is not yet clear what the density of these settlements is on the Coastal Plain, nor are the factors affecting site location fully understood, but both Oving and Oldplace Farm, Westhampnett are situated on soils derived from freshwater alluvium.

The economic basis of these settlements is mixed farming: large numbers of animal bones were present at both North Bersted and Oving, cattle being by far the most important species. In spite of extensive flotation, little charred grain has been isolated. At Oving, barley, spelt, bread wheat and oats were all present in small amounts (P. Hinton, pers. comm.).

The Chichester dykes and the southern Atrebatic oppidum

Along the northern edge of the Coastal Plain are the complex and extensive series of linear earthworks known as the Chichester dykes (Fig. 3.4). Excavation has indicated that they were almost certainly constructed towards the end of the Iron Age (e.g. Murray 1956; Bradley 1971; Bedwin and Orton 1984). It has been accepted that these dykes form the northern limit of the southern Atrebatic oppidum, but it remains to be established where within the Coastal Plain the major foci of settlement are located. The finds of gold coins along the coast to the west of Selsey Bill (Fig. 3.4) have suggested an important site here, but this location has recently come under critical scrutiny (Champion and Champion 1981, 43; Bedwin 1983). The logic of the dyke lay-out has persuaded many authors that a location in the Fishbourne area, just west of Chichester, is more likely.

The coin-mould fragments recently found at Ounces Barn, Boxgrove at the eastern extremity of the dyke system (Bedwin 1983) come from an early Roman rubbish-deposit, with no late Iron Age settlement in the vicinity. It is therefore unlikely that they represent an important centre producing coins before AD 43. It may be more probable that they indicate coin-production in the period 43 to c. 70, after the conquest, up to the time when the client kingdom was absorbed into the empire; however, no such coins are known at present.

References

ARTHUR, P. 1978: Seeds. In Hartridge, R., Excavations at the prehistoric and Romano-British site on Slonk Hill. *Sussex Archaeol. Coll.* 116, 131.

BEDWIN, O. 1978: Iron Age Sussex. In Drewett, P.L. (editor), *The archaeology of Sussex to AD 1500* (London CBA Res. Rep. 29), 41–51.

BEDWIN, O. 1979: Excavations at Harting Beacon, West Sussex: 2nd season. *Sussex Archaeol. Coll.* 117, 21–36.

BEDWIN, O. 1980: Excavations at Chanctonbury Ring, Wiston, West Sussex 1977. *Britannia* 11, 173–222.

BEDWIN, O. 1981: Excavations at the Neolithic enclosure on Bury Hill, Houghton, West Sussex 1979. *Proc. Prehist. Soc.* 47, 69–80.

BEDWIN, O. 1982: The pre-Roman Iron Age. In Drewett, P.L., *The archaeology of Bullock Down, Eastbourne* (Lewes, Sussex Archaeol. Soc. Monograph No. 1), 73–96.

BEDWIN, O. 1983: The development of prehistoric settlement on the West Sussex Coastal Plain. *Sussex Archaeol. Coll.* 121, 31–44.

BEDWIN, O. 1984a: Excavations at Halnaker Hill, West Sussex. *Bull. Inst. Archaeol. Lond.* 21.

BEDWIN, O. 1984b: Excavations at Seaford Head, East Sussex. *Bull. Inst. Archaeol. Lond.* 21.

BEDWIN, O. and ORTON, C. 1984: The excavation of the eastern terminal of the Devil's Ditch (Chichester dykes), Boxgrove, West Sussex 1982. *Sussex Archaeol. Coll.* 122.

BEDWIN, O. and PITTS, M.W. 1978: The excavation of an Iron Age settlement at North Bersted, Bognor Regis 1975–76. *Sussex Archaeol. Coll.* 116, 293–346.

BELL, M.G. 1977: Excavations at Bishopstone. *Sussex Archaeol. Coll.* 115.

BRADLEY, R.J. 1971: A field survey of the Chichester entrenchments. In Cunliffe, B.W., *Excavations at Fishbourne* vol. I (London, Rep. Res. Soc. Antiq. 26), 17–36.

BURSTOW, G.P. 1961–62: Notes on two seasons' work at Balcombe Pit, Glynde Quarry. (Sussex Archaeological Society Library, Lewes).

CHAMPION, T.C. and CHAMPION, S.T. 1981: The Iron Age in Hampshire. In Shennan, S.J. and Schadla-Hall, R.T. (editors), *The archaeology of Hampshire* (Winchester, Hampshire Field Club and Archaeol. Soc. Monograph No. 1), 37–45.

CUNLIFFE, B.W. 1976a: *Iron Age sites in central southern England* (London, CBA Res. Rep. 16).

CUNLIFFE, B.W. 1976b: The origins of urbanisation in Britain. In Cunliffe, B.W. and Rowley, T. (editors), *Oppida in barbarian Europe* (Oxford, BAR S11), 135–162.

CURWEN, E.C. 1930: Wolstonbury. *Sussex Archaeol. Coll.* 71, 237–45.

DREWETT, P.L. 1982: *The archaeology of Bullock Down, Eastbourne* (Lewes, Sussex Archaeol. Soc. Monograph No. 1).

GEBBELS, A. 1977: The animal bones. In Bell, M.G., Excavations at Bishopstone. *Sussex Archaeol. Coll.* 115, 277–84.

HARCOURT, R. 1979: The animal bones. In Wainwright 1979, 150–60.

HOLLEYMAN, G.A. 1937: Harrow Hill excavations, 1936. *Sussex Archaeol. Coll.* 78, 230–54.

MURRAY, K.M.E. 1956: The Chichester earthworks. *Sussex Archaeol. Coll.* 94, 139–41.

WAINWRIGHT, G.J. 1979: *Gussage All Saints* (London, Department of the Environment Archaeological Report No. 10).

WOLSELEY, G.R. and SMITH, R.A. 1924: Discoveries near Cissbury. *Antiq. Journ.* 4, 347–59.

Aspects of Iron Age Settlement in the Upper Thames Valley

Richard Hingley and David Miles

'When measured against the intensity of archaeological activity which has taken place in the Upper Thames Region, the results which have been achieved in terms of a coherent historical interpretation, and which might have served as a model for other regions, have been singularly disappointing.'

D. Harding

'The further we progress in knowledge the more clearly we can discern the vastness of our ignorance.'

Karl Popper

It is 127 years since Stephen Stone delivered his communication of work at Standlake to the Society of Antiquaries, when the first excavation of an Iron Age settlement (and probably house site) in the Upper Thames Valley was recorded. Even then local archaeology was in the gravel-pits. Stone brought remarkably modern methods and theory to the study of this settlement. He produced scale models of the site from which a ground plan can be restored and was well aware of the significance of his work.

'From the variety and extent of these discoveries it may fairly be concluded that Standlake offers a wide if not rich field for the investigation of the antiquary. He may indeed fail to find relics of that costly description which have been found in some other districts; but if a collection of facts tending to elucidate an interesting but obscure subject be to him, as it ought to be, of greater importance than a mere collection of curiosities, however valuable they may be — if the acquisition of knowledge be more his object than the acquisition of wealth, he may perchance reap a rich harvest here.' (Stone 1857, 99)

Other excavations in the 19th and earlier 20th centuries were far more limited in their methods and usually in the excavations' objectives. As Cunliffe has noted, no solid framework existed for Iron Age studies before the 1930s (Cunliffe 1978, 4). Cunliffe has suggested that the theorising and consolidation of 1930 and 1931 focused archaeological activity firmly on the Iron Age. In the Upper Thames Region this is demonstrated by an outburst of activity: excavations were conducted on enclosed sites and earthworks (hillforts and the North Oxfordshire Grims Ditch) and on Iron Age settlements. The threat of gravel-quarrying in close proximity to Oxford continued to attract attention to sites in the valley. Before the introduction of planning legislation in the late 1940s most of the gravel pits were small-scale and uncontrolled; the possibilities for archaeological work were therefore limited. Nevertheless standards of excavation continued to improve, notably with W.F. Grimes' (1943) wartime work at Stanton Harcourt. Aerial photography also contributed a major advance to Iron Age studies in the Thames Valley. The work was pioneered by Major G. Allen (1938) and carried forward by D.N. Riley who in 1943 produced a gazetteer of cropmark sites in the Upper Thames Valley (Riley 1943).

After the war excavations continued to congregate on the gravel terraces. These were occasionally on a larger scale but more often were essentially salvage operations. Until the 1970s archaeology suffered from an absence of implemented research designs; it reacted to threats more often than it posed questions.

The late 1960s and 1970s saw a more organised approach to the problems of late prehistoric settlement-archaeology. In an attempt to rationalise the outburst of Excavation Committees (Oxford, Upper Thames Valley, Abingdon, M40 etc) the Oxford Archaeological Unit was established in 1973. A survey of the cropmark evidence rapidly followed — made possible by the pioneering Sites and Monuments Record in the Oxford City and County Museum, Woodstock (Benson and Miles 1974). This was the first major survey of cropmark evidence since 1943 and acted as a basis for problem-orientated, excavation-based research.

The Unit's excavation policy has involved the large-scale excavation of a few sites, rather than the piecemeal excavation of many, systematised retrieval of data and stated objectives.

In the context of present-day government-funded archaeology the excavation policy is governed by rescue considerations. This has major effects: archaeological research follows in the wake of modern develpment and inevitably, if unsatisfactorily, there is an increased emphasis and bias towards the gravel terraces of the Thames Valley. Up to 1970 almost half of the Iron Age sites excavated in the area were on soils other than on gravel (19 out of 40 or 48% in a recent survey of part of the region, Hingley unpublished), in the 1970s only one sixth (2 out of 12 or 16%) were on soils other than gravel; and these were both minor excavations. When we consider that the gravels form less than 15% of the total survey area then (ignoring rescue considerations) the gravel areas have received twelve times their due level of attention.

This bias is exacerbated by aerial photography, which like excavation, tends to trawl the productive grounds of the gravel terraces. The number of photographs taken over the country as a whole has grown almost exponentially (Palmer 1978). In the much-flown Thames Valley the rate of increase has been less than in other recently explored areas. Nevertheless, in the years following the Benson and Miles survey (1974), the cropmark discoveries have increased by as much as 30% (Hingley 1980a) in the Oxfordshire stretch of the valley, and by more than 50% in the Gloucestershire/Wiltshire area (current re-survey of the Cotswold Water Park: for previous information see Leach 1977).

The information that is available for Iron Age settlement comes from a number of sources, in particular excavation, fieldwork and aerial photography. Excavation is, in many ways, the most reliable of the three techniques, but it is also subject to severe limitations. Excavation is expensive in time and money; as a consequence it is often restricted to only part of a site. The concept of the 'site' itself causes problems; excavation often concentrates on the focal point of settlement where the archaeological record indicates concentrations of artefacts, installations and structures. The full extent and complexity of activity areas in the surrounding landscape (what Foley (1981) has termed the 'off-site' archaeology and Thomas more confusingly the 'non-site' archaeology) has been relatively unexplored. Even the limits of any centralised occupation-area are rarely discovered (for example Parrington 1978; Halpin 1983; Hingley 1983b) and the definitions of the settlement area is 'essentially a subjective judgement' (Best and Rogers 1973, quoted in Fletcher 1981). The emphasis on the excavation of threatened sites also creates a gross regional bias in which detailed evidence of site structure, aspects of material culture and economic environmental data are almost totally restricted to lower levels of the river valleys. The gravel terraces do, however, present the opportunity for large-scale excavation, ranging across contemporary and successive settlements, fields, trackways and watercourses (Miles and Palmer 1983a). There has also, in recent years, been a welcome effort to study the previously neglected river floodplain (Lambrick and Robinson 1979; Lambrick 1981a; 1982).

The techniques of aerial photography and field survey are less labour-intensive but have serious limitations. Aerial photography can provide plans of site layout and information on the distribution of sites. However, an aerial photographic plan is not definitive. Even a large number of good-quality cropmark photographs may only reveal a sample of the buried features (Miles 1983). It is usually not possible from this evidence to understand fully the chronological complexities of the site. In addition, not all soils are equally productive of cropmarks. Clay soils are notoriously less photogenic than gravels, a problem further biased by the less intensive aerial survey which they have received.

Fieldwork is an essential supplementary technique for locating and dating individual sites and for examining regional patterns of settlement. Dating evidence can be found on ploughed sites, but not inevitably so (Miles 1983, 79; in contrast Lambrick 1979, fig. 32; Jones 1978). Much depends on the nature of the soil and the durability of the cultural debris. The factors that determine the presence of surface finds are complex, and negative evidence from fieldwork is never entirely conclusive.

As a conclusion to the assessment of these techniques it is necessary to stress that the information-base for the Upper Thames Valley is the consequence of unsystematic recovery and hence is very inadequate. The majority of the sites known in the area are on the gravels of the Thames Valley and those of the main tributaries. By contrast recent field and aerial survey has produced new sites on the limestone hills north-west and south-east of Oxford (Hingley 1980b; unpublished; Edward et al 1979, Cowell and Miles 1980). In spite of this the uplands have yet to see any major excavations.

The Region

The tradition of regionally based studies of the British Iron Age goes back to the work of Williams-Freeman (1915) in Hampshire. In the Upper Thames area both Leeds and Bradford attempted to develop a coherent local framework before Hawkes (1959) produced his wider definition of regions within the British Iron Age. Cunliffe (1974) furthered the regional approach, but largely from the perspective of ceramic studies. Lacking a comprehensive settlement data-base, Iron Age students continued for too long to utilise Highland/Lowland zone generalisations and simplified type-site models.

A more logical, integrated approach to regional studies was advocated twenty years ago (Binford 1964), stimulated in the United States by the need for large-scale survey in relatively unknown areas of usually low modern population. The processualist school of the succeeding two decades has nevertheless sometimes seemed fixed on the general law and the simple theory. A methodology of regional archaeology has not been fully developed: at times it seems that the Little Woodbury culture has been replaced by David Clarke's (1972) inspirational reconstruction of Glastonbury based on a modular concept.

There has been a growing awareness of the value of regionally-based archaeology. Dissatisfaction with the culture concept has led to new studies of patterning in the archaeological record (e.g. Blackmore et al. 1979) but society is still tentatively glimpsed through objects which are lacking even an adequate archaeological context. In the past decade nomadic archaeologists have themselves settled down, within the framework of government-funded regional units. This has served to institutionalise the interest in regions and in regional settlement-systems. Unfortunately this work has often continued to be piecemeal and haphazard. Nevertheless it is now widely appreciated that late prehistoric settlements are frequent, varied and discoverable. 'We are thus forcibly reminded that the site can only be meaningfully modelled against a network of related and different sites within an interrelated system.' (Clarke 1972, 838).

This has led in the Upper Thames region to a concerted attempt to investigate settlement variation and interrelationships. Opportunities have been taken, within the framework of rescue archaeology, to investigate settlements of different form and location. A strong emphasis has been placed on biological studies (see Robinson and Jones this vol.) and on the selection of sites where preservation is relatively good because of waterlogging or where ploughing has been limited. The desire to compare sites has also encouraged probabilistic sampling strategies and standardised methods of data-collection (Jones 1978; Wilson 1978).

This does not mean that the study of regional archaeology can be reduced to mechanistic formulae. As Paul Levilliot has said of local history it 'cannot build carefully planned edifices, it must in a sense be modulated to conform to the imperatives of its subject' (Levilliot 1977, 13). A region has its own deeper characteristics and qualities, its own rates of adaptation to the processes of change. In a sense, no regional study should be too 'period'-oriented; it is necessary to look both backwards and forwards. For this reason in particular, recent studies of regional patterning and change in what is conventionally called the late Bronze Age are particularly welcome (Barret and Bradley 1980; Barrett 1980a; Rowlands 1980; Ellison 1981; Thomas forthcoming).

The Upper Thames region is one of relatively few to have had a detailed individual study of its Iron Age (Harding 1972). Harding laid considerable emphasis on the chronological development of pottery sequences against the background of an invasion theory of change. Settlement-data were in short supply, large-scale excavations were scarce, environmental information was negligible and limited mapping and analysis of crop-marks had taken place. 'Major settlements' (Harding 1972, pl 1) qualified for that description largely on the basis of who had dug in them. Nevertheless Harding's description of the region's characteristics hold good: an area of contrasting landscapes and ecological zones; a frontier zone in prehistoric, Roman and early historic times; a region in part open to outside influences and in part conservative and traditional. Harding also emphasised the shortcomings of the disparate and unco-ordinated archaeological efforts up to that time (see quote which opens this paper).

The Iron Age Settlement-Evidence in the Upper Thames Valley

The main point which should be stressed at this stage is the complexity of the settlement evidence for the area. The most prominent sites, but ones which have received little recent attention, are defended enclosures — so called because their substantial ramparts are of defensive proportions. Most of these sites occur on upland positions, but others are on hillslopes or even valley bottoms.

Only limited excavation has been conducted, in contrast with Wessex (see Cunliffe this vol.), and knowledge of these sites is partly from earthwork survey and surface examination (Hingley 1981). Small univallate hillforts at Lyneham (Bayne 1957) and Chastleton (Leeds 1931) have been shown by excavation to have phases of Late Bronze Age/Early Iron Age occupation, and many of the other undated defended enclosures in the region may begin at this time. (These hillforts possibly fall into a class with the small univallate hillforts of the Cotswolds discussed by Marshall (1978). At Blewburton Hill (Harding 1976), prominently posi-

tioned on an outlying hill of the Berkshire Downs, a stockaded enclosure of c. 2 ha has been dated to the 7th–6th centuries BC, followed by a timber-laced rampart in the 6th–5th centuries, a dump rampart about 100 BC and abandonment shortly afterwards.

More extensive defensive sites are known which are not in particularly prominent positions. At Salmonsbury (c. 23 ha), between the River Windrush and the River Dickler, the main defensive phases belonged to the mid to late Iron Age (Dunning 1976; RCHM (E) 1967, 17–19). Dyke Hills, Dorchester (c. 47 ha) at the confluence of the River Thames and the Thame (Benson and Miles 1974, 91–4) is completely undated, though often *assumed* to be of late Iron Age date on the basis of its position between the hillfort at Castle Hill and the Roman fort just outside its ramparts. Aerial photography shows the site to have been densely occupied (Fig. 4.9). The ?defended enclosure at Cassington Mill (c. 5.5 ha) had six causeways, and it has been suggested that the earthwork was unfinished (Startin in Case 1982, 150–1). This site dates to the late Iron Age, but the scatter of salvage excavations which peppered it has not clarified its role or the nature of its occupation. Traces of round houses were recorded behind the ramparts, but these were thought to date to the later first and second centuries AD (Case 1982). Another low-lying defended site is Burroway, Clanfield. This 3 ha enclosure lies on a long island formed by the Thames and Burroway Brook (Benson and Miles 1974, 36, Map 11). Trial excavations in 1962 produced indeterminate Iron Age pottery and in 1983 revealed a burnt timber-laced rampart (Lambrick pers comm.). Its chronology, however, remains uncertain.

The small, multivallate, defended enclosure at Cherbury (Fig. 4.2, 3796) is of middle Iron Age date (Bradford 1940; Hingley 1983b). Although this site is of limited extent, it appears to be associated with an extensive open settlement, which may make the total occupation at Cherbury comparable with Salmonsbury. Castle Hill, Long Wittenham has also produced evidence of external occupation (Hingley 1983a).

It is apparent that the defended enclosures of the Upper Thames region show a great complexity of form, a wide range of size and chronology, and probably a considerable variation of function. In the absence of the number and scale of excavations which have taken place in Wessex, it is impossible at present to assess the role of these sites in the Upper Thames region.

Other types of settlement are well known from the larger number of excavations on the gravels of the Oxford Clay Vale (Lambrick 1978). In addition many further sites are familiar from aerial photography. Recent excavations by the Oxford Archaeological Unit (at Ashville, Abingdon (Parrington 1978; Halpin 1983); Farmoor (Lambrick and Robinson 1978); Appleford (Hinchliffe and Thomas 1980); Barton Court Farm Abingdon (Miles 1983; forthcoming); Mount Farm, Berinsfield (Lambrick 1981b); Claydon Pike, Fairford/ Lechlade (Miles and Palmer 1981; 1983a, b); Mingies Ditch Hardwick (Allen and Robinson 1979); and cur-

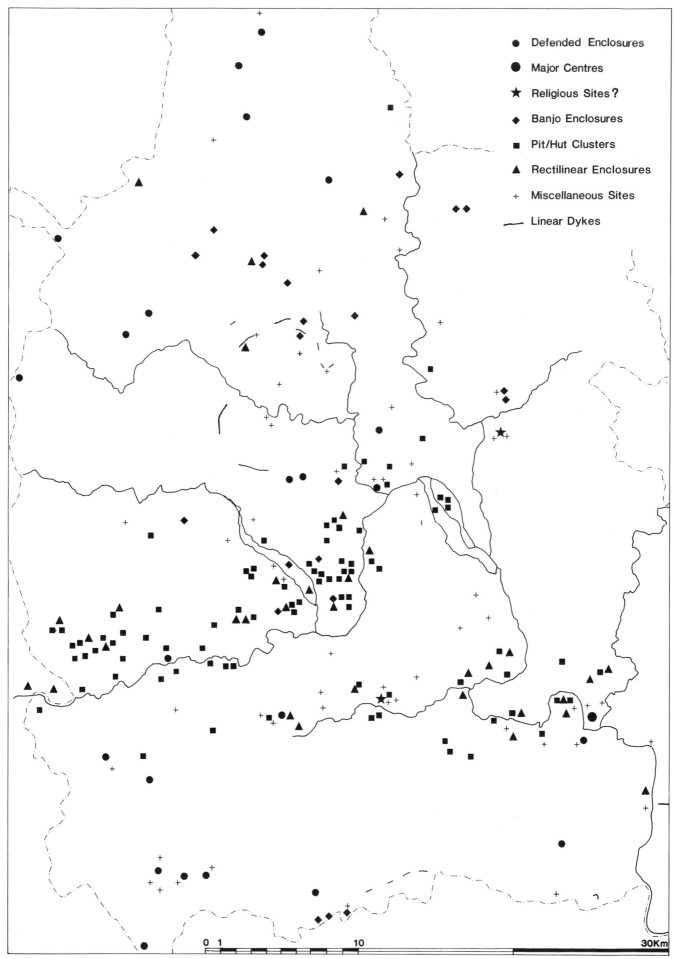

Figure 4.1 *Iron Age Settlement in the Upper Thames region.*

The legend reads:

- ● Defended Enclosures
- ⬤ Major Centres
- ★ Religious Sites?
- ◆ Banjo Enclosures
- ■ Pit/Hut Clusters
- ▲ Rectilinear Enclosures
- + Miscellaneous Sites
- — Linear Dykes

0 1   10   30Km

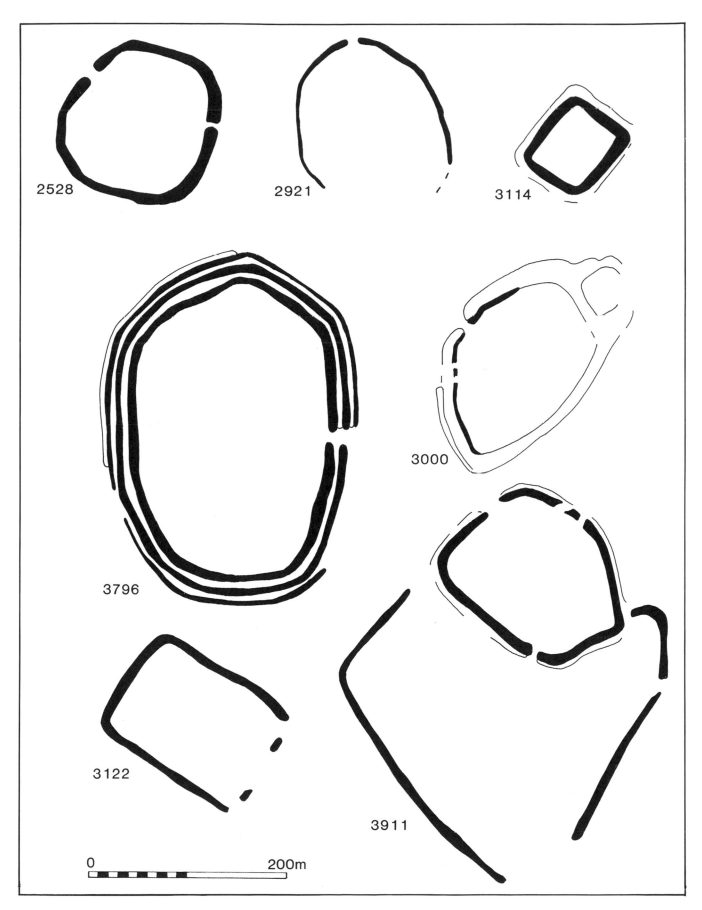

Figure 4.2 *A selection of Iron age defended enclosures in the Upper Thames region. The numbers refer to 1 km grid squares.*

2528 *Chastleton*   3122 *Knowlbury*
2921 *Lyneham Camp*   3796 *Cherbury*
3000 *Burroway*   3911 *Eynsham Hall Park.*
3114 *Lowbarrow Leafield*

rently at Stanton Harcourt and Northmoor) demonstrate the variability exhibited by settlements in the lower part of the valley. The excavations emphasise the problems of simple classification, particularly in a changing landscape. No classification can be foolproof or cut and dried; as Clarke emphasised (1972, 843) settlement-types may be only phases in the life-cycle of a community and not necessarily independent classificatory taxa. Classification will vary along with the questions being posed and the perception of the questioner (Hill and Evans 1972). In general, however, Iron Age settlement-studies have been typified by over-simplistic site-typologies that have discouraged closer investigation of complexity.

Within the region cropmark and excavation evidence suggest a variety of site types connected with particular zones of the landscape. On the low-lying floodplain of the Thames, loosely scattered hut and pen sites, a lowland version of the shieling, have been excavated at Farmoor (Lambrick and Robinson 1979). Biological evidence indicates that these occupied an open, grassland environment and were used seasonally, but only over a short period of four or five years. Similar features are also known at Port Meadow, Oxford (Atkinson 1942; Lambrick 1982, fig. 34) and there are possible traces on aerial photographs of Abingdon Common. These floodplain sites are not easy to locate as they are usually buried beneath late Iron Age and post-Roman alluvial deposits.

Another type of floodplain settlement which has been excavated is in the valley of the River Windrush at Mingies Ditch, Hardwick (Fig. 4.3, 3905) (Allen and Robinson 1979; Benson and Miles 1974, Map 21, SP 3905). This double-ditched enclosure with external antennae ditches contained a sequence of round houses and four-post structures. The space between its concentric ditches is thought to have acted as a corral for animals. The landscape around the Mingies Ditch settlement was not so open as at Farmoor, but grassland probably predominated. It is impossible to say whether occupation was seasonal, but the settlement seems to have been a longer-term one than Farmoor.

On the first gravel terrace patches of dry ground provide occupation-sites above all but exceptional levels of flooding. Round houses have been excavated at Claydon Pike in such a situation, where they were integrated into a rare example of a ditched field-system (Fig. 4.4). At Claydon Pike these drainage ditches were an essential element in the long-term viability of the settlement and enabled the community to live close to the rich pasture which, traditionally, is a notable feature of this area of the valley.

On the higher, second gravel terrace open settlements consisting of scattered round houses are also a common feature of aerial photographs (Fig. 4.5). Many cropmarks indicate that these are associated with dense clusters of pits, which are assumed to be principally for grain and other food-storage. Such pit clusters are clearly visible at Linch Hill, Stanton Harcourt (Harding 1972, pl 35) and Gravelly Guy, Stanton Harcourt (Benson and Miles

1974, frontispiece). Current excavation at the latter site also emphasises that Iron Age post-ring houses may not be visible as cropmarks (Lambrick pers comm). The investigations at Ashville, Abingdon (Parrington 1978) have shown the importance of cereal production on these second-terrace sites (see Jones this vol.) though animal rearing was also an important aspect of their mixed economy (Grant this vol.). This type of site has also been identified from the air on the Corallian ridge, near Frilford, and by salvage excavation on the plateau gravels at Milton Common (Rowley 1973).

The densely populated second gravel terraces have other types of site. Three banjo enclosures have been recognised in the Stanton Harcourt area, but as Hingley argues in the following paper, these may have had a different function to those of the more isolated examples on the limestone uplands to the north. Individual rectangular enclosures are also a common cropmark feature. Some of these certainly belong to the Roman period but an example at Barton Court Farm, Abingdon (Miles 1983 and forthcoming) was established in the early decades of the first century AD. This contained pit clusters and an internal occupation area with a circular structure.

Other rectangular enclosures on the higher gravel terraces and on the limestone uplands form complex blocks and are often associated with trackways. Surface evidence tends to point to a Roman date for their use; but Iron Age origins have been attested at Mount Farm, Berinsfield; Ashville, Abingdon and Claydon Pike, Fairford. The enclosures have, in some cases, been associated with animal-rearing. There were certainly occupation-areas within them but house sites have proved difficult to define (see Allen et al. this vol.). Some enclosure systems appear very irregular in plan. At Claydon Pike, Fairford, irregular oval enclosures were attached to a more rectilinear block. The arrangement appears in this case to have functioned as an animal-rearing site with only a small human population.

On the higher, limestone uplands of the Cotswolds Iron Age settlements are of distinctly different form. In addition to the hillforts there are other enclosed, banjo sites (Fig. 4.3). These are characteristically sited on hillslopes with well-watered valleys in front of them and limestone plateau behind. The locations suggest that a mixed economy was practised in a landscape with a considerably more scattered population than in the valley bottom.

Intra-site organisation

In the past decade a series of excavations has revealed substantial areas of a number of Iron Age settlements. While it is to be expected that such settlements will to a degree reflect the social structure and organisation of the communities which occupied them, it is obvious that the archaeological evidence does not speak to us directly.

In some cases it is difficult to establish the boundaries of settlement, and keyhole trenches, even quite large ones, can be misleading. At Ashville, Abingdon, for

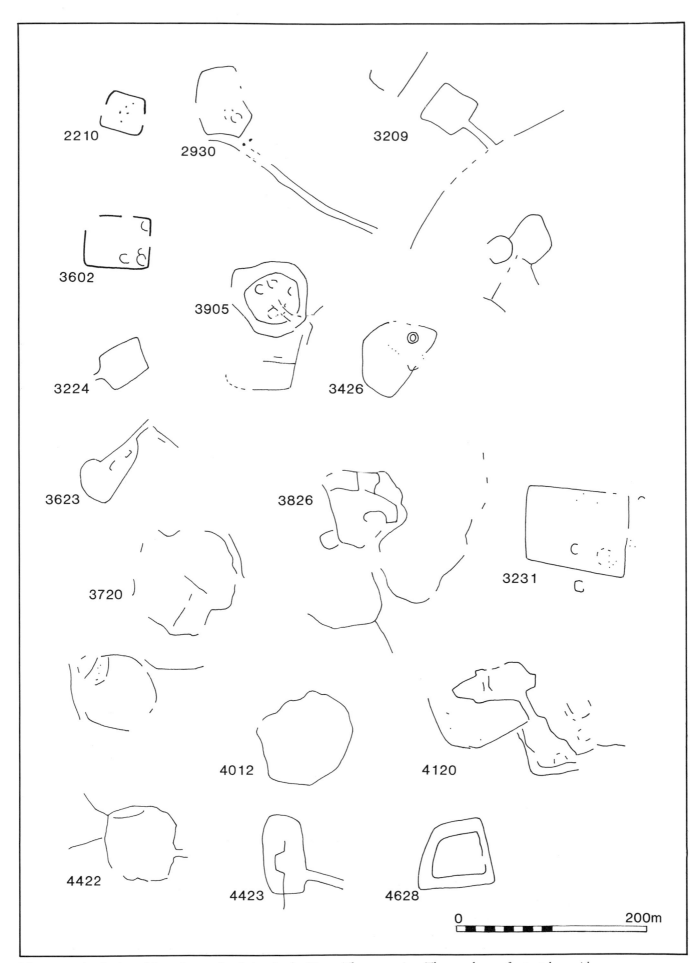

Figure 4.3 *A selection of Iron Age enclosed sites in the Upper Thames region. The numbers refer to 1 km grid squares.*

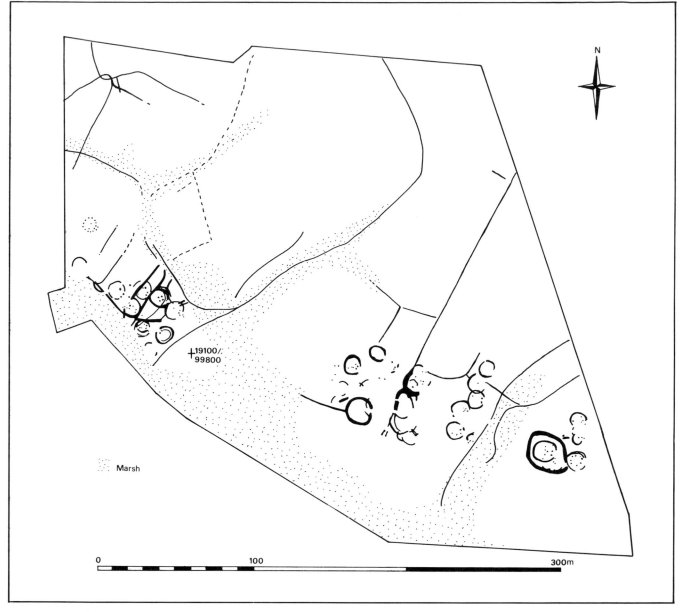

Marsh

Figure 4.4 *Middle Iron Age settlements and enclosures at Claydon Pike, Lechlade.*

example, excavations in 1982/3, following the publication of the 1976 investigation, showed that occupation or (more precisely) activity covered several more hectares but was of a very different character. Many cropmark complexes highlight this problem. This has in part been overcome by observation and excavation of Iron Age landscapes on a massive scale, the investigation of enclosed settlements and the area around them, and the excavation of topographical features such as dry islands of gravel surrounded by marsh.

Even after excavation, settlements present major problems of interpretation; site plans can be misleading. This particularly applies to open settlements where structures are spaced so as to have no stratigraphical relationship with each other and where chronological indicators are not sufficiently precise to allow for accurate or even relative dating. The problem is clear at Claydon Pike (Fig. 4.6). On the westerly platform of gravel a dozen house sites superficially appear to form a

compound arrangement. However, linear ditches provide a series of horizontal relationships which show that the number of contemporary houses could have been no more than four, and in several sub-phases fewer than that. There are also structures which cannot be tied in precisely into any of the sub-phases and therefore must be shown as 'floating'.

Other sites have produced sufficient stratigraphical evidence to sub-divide the complex of structure plans. At Mingies Ditch (Fig. 4.7) the excavators see the arrangement of buildings not in terms of a single group, but as a series of buildings moving anti-clockwise around the enclosure (Allen pers comm). At Danebury, also, the exceptional preservation within an infilled quarry area behind the rampart has highlighted the kaleidoscopic shifting of structures (Cunliffe 1984). As Denyer (1978, 19) has emphasised, among communities using local resources for house-building, 'Villages and houses were built round people and their groupings;

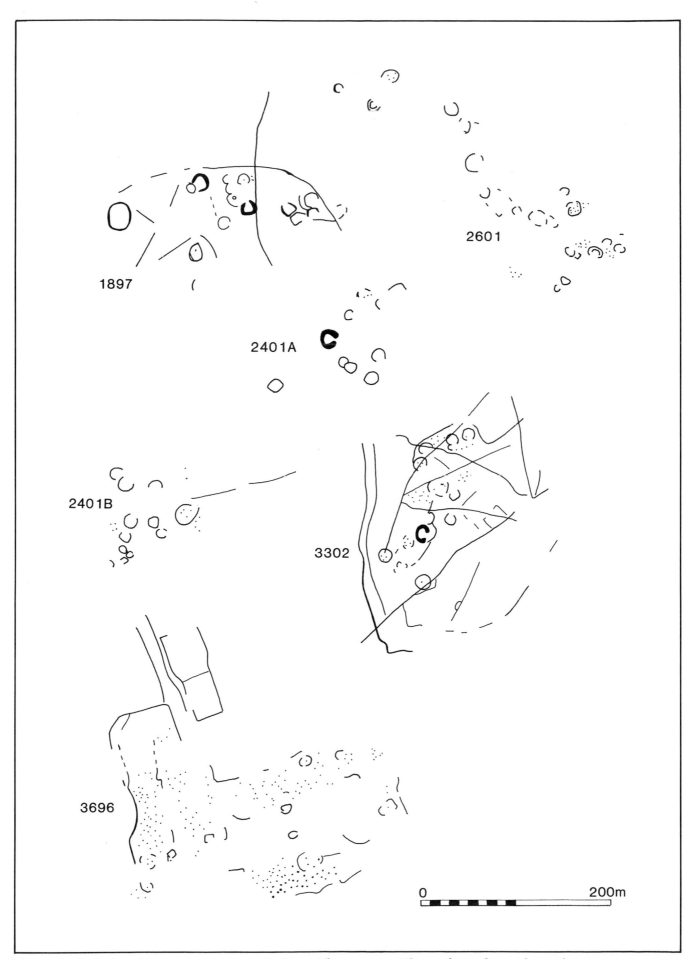

1897

2601

2401A

2401B

3302

3696

0   200m

Figure 4.5 *A selection of Iron Age open sites in the Upper Thames region. The numbers refer to 1 km grid squares.*

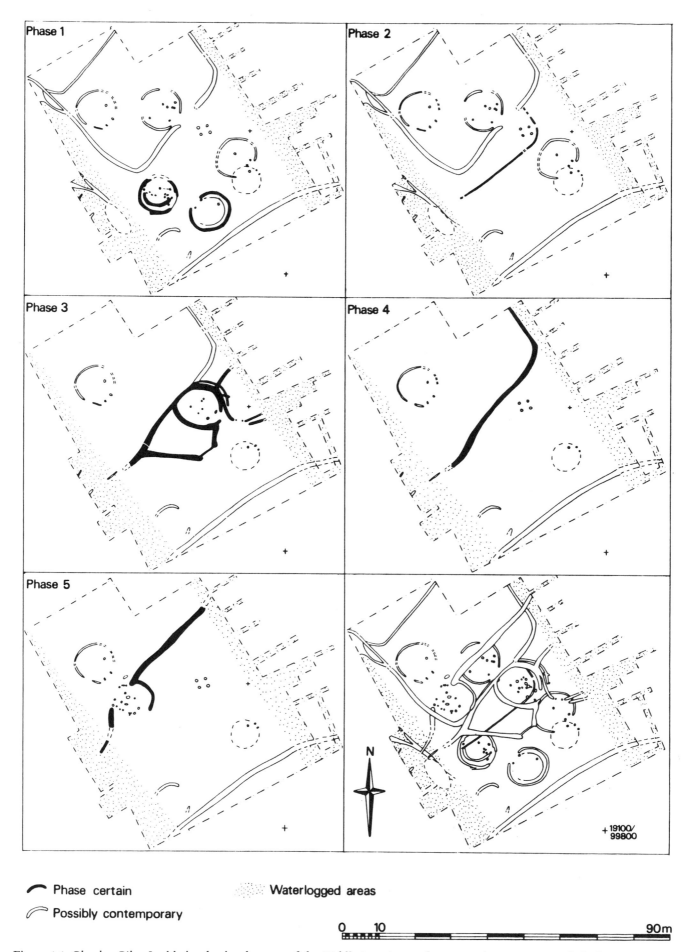

Phase 1

Phase 2

Phase 3

Phase 4

Phase 5

N

+ 19100/
  99800

🌑 Phase certain

◠ Possibly contemporary

▒ Waterlogged areas

0   10   90m

Figure 4.6 *Claydon Pike, Lechlade: the development of the Middle Iron Age settlement on the western gravel platform (see Fig. 4.4 for its relationship to the rest of the site).*

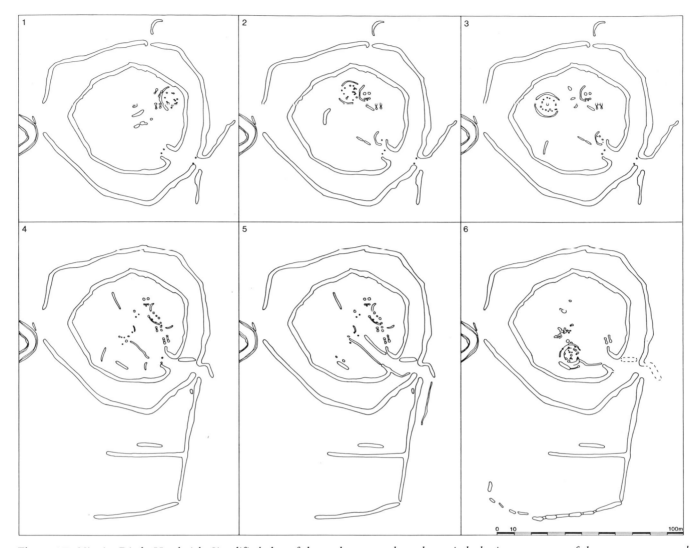

Figure 4.7 *Mingies Ditch, Hardwick. Simplified plan of the settlement to show the anti-clockwise movement of the structures around the compound (Information from T. Allen).*

there was no question of people adapting themselves to fixed houses and villages, which may have been unsuitable or inadequate.'

Where these problems are not fully appreciated all too often unjustified terms are adopted for settlement types. At Ashville, Abingdon, for example, the ravelled knot of oval enclosures has often been referred to as a village: in fact no more than six enclosures could have been in use at any one time and possibly fewer. It is impossible, therefore, on the present evidence even to estimate the population or extent of the settlement.

Even when they are better understood archaeologically, site plans do not submit to easy interpretation. Fletcher (1977, 52) has made the valid point that settlements which look to be haphazard agglomerations of structures to the outside observer nevertheless maintain an intricate formal order and deliberate planning. Any settlement plan then is likely to contain potentially coherent patterns, albeit masked by the background noise of short-term changes and strategies, and the presence of 'invisible' boundaries.

Iron Age settlements in the Upper Thames region present certain regularities even if they do not conform to modern or even Classical ideas of planning. Certain lines of communication have been observed in the form of pathways on low-lying sites: at Farmoor and Mingies Ditch gravel paths were preserved beneath alluvium. The linear layout of enclosures and houses at Farmoor and Claydon Pike suggests that trackways or boundaries may have run alongside them. At Farmoor a Roman trackway maintained the same alignment as the middle Iron Age houses and may reflect the continuity of an earlier line of communication from the higher ground.

With the second terrace settlements zoning is apparent, notably in the concentrations of storage pits. Clustering of pits into groups or bands can be seen at Ashville, Abingdon; Gravelly Guy, Stanton Harcourt and City Farm, Hanborough; at Barton Court Farm, Abingdon pits were within the square enclosure but separated from the main living area. Some pit groups appear to be associated with and respect individual house sites or enclosures (Parrington 1978, fig. 3; Harding 1972, pl 26). Other groups form discreet linear clusters edged by boundaries which are invisible, at least on aerial photographs (Harding 1972, pl 29 and 35; Benson and Miles 1974, frontispiece). Excavation has shown that these groups are the result of pit digging over a considerable period. The number of pits is therefore governed by the length of occupation as much as by the size of the community using them and the amount of grain which they produced.

Four-post structures are most obvious in the Upper Thames Valley on low lying sites, where storage pits are not appropriate (Mingies Ditch, Claydon Pike, Appleford). Possible examples on drier terrace settlements are fewer in number. In no case do the four-posters cluster in groups, as can be observed in a number of hillforts (eg Danebury in Wessex, Crickley Hill and Norbury on the Cotswolds (Gent 1983; Saville 1983; Guilbert 1975, fig. 2)). In the lower valley sites single four-posters appear to be associated with a particular house or group of buildings.

The difficulty of assessing the arrangement of houses on Iron Age sites has already been discussed. Certain patterns do however emerge. Clarke's (1972) 'tentative' Glastonbury model of an Iron Age community was based on a poorly-implemented excavation of a superbly preserved settlement. Rarely today are such conditions repeated. A basic module was postulated consisting of a major residential unit, an ancilliary hut, storage facilities and an open-air activity area. On the basis of the archaeological evidence a kinship organisation which was patrilineal and patrilocal was suggested. This was supported by the statements of ancient ethnographers. The compound arrangement also fitted patterns found among round-house users in present day societies. Other excavators, particularly of Bronze Age settlements, have found this model a convincing one (Ellison 1981).

The buildings in a compound group do not necessarily have to take on a circular arrangement around an open space. At Black Patch, Sussex, for example, Drewett (1982, 341–2) proposed a 'united, sharing compound with independent units' for an extended family. This settlement had an essentially linear layout, with south-easterly-facing round houses fronting onto individual fenced yards.

In Upper Thames Valley settlements round houses predominantly face east or south-east. The conventional functionalist interpretation for this is in terms of environmental stimuli. South-eastern facing doorways are away from dominant westerly and north-easterly winds (Smith 1954, fig. 12), a factor which may have been exacerbated in the Iron Age (Lamb 1981; but see Robinson this vol.). Doorways in this position would also be best placed to take advantage of daylight, which would be necessary when buildings were used for cooking and craft activities. A more formal approach would regard the location of doorways as at least a partial reflection of human behaviour. Does the linear arrangement of structures at Claydon Pike, for example, indicate a degree of privacy or independence between units (though not separated by fences as at Black Patch)?

At Claydon Pike, one of the more coherent Upper Thames sites, houses are positioned on three discrete platforms or islands of gravel. The initial phase of settlement began on the western platform probably in the 3rd century BC. It then expanded to the east, and the latest phase is identifiable on the most easterly island (Figs. 4.4 and 4.6). The buildings were integraged into a ditched field-system and maintain a degree of linearity. Thus on the central platform three rows of structures are positioned one behind the other. Stratigraphy indicates that not all of the structures in each of these rows was occupied at one time. Although the site plan (Fig. 4) suggests a community of substantial size, detailed analysis favours a family group increasing and shifting through a century or more of occupation.

It is possible to identify tentatively areas for cooking, outdoor-working, sleeping, craft activity and penning of animals, but the Glastonbury module of main house, ancilliary building etc. is not clear-cut. As at other Thames Valley sites the round house (with an average diameter of c. 9 m, sometimes with an annexe) seems to act as the basic unit. Claydon Pike had a single example of a paired unit: Building 15 faced north-west directly into Building 17. To the south of these structures was an arc of curving gully which may indicate a pen or sheltered working area. Other possible groups were formed by Buildings 12 and 7 on the central platform (angled towards each other, also with a nearby curving gully) and Buildings 2 and 3 on the eastern platform. Building 3 had an annexe to the south and inside Building 2 was a semicircular stone floor, possibly acting as a hardstanding for livestock. There was a single four-post structure on each of the western and central platforms. As on other Thames Valley settlements no house stood out as significantly larger than the rest, though a single structure, on the eastern platform, sat within a ditched enclosure.

Systematic sampling of Upper Thames settlements has shown them to be rich in biological evidence; carbonised plant remains for example are ubiquitous and exhibit an interesting degree of patterning (see Jones this vol.). Artefacts are notably scarce and are mostly, in the jargon of post-depositional studies, secondary rubbish — that is discarded away from the place of use. House floors, even when unploughed and protected by alluvium, are unfortunately almost entirely free of debris, although the surrounding drainage gullies are not.

The deposits of animal bones and pottery in the terminals of house gullies suggest that food preparation and consumption took place in most of the round-house sites. No specialised buildings for cooking have been recognised. Specifically male-orientated artefacts are notably rare. In contrast, equipment connected with textile production and usually, in farming communities, associated with women (Sherratt 1981, 283) is a feature of most settlements. This is not surprising among the permanent, mixed farming communities of the higher terraces (where infant burials are also not infrequent). Textile equipment has also been found, however, on floodplain and first-terrace sites such as Farmoor, Claydon Pike and Appleford. Cunliffe (see this vol.) has drawn attention to the preponderance of loomweights in Wessex hillforts, as opposed to spindle whorls in other sites, and has suggested that this reflects centralised collection of yarn. The Thames Valley-bottom sites also show clear evidence of weaving: loomweights and polished sheep metatarsals/tibia which probably served as bobbins. This is particularly interesting at Farmoor and suggests that these summer shielings were not simply occupied by a single sex and age set, but by a mixed group. The equipment also suggests that weaving was not necessarily a seasonal, winter activity but, in this case at least, was carried out in summer.

Inter-site relationships

It is a characteristic of western thought to seek order and ranking in complex variation. In Iron Age studies this has been much in evidence with the concern for social and site hierarchies. Archaeologists are encouraged in this pursuit by the traditional view of the Celts as tribal, rural, hierarchical and familiar.

Burial evidence is limited for this period (Whimster 1981, 216–7, but for a sword-burial at Sutton Courtenay see his p 135), so hierarchies must be seen in settlement terms.

The simple pyramid of settlement, with the hillfort (in the early to middle Iron Age) at the peak, may be too simple a model in the Upper Thames region. The dense population from Lechlade down river to Abingdon does not conveniently fall into the catchment of hillfort territories (see Hingley this vol.). The landscape is nevertheless a complex one in which settlements are interrelated.

There are a variety of low-lying settlements. The Farmoor floodplain settlements seem to reflect the movement of small mixed groups, possibly single families, and their (or the community's) flocks down to the riverside pasture in summer. Artefacts are few; the pottery is of a limited range but could have been produced in the sites on the higher ground (see Lambrick this vol.). These herders need not be a separate, independent group but more probably were part of the community of mixed farmers with homes on the upper slopes of the valley and grazing rights by the river. This use of land is not unlike the linear parishes of the Medieval period.

Other groups, such as those at Claydon Pike and Mingies Ditch may have occupied these rather drier sites on a longer-term and not necessarily seasonal basis. Claydon Pike was involved in a long-distance exchange-network for salt, and with it fine Malvernian pottery crossed the Cotswolds from the Droitwich area. Here, as at many other sites, a variety of quernstones was introduced, some from as far afield as Derbyshire. At the local level these sites may have been dependent on arable neighbours for cereal foodstuffs (see Jones this vol.). In return meat, milk products and textiles may have been exchanged.

The storage facilities at arable settlements such as Ashville and City Farm suggest that a substantial part of the produce was kept there. Only when defended sites are excavated in the area will it be possible to test the Wessex hypothesis that such places act as central storage and redistribution centres.

The Process of Change

To understand more clearly the process of change in the region it is necessary to have a chronological framework. At present this exists only in a crude and blurred form. Harding (1972) outlined a sequence of pottery-development which is in part still valid, though subject to recent modification: for example his 'early' T-shaped rims, thought to be skeuomorphs of bronze cauldrons which appear from the 10th century BC, can now be seen to belong to straight-sided or shouldered vessels (De Roche 1977; 1978). Late Bronze Age–Early Iron Age pottery has been the subject of considerable discussion, but the development, and in particular the precise chronology, remains unclear (Barrett 1980b). The development of an accurate Iron Age chronology has been hindered by the failure to excavate well-stratified sites with long-term occupation. The pit-complexes and ditches at Ashville have produced the best, though still highly unsatisfactory, sequence of pottery (De Roche 1978). It is uncertain whether the local pottery types will demonstrate the useful morphological changes observable in Wessex (see Cunliffe and Lambrick this vol.).

The Upper Thames region is also lacking an adequate collection of radiocarbon dates for the first millennium BC. Only a handful are so far available and a number of these seem to be erratic (Parrington 1978, 39; Lambrick and Robinson 1979, 37–8, 144; unpublished dates from Mount Farm, Claydon Pike, and Mingies Ditch).

A general sequence of development can be postulated.

Mid to late Bronze Age

In the middle to late Bronze Age settlement-evidence in the Upper Thames region is sparse. Barrett and Bradley (1980) have suggested that the more populous lower Thames Valley communities controlled the distribution of prestige bronzework; in contrast the Upper Thames was a backwater, perhaps with the population attracted down river.

There is evidence for the development of a complex network of sedentary farming communities in Wessex and the Lower Thames. The 'desertion' of the Upper Thames may reflect the nature of the archaeological record more than the true state of settlement.

Late Bronze Age/Early Iron Age

Apparently new settlements can be recognised from ceramic evidence at a number of sites in the Upper Thames Valley: Ashville, Mount Farm, Long Wittenham, Allen's Pit, Wallingford and Appleford. These can be tentatively dated from the 8th century BC. In the early Iron Age there is a decline in the number of settlements in the lower part of the valley. These shifts of emphasis in regional settlement-patterns may be associated with the changes brought about by the use of iron and the collapse of the networks based on the distribution of prestige bronzework (though the causes and sequence are debatable: see Thomas forthcoming).

The character of these new sites is unknown but most

are located on free-draining, second-terrace soils, which develop as 'favoured' settlement sites, in use through the Iron Age and Roman period.

Occupation probably begins on hillfort sites around the fringes of the region, but except at Blewburton Hill and to a lesser extent Lyneham and Chastleton there is little evidence.

Middle Iron Age

For the first time settlement evidence is prolific. The second gravel terrace is densely occupied with mixed farming communities. The floodplain and damper part of the first gravel terrace are colonised and drainage ditches are constructed. In the Thames Valley the landscape is predominantly an open one. Settlements in the form of banjo-enclosures colonise the limestone slopes. These may represent a form of assarting by family groups, breaking away from the closely-knit kin-groupings in the valley. Numbers are impossible to estimate with precision, but the general impression is of population-growth and an increasingly controlled landscape. The resources of the area are fully used and specialist exploitation of a variety of plants and animals utilise the varying available niches. There is little evidence of settlement hierarchies in the Upper Thames Valley, but the roles of hillforts and defended enclosures as perhaps predominantly redistribution-centres has not been investigated.

Late Iron Age

Considerable changes are apparent in the last decades before the Roman Conquest. The inability to date settlements with accuracy creates problems in understanding this proto-historic period. Rectilinear paddocks and trackways are prolific on aerial photographs of the valley but the date of origin of most is uncertain. At Ashville, Claydon Pike, (Fig. 4.8) Mount Farm and possibly Northfield Farm, Long Wittenham, tracks and enclosures are known at this time, sometimes overlying more dispersed middle Iron Age settlements. House-sites are few, but the impression is of a more nucleated and tightly organised landscape.

New types of settlement, such as Barton Court Farm, infill the valley and may represent less traditional agricultural units. On the floodplain seasonally occupied sites are no longer found. In part these may have been abandoned because of the increasingly heavy deposition of alluvium, as soil was eroded within the catchment area of the Thames. This may be caused by the increasing level of arable farming in relation to woodland and pasture, as land and food-production become increasingly important.

Hillforts were probably abandoned by this time. Defended valley-settlements at nodal points, such as Dyke Hills, Dorchester (Fig. 4.9) may function as regional centres or entrepôts between tribal groups. The concentration of coinage and imported pottery in the Dorchester–Abingdon area suggests that this was a particularly important zone of contact between groups north, south and east of the Thames. High-status objects such as swords have also been found in this area and at Frilford and Woodeaton religious centres existed in the Roman period (Sherratt 1983; Harding 1972).

Dyke Hills has not been excavated in this century but cropmarks show that it was densely occupied, probably for a substantial period, not just during the final decades before the Roman Conquest. The location of a Roman fort, walled town and the official known as a *beneficarius consularis* may reflect the earlier importance of the site in the late Iron Age. This importance probably declined in the Roman province as Dorchester lost its role at the interface of different socio-political groupings. Abingdon also has concentrations of imported pottery, Celtic coins and early Roman coinage. Although little is known in detail of the organisation of the place in the early to mid first century BC, it may represent the emergence of new marketing centres on the eve of the Conquest.

Appendix 1

Major Excavations

1. Salmonsbury, Bourton-on-the-Water
   RCHM(E) 1976, 17–19
   Dunning 1976
2. Claydon Pike, Fairford/Lechlade
   RCHM(E) 1976, 55
   Jones & Miles 1979, 321
   Miles 1979
   Miles & Palmer 1981; 1983 a & b
3. Roughground Farm, Lechlade
   RCHM(E) 1976, 73
   Jones 1978, 171
   Allen & Jones forthcoming
4. Langford Down, Lechlade
   Williams 1946
   Harding 1972, fig. 5
5. Cherbury Camp
   Bradford 1940
   Harding 1972, 140
6. Rams Hill, Uffington
   Piggott, S. & C.M. 1940
   Bradley & Ellison 1975
7. Mingies Ditch, Hardwick-with-Yelford
   Lambrick 1978, 114, fig. 4
   Allen & Robinson 1979, 115–7
8. Vicarage Field, Stanton Harcourt (and neighbouring sites)
   Grimes 1943
   Hamlin 1963
   Harding 1972, 143
   Benson & Miles 1974, 81. fig. 11
   Mytum & Taylor 1981
   Case & Whittle 1982, 113–5, fig. 63
   Riley 1983, 59–61
9. Gravelly Guy, Stanton Harcourt
   Benson & Miles 1974, frontispiece, 81, fig. 11
   current excavations by OAU (Lambrick) 1983/4
10. Watkins Farm, Northmoor
    current excavations by OAU (Allen) 1983/4
11. City Farm, Hanborough

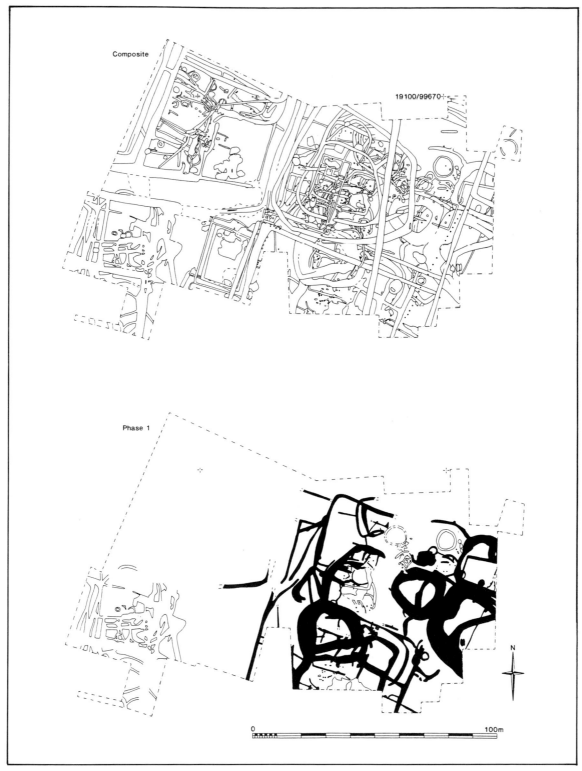

Figure 4.8 *Late Iron Age settlement at Claydon Pike, Fairford. The earlier settlements on Fig. 4.6 are 200 m to the north across the present parish boundary.*

    Case *et al.* 1964
    Harding 1972, pl 26
12. Frilford
    Bradford & Goodchild 1939
    Stevens 1940
    Hingley 1982
13. Farmoor
    Lambrick & Robinson 1979

14. Cassington
    Harding 1972, 139
    Benson & Miles 1974, 84–7, fig. 13
    Case & Whittle 1982, 129-36
15. Ashville Abingdon
    Parrington 1978
    Halpin 1983
16. Barton Court Farm, Abingdon

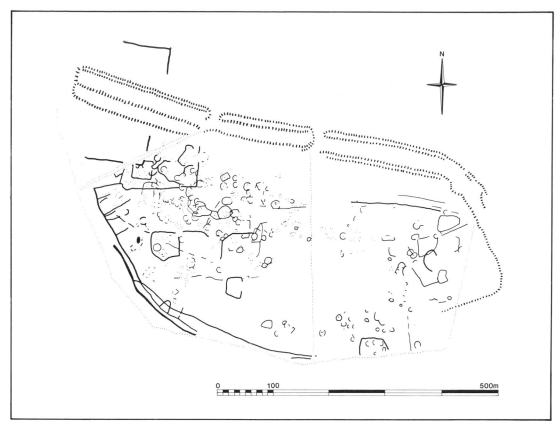

Figure 4.9 *Dyke Hills, Dorchester and interior cropmarks.*

Benson & Miles 1974, 87–90, fig. 15, 19
Miles 1978a; 1982, 76; forthcoming
17. Appleford
 Hinchliffe & Thomas 1980
18. Mount Farm, Berinsfield
 Myres 1937
 Harding 1972, 29
 Lambrick 1979; 1981b

Minor Excavations

19. The Loders, Lechlade
 RCHM 1976, 73
20. Little Faringdon
 Benson & Miles 1974, map 3
 Chambers
21. Castle Hill, Uffington
 Harding 1972, 48–9, 143
22. Chastleton
 Leeds 1931
 Sutton 1966, 35–6
23. Burroway
 Sutton 1966, 37
 Benson & Miles 1974
 recent excavations by OAU (Lambrick)
24. Lyneham Camp
 Bayne 1957
25. Hatford
 Harding 1972
 recent excavation by Hingley

26. Ducklington
 Chambers & Williams 1976
27. Model Farm, Grims Ditch
 Harden 1937
28. Grims Ditch, North Leigh
 Fine 1976
29. Hardwick-with-Yelford
 Allen 1981
30. Standlake
 Stone 1857; 1858
31. Standlake
 Bradford 1942c
 Riley 1946
32. North Leigh
 Harding 1972, 142
33. Kingston Hill Farm, Kingston Bagpuize
 Cowell & Miles 1980
34. Foxley Farm, Eynsham
 Bradford 1942a
35. Callow Hill, Stonesfield
 Thomas 1957
36. Tomlin's Gate, Kiddington
 Hingley 1981
37. Grims Ditch, Blenheim Park
 Harden 1937
38. Purwell Farm, Cassington
 Harding 1972
39. Yarnton
 VCH Oxon 1, 251–266a
 Boyd-Dawkins 1862
 Harding 1972, 143

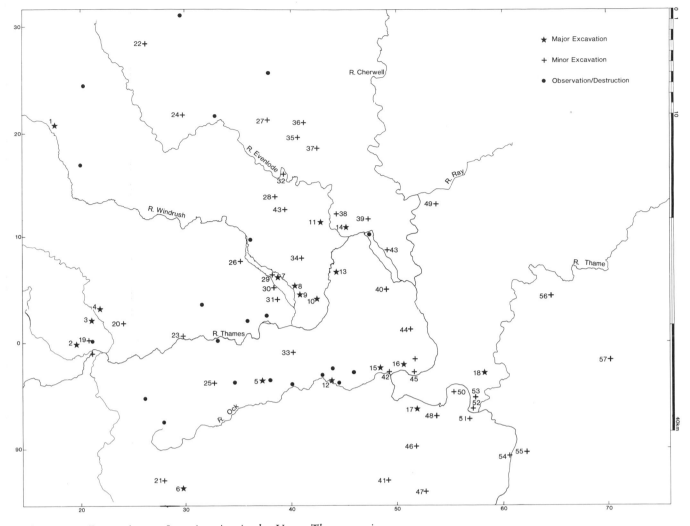

Figure 4.10 *Excavations at Iron Age sites in the Upper Thames region.*

40. Cumnor Hill/Hinksey Hill
    Myres 1930
41. Hagbourne Hill
    King 1812
    Harding 1972, 141, pl 77
42. West St Helen St, Abingdon
    Miles 1975
43. Port Meadow, Oxford
    Atkinson 1942
    Rhodes 1949
    Lambrick 1982
44. Sugworth Farm, Radley
    Miles 1976
45. Thrupp Farm, Abingdon
    Jones, Thomas & Wallis 1979
46. Didcot
    recent excavations OAU (Chambers)
47. Blewburton Hill
    Bradford 1942b
    Collins 1947; 1952
    Collins & Collins 1959
    Harding 1976
48. Wigbalds Farm, Long Wittenham
    Savory 1937

Harding 1972, 34
49. Northfield Farm, Long Wittenham
    Gray 1977
50. Woodeaton
    VCH Oxon 1 251–266a
    Harding 1972, 143
51. Wittenham Clumps
    Rhodes 1948
    Hingley 1983a
52. Dyke Hills, Dorchester
    Lane Fox 1870
    Sutton 1966
    Benson & Miles 1974
53. Allens Pit, Dorchester
    Leeds 1935
    Bradford 1942a
54. Nuneham Murren, Wallingford
    Moorey 1982
55. Grims Ditch, Mongewell
    Hinchliffe 1975
56. Heath Farm, Milton Common
    Rowley 1975
57. Chinnor
    Richardson & Young 1951

References

ALLEN, T. 1981: Hardwick-with-Yelford. *CBA Group 9 Newsletter* 11, 124–7.

ALLEN, T. and ROBINSON, M. 1979: Mingies Ditch, Hardwick. *CBA Group 9 Newsletter* 9, 115–7.

ATKINSON, R.J.C. 1942: Archaeological sites in Port Meadow. *Oxoniensia* 7, 24–35.

BARRETT, J.C. 1980a: The Evolution of later Bronze Age settlement. In Barrett, J.C. and Bradley, R.J. (editors), *The British Later Bronze Age* (Oxford BAR 83, part 1), 181–208.

BARRETT, J.C. 1980b: The Pottery of the Later Bronze Age in Lowland England. *Proc. Prehist. Soc.* 46, 297–319.

BARRETT, J.C. and BRADLEY, R. 1980: The later Bronze Age in the Thames Valley. In Barrett, J.C. and Bradley, R.J. (editors), *The British Later Bronze Age* (Oxford, BAR 83), 247–69.

BAYNE, N. 1957: Excavations at Lyneham Camp, Lyneham, Oxon. *Oxoniensia* 22, 1–10.

BENSON, D. and MILES, D. 1974: *The Upper Thames Valley: an archaeological survey of the river gravels* (Oxford).

BERSU, G. 1940: Excavations at Little Woodbury, Wiltshire. Part I: the settlement as revealed by excavation. *Proc. Prehist. Soc.* 6, 30–111.

BINFORD, L.R. 1964: A consideration of archaeological research design. *American Antiquity* 29, 425–41.

BOYD-DAWKINS, W. 1862: Traces of the Early Britons in the neighbourhood of Oxford. *Proc. Oxford Architectural & Hist. Soc.* new series 1 (1860–4), 108–16.

BRADFORD, J.S.P. 1940: The excavation at Cherbury Camp 1939. *Oxoniensia* 5, 13–20.

BRADFORD, J.S.P. 1942a: An Early Iron Age site at Allen's Pit, Dorchester. *Oxoniensia* 7, 36–60.

BRADFORD, J.S.P. 1942b: An Early Iron Age site on Blewburton Hill, Berks. *Berks. Archaeol. Journ.* 46, 97–104.

BRADFORD, J.S.P. 1942c: An Early Iron Age settlement at Standlake, Oxon. *Antiq. Journ.* 22, 202–14.

BRADFORD, J.S.P. and GOODCHILD, R.G. 1939: Excavation at Frilford, Berks, 1937–8. *Oxoniensia* 4, 1–80.

BRADLEY, R. and ELLISON, A. 1975: *Rams Hill* (Oxford, BAR 19).

CASE, H.J. 1982: Cassington, 1950–2: Late Neolithic pits and the Big Enclosure. In Case, H.J. and Whittle, A.W.R. (editors), *Settlement Patterns in the Oxford region* (London, CBA Res. Rep. 44).

CASE, H.J., BAYNE, N., STEELE, S., AVERY, G. and SUTERMEISTER, H. 1964: Excavations at City Farm, Hanborough, Oxon. *Oxoniensia* 29–30, 1–98.

CASE, H.J. and WHITTLE, A.W.R. 1982: *Settlement patterns in the Oxford region: excavations at the Abingdon causewayed enclosure and other sites* (London, CBA Res. Rep. 44).

CHAMBERS, R.C. 1979: Little Faringdon. *CBA Group 9 Newsletter* 9, 129–30.

CHAMBERS, R.C. and WILLIAMS, G. 1976: A late Iron Age and Romano-British settlement at Hardwick. *Oxoniensia* 41, 21–35.

CLARKE, D.L. 1972: A provisional model of an Iron Age society and its settlement system. In Clarke, D.L. (editor), *Models in Archaeology* (London), 801–69.

COLLINS, A.E.P. 1947: Excavations on Blewburton Hill, 1947. *Berks. Archaeol. Journ.* 50, 4–29.

COLLINS, A.E.P. 1952: Excavations on Blewburton Hill, 1948–49. *Berks. Archaeol. Journ.* 53, 21–64.

COLLINS, A.E.P. and COLLINS, F.J. 1959: Excavations at Blewburton Hill, Berks, 1953. *Berks. Archaeol. Journ.* 57, 52–73.

COWELL, R. and MILES, D. 1980: Kingston Bagpuize. *CBA Group 9 Newsletter* 10, 145–7.

CUNLIFFE, B.W. 1978: *Iron Age Communities in Britain* (London).

CUNLIFFE, B.W. 1984: *Danebury: an Iron Age hillfort in Hampshire Vol. 1 The excavations, 1969–1978: the site* (London, CBA Res. Rep. 52).

DENYER, S. 1978: *African traditional architecture* (London).

DE ROCHE, C.D. 1977: *An analysis of selected groups of early Iron Age pottery from the Oxford Region* (Unpublished thesis for the degree of Bachelor of Letters (1977) Univ. of Oxford).

DE ROCHE, C.D. 1978: The Iron Age pottery. In Parrington, M. (editor), *The excavation at Ashville, Abingdon (Oxfordshire) 1974–76* (London, CBA Res. Rep. 28), 40–74.

DREWETT, P.L. 1982: Excavations at Black Patch, Sussex. *Proc. Prehist. Soc.* 48, 321–400.

DUDLEY, D. 1959: An excavation at Bodrifty, Mulfa Hill, near Penzance, Cornwall. *Archaeol. Journ.* 113, 1–32.

DUNNING, G.C. 1976: Salmonsbury, Bourton-on-the-Water, Gloucestershire. In Harding, D.W. (editor), *Hillforts: Later Prehistoric Earthworks in Britain and Ireland* (London), 75–118 and 373–401.

EDWARD, K., GOULD, C., MILES, D. and WRIGHT, G. 1979: Great Coxwell. *CBA Group 9 Newsletter* 10, 144–5.

ELLISON, A. 1981: Towards a socio-economic model for the Middle Bronze Age in Southern England. In Hodder, I., Isaac, G. and Hammond, N. (editors), *The Pattern of the Past* (Cambridge), 413–38.

FINE, D. 1976: An Excavation of the North Oxfordshire Grim's Ditch at North Leigh. *Oxoniensia* 41, 12–16.

FLETCHER, R. 1977: Settlement Studies (Micro and Semi-micro). In Clarke, D.L. (editor), *Spatial Archaeology* (London), 47–162.

FLETCHER, R. 1981: People and space: a case study on material behaviour. In Hodder, I., Isaac, G. and Hammond, N. (editors), *Pattern of the Past* (Cambridge), 97–128.

GENT, H. 1983: Centralized storage in later prehistoric Britain. *Proc. Prehist. Soc.* 49, 243–67.

GRAY, M. 1977: Northfield Farm, Long Wittenham. *Oxoniensia* 42, 1–29.

GRIMES, W.F. 1943: Excavations at Stanton Harcourt, Oxon, 1940. *Oxoniensia* 8–9, 19–63.

GUILBERT, G. 1975: Planned hillfort interiors. *Proc. Prehist. Soc.* 41, 203–21.

HALPIN, C. 1982: Abingdon: the ex-MG car factory site. *CBA Group 9 Newsletter* 13, 113–4.

HAMLIN, A. 1963: Excavations of ring-ditches and other sites at Stanton Harcourt. *Oxoniensia* 28, 1–19.

HARDEN, D.B. 1937: Excavations at Grim's Dyke, North Oxfordshire. *Oxoniensia* 2, 74–92.

HARDING, D.W. 1972: *The Iron Age in the Upper Thames Basin* (Oxford).

HARDING, D.W. 1976: Blewburton Hill, Berkshire: re-excavation and re-appraisal. In Harding, D.W. (editor), *Hillforts: Later Prehistoric Earthworks in Britain and Ireland* (London), 133–146.

HAWKES, C. 1959: The ABC of the British Iron Age. *Antiquity* 33, 170–82.

HILL, J.N. and EVANS, R.K. 1972: A model for classification and typology. In Clarke, D. (editor), *Models in Archaeology* (London), 231–73.

HINCHLIFFE, J. 1975: Excavations at Grim's Ditch, Mongewell, 1974. *Oxoniensia* 40, 122–135.

HINCHLIFFE, J. and THOMAS, R. 1980: Archaeological Investigations at Appleford. *Oxoniensia* 45, 9–111.

HINGLEY, R. 1980a: The Upper Thames Valley survey. *CBA Group 9 Newsletter* 10, 141–3.

HINGLEY, R. 1980b: The Frilford/Marcham/Garford Survey. *CBA Group 9 Newsletter* 10, 143–4.

HINGLEY, R. 1981: The Upper Thames Valley Survey. *CBA Group 9 Newsletter* 11, 104–7.

HINGLEY, R. 1982a: Frilford. *CBA Group 9 Newsletter* 12, 150–3.

HINGLEY, R. 1982b: Kiddington, Tomlin's Gate. *CBA Group 9 Newsletter* 12, 154–5.

HINGLEY, R. 1983a: Excavations by R.A. Rutland on an Iron Age site at Wittenham Clumps. *Berks. Archaeol. Journ.* 70, 21–55.

HINGLEY, R. 1983b: Charney Bassett: Cherbury Camp. *CBA Group 9 Newsletter* 13, 123.

HINGLEY, R. 1983 (unpublished): *Iron Age and Romano-British society in the Upper Thames Valley: an analysis of settlement data in terms of modes of production.* (Unpublished thesis for the degree of Doctorate of Philosophy (1983) Univ. of Southampton).

JONES, G., THOMAS, R. and WALLIS, J. 1979: Thrupp Farm, Radley. *CBA Group 9 Newsletter* 10, 180–2.

JONES, M. 1978: Sampling in a rescue context; as case study in Oxfordshire. In Cherry, J.F., Gamble, C. and Shennan, S. (editors), *Sampling in Contemporary British Archaeology* (Oxford, BAR 50), 191–205.

JONES, M. and MILES, D. 1979: Celt and Roman in the Upper Thames Valley: approaches to culture change. In Burnham, B. and Johnson, H.B. (editors), *Invasion and Response* (Oxford, BAR 73), 315–25.

JONES, M.U. 1978: Roughground, Lechlade and Mucking, Essex. In Fowler, P.J. and Bowen, H.C. (editors), *Early Land Allotment in the British Isles* (Oxford, BAR 48), 171–3.

LAMB, H.H. 1981: Climate from 1000 BC to AD 100. In Jones, M. and Dimbleby, G.W. (editors), *The Environment of Man: the Iron Age to Anglo-Saxon period* (Oxford BAR 87), 53–65.

LAMBRICK, G. 1978: Iron Age settlements in the Upper Thames Valley. In Cunliffe, B and Rowley, T. (editors), *Lowland Iron age Communities in Europe* (Oxford, BAR International Series 48), 103–19.

LAMBRICK, G. 1979: Mount Farm, Berinsfield. *CBA Group 9 Newsletter* 9, 113–5.

LAMBRICK, G. 1981a: The Thames Flood Plain survey. *CBA Group 9 Newsletter* 11, 102–4.

LAMBRICK, G. 1981b: Mount Farm, Berinsfield. *CBA Group 9 Newsletter* 11, 148.

LAMBRICK, G. 1982: The Thames Floodplain Survey. *CBA Group 9 Newsletter* 12, 129–34.

LAMBRICK, G. 1983: *The Rollright Stones* (Oxford).

LAMBRICK, G. forthcoming: *Excavations at Mount Farm, Oxfordshire.*

LAMBRICK, G. and ROBINSON, M. 1979: *Iron Age and Roman riverside settlements at Farmoor, Oxfordshire* (London, CBA Res. Rep. 32).

LANE-FOX, A. 1870: *Journ. Ethnological Soc. Lond.* new series II, 412–5.

LEACH, R. 1977: *The Upper Thames Valley in Gloucestershire and Wiltshire: an archaeological survey of the river gravels* (Cheltenham, CRAAGS Survey 4).

LEEDS, E.T. 1931: Chastleton Camp, Oxfordshire, a hillfort of the early Iron Age. *Antiq. Journ.* 11, 382–92.

LEEDS, E.T. 1935: Recent Iron Age discoveries in Oxfordshire and North Berkshire. *Antiq. Journ.* 15, 30–41.

LEVILLIOT, P. 1977: A manifesto: the defense and illustration of local history. In Forster, R. and Ranum, O. (editors), *Selection from the Annales: Economies, Societies, Civilisations* (Baltimore), 6–30.

MARSHALL, A.J. 1978: The Pre-Belgic Iron Age in the northern Cotswolds. *Trans. Bristol and Gloucs. Archaeeol. Soc.* 96, 17–26.

MILES, D. 1975: Excavations at West St Helen Street, Abingdon. *Oxoniensia* 40, 79–101.

MILES, D. 1976: Excavations at Sugworth Farm, Radley. *Oxoniensia* 41, 6–11.

MILES, D. 1978a: Barton Court Farm, Abingdon/Radley 1972–6. *CBA Group 9 Newsletter* 8, 11–13.

MILES, D. 1978b: The Upper Thames Valley. In Fowler, P.J. and Bowen, H.C. (editors), *Early Land Allotment in the British Isles* (Oxford, BAR 48), 81–88.

MILES, D. 1979: Claydon Pike, Fairford/Lechlade. *CBA Group 9 Newsletter* 10, 160–4.

MILES, D. 1982: Confusion in the countryside: some comments from the Upper Thames region. In Miles, D. (editor), *The Romano-British Countryside: studies in rural settlement and economy* (Oxford, BAR 103), 53–79.

MILES, D. 1983: An integrated approach to the study of ancient landscapes: the Claydon Pike project. In Maxwell, G.S. (editor), *The Impact of Aerial Reconnaissance on Archaeology* (London, CBA Res. Rep. 49), 74–84.

MILES, D. forthcoming: *Archaeology at Barton Court Farm, Abingdon* (London, CBA Res. Rep.).

MILES, D. and PALMER, S. 1981: Claydon Pike, Fairford/Lechlade. *CBA Group 9 Newsletter* 11, 144–7.

MILES, D. and PALMER, S. 1983a: *Figures in a Landscape: archaeological investigations at Claydon Pike, an interim report* (Oxford).

MILES, D. and PALMER, S. 1983b: Claydon Pike. *Current Archaeology* 86, 88–92.

MOOREY, P.R.S. 1982: A Neolithic ring-ditch and Iron Age enclosure at Newnham Murren, near Wallingford. In Case and Whittle 1982, 55–9.

MYRES, J.N.L. 1930: A prehistoric settlement on Hinksey Hill, near Oxford. *Journ. British Archaeol. Assoc.* 36, 360–90.

MYRES, J.N.L. 1937: A Prehistorical and Roman site on Mount Farm, Dorchester. *Oxoniensia* 2, 12–40.

MYTUM, H. and TAYLOR, J.W. 1981: Stanton Harcourt, Linch Hill Corner. *CBA Group 9 Newsletter* 11, 139.

PALMER, R. 1978: Aerial archaeology and sampling. In Cherry, J.F., Gamble, C. and Shennan, S. (editors), *Sampling in Contemporary British Archaeology* (Oxford, BAR 50), 129–49.

PARRINGTON, M. 1978: *The excavation at Ashville, Abingdon (Oxfordshire) 1974–76* (London, CBA Res. Rep. 28).

PIGGOTT, S. and PIGGOTT, C.M. 1940: Excavations at Rams Hill, Uffington, Berks. *Antiq. Journ.* 20, 415–80.

R.C.H.M.(E). 1976: *The County of Gloucestershire. Vol. 1 Iron Age and Roman Monuments in the Cotswolds.*

RHODES, P.P. 1948: A Prehistoric and Roman site at Wittenham Clumps, Berks. *Oxoniensia* 13, 18–31.

RHODES, P.P. 1949: New Archaeological sites at Binsey and Port Meadow, Oxford. *Oxoniensia* 14, 81–4.

RICHARDSON, K. and YOUNG, A. 1951: An Iron Age A site on the Chilterns. *Antiq. Journ.* 31, 132–48.

RILEY, D.N. 1943: Archaeology from the air in the Upper Thames valley. *Oxoniensia* 8–9, 64–101.

RILEY, D.N. 1946: A late Bronze Age and Iron Age site on Standlake Downs, Oxon. *Oxoniensia* 11–12, 27–43.

RILEY, D.N. 1983: The frequency of occurrence of cropmarks in relation to soils. In Maxwell, G.S. (editor), *The Impact of aerial reconnaissance on archaeology* (London, CBA Res. Rep. 49), 59–73.

RODWELL, W. 1978: Buildings and Settlements in South-East Britain in the late Iron Age. In Cunliffe, B. and Rowley, T. (editors), *Lowland Iron Age Communities in Europe* (Oxford, BAR International Series 48), 25–41.

ROWLANDS, M.J. 1980: Kinship, exchange and regional economies of the later Bronze Age. In Barrett and Bradley 1980, 15–56.

ROWLEY, T. 1973: An Iron Age Settlement Site at Heath Farm, Milton Common. *Oxoniensia* 38, 23–40.

SAVILLE, A. 1983: *Uley Bury and Norbury Hillforts* (Bristol, Western Archaeological Trust excavation monograph 5).

SAVORY, H.N. 1937: An Early Iron Age site at Long Wittenham, Berks. *Oxoniensia* 2, 1–11.

SHERRATT, A. 1981: Plough and pastoralism: aspects of the secondary products revolution. In Hodder, I., Isaac, G. and Hammond, N. (editors), *Pattern of the Past* (Cambridge), 261–305.

SHERRATT, A. 1983: An Iron Age sword from Little Wittenham *Oxford Journ. Archaeol.* 2(1), 115–118.

SMITH, C.G. 1954: Climate. In Martin, A.F. and Steel, R.W. (editors), *The Oxford Region: a scientific and historical survey* (Oxford), 37–49.

STEVENS, C.E. 1940: The Frilford site — a postscript. *Oxoniensia* 5, 166–7.

STONE, S. 1857: Account of Certain (supposed) British and Saxon remains. *Proc. Soc. Antiq. Lond.* 1st series, 4 (1856–9), 92–100.

STONE, S. 1858: *Proc. Soc. Antiq. Lond.* 1st series, 4 (1856–9), 213–9.

SUTTON, J.E.G. 1966: Iron Age hillforts and some other earthworks in Oxfordshire. *Oxoniensia* 31, 28–42.

THOMAS, N. 1957: Excavations at Callow Hill. *Oxoniensia* 22, 11–53.

THOMAS, R. forthcoming: The Bronze–Iron transition in Southern England.

VICTORIA COUNTY HISTORY 1939: *Oxfordshire Vol. 1* (London, OUP).

WILLIAMS, A. 1946: Excavations at Langford Downs, Oxon (near Lechlade) in 1943. *Oxoniensia* 11–12, 11–64.

WILLIAMS-FREEMAN, J.P. 1915: *Field Archaeology as Illustrated by Hampshire.*

WILSON, R. 1978: Sampling bone densities at Mingies Ditch. In Cherry, C.F., Gamble, C. and Shennan, S. (editors), *Sampling in Contemporary British Archaeology* (Oxford, BAR 50), 355–61.

Towards Social Analysis in Archaeology: Celtic Society in the Iron Age of the Upper Thames Valley (400–0BC)

R. Hingley

Introduction

The approach that will be followed in this paper is a consequence of the author's dissatisfaction with contemporary archaeological practice. Archaeologists require theoretical orientations that enable the placing of material culture within its social context. Such theory can only be derived through a study of the social 'whole' of which artefacts and sites are part.

It will be argued that 'cultural' analysis (the term is used in a specific sense, as explained below) results in an emphasis within archaeology on observation/description rather than on any form of explanation or understanding. The approach to the analysis of culture is founded on the detailed typological/morphological analysis of classes of material evidence (this tendency can be traced back to Childe's initial definition of archaeological culture (1929, v–vi), and also through much more recent archaeological theory (see Hodson 1964; 1980 and Clarke 1978, 150)). The assumption behind such archaeological theory appears to be that something useful can be inferred about human society through the construction (? or elucidation) of a hierarchy of expanding 'artefact', 'assemblage' and 'cultural' types (Fig. 5.1a).

This 'cultural' perspective will be criticised in more detail later in the paper (p. 73). In the context of the arguments put forward in this study it will be suggested that, as the past societies that archaeologists study were responsible for creating the material relics that survive them, an attempt must be made to comprehend the nature of social organisation at the scale of 'society' before the archaeologist can turn to lower-order entities (such as artefact types and site types) which were actually a product of these societies. This is a claim that

has been made recently by Klejn (1982): that we require a 'contextual' rather than a typological/morphological archaeology.

It is the purpose of this paper to attempt to make a first start in the construction of a coherent 'contextual' theory for archaeology. In order to achieve this it will be argued that it is necessary to develop some theory that can relate the structure of material data to the organisation of society. In addition it is suggested that the most effective approach to the archaeological study of social organisation is through the analysis of spatial relationships in human settlement systems. The theory outlined in this paper functions by distinguishing the regional organisation of 'societies' (large-scale social groups) and then attempting to comprehend the nature of this organisation in terms of more localised social groupings (Fig. 5.1b).

Before proceeding with the construction of this interpretative theory it is necessary to provide a fuller critique of the 'cultural' or typological/morphological approach to the study of material culture.

A Critique of Studies concerning aspects of the Spatial Organisation of Iron Age Society

Theory must take primacy of place over data in any coherent philosophy of archaeology. The primacy of theory is a consequence of the consideration that all observation and description of phenomena are derived from underlying presuppositions about the world and the place of observed phenomena within the analyst's 'world-view' (Clarke 1972; Hill and Evans 1972; for anthropological perspectives see Scholte 1972; 1981; Lowry 1981; Gudeman and Penn 1982; Parkin 1982;

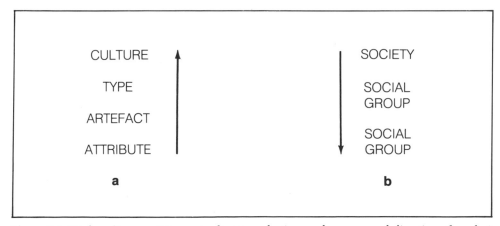

Figure 5.1 'Cultural' versus 'Contextual' approach. Arrow shows general direction of analysis.

Tonkin 1982). All observations/descriptions are selective and partial. Pure description, as any form of objective activity, is an impossibility; it is only those archaeologists who refuse to acknowledge their biases/assumptions/presuppositions who can claim that they have no need for theory.

A purely observational (or inductive) classification may have very little meaning (in other words categories within the classification may have very little significance, as boundaries may be blurred). Foucault has discussed a classification of animals from a Chinese Encyclopedia in which animals are ordered into the following classes:

'(a) belonging to the Emperor, (b) enbalmed, (c) tame, (d) suckling pigs, (e) sirens, (f) fabulous, (g) stray dogs, (h) included in the present classification, (i) frenzied, (j) innumerable, (k) drawn with a very fine camelhair brush, (l) etcetera, (m) having just broken the water pitcher, (n) that from a long way off look like flies'. (1970, xv).

This classification was constructed from the perspective of a particular 'world-view'; however to a westerner, educated with the knowledge of Darwinian evolutionary theory, the scheme seems nonsensical. Whether an animal is enbalmed, frenzied, drawn with a very fine camelhair brush or looks like a fly from a long distance off has little significance in any form of genetic theory; while distinct classifications would have to be set up in order to describe factors such as ownership (belonging to the Emperor), or state of mind (eg frenzied) of the animals concerned. There is no form of consistent theory behind the classification (such as genetics) which would enable relevant factors of form (in other words morphological characteristics) to be distinguished and a consistent classificatory scheme to be put forward.

We require theoretical orientations and an understanding of the factors of site-form that will enable a study of specific theoretical orientations. Without this archaeological classification is as lacking in analytical selfconsciousness as the Chinese classification of animals.

The dominant philosophy within later Prehistoric settlement research has been the 'site-type' approach. This theory involves the excavation and detailed analysis of individual sites/settlements and the attempt to recognise 'site-types'/'type-sites' within the archaeological record. Site-types are generally recovered through an inductively-orientated study of the evidence which leads to the identification of superficially similar site-forms (on a space/time dimension) as site-types.

The historical development of Iron Age archaeology perhaps made the site-type approach unavoidable. Certain forms of site appear fairly distinct within the archaeological record. For instance the 'hillfort' was recognised as typically Iron Age at an early date within the development of Iron Age studies (Hawkes 1931). The excavation of the site at Little Woodbury resulted in the creation of a second type of site (Bersu 1940); the Little Woodbury settlement was taken as the typical rural settlement for much of the Iron Age of Wessex and southern Britain (Bowen 1961; Hodson 1964; Bowen and Fowler 1966).

In the 1960s it came to be realised that the definition of Little Woodbury as typical of Iron Age settlement over much of southern Britain was over-simplistic. In a 'preliminary sorting' of aerial-photographic evidence for the Hampshire chalklands, Perry has distinguished six classes of site (unenclosed settlements and five types of enclosed settlement: Perry 1969). Cunliffe has also discussed the range of settlement-evidence for the Iron Age in southern Britain (1978).

We may consider some of the types of settlement that are commonly distinguished in the settlement record.

Defended enclosures have long been recognised as a site type for the Iron Age (see above). In addition they appear to form one of the most widespread settlement-forms for the European Iron Age. These sites are those in which an enclosure has been constructed to act as a defence against attack. However the class of sites that are included within the category of defended enclosures vary in a wide variety of ways. They vary in terms of the area enclosed by the defences (from less that 1 hectare to several square kilometers); in the magnitude of their defences; in the shape of the enclosure (from oval to rectangular); in the geographical location of the enclosure (from hilltop to valley-bottom) and in terms of dating (from Bronze Age to late Iron Age). It would seem that the broad class of defended enclosures probably subsumes a wide variety of sites with multiple functions. Sites are recognised through the observation of one aspect of site-form (the defensive earthwork); in reality the sites had varying significance and this can only be understood through the analysis of the place of individual enclosed sites within the larger-scale social systems of which they were part.

Other forms of enclosed settlements can be subdivided in a number of ways. Perry's classification into five sub-groupings (1969) does not seem to rest on any logical foundations and has not been applied in other areas of southern Britain. However, while it would seem clear that oval and rectangular enclosures of Iron Age date are widespread across southern Britain, it is also clear that these enclosures vary widely in terms of extent and form. In particular cases enclosures appear to enclose settlements, see Fig. 5.2a; this appears to be so at Little Woodbury (Bersu 1940) and Gussage All Saints (Wainwright 1979), and also at Orsett in Essex (Rodwell 1974) and Holcombe in Devon (Pollard 1974), while elsewhere enclosures occur as elements within larger settlement-complexes; see Fig. 5.2b; as at Moulton Park in Northamptonshire (Williams 1974), Ryton-on-Dunsmore in Warwickshire (Bateman 1976) and Hod Hill (Richmond 1968): in these examples the enclosure presumably functioned as an area with a specialised function within a more extensive open or unenclosed settlement.

Banjo enclosures form a subdivision of the class of Iron Age enclosures. These sites, which were first studied in detail by Perry (1972), occur across Britain and in continental Europe. At Hamshill Ditches and Gussage Cowdown in Wessex Perry was unable to locate surface material over enclosures which clearly formed an element within larger settlement complexes; it

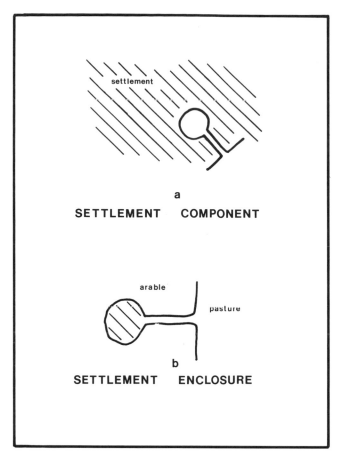

Figure 5.2 *Banjo enclosures as: a. settlement component; b. settlement enclosure.*

seemed probable that some banjo enclosures represented specialised stock-corralling enclosures within more extensive settlement complexes (Fig. 5.2a).

However an alternative interpretation can be proposed; this is that some of them represent individual enclosed settlements with a division into arable and pastoral territory at the local level (Fig. 5.2b; for this argument in more detail see p. 80). Thus, for banjo enclosures (as with others), at least two distinct functions (as settlement-enclosures and settlement-components) may be indicated. As with defended enclosures, the presence of a feature within the settlement record is observed without any clear understanding of the significance of this feature. Enclosures as settlement-components are liable to have a very different significance from those that mark the edges of an area of domestic occupation (as we shall see in detail below).

Finally in this discussion of settlement types we may consider Perry's class of unenclosed sites. Unenclosed (or 'open') settlements were common in Iron Age Britain (see particularly Harding 1974). Open settlements are those that lack any form of enclosing earthwork. Nevertheless open settlements vary greatly in size and form. It is also clear that the significance of the open settlement varies from site to site. Thus work by members of the Oxford Archaeological Unit in the Upper Thames Valley indicates that diverse economic functions can be represented at open settlements of superficially similar form (seasonal pastoral camps and

permanent mixed-farming settlements both appear to exist; see p. 83).

During this discussion of classification, examples have been given of the failings of an over-inductive approach to the analysis of settlements. The site-type approach functioned by basing classification on factors of site typology which were clearly distinct. Defended enclosures, banjo enclosures and open settlements were recognised because they *appeared* to represent fairly distinct forms. In fact the significance of these types of settlement is dubious when the evidence is reviewed in greater detail.

It will be recalled that the Chinese classification of animals was considered unworkable because it incorporated inconsistent classes of information (for instance genetic factors, but also ownership and state of mind). This is a consequence of the fact that the classification does not involve any coherent form of theoretical scheme. If we consider genetics and evolutionary theory, factors which seem of significance in a superficial inductive analysis of differing animals are not necessarily relevant in classifying species (eg Lyell 1970; in this I am at a variance of opinion with Hodson, who appears to consider that animal species are 'naturally given' and can be distinguished through pure observation of evidence (1980, 8); much biological writing indicates that this is not so (eg Lowenberg 1970)). Species can only be distinguished by reference to a coherent theory of genetics and evolution which enables significant factors to be isolated and studied. This is also true of the analysis of classes of material evidence. Aspects of site morphology which seem important in a superficial review of settlement evidence are of little value in actually understanding the significance of settlement evidence.

It has been argued that items of material culture can only be understood through a consideration of the social context of this information. In other words the attempt in this analysis must be to produce a classification of sites that relates to the social organisation of the societies that created the sites. We must not adopt an approach to settlement-typology which is based on a whole set of unspecified assumptions about the significance of site form, for such an approach will act to condition the process of research.

At the start of this paper it was argued that a 'cultural' or typological/morphological philosophy in archaeology results in observation/description rather than any form of explanation or understanding of material evidence. In addition it was suggested that an understanding of the social significance of material evidence can only be gained through a contextual analysis. In order to proceed with the contextual analysis of settlement evidence it is necessary to develop some theory that can relate the structure of material data to the organisation of society. My concern in this paper is with the analysis of social organisation in terms of social relations of production. Therefore, the purpose of the site classification adopted in this paper must be to distinguish factors in the settlement-record that are of use in understanding social relations of production amongst Iron Age social groups in the Upper Thames Valley.

Some Notes Towards Interpretative Theory for Settlement Analysis: Social Relations of Production and the Spatial Organisation of Society

In this section a number of topics will be discussed which relate to the social analysis of settlement-patterns. First an attempt will be made to review the significance of settlement-pattern analysis in the understanding of social organisation. Secondly an attempt will be made to justify the use of the concept of social relations of production in the analysis of Iron Age society. Thirdly some ways in which settlement evidence can be interpreted in terms of social relations of production will be discussed.

Settlement Evidence and Social Organisation

The value of settlement evidence for an understanding of social organisation is that each individual society represents a unique adaptation involving social conventions and the constraints of the human environment and that each society may be visualised as having a unique method for structuring space and spatial relations (Grossman 1971). In order to gain an understanding of the social significance of settlement data it is necessary to comprehend the manner in which a particular society ordered space. According to Thornton:

> 'Before space can represent anything at all, there must be imposed upon it a structure of differentiation or topology, which allows other relationships to be expressed in its terms.' (1980, 14).

In order to be able to isolate factors in the archaeological settlement-record that are of significance for classification (and to be able to construct any coherent form of typology of sites) it is first necessary to understand something of the topology of space of the society concerned. The typology of sites will follow on from an understanding of the society's topology of space, and it is only through this type of analysis that the site can be set in context.

Thus settlement-evidence encodes information on the social organisation of space. It is now necessary to discuss how this code can be broken.

Social Relations of Production and Iron Age Society

The concept of the mode of production and of social relations of production have been defined in a variety of ways (for reviews of the literature see Law 1978; Copans and Seddon 1978; Bonte 1979; Kahn and Llobera 1981). The approach adopted in this paper relates the mode of production to the organisation of each individual society (rather than attempting to impose preconceived notions of six supposed phases of world history on the evidence). Thus, as Bonte has suggested:

> '. . . only concrete analysis, and not theoretical deductions, will allow us to construct the concept of the constitution, variation and transformation of differing modes of production.' (1979, 161).

In a number of recent publications several anthropologists have demonstrated that this approach to the analysis of modes of production enables a subtle and sophisticated study of certain non-Capitalist societies (see Bonte 1977, 1981; Godelier 1978; 1979 and articles in Crummey and Stewart (eds) 1981).

The mode of production of a society combines the 'technical forces of production' and 'social relations of production' (Marx 1857–8, 109). The technical forces of production are the direct labour processes by which material value is produced (these include the labour activity itself and the tools that are used in labour). Social relations of production are the rules/norms through which production is organised. Shaw has attempted to distinguish 'work-relations' and 'property-relations' (1978, 28). Work-relations are the social relations through which work is organised (as opposed to the actual activity of labour itself). Property-relations are the abstract rules that relate to access, control and transmission of any form of resource susceptible to dispute (Godelier 1978).

The concept of social relations of production may be of use in the analysis of Iron Age society. This is a consequence of the consideration that many of the societies of the Iron Age in southern Britain may have been characterised by an emphasis on intensive agricultural production.

Bradley has suggested that, with the eclipse of regional exchange-systems in the late Bronze Age/early Iron Age (which is demonstrated clearly by the absence of 'imported' metalwork from the archaeological record by 400 BC), an increased emphasis on intensive arable production occurs. According to Bradley:

> 'The intensification of arable farming is widely documented' (1978, 123)

at this time (see also Bradley 1980, 70). This tendency is for instance clearly demonstrated at the Bronze Age/Iron Age site at Ashville (Oxfordshire) by the 'high level of development' of cereal agriculture in the Iron Age as contrasted to the Bronze Age (Jones, 1978, 108).

In the context of increased agricultural production the reproduction of individual Iron Age social groups may have been organised to a greater degree via the control of access to territory rather than, as with some Bronze Age societies (see Rowlands 1980; Barrett 1980), through integration into regional exchange-networks. This is not to say that participation in the exchange of prestige goods was never a practical strategy for Iron Age social groups, as the history of eastern Britain in the century before Claudius's invasion demonstrates (Haselgrove 1982); merely that the potential to participate in exchange-networks was latent for many of the societies that we are studying (see p. 83).

If Iron Age society was characterised by intensive agricultural production, and if control and exploitation of territory were significant, what form did social relations of production take in Iron Age society? Literary evidence indicates a degree of social ranking within Celtic society. Chieftains/kings are mentioned in Classical accounts of Celtic society in Gaul before the Roman conquest of these societies (Nash 1975) and also in texts concerning early historical Ireland (MacNiocaill 1972; Powell 1958; Hamilton 1969). However these 'kings' appear to have had fairly restricted powers and Celtic society would seem to have been primarily de-centralised (Nash 1975; Crumley 1974; MacNiocaill 1972).

In the absence of a strong political/administrative elite class, kinship may have been of significance in structuring access to territory. It has been argued by a number of anthropologists that in many non-Capitalist societies kinship functions as the social relations of production (eg Godelier 1978; Bonte 1979); in other words in these societies property and labour relations are organised through kinship. The Irish evidence has been taken to indicate that a local social group of four generations, defined by patrilineal descent, may have determined much of a man's rights and duties (Charles-Edwards 1972; Friedrich 1966; MacNiocaill 1972), and the same may have been true in Celtic Gaul and Britain (see Nash 1975, 371). It seems fairly likely that kinship functioned as the social relations of production in Iron Age society; however the literary sources do not enable a detailed understanding of kinship relations, or of variation in the structure of kinship through space and time (Crumley 1974).

Kinship may thus have had this function within the Iron Age societies of the Upper Thames Valley. In order to understand the way in which territory was controlled among Iron Age social groups it may be necessary to reconstruct the organisation of kinship.

However, in analysing the significance of kinship to Iron Age studies it is necessary to avoid the trap of an idealist perspective. Even in societies in which kinship does act to order work and property relations it does not represent a reified analytical principle (as it often appears to in the anthropologist's mind). Kinship will not act to dominate production in independence from the forces of production and the environment (see Bourdieu 1977 and Holy 1976). As Bonte has remarked:

> '. . . kinship structures are dominant in certain societies not because these societies are institutionally organised through kinship, but because kinship performs a particular series of functions.' (1979, 148).

If kinship represents (at one moment in time) the way in which a particular society relates to its environment through production, kinship relations are also a consequence of past practical experiences gained through exploitation of the environment.

Thus in order to understand the potential significance of kinship as the social relations of production in Iron Age society it is necessary to view kinship as a product of past/present social conventions of a society developed through adaptation to the material environment that constrains the group.

Where does this discussion of social relations of production place us in the context of an attempt to analyse social organisation from settlement-evidence? If we can form some type of link between the spatial organisation of society and kinship relations it will be possible to reconstruct the social relations of production from the archaeological record.

Settlement Evidence and Social Relations of Production

A number of anthropological studies appear to indicate that significant units of the control and exploitation of territory are reflected in 'corporate' social groupings. For instance Godelier and Bonte have discussed the corporate nature of the 'tribe' among nomadic pastoralists and have related this to communal control of pasture (see p. 84). According to Afigbo, the Igbo communities that were able to work out some arrangement for the exploitation of land became 'political-units', while any group (such as the clan) which did not have land-administering functions failed to become a political unit (1980, 316). Also communal control and exploitation of territory appears to have been present in societies in which nucleated forms of settlement occurred (for European examples see Stahl 1980; Protero 1912; Jones 1961a; 1961b; Graham 1954; for Third World societies see Horton 1971; Mitchell 1956; Harris 1965; Wolfe 1957 etc).

Thus it will be argued that a start can be made to the analysis of social relations of production within Iron Age society through the study of corporate scales of social organisation. At this point something must be said about terminology: The term 'society' as used in this paper refers to a large-scale social group, while a social group is a unit of social organisation at any level of scale within society (social groups may vary from individual domestic groups ('nuclear' or 'extended' families) to whole communities (eg 'bands', 'tribes' and 'chiefdoms') with any number of intermediate levels). The term 'corporate' is not used in a technical sense in this paper; a corporate social group is merely a social group which is clearly defined in relation to other social groups.

Thus it will be argued that in Iron Age society social groupings varied widely in scale within and between societies. These social groups were based on productive relations in societies in which control of territory was vital to the maintenance of intensive agricultural production. It seems possible that individual societies can by 'typed' through the nature of the organisation of levels of corporate significance, as each individual society has a unique topology of spatial relations.

But how are archaeologists to attempt to recognise corporate social groupings from the evidence at hand? For the purpose of this study it will be argued that space is utilised in human society to symbolise social relations (eg Fletcher 1977). Corporate social groupings may be symbolised through the creation and maintenance of some form of boundary which divides the group from others.

Hodder has concentrated on the display of ethnic identity through symbolism in items of material culture (1978). In this paper I shall concentrate on the organisation of society in terms of spatial boundaries. In an archaeological and historical study of land-units in the Hawaiian Islands Cordy and Kaschko have suggested that various hierarchically-structured and spatially-bounded levels exist within the archaeological record (1980). These levels of scale are defined by what the authors title 'buffer-zones'. The size (ie width) of the buffer-zone is said to vary with the scale of the social group bounded (buffer-zones between 'households' are narrow, between 'residence groups' they are wider and between 'communities' wider still; Cordy and Kaschko 1980, 419).

This concept — that corporate social groups are bounded by space — finds support in historical and ethnographic accounts. For instance according to Tacitus:

> '. . . the peoples of Germany . . . will not . . . have their houses set close together.' (*Germania*, 16).

While Caesar records that:

> 'the various (Germanic) tribes regard it as their greatest glory to lay waste as much as possible of the land around them and to keep it uninhabited.' (*The Conquest of Gaul*, vi, 23).

Numerous anthropologists have provided accounts of boundaries between social groups of the Third World (see for instance Afigbo 1980; Agbolla 1961; Buxton 1958; Cordy and Kaschko 1980; Davidson 1969; Gleave 1965; Hoffman 1967; Mitchell 1956; Scudder 1962; Udo 1963).

Clearly at some levels of scale within society and perhaps in some societies as a whole, the concept of the corporate group is of limited significance. In a 'kindred' for instance, social groups ideally form networks of overlapping relations and no corporate groups are formed (see Goodenough 1955; 1970, 46). However, it

will be argued in this paper that many societies can be characterised through the analysis of corporate social groups at whatever level of scale they occur.

In conclusion, it has been argued that Iron Age society can be effectively analysed through the use of the concept of social relations of production. An attempt has also been made to argue that corporate social groups within society can be identified from the archaeological record, and that differing societies are liable to be characterised by varying topologies of space (in other words; differing scales of corporate significance will exist within the archaeological record for these differing societies).

We must attempt to recognise corporate social groupings at whatever levels of scale they exist within the archaeological record. We must then attempt to relate these corporate social groupings to social relations of production in terms of the control and exploitation of territory.

Social Relations of Production and the Spatial Organisation of Celtic Society in the Upper Thames Valley

The area with which this discussion is concerned is in the Upper Thames Valley of Southern Britain (Fig. 5.3). This area includes about half of the region considered by Harding (Harding 1972, fig. 1) and is only part of the Upper Thames Valley Basin as defined elsewhere in this

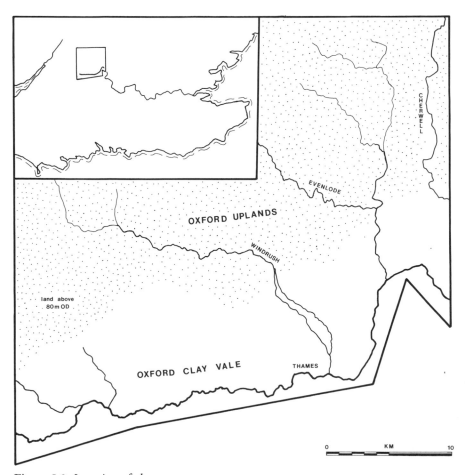

Figure 5.3 *Location of the survey area.*

publication. In contrast to Harding no attempt has been made to select a region with well-defined natural boundaries; in this study a transect was taken across a series of physiographical/ecological zones and an attempt made to distinguish significant social groups within it (Hingley 1983; forthcoming b).

The main series of geological deposits in the area is the Jurassic system of clay vales and limestone uplands (Edmonds 1954; Curtis *et al.* 1976). To the north of the area are the limestone hills of the Oxford Uplands (an area around Woodstock and Witney and to the south of Chipping Norton and Banbury). The landscape over much of this area is fairly broken, being divided by tributary rivers of the Thames (the Evenlode, Windrush and Cherwell; Fig. 5.3). In the Oxford Uplands corn-brash soils predominate; these soils are in general fertile, although fertility varies from area to area (Orr 1916). The best arable land is commonly on hill slopes (Barker and Webley 1978), while the river valleys (particularly those of the major rivers) provide valuable meadow/pasture (Berkinsale 1954).

To the south of the Oxford Uplands is the Oxford Clay Vale. This is the clay vale of the river Thames (to the west of Oxford; Fig. 5.3) and is relatively low-lying. Soils vary from heavy and wet clay lands to the relatively extensive, flat and fertile gravel terraces of the Thames. The gravels are valuable lands for arable exploitation, as they are easy to work, freely draining and high in loam content (Pocock 1926, 127). The floodplain alluvium of the Thames gives valuable summer pasture land, as the high water-table allows grass to grow throughout the summer months without withering (Lambrick and Robinson 1979, 125).

Observations on the Nature of the Settlement Record

What forms of archaeological data exist for the Upper Thames Valley that might be of value in the analysis of social relations of production?

Before discussing this point it must be stated that, in spite of the intensive archaeological work conducted in Oxfordshire over the last 150 years, the record of settlement is inadequate (see p. 52n). It is therefore only possible to search for gross variation in settlement-form within the record. Any attempt at detailed quantitative analysis would be a misuse of the data. One gross variation involves the nature of boundaries to settlement space in the two regions discussed above.

On the gravels of the Oxford Clay Vale occupation in the Iron Age would appear to have been fairly intensive. A dense distribution of huts occurs on the gravel terraces (if an arbitrary 150-metre division is used to isolate individual settlements from each other the average distance between settlements so defined is about 0.8 kilometres (Fig. 5.4)). In addition sites on the gravel are commonly unenclosed (Harding 1972; 1974; this publi-

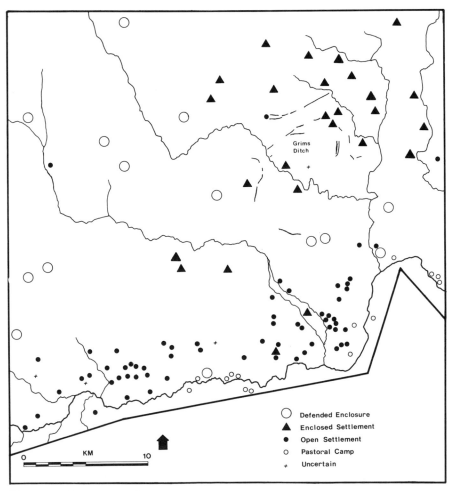

Figure 5.4 *Iron Age settlement.*

cation, p. 57). For the purpose of this paper 'open settlements' are those that have no boundary around the area of domestic occupation: enclosures may occur within the area of the open settlement but these enclosures are settlement-components; Fig. 5.5a.

By contrast to the Oxford Clay Vale, settlements in the Oxford Uplands would appear to have been far more isolated. The average distance between settlements (as defined above) is about 2.7 kilometres. In addition settlements in the Oxford Uplands are commonly enclosed. Enclosed settlements are those in which the area of occupation lies within the boundary of an enclosure (whether this enclosure is defensive or non-defensive; Fig. 5.5b).

In conclusion two factors relating to the bounding of space seem to be important in characterising regional variation in settlement patterning. First there is the presence or absence of a physical boundary around the settlement; secondly there is the degree of spatial isolation of each social group from others in its neighbourhood.

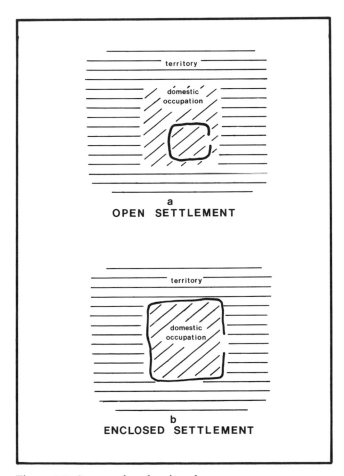

Figure 5.5 *Open and enclosed settlements.*

Corporate Groups in the Settlement Data

Archaeologists have noted and commented on the nature of enclosed and unenclosed settlements (see Bradford 1942, 209; Harding 1972; 1974, 36; Cunliffe 1978); however little attempt has been made to explain the variation. What is the explanation for the open or enclosed nature of settlement patterning? A related

question is the meaning of differing degrees of spatial isolation between local groupings?

One possible function for the enclosure is economic and ecological. If the social group is resident in a sparsely-populated or unsettled landscape it may require an enclosure to keep wild men and animals out of the settlement and domestic animals inside.

In addition it is possible to suggest a social significance for the enclosure, a significance related to the meaning of space; the existence of a boundary may represent a discontinuity in social space. If we consider three hypothetical social groups the boundary between each and its neighbour(s) may symbolise and be a consequence of their social relationship one to the other.

If a narrow spatial boundary exists between the groups (Fig. 5.6a), these may have close social relations. By contrast if the boundary is wide (Fig. 5.6b) the groups may be, in practical terms, socially isolated from one another. The significance of the enclosure around the settlement is that, in certain circumstances, it might have the purpose of defining the extent of the social group (Fig. 5.6c). This is the social significance of the settlement enclosure; the enclosure may result from and be a symbol of the isolation of a local social group.

From these arguments about the social significance of spatial and physical boundaries in the settlement land-

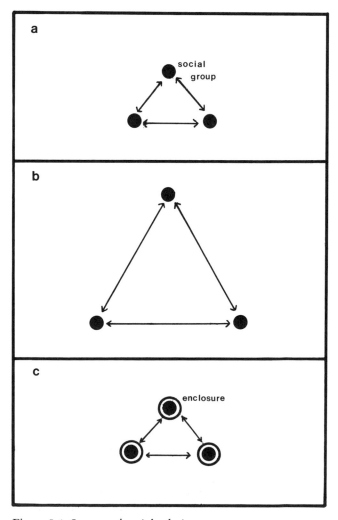

Figure 5.6 *Space and social relations.*

scape we may attempt to construct models for a series of situations which will represent varying modes of spatial and social organisation.

One landscape involves a dense distribution of open settlements (Fig. 5.7b) in which the individual social group is bound into a larger-scale co-operative group (in this case the former is not corporate). The integration of the local social group into society as a whole is demonstrated by (i) the narrow spatial gap between individual examples and (ii) by the open nature of the individual settlement.

A second idealised settlement-landscape involves a widely-dispersed distribution of enclosed settlements (Fig. 5.7a) in which the local social group is clearly-defined and corporate in nature. The (comparative) isolation of the individual social group is demonstrated (i) by the wide spatial boundaries between individual examples and (ii) by the enclosed nature of the settlements.

Two further settlement-landscapes can be envisaged: widely-dispersed open settlements, and densely-distributed enclosed settlements. The potential significance of these seems less clear. Examples of such settlement-landscapes do not occur within the survey area.

The first two idealised settlement-landscapes bear a resemblance to the observed settlement-patterning in the survey area (Fig. 5.8). On the gravels of the Oxford Clay Vale settlement appears to be dense and settlements are typically open. The model suggests interpretation of these densely-distributed open settlements as being integrated into larger-scale communities.

By contrast in the Oxford Uplands settlements are far more spatially isolated, and are also typically enclosed. This pattern suggests the isolation of the local social group from society as a whole.

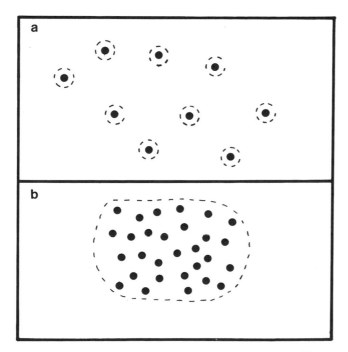

Figure 5.7 *Two idealised settlement landscapes. Dashed lines represent boundary of corporate social group.*

Social Relations of Production and the Settlement Data

It has been suggested that the survey area is characterised by societies with two differing topologies of space. An attempt will now be made to relate these observations on the nature of the settlement-landscape to arguments about the social organisation of Iron Age social groups. The link between spatial organisation and social relations of production can be made through the analysis of the significance of the corporate groups discussed above. The corporate social groups of the Upper Thames Valley appear to have varied from the local groups resident in the single enclosed settlements in the Oxford Uplands to larger communities in the Oxford Clay Vale. It remains to show the way in which corporate groups in these two forms of society were based on productive relations.

An attempt will be made to demonstrate that control and exploitation of territory are reflected in the form and organisation of the landscape associated with the corporate groups that have been identified above.

In the Oxford Uplands production was organised by the social groups within the isolated settlement, who controlled and exploited the territory. The physically-isolated groups of the Oxford Uplands had social relations of production which involved the control and exploitation of territory by the social group resident within the individual settlement.

Settlement-forms vary in the Oxford Uplands, although nearly all settlements are enclosed. Defended and non-defended enclosures occur, as do more complex forms of enclosure (see p. 54). Of particular importance in this discussion are the banjo enclosures. Above it was argued that banjo enclosures may have had at least two distinct functions; it would seem possible that banjo enclosures in the Oxford Uplands are distinct farming units rather than specialised stock-corralling enclosures within more extensive open settlements. In this region the settlement may have lain within the enclosure and the arable land have surrounded it; the neck of the enclosure could then have pointed towards the pasture, and the arable land was protected from livestock by boundaries running from the entrance trackway. This interpretation is similar to that for some Scandinavian sites of the late Roman Iron Age/Migration period (see Myhre 1973; 1974; Lindquist 1974; Widgren 1979). A forceful point for interpreting some banjo enclosures in this way is their location in the landscape; Owslebury and at least three of Perry's sites (1972, 71) are located on hillslopes and face downhill towards valley bottoms. These enclosures are located at the point at which the heavy soils of the valley and light soils of the hilltop meet (Collis 1970), and this is an ideal location for cultivation (Widgren 1979; Barker and Webley 1978).

If banjo enclosures in the Oxford Uplands are systems for the organisation of mixed farming at the scale of the single settlement, then there is additional evidence that the corporate local group in this area had social relations of production based on the appropriation of territory from an individual settlement (Fig. 5.9a).

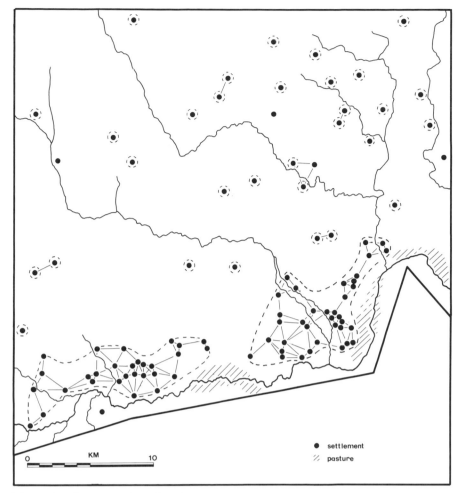

Figure 5.8 *Interpretation of settlement patterns.*

If the structural organisation of the banjo enclosure in the Oxford Uplands indicates control of territory by the local social group, territory was presumably organised in an analogous fashion at other defensive and non-defensive enclosures in this area (although the structural evidence for land-use at these sites has not been recovered).

Defended and non-defended enclosures occur in the Oxford Uplands. The ramparts of defended enclosures are (by definition) more massive than those of non-defended enclosures; however the actual significance of the defensive rampart is uncertain. In the survey area the size-distribution of enclosures with defensive ramparts overlaps that of non-defensive enclosures (Fig. 5.10). In addition the strength of the defences of enclosed settlements may vary along a continuum. We require more information on the degree to which defended and non-defended enclosures actually form distinct classes of sites.

Following on from the work of Ellison (1978; 1980) and some suggestions of Rowlands (1980) concerning Bronze Age settlement, it may be possible to argue that the scale of the enclosed settlement is related to the scale of the social group resident on the site, large enclosures representing fairly large-scale groups, while small enclosures may indicate small-scale groups. In addition it would seem possible that the magnitude of the enclosure

(in terms of the area enclosed and the scale of the rampart) symbolises the status of the group which was resident in the settlement. Rowlands has argued that the scale of the social group indicates its success in attracting followers, and that a large following indicates high rank (1980).

The evidence for the Oxford Uplands is inadequate for testing these propositions (see p. 52). Although a wide range of enclosure-sizes are represented (Fig. 5.10), the excavation of some of these sites will be a necessity before they can be more fully understood. However some evidence from Wessex could indicate that the size of the enclosure is connected with the scale and social status of the group that is represented. Analysis of pit capacity for the 1.2-hectare enclosed settlement at Gussage All Saints would appear to indicate a population of about 40 persons (Jefferies 1980). By contrast to such large enclosed sites, small enclosures commonly do not produce evidence of extensive settlement (see Perry 1972 on the banjo enclosure at Bramdean and Wainwright 1968 on the rectangular enclosure at Tollard Royal). In addition to the evidence for the scale of the local social group it is possible that certain aspects of the morphology of large enclosures (such as Little Woodbury and Gussage All Saints) may indicate that these were the sites of high-ranking social groups (see Bersu 1940; Bowen and Fowler 1966; although in the absence

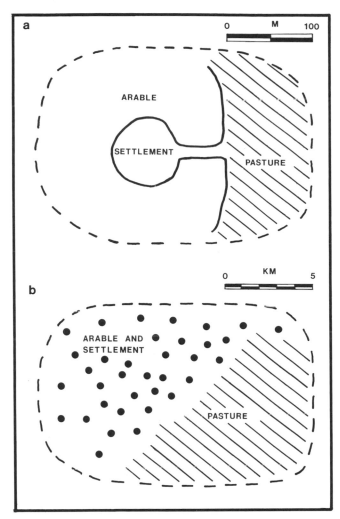

Figure 5.9 *Corporate social groups and social relations of production. Scales are approximate.*

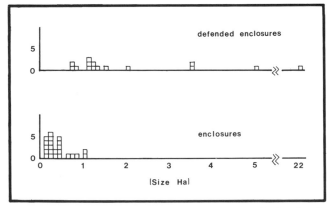

Figure 5.10 *Size distribution of enclosures in Oxford uplands.*

of further evidence to this effect these arguments are not fully conclusive).

Thus in discussing the evidence for Iron Age settlement in the Oxford Uplands it is possible to suggest that social relations of production were based on the local group which was resident in the isolated and enclosed settlement. In addition it is possible that the scale of the individual social group varied from settlement to settlement, and that variation in the scale of the enclosure indicates the position of the local group within larger-

scale systems of interaction. In other words at this point our idealised model for the organisation of the settlement landscape (Fig. 5.7a) may begin to break down.

Certain Irish societies were organised with so-called 'lineage' as the basis of productive relations (see p. 76). However, social ranking existed within Irish society and was probably based on the practice of cattle clientage (Crumley 1974). Cattle clientage involved the initial donation of a grant of cattle from a patron to a client. The client then donated an annual levy of produce to the patron and also owed him duties of loyalty (MacNiocaill 1972). Relations in this form of clientage are based on mutual agreement over productive relations; however, cattle clientage enables the patron to live (at least in part) from the activity of others. Cattle clientage may have created relations of exploitation within Irish society to be extended beyond the direct kin of the patron.

There is a possibility that social groups in the Oxford Uplands were linked together by a form of property (cattle) which is at present archaeologically invisible. In addition it is possible that social ranking between local domestic groups was in part a consequence of the ownership and distribution of cattle.

Iron Age society in the Oxford Uplands is impossible to understand without some consideration of the origins of that society. In order to comprehend the significance of kinship as the social relations of production it is important that we consider the past history of the societies that we are studying (p. 76). Evidence for Bronze Age settlement in the area of the Oxford Uplands is fairly scarce (Hingley 1983). The only evidence that is prolific is the distribution of round barrows or ring ditches (Fig. 5.11). The sparse and dispersed distribution of these monuments in the Oxford Uplands forms a marked contrast to the extensive barrow cemeteries in the area of the Oxford Clay Vale. This may indicate, as Case has argued (1963), that the Oxford Uplands were marginal to settlement in the Bronze Age. The Oxford Uplands are physiographically more broken-up than is the Oxford Clay Vale. In addition some evidence exists for possible woodland in the area in the Iron Age. Iron Age settlement in the Oxford Uplands may have occurred in a broken and wooded landscape in which local social groups settled and existed in partial isolation from one another. This is not to say that the nature of the environment is a total explanation for social organisation.

It has been suggested that a degree of social ranking occurred between groups in the Oxford Uplands; however the evidence would not appear to indicate that society was highly centralised. If the North Oxfordshire Grims ditch represents a 'territorial oppidum' of Late Iron Age date (Cunliffe 1978), we may have some evidence for appropriation of communal labour at a scale above that of the individual social group. However the evidence for the dating of the earthwork(s) is not conclusive, and it is possible that the earthwork relates (at least in part) to the group of Roman villas that lie within it (Copeland, pers. comm.). Thus the evidence for

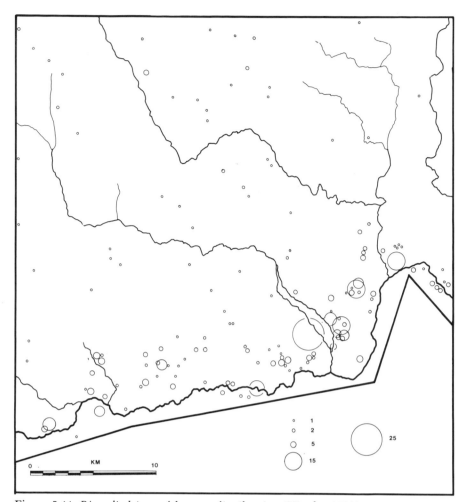

Figure 5.11 *Ring ditch/round barrow distribtution (Hingley 1983).*

any form of centralised social system in the region is tentative.

It can be argued that the potential for social inequality in the region in the Iron Age was largely latent (see p. 75). However, in the Roman period the situation changes dramatically. It will be argued in more detail elsewhere that, where the local social group is fairly independent, the integration of society into larger-scale systems of interaction may stimulate it into dynamism (see Rowlands 1980; Hingley 1982 and forthcoming b). The independent social group represents the basic unit of production, and if society becomes 'peripheralised' within an expanding political/economic system these local groups will be in direct competition. This may result in increased production and the development of some form of stratification.

These ideas cannot be discussed in detail in this paper; however it can be briefly noted that the Oxford Uplands become highly 'Romanised'. Large villas are known in the region (for instance at Northleigh, Stonesfield and Fawler) and some local villas appear to have their origins at the end of the first century AD (Ditchely and Shakenoak, see Smith 1978). In addition 'minor towns', which may represent local exchange-centres are common in the Oxford Uplands, and Roman coinage also appears to be fairly common over much of the region (Fig. 5.12).

On the *Gravels of the Oxford Clay Vale* it would seem possible that larger-scale communities controlled access to territory. Elsewhere it has been argued that two such communities existed in the survey area (Hingley 1983), and an attempt will now be made to discuss these communal groups in terms of the social relations of production.

It can be argued that each group had a territory divided between areas of arable and pastoral. In the Oxford Uplands this division was organised at the scale of the local social group (the settlement); on the gravels it was organised at the scale of the community (Fig. 5.9).

Archaeological evidence would appear to indicate that open settlements on the gravel terraces were occupied by communities practising an arable strategy. By contrast the seasonally-occupied open settlements of the Thames floodplain were associated with the pasturing of cattle (the seasonal nature of these settlements was demonstrated clearly through biological analysis of samples from the recently-excavated floodplain site of Farmoor; Lambrick and Robinson 1979).

The agricultural cycle for communities on the gravel may have been as follows (Fig. 5.13). In the spring cattle may have been driven from the gravel terraces onto the Thames floodplain in order to remove them from the area of the growing crops. Lindquist, discussing Iron Age settlement in Gotland (1974), has proposed that

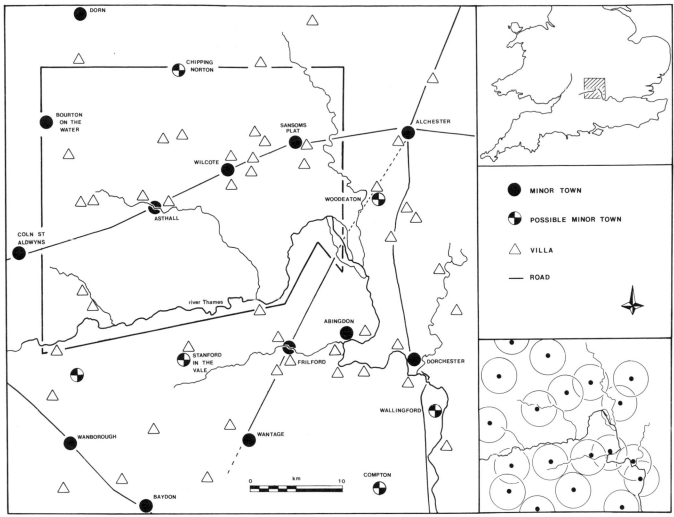

Figure 5.12 *Romano–British settlement in the Upper Thames Valley.* (Box shows location of survey area).

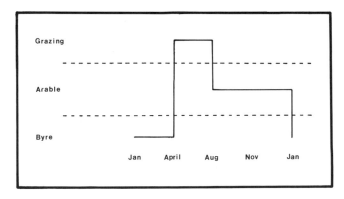

Figure 5.13 *Agricultural cycle on the gravels (the movement of cattle).*

cattle were transhumed to seasonal pasture in order to remove them from the area of (unenclosed) arable fields; the same practice is attested historically in medieval Ireland (McCourt 1950). During the spring and summer months crops may have been grown over much of the area of the gravel terraces (it has been remarked that the gravel terraces are fertile arable land).

Cattle may have been kept on the floodplain throughout the late spring and summer (the value of the floodplain as pasture was discussed above). After harvest, in the early autumn, livestock could have been returned to graze the stubble and also to fertilise the area for the next season's growth.

Thus the form of settlement on the gravels indicates the integration of the local social group into a wider-scale group, and this communal group was a consequence of communal ownership of territory. The division of arable and pastoral territory is drawn at the scale of the community (rather than of the settlement) and the archaeological evidence can be seen to embody this division into distinct areas of arable and pasture (Fig. 5.9). Is it possible to say anthing more about the nature of the community on the gravel?

The concept of the 'tribe' was widely used in late nineteenth- and early twentieth-century accounts of Celtic society (see Seebohm 1884; Vinogradoff 1904; Lang 1900; Jolliffe 1926). In more recent times the general use of the concept has been challenged on anthropological grounds (that Third World tribes as corporate entities are the product of colonial expansion by Western powers; Fried 1969) and also on specifically historical grounds (Jones 1961a). However in this paper it will be argued that it is possible to provide support for a form of communal organisation that may be called tribal amongst societies of north-western Europe in the first millennium BC/first millennium AD.

Tribes may be seen as corporate social groups and have owed their existence to communal relations of social reproduction. Godelier and Bonte have discussed the corporate nature of the tribe among nomadic pastoralists, and have related corporate structure to communal control of pasture. In these societies two forms of 'property' are thought to exist. Cattle and agricultural land are 'domesticated' property (through the input of human energy in the maintenance of these resources); by contrast, pasture is a 'wild' (if vital) resource (as little effort is expended in its maintenance). Domestic resources are exploited by a domestic social group within society, while wild resources are controlled, exploited and defended by the community. The corporate tribal community is a consequence of the communal ownership of pasture (Bonte 1977; 1981; Godelier 1978; 1979).

Bonte has suggested that, in discussing Germanic society, Marx refers to this tribal mode of organisation (Bonte 1977; Marx 1857–8). Seebohm, in discussing the evidence of Irish and Welsh historical law-tracts, has proposed a similar model for the organisation of Celtic society in the early historic period (1884, 203). Thus it is possible to argue that tribal solidarity among some German and Celtic social groups was related to control and exploitation of certain wild resources which were vital to the reproduction of society as a whole. The tribe was corporate through communal defence and appropriation of pasture.

We must discuss the details of settlement-form on the gravel in more detail. It seems clear that enclosures occur within the open settlement-landscape (see p. 57). However, in contrast to the Oxford Uplands, these enclosures are settlement-components rather than the boundaries to areas of domestic occupation. Although superficially the enclosures of the Oxford Clay Vale may appear to resemble those of the Oxford Uplands, the context and hence significance of the enclosure in the two regions are quite different. If we take the banjo enclosures, it has been argued that examples on the gravels represent specialised stock-enclosures within larger open settlements (Fig. 5.2), while examples in the Oxford Uplands are enclosed settlements (Fig. 5.2).

It remains to discuss the origin and transformation of Iron Age communities on the gravels of the Oxford Clay Vale. The distribution of Neolithic and Bronze Age monuments could be taken to indicate that the region was settled relatively intensively throughout the earlier prehistoric period (Hingley 1983). The ring-ditch distribution involves a dense concentration of sites on the gravel terraces and is in marked contrast to the situation in the Oxford Uplands (Fig. 5.11). The gravel terraces may have been intensively settled in the Bronze Age (the supposed evidence for a late Bronze Age 'depopulation' (Barrett 1980) is mostly negative and late Bronze Age sites almost certainly exist in the area). The context of Iron Age communities was that of close communications with neighbours. In addition the extensive areas of fertile arable soil and restricted areas of valuable floodplain may have favoured communal social formations in the Iron Age.

In the Roman period these tribal communities became integrated into wider systems of interaction. It seems probable that the practice and ideology of communal control of territory resulted in a situation in which conflict and competition between local social groups was not a practical strategy. As a consequence increased production and the development of social stratification was of limited significance in this area (see the arguments of Vinogradoff 1904).

The gravels of the Oxford Clay Vale failed to become particularly Romanised. Villas are uncommon on the gravels in the area: when they do occur they are on the borders of the tribal territory. In addition the distribution of sites that may represent 'minor towns' covers much of the South Midlands but avoids this area (Fig. 5.12). Roman coins, too, are fairly rare in the area (Hingley 1983; forthcoming b). The inherent structure of social relations may have caused a lack of dynamism and consequential underdevelopment of the societies of the Oxford Clay Vale (Hingley 1983).

Conclusion

It has been suggested that two distinct forms of society existed in the Iron Age of the Upper Thames Valley. The societies had contrasting topologies of space, and these systems have been analysed in terms of the organisation of corporate social groups and the structure of social relations of production.

Communalistic societies of the Oxford Clay Vale are characterised in the archaeological record by densely-distributed open settlements and by social relations of production based on the communal control of pasture. By contrast individualistic social groups in the Oxford Uplands lived in spatially-isolated, enclosed settlements and had social relations of production involving the appropriation of territory by the individual social group.

Clearly the specific significance of these arguments to the archaeology of Iron Age Britain is that we may expect similar patterns in other areas. The whole area of southern Britain may be typified by (fairly) small-scale social formations which differ from one another in their social organisation (e.g. Hingley forthcoming a).

In terms of an approach to the analysis of social formations of this type it has been argued that we require the construction of theory that will enable the interpretation of the spatial organisation of human society in terms of the social relations of production. Some particular themes may be of importance in understanding social groups in other areas of Britain.

The regional approach is of particular importance. By studying two societies with contrasting topologies of space a fuller understanding can be gained of each individual society (as I hope that the case-study has demonstrated). As an alternative to this regional approach it would be possible to study society in terms of temporal transformation (Udo has discussed a transition from nucleated to dispersed settlement among the Ibo of Nigeria; Udo 1963). It is possible that this approach to the contrasting of varying topologies of space is the only practical strategy in settlement analysis, as the significance of one pattern is relative and can only be understood when contrasted to another (for instance a dispersed settlement-pattern is most easily defined in relation to a contrasting nucleated pattern).

Throughout this paper stress has been put on the significance of scales of corporate organisation within society. It has been argued that the topology of spatial relations within an individual society can be comprehended through an analysis of scales of corporate organisation. Clearly space and scale are also problems of significance in geography and anthropology, and archaeologists must now make an effort to broaden their understanding of the social significance of space.

In more general terms this paper has also been concerned with the discussion of an alternative philosophy for archaeology. It has been contended that much archaeological theory is misguided. Whilst the detailed typological/morphological analysis of classes of material data may condemn archaeology to a descriptive and materialistic dustbin, there are alternatives to this approach. The claim made in this paper is not that the concepts of society and social group are units of validity equal to those of artefact- and site-type in social analysis, but that they are the only valid concepts. After all it is society that created material culture and not vice versa. In order to construct a social archaeology we require a contextual philosophy. It can be argued that a contextual philosophy is most easily achieved through analysis of the human use of space.

In addition a further concern in this paper was to avoid an overtly idealist or materialist perspective. As Marx stated on several occasions, social relations of production tend in the long run to determine other factors (such as the material foundations of society and the ideas of an individual within society). Thus an understanding of social relations of production is vital to a comprehension of society. This is not to say that studies concerning the ecology of individual societies, or studies concerned with the symbolic significance of items of material culture are invalid, but merely that an understanding of the social relations entered into by individuals and groups in the process of production provides a necessary background for the examination of ecology and symbolism.

The approach to the study of social relations of production through settlement-evidence requires a revolution in archaeological theory. The site is no more a valid unit of archaeological analysis than is the artefact. The organisation of the society that created the site must be the aim of analysis as it is only through an understanding of the topology of space of individual societies that a typology of sites can be created.

Acknowledgements

I should like to thank Steve Shennan, Clive Gamble, Tim Champion and Richard Bradley for comments on my thesis, and Colin Haselgrove and Ian Hodder for comments on an earlier version of this paper.

References

AFIGBO, A.E. 1980: Prolegomena to the study of the Culture History of the Igbo-speaking Peoples of Nigeria. In Swartz, R.K. and Dumett, R.E. (editors), *West African Culture Dynamics: Archaeological and Historical Perspectives* (Paris), 305–26.

AGBOLLA, S.A. 1961: The Middle Belt of Nigeria: The Basis of its Unity. *Nigerian Geograph. Journ.* 4, 41–6.

AUGE, M. 1982: *The Anthropological Circle: Symbol, Function, History* (London).

BARKER, G. and WEBLEY, D. 1978: Causewayed Enclosures and Early Neolithic Economies in Central Southern England. *Proc. Prehist. Soc.* 44, 161–86.

BARRETT, J. 1980: The Evolution of Later Bronze Age Settlement. In Barrett, J. and Bradley, R. (editors), *The British Later Bronze Age* (Oxford), 77–100.

BATEMAN, J. 1976: A Late Bronze Age Cremation Cemetery and Iron Age/Romano-British Enclosure in the parish of Ryton-on-Dunsmore, Warwickshire. *Trans. Birmingham and Warwicks. Archaeol. Soc.* 88, 11–47.

BERKINSALE, R.P. 1954: Geomorphology. In Martin, A.F. and Steele, R.W. (editors), *The Oxford Region: A Scientific and Historical Survey* (Oxford), 24–36.

BERSU, G. 1940: Excavations at Little Woodbury, Wiltshire: Part 1: The Settlement as Revealed by Excavation. *Proc. Prehist. Soc.* 6, 30–111.

BIDET, J. 1979: Questions to Pierre Bourdieu. *Critique of Anthropology* 4, 203–8.

BONTE, P.P. 1977: Non-Stratified Social Formations among Pastoral Nomads. In Friedman, J. and Rowlands, M. (editors), *The Evolution of Social Systems* (London), 173–200.

BONTE, P.P. 1979: Marxist Analysis and Social Anthropology: A Review Article. *Critique of Anthropology* 4, 145–64.

BONTE, P.P. 1981: Marxist Theory and Anthropological Analysis: The Study of Nomadic Pastoralist Society. In Kahn, J.S. and Llobera, J.R. (editors), *The Anthropology of Pre-Capitalist Societies* (London), 22–56.

BOURDIEU, P. 1977: *Outline of a Theory of Practice* (Cambridge).

BOWEN, H.C. 1961: *Ancient Fields* (London).

BOWEN, H.C. and FOWLER, P.J. 1966: Romano-British Rural Settlement in Dorset and Wiltshire. In Thomas, C. (editor), *Rural Settlement in Roman Britain* (London), 43–67.

BRADFORD, J.S.P. 1942: An Early Iron Age site at Allen's Pit, Dorchester. *Oxoniensia* 7, 36–70.

BRADLEY, R. 1978: *The Prehistoric Settlement of Britain* (London).

BRADLEY, R. 1980: Subsistence, Exchange and Technology: A Social Framework for the Bronze Age in Southern Britain c1400–700 BC. In Barrett, J. and Bradley, R. (editors), *The British Later Bronze Age* (Oxford), 57–76.

BUXTON, J. 1958: The Mandari of Southern Sudan. In Middleton, J. and Tait, D. (editors), *Tribes Without Rulers* (London), 67–96.

CAESAR, J.: *The Gallic War*. Trans. Edwards, H.J. Loeb Classical Library (London).

CASE, H. 1963: Notes on the Finds and on Ring Ditches in the Oxford Region. In Hamlin, A., Excavations on Ring Ditches and other sites at Stanton Harcourt. *Oxoniensia* 28, 19–52.

CHARLES EDWARDS, T.M. 1972: Kinship, Status and the Origin of the Hide. *Past and Present* 56, 3–33.

CHILDE, V.G. 1929: *The Danube in Prehistory* (Oxford).

CHILDE, V.G. 1958: Retrospect. *Antiquity* 32, 69–74.

CLARKE, D.L. 1972: A Provisional Model of an Iron Age Society and its Settlement System. In Clarke, D.L. (editor), *Models in Archaeology* (London), 801–869.

CLARKE, D.L. 1978: *Analytical Archaeology* (first published 1968, London).

COLLIS, J. 1970: Excavations at Owslebury, Hants: A Second Interim Report. *Antiq. Journ.* 50, 246–61.

COPANS, J. and SEDDON, D. 1978: Marxism and Anthropology: A Preliminary Survey. In Seddon, D. (editor), *Relations of Production: Marxist Approaches to Economic Anthropology* (London), 1–46.

CORDY, R. and KASCHKO, M.W. 1980: Prehistoric Archaeology and the Hawaiian Islands: Land Units Associated with Social Groups. *Journ. Field Archaeol.* 7, 403–16.

CRUMLEY, C.L. 1974: *Celtic Social Structure: The Generation of Archaeologically Testable Hypotheses from Literary Evidence* (Michigan).

CRUMMEY, D. and STEWART, C.C. 1981: The Poverty of Pre-Colonial African Historiography. In Crummey, D. and Stewart, C.C. (editors), *Modes of Production in Africa* (London), 11–14.

CRUMMEY, D. and STEWART, C.C. (editors) 1981: *Modes of Production in Africa* (London).

CUNLIFFE, B.W. 1978: *Iron Age Communities in Britain* (London).

CURTIS, L.M., COURTENAY, F.M. and TRUDGILL, S.T. 1976: *Soils in the British Isles* (London).

DAVIDSON, J.M. 1969: Settlement Patterns in Samoa before 1800. *Journ. Polynesian Soc.* 78, 44–82.

EDMONDS, J.M. 1954: Geology. In Martin, A.F. and Steele, R.W. (editors), *The Oxford Region: A Scientific and Historical Survey* (Oxford), 7–20.

ELLISON, A. 1978: The Bronze Age in Sussex. In Drewett, P.L. (editor), *The Archaelogy of Sussex to AD 1500* (London), 30–8.

ELLISON, A. 1980: Settlement and Regional Exchange: A Case Study. In Barrett, J. and Bradley, R. (editors), *The British Later Bronze Age* (Oxford), 127–40.

FLETCHER, R. 1977: Settlement Studies (Micro and Semi-Micro). In Clarke, D.L. (editor), *Spatial Archaeology* (London), 47–164.

FOUCAULT, M. 1970: *The Order of Things* (London).

FRIED, M.H. 1969: *The Evolution of Political Society: An Essay in Political Anthropology* (New York).

FRIEDRICH, P. 1966: Proto-Indo-European Kinship. *Ethnology* 5, 1–36.

GLEAVE, M.B. 1965: The Changing Frontiers of Settlement in the Uplands of Northern Nigeria. *Nigerian Geograph. Journ.* 8, 127–41.

GODELIER, M. 1978: Territory and Property in Primitive Society. *Information sur les Sciences Sociales* 17, 399–422.

GODELIER, M. 1979: The Appropriation of Nature. *Critique of Anthropology* 4, 17–27.

GOODENOUGH, W.H. 1955: A Problem in Mayo-Polynesian Social Organisation. *American Anthropology* 62, 71–83.

GOODENOUGH, W.H. 1970: *Description and Comparison in Cultural Anthropology* (London).

GRAHAM, J.M. 1954: *Transhumance in Ireland with special reference to its bearing on the evolution of rural communities in the West.* Thesis presented for the degree of Ph.D. at Queens University, Belfast.

GROSSMAN, D. 1971: Do we have a Theory for Settlement Geography? The Case of Iboland. *The Professional Geographer* 23, 197–203.

GUDEMAN, S. and PENN, M. 1982: Models, Meaning and Reflexivity. In Parkin, D. (editor), *Semantic Anthropology* (London), 89–106.

HAMILTON, J.R.C. 1969: *Excavations at Clickhimin, Shetland* (London).

HARDING, D.W. 1972: *The Iron Age in the Upper Thames Basin* (Oxford).

HARDING, D.W. 1974: *The Iron Age in Lowland Britain* (London).

HARRISS, R. 1965: *The Political Organisation of the Mbembe* (London).

HASELGROVE, C.C. 1982: Wealth, Prestige and Power: The Dynamics of Late Iron Age Centralization in South Eastern England. In Renfrew, C. and Shennan, S. (editors), *Ranking, Resources and Exchange: Aspects of the Archaeology of European Society* (London), 79–88.

HAWKES, C.F.C. 1931: Hill Forts. *Antiquity* 5, 60–97.

HAWKES, C.F.C. 1959: The ABC of the British Iron Age. *Antiquity* 33, 170–82.

HILL, J.N. and EVANS, R.K. 1972: A Model for Classification and Typology. In Clarke, D.L. (editor), *Models in Archaeology* (London), 231–273.

HINGLEY, R.C. 1982: Roman Britain: The Structure of Roman Imperialism and the Consequence sof Imperialism on the Development of a Peripheral Province. In Miles, D. (editor), *The Romano-British Countryside: Studies in Rural Settlement and Economy* (Oxford), 17–52.

HINGLEY, R.C. 1983: *Iron Age and Romano-British Society in the Upper Thames Valley: An Analysis of Settlement Data in terms of Modes of Production.* Thesis submitted for the degree of Ph.D. at Southampton University.

HINGLEY, R.C. forthcoming a: *Space and Society: Iron Age and Romano-British Settlement in the Upper Thames Valley.*

HINGLEY, R.C. forthcoming b: The Archaeology of Settlement and the Social Significance of Space. *Scottish Archaeological Review.*

HODDER, I.R. 1978: The Maintenance of Group Identities in the Baringo District, West Kenya. In Green, D., Haselgrove, C. and Spriggs, M. (editors), *Social Organisation and Settlement* (Oxford), 47–74.

HODSON, F.R. 1964: Cultural Groupings in the British Pre-Roman Iron Age. *Proc. Prehist. Soc.* 30, 99–110.

HODSON, F.R. 1980: Cultures as Types: Some Elements of a Classification Theory. *Bull. Instit. Archaeol.* 17, 1–10.

HOFFMAN, B.G. 1967: *The Structure of Traditional Moroccan Society* (The Hague).

HOLY, I. 1976: Kin Group: Structural Analysis and the study of Behaviour. *Annual Rev. Anthrop.* 5, 107–131.

HORTON, R. 1971: Stateless Societies in the History of West Africa. In Ajayi, J.F.A. and Crowder, M. (editros), *History of West Africa, Volume 1* (London), 72–113.

JEFFERIES, J.S. 1979: The Pits. In Wainwright, G.J., *Gussage All Saints: An Iron Age Settlement in Dorset* (London, HMSO), 9–15.

JOLLIFE, J.E.A. 1926: Northumbrian Institutions. *English Hist. Rev.* 51, 1–42.

JONES, G.R.J. 1961a: The Tribal System in Wales: A Re-assessment in the light of Settlement Studies. *Welsh Hist. Rev.* 1, 111–132.

JONES, G.R.J. 1961b: Early Territorial Organisation in England and Wales. *Geografiska Annaler* 43, 174–81.

JONES, M. 1978: The Plant Remains. In Parrington, M., *The Excavation of an Iron Age Settlement, Bronze Age Ring Ditches and Roman Features at Ashville Trading Estate, Abingdon (Oxfordshire), 1974–6* (London), 93–100.

KAHN, J.S. and LLOBERA, J.R. (editors) 1981: *The Anthropology of Pre-Capitalist Societies* (London).

KLEJN, L.S. 1982: *Archaeological Typology* (Oxford).

LAMBRICK, G. 1978: Iron Age Settlement in the Upper Thames Valley. In Cunliffe, B.W. and Rowley, T. (editors), *Lowland Iron Age Communities in Europe* (Oxford), 103–20.

LAMBRICK, G. and ROBINSON, M. 1979: *Iron Age and Romano-British Riverside Settlements at Farmoor, Oxfordshire* (London).

LANG, L. 1900: *A History of Scotland from the Roman Occupation, Volume 1* (London).

LAW, R. 1978: In Search of a Marxist Perspective on Pre-Colonial Tropical Africa. *Journ. African History* 19, 441–52.

LINDQUIST, S.O. 1974: Development of Agrarian Landscapes on Gotland during the Early Iron Age. *Norwegian Archaeol. Rev.* 7, 6–32.

LOWENBERG, B.J. 1970: The Mosaic of Darwinian Thought. In Appleman, P. (editor), *Darwin* (London), 211–9.

LOWRY, J. 1981: Theorising 'Observation'. *Communication and Cognition* 14, 7–23.

LYELL, C. 1970: Principles of Geology (1830–1833). In Appleman, P. (editor), *Darwin* (London), 10–14

MACNIOCAILL, I. 1972: *Ireland before the Vikings* (London).

MARX, K. 1857–8: *Grundrisse: Foundation of the Critique of the Political Economy* (London).

MCCOURT, D. 1950: *The Rundale System in Ireland: A Study of its Geographical Distribution and Social Relations.* Thesis submitted for the degree of Ph.D. at Queens University, Belfast.

MITCHELL, J.C. 1956: *The Yao Village: A Study of the Social Structure of a Nyasaland Tribe* (Manchester).

MYHRE, B. 1973: The Iron Age Farm in South Western Norway. *Norwegian Archaeol. Rev.* 6, 14–29.

MYHRE, B. 1974: Iron Age Farms in South Western Norway: The Development of the Agrarian Landscape on Jaeren. *Norwegian Archaeol. Rev.* 7, 39–83.

MYHRE, B. 1978: Agrarian Development, Settlement History and Social Organisation in South Western Norway in the Iron Age. In Kristiansen, K. and Paludan-Muller, L. (editors), *New Directions in Scandinavian Archaeology* (Copenhagen), 224–71.

NASH, D. 1975: *The Celts of Central Gaul: Some Aspects of Social and Economic Development as Background to the Roman Conquest in the Light of Numismatic and Archaeological Evidence.* Thesis submitted for the degree of D. Phil. at Oxford University.

ORR, J. 1916: *Agriculture in Oxfordshire: A Survey* (Oxford).

PARKIN, D. 1982: Introduction. In Parkin, D. (editor), *Semantic Anthropology* (London), xi–li.

PERRY, B.T. 1969: Iron Age Enclosures and Settlements on the Hampshire Chalklands. *Archaeol. Journ.* 126, 29–43.

PERRY, B.T. 1972: Excavations at Bramdean, Hampshire, 1965 and 1966, and a discussion of similar sites in Southern England. *Proc. Hants. Field Club and Archaeol. Soc.* 29, 41–78.

POCOCK, T.I. 1926: *The Geology of the Country around Oxford* (London).

POLLARD, S. 1977: A Late Iron Age Settlement and a Romano-British Villa at Holcombe, near Uplyme, Devon. *Devon Archaeol. Exploration Soc.* 31–4, 60–159.

POWELL, T.G.E. 1958: *The Celts* (London).

PROTHERO, R.E. 1912: *English Farming, Past and Present* (London).

RENFREW, C. 1977: Space, Time and Polity. In Freidman, J. and Rowlands, M. (editors), *The Evolution of Social Systems* (London), 89–112.

RICHMOND, I.R. 1968: *Hod Hill, Volume 2: Excavations carried out between 1951 and 1958* (London).

RODWELL, W. 1974: The Orsett 'Cock' Crop Mark Site. *Essex Archaeol. Journ.* 6, 1–12.

ROWLANDS, M. 1980: Kinship, Alliance and Exchange in the European Bronze Age. In Barrett, J. and Bradley, R. (editors), *The British Later Bronze Age* (Oxford), 15–56.

SCHOLTE, B. 1972: Towards a Reflexive and Critical Anthropology. In Hymes, D. (editor), *Reinventing Anthropology* (The Hague), 430–57.

SCHOLTE, B. 1981: Critical Anthropology since its Reinvention. In Kahn, J.S. and Llobera, J.R. (editors), *The Anthropology of Pre-Capitalist Societies* (London), 148–84.

SCUDDER, T. 1962: *The Ecology of the Gwembe Tonga* (Manchester).

SEEBOHM, F. 1884: *The English Village Community* (London).

SHAW, W.H. 1978: *Marx's Theory of History* (London).

SMITH, D.J. 1978: Regional Aspects of Winged Corridor Villas in Britain. In Todd, M. (editor), *Studies in the Romano-British Villa* (Leicester), 117–48.

STAHL, H.H. 1980: *Traditional Romanian Village Communities: The Transition from the Communal to the Capitalist Mode of Production in the Danube Region* (Cambridge).

TACITUS, P.C.: *The Germania.* Trans. Mattingly, H. (London).

THORNTON, R.J. 1980: *Space, Time and Culture among the Iraqw of Tanzania* (London).

TONKIN, E. 1982: Language vs the World: Notes on Meaning for Anthropologists. In Parkin, D. (editor), *Semantic Anthropology* (London), 107–22.

UDO, R.K. 1963: Patterns of Population Distribution and Settlement in Eastern Nigeria. *Nigerian Geograph. Journ.* 6, 73–87.

VINOGRADOFF, P. 1904: *The Growth of the Manor* (London).

WAINWRIGHT, G.J. 1968: The Excavation of a Durotrigian Farmstead near Tollard Royal in Cranborne Chase, Southern England. *Proc. Prehist. Soc.* 34, 102–7.

WAINWRIGHT, G.J. 1979: *Gussage All Saints: An Iron Age Settlement in Dorset* (London).

WIDGREN, M. 1979: A Simulation Model of Farming Systems and Land Use in Sweden during the Early Iron Age, c 500 bc–ad 550. *Journ. Historical Geography* 5, 21–32.

WILLIAMS, J.H. 1974: *Two Iron Age Sites in Northamptonshire* (Northampton).

WOLFE, E.R. 1957: Closed Corporate Peasant Communities in Meso-america and Central Java. *Southwestern Journ. Anthrop.* 13, 7–12.

WOLPE, H. 1980: Introduction. In Wolpe, H. (editor), *The Articulation of Modes of Production: Essays from Economy and Society* (London), 1–43.

Iron Age Buildings in the Upper Thames Region

Tim Allen, David Miles and Simon Palmer

Introduction

The past fifteen years have seen a dramatic increase in the amount of evidence available to the student of late prehistoric structures in Britain. The data-base has increased not only in quantity but also in quality. At the same time approaches to this evidence have become more critical and sophisticated. There is now a greater awareness of the problems of reconstructing vernacular architecture, of the formation-processes of the archaeological record, and of the methods required to uncover it. There is also, thanks to the work of ethnographers, an increased awareness of the social and symbolic implication of structures and their arrangement. (Close-Brooks and Gibson 1966; Denyer 1978; Hodder 1983; Oliver 1971).

In the past, Iron Age structures have often been regarded as primitive (pit dwellings) or seen largely in terms of type-sites (Little Woodbury) that are not necessarily typical of their own, let alone other, regions. A number of recent studies have illustrated clearly that the range of construction-methods, even within the round-house tradition, was wide, relatively sophisticated, and well adapted to local materials (e.g. Musson 1970; Guilbert 1975; 1981; 1982). Experimental archaeology (Reynolds 1979; 1982) has made excavators more aware both of the problems of reconstruction, and of the favourable qualities of prehistoric housing.

The Upper Thames Region

The common tendency of archaeologists to generalise from the particular has led to many appeals for more systematic, regionally-based research-programmes. The Wessex-hillfort-Little-Woodbury syndrome has persistently been attacked by those in search of their own regional identity. From the perspective of the Scottish borders Hill (1982) has emphasised that 'early housing appears to be one of the North's most fruitful archaeological resources and it is attractive to think that their potential can be realised without constant recourse to the Wessex Downlands (and in particular to Little Woodbury) which blights much northern literature and produces irrelevant contrasts and inadequate comparisons'.

English lowlanders are no happier: 'The Iron Age is seen from a multivallate hilltop somewhere well to the west of Watford . . . lowland inter-site interpretation is often seen through upland eyes' (Pryor 1983, 190). The English landscape is notable for its variety, but this has not always sufficiently been taken into account. The Highland zone includes valleys and fertile plains as well as moorland and mountain; Wessex is not simply chalk downland.

The variety of landscape in the Upper Thames region is considerable and provides a wide choice of building-resources, as can be seen from surviving vernacular architecture today. In the south is the chalk; from the centre and north of the region comes the limestone of the Corallian ridge and of the Cotswolds. Environmental studies (see Robinson this volume) indicate that during the Iron Age the landscape was essentially open with extensive pasture on the floodplain and increasingly large areas of arable on the gravel terraces and higher ground. Much of the clay slopes was wooded and would have supplied timber, while straw and reed thatch would have been abundantly available on the arable and floodplain areas. Reynolds has pointed out that the quantities of timber required were substantial: the Pimperne house, he estimates, would have needed a minimum of 200 trees. Alluvial and boulder clays were plentiful for daub and cob walling; in historical times cob has been extensively used in that part of the valley below Oxford.

In the Cotswolds a history of skilled dry-stone walling stretches back to middle Neolithic chambered tombs such as Hazleton (Saville 1983), and was commonly used in Cotswold hillforts and on the fringes of the Ock valley at Cherbury. However there is no good evidence for the use of stone in the walling of Iron Age houses in the region, though stone foundations to daub-walled structures were claimed at Salmonsbury (Dunning 1976, 377, fig. 6). Considerable quantities of stone were transported upwards of 6 km to middle Iron Age sites such as Claydon Pike at Lechlade (Miles and Palmer 1983), Mingies Ditch and Gravelly Guy in the Windrush valley.

The Evidence of Structures in the Upper Thames Region

When D.W. Harding published his survey of the Upper Thames region in 1972 the evidence of Iron Age structures was extremely limited. Only a handful of relevant excavation plans existed, mostly from the upper part of the valley above Oxford: City Farm, Hanborough; Purwell Farm, Cassington; Standlake Down; Beard Mill, Stanton Harcourt; Langford Down and Lechlade (Harding 1972, 22–35 pl. 26). South of Oxford a circular structure was known at Frilford (Harding 1972, pl. 33) beneath the Romano-Celtic temple, now thought by Harding (pers. comm.) to be a domestic structure. At Radley curving gullies were believed to demarcate round-house sites 45–50 ft in diameter. Harding noted that the structures in the upper reaches of the valley were 'less grandiose in proportions than their Wessex counterparts' — as exemplified by Little Woodbury, Longbridge Deverill and Pimperne. As the settlement contexts of few of the Thames Valley houses were known it is dubious whether the structures can in any way be regarded as 'counterparts'.

The evidence of these Iron Age structures in the Upper Thames had mostly been retrieved in difficult conditions, notably on the over-stripped surfaces of gravel pits. Relatively deep gullies, such as those at Radley, survived such treatment, but traces of timber foundations were rare. When these were found they tended to conform to the post-ring mode. In recent years such forms have been found less frequently (though two are currently being excavated at Gravelly Guy, Stanton Harcourt). It is impossible to say to what extent excavators have been influenced by this model. Like any other observer excavators are not entirely free to describe nature with absolute impartiality. As B.L. Whorf (1940) has emphasised: 'The categories and types that we isolate from the world of phenomena we do not find there because they stare every observer in the face; on the contrary the world is presented in a kaleidoscopic flux of impressions . . . We cut nature up, organise it into concepts and ascribe significances as we do largely because we are parties to an agreement to organise it in this way.'

The growing awareness of the archaeological complexities has led, since 1972, to excavation-strategies designed specifically to recover the evidence of buildings, and their relationship to each other. The location of structures has been discovered in a number of ways: from aerial photography, where hut gullies in particular are often discernible as cropmarks, by excavations, by geophysical survey and by phosphate analysis (Miles 1984; Miles and Palmer 1983a and b).

Experimental archaeologists such as Peter Reynolds have emphasised that the foundations of Iron Age round houses need not penetrate the subsoil. Excavation must therefore proceed with considerable care if structural evidence is to be recovered. Even then results can be disappointing. At Appleford a possible wall-slot inside a ditched enclosure was clearly visible on aerial photographs (Hinchliffe and Thomas 1980, 34–35, pl. 1); meticulous excavation nevertheless failed to reveal any trace of it within the deep soil overlying the gravel terrace.

For the most part the gravel terraces of the Thames Valley have been subject to generations of ploughing. In many cases this has resulted not only in the loss of the Iron Age ground-surface but in the disturbance of the gravel beneath. The pebbly gravel surfaces are not an ideal medium for retaining the fine details of earth-fast timbers, and the surface has to be carefully cleaned if any traces of structures are to be observed. In addition many of the Iron Age settlements are on the kind of 'favoured' sites where long-term occupation has disturbed the remains of earlier structures (e.g. Ashville, Abingdon; Parrington 1978).

Not surprisingly some of the most illuminating evidence has come from those sites where conditions are more appropriate for the retrieval of building-detail.

Protection from ploughing was afforded to sites at Farmoor (Lambrick and Robinson 1979) and Mingies Ditch by later deposits of alluvium. At this latter site the Iron Age ground-surface with occupation deposits was preserved. Waterlogging, another potential source of structural information, had also preserved the bottom of an oak door-post. Unfortunately no site in the Upper Thames region has produced the quality of preservation which makes the Glastonbury settlement so exceptional (Bulleid and Gray 1911; 1917).

The alluvium can, at the same time, mask archaeological remains so that they are invisible to the field-walker and aerial photographer. Observation of ground disturbance — drainage ditches, pipelines, new reservoirs (as at Farmoor) or gravel pits — is essential if some of the best-preserved sites are to be located (Pryor 1983, 190). At Claydon Pike, Fairford, a substantial stone-based Roman shrine was found beneath alluvium with the aid of a metal detector, which pinpointed a mass of votive coins. Unfortunately no Iron Age structures in the region have been rich in metal finds.

The classification of Iron Age structures has often depended on a small number of isolated excavated examples of different, and often indifferent, states of preservation. This has led to idiosyncratic interpretations, in which excavated elements, especially post-holes, have been joined together like a child's dot puzzle. Edward Hall's comment is particularly appropriate. 'To try to deal with a foreign culture by learning more and more sets is a hopeless task. To collect sets in your mind is easy, but to decipher a pattern is difficult. Talking about sets without bringing in patterns is like talking about bricks without saying anything about houses' (Hall 1973, 106).

In British Iron Age studies the patterns have begun to emerge as a result of controlled, large-scale excavations. At Moel y Gaer (Guilbert 1975; 1976) and Danebury (Cunliffe 1984), for example, large number of structures have been examined; it is possible, therefore, to see the patterns of regularity and processes of change. In particular the varying states of preservation can be taken into account so that classification of structures is not governed simply by the unrecognised formation-processes affecting the archaeological record.

At Claydon Pike a sizeable settlement has recently been excavated. Here the best-preserved house, xv (Fig. 6.7) consisted of a circular wall-slot attached to a pair of stone-packed postholes, about 2 m apart. Inside the structure was a clay-lined pit, and outside it was surrounded by a penannular gully. The gully had silted up and was probably for drainage; occupation-debris from use of the house was concentrated in the gully terminals close to the door. This last phenomenon has also been observed in the gullies around houses at Mingies Ditch, Hardwick (see also Pryor 1983, 194). Study of the distribution of finds in the gullies at Claydon Pike (Fig. 6.3) has shown this pattern to be general. There were no other wall lines preserved, but varying combinations of at least two of the other elements — doorposts, clay-lined pit, penannular gully and concentrations of occupation-debris — were present in almost twenty other places, and can plausibly be interpreted as other house sites. The most persistent elements from such a structure are the pair of doorposts and the penannular gullies. Paried postholes, identified by Bersu (1940) as drying racks in the Little Woodbury culture complex, may, therefore, indicate house sites by themselves (Fig. 6.6).

House Types

Post-Ring Houses

Attempts to categorise house types on the basis of archaeological evidence have often been inconsistent (Hill 1982). 'Post-ring' houses for example may imply either a structure whose outer wall is formed of posts, or one with an inner ring of posts supporting the roof and forming an aisle, with the wall further out. Guilbert has pointed out that in well-preserved double-ring houses the outer wall may leave substantially less trace than the inner ring of support posts (for example Moel y Gaer, Pimperne and Shearplace Hill: Guilbert 1981, fig. 7). Little Woodbury House 1 (Bersu 1940, fig. 20) is exceptional in having an outer, though incomplete, set of relatively substantial postholes. Guilbert has convincingly re-interpreted some of the 'single' post-ring houses as double-ring, aisled types — where they have projecting doorposts to which an outer wall could be attached. Possible Upper Thames examples include round houses from City Farm and Standlake Down (Guilbert 1976, fig. 8, J and K). A more recent example from the Upper Thames region, House 2 at Groundwell Farm, Wilts (Gingell 1981) (Fig. 6.5) had a continuous wall groove, with an inner ring of widely-spaced and deep-set ramped postholes. At Claydon Pike, Lechlade, another possible structure of this kind (house XVIII) has recently been excavated (Fig. 6.7). Twelve posts formed a ring c. 7 m in diameter. A pair of posts, 2 m apart, projected to the south-east. An outer wall attached to these posts would have formed a ring of c. 10 m in diameter. An increase of 3 m in diameter would, in this case, therefore, almost double the floor area of the house.

Structures with outer walls formed by single post-rings cannot however be discounted. At Salmonsbury a pair of post-ring structures were closely bounded by a drainage gully (Dunning 1976, fig. 80, (Fig. 6.1b) which if contemporary would have left no room for an outer wall. At Claydon Pike a second post-ring structure of c. 7 m diameter could not be associated with projecting doorposts. Other structures, such as those at Longbridge Deverill (S. Hawkes, unpublished excavation) and Frilford (Harding 1972, 133) (Fig. 6.2(1)), have a ring of posts so clearly set that they are likely to represent wall supports. This ring is also attached to an inner, larger pair of doorposts.

'Ring-groove' or Trench-built houses

These buildings, in which the house wall is set in a continuous slot, are of two distinct types. Differing preservation does not seem to be the main factor. In some cases the groove is slight and narrow as in House XV at Claydon Pike (Fig. 6.7). The outer wall of the aisled house at Groundwell Farm (Fig. 6.5, house 3) is similarly slight but markedly wider.

However, more frequently examples of the 'ring-groove' house have a wall of substantial timbers deeply embedded in vertical-sided trenches. Several well-preserved buildings of this type have been excavated at Danebury, Hants (Cunliffe 1984). In some of these the outlines of individual planks have been detected in the chalk-cut slots. The method of construction is not altogether dissimilar to the continuous-post wall of the Longbridge Deverill house which, like the Danebury houses, belongs to the early Iron Age. This trench-built construction has been claimed for many Iron Age houses in northern and southern Britain, but no convincing example is known from the Upper Thames. Whether this reflects variations in Iron Age vernacular architecture or patterns of contemporary archaeological interpretations is difficult to say.

Circular drainage gullies

In the Upper Thames valley penannular gullies are a common element of Iron Age sites. Their size and shape, silting pattern (including flood deposits) and distribution of artefacts show that these were normally open gullies (Fig. 6.3). Excavations in recent years indicate that many, in fact, surround house sites as at Hardwick, House 5 (Fig. 6.8), Claydon Pike, House XV (Fig. 6.7). The modern Italian round 'hut' described by Close-Brooks and Gibson (1960) was provided with a similar gully to act as a storm-water drain. On the flat Thames-side terraces these gullies would have acted as sumps to drain surface water and help keep the house foundations and immediate vicinity dry.

Such gullies have been interpreted as possible wall-trenches, for example at Groundwell Farm, Wilts, where House 4 has gullies of 17.5 m and 19 m in diameter (Fig. 6.5) and Heath Farm, Milton Common (Fig. 6.4(2)). The recut gullies at the latter site ranged in diameter from 12 m to 14 m, similar to those at Radley and Ashville, Abingdon (Fig. 6.4(5)). None of them has produced convincing evidence for foundations set within these slots. In addition the diameters of the larger gullies make their interpretation as buildings highly unlikely. (But see Hill 1982 for northern huts with supposed integral, internal ditches).

Although it is common in this region for these gullies to be associated with houses, this is not invariably so. At Claydon Pike (excavations in 1983 by Miles and Palmer) considerable numbers of shallow circular gullies, ranging in diameter from 3 to 9 m were thought to define stacking areas for animal fodder. At Farmoor some of them may have served as animal pens (Lambrick and Robinson 1979). Others, often shaped like a shepherd's crook, probably acted as annexes alongside round houses for working-areas, livestock, storage, or subsidiary buildings.

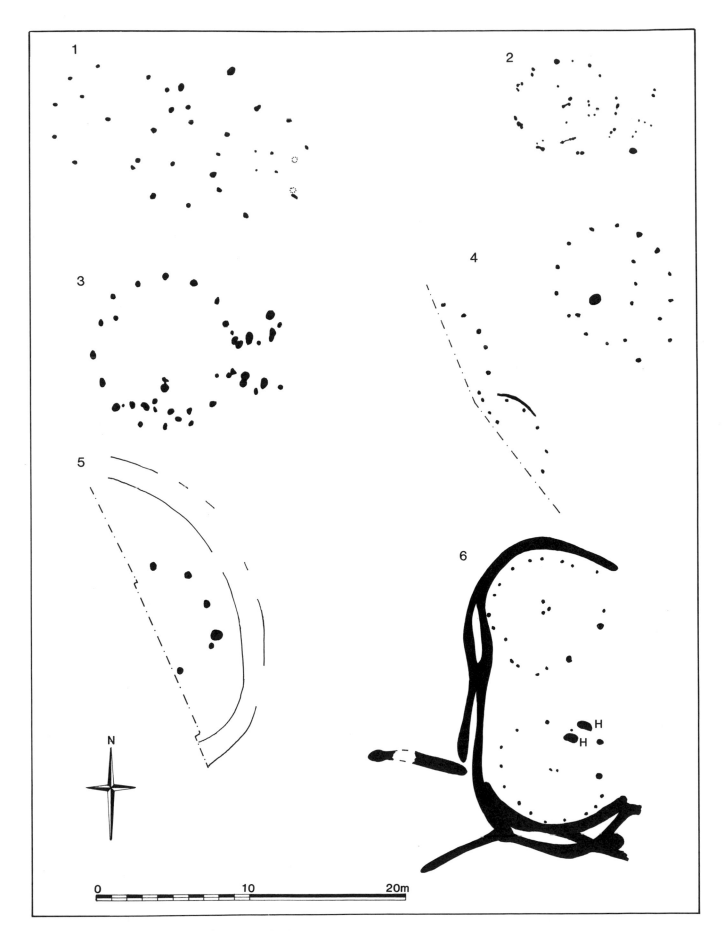

Figure 6.1 *Post-ring structures in the Upper Thames region*
1. *Rams Hill (Bradley and Ellison 1975)*
2. *Lechlade (from Harding 1972)*
3. *City Farm, Hanborough (Harding 1972)*
4. *Standlake Down (Riley 1946)*
5. *Beard Mill, Stanton Harcourt (Williams 1951)*
6. *Salmonsbury (Dunning 1976)*

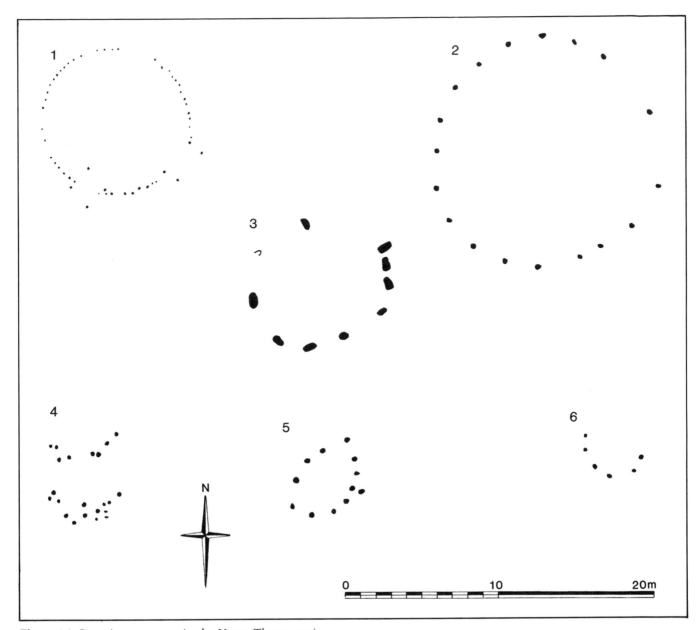

Figure 6.2 *Post-ring structures in the Upper Thames region*
1. *Frilford (Harding 1972)*
2. *Langford Downs (Williams 1946)*
3. *Langford Downs (Williams 1946)*
4. *Barton Court Farm, Abingdon (Miles forthcoming)*
5. *Barton Court Farm, Abingdon (Miles forthcoming)*
6. *Shakenoak (Brodribb, Hands and Walker 1971)*

Stake-walled houses

At Mingies Ditch traces of a circular stake-walled house sealed by alluvium were preserved in the subsoil, House 5 (Fig. 6.8). Not only were the holes of the vertical stakes clearly visible, but the impression of the bottom course of continuous wattle-walling also survived. The vertical stakes were set at 0.15–0.30 m intervals and joined onto substantial doorposts. Presumably a continuous circular ringbeam would have run around the top of the basket construction to distribute the weight of the roof evenly.

The slight ring-groove of House xv, Claydon Pike (Fig. 6.7) may represent the bottom of a stake-wall. The survival of individual stake-holes in such a coarse medium as gravel would be surprising. Numbers of these stake-walled houses similar to the Mingies Ditch example have been excavated at Danebury (Cunliffe 1984, 67, 78), well preserved in the unploughed chalk (and not subject to sub-aerial denudation, as is often exaggeratedly claimed on Downland sites). Most of the Danebury examples were 7–8 m in diameter. However some were as much as 10.5 m across, showing that larger structures are possible using this technique. Danebury also had an unusual variant of the stake-walled house: two buildings had double-stake walls (Cunliffe 1984). The Danebury stake-walled houses have well-preserved dooorways. The postpipes show that in several cases there were two posts in each; presumably one supporting the roof and walls and the other forming the doorframe. Double doorposts have also been observed at Claydon Pike and Mingies Ditch. Also at Danebury threshold-slots indicate that timber sills were provided to brace the doorframes.

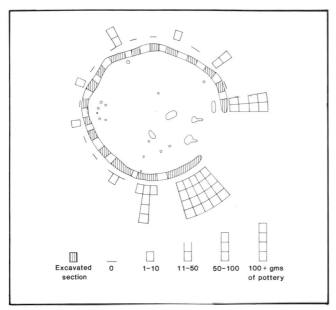

Figure 6.3 *Distribution of pottery in drainage gully around House 1 Claydon Pike, Lechlade (Miles and Palmer 1982)*

Other forms of house construction

It has already been noted that in several otherwise well-preserved houses there was no trace of the outer wall. Dixon has suggested that at Crickley Hill walls were bedded into sleeper beams (Dixon 1976). This technique is not particularly suited to circular structures, as many short lengths of selected timber would be required. At Danebury several houses were represented by circular floor areas and by doorposts with linking thresholds but with no trace of the wall. House 4 at Mingies Ditch (Fig. 6.8) was also represented by doorposts, a central hearth and floor layers respecting the wall-line inside and out, but without any trace of the wall. At both Danebury and Hardwick the evidence suggests that the walls of these buildings were relatively narrow.

Musson (1970, 274) noted the use of a mass-wall construction in an Iron Age context: dwarf stone walls with an inner ring of posts were excavated at Maiden Castle (Wheeler 1943, 94–95), and at other south-western sites such as Bodrifty, Cornwall (Dudley 1957). Surprisingly perhaps, stone-walled houses have not been found as yet in the Cotswolds. In the Thames Valley mass-wall construction could have utilised the abundant turf which was available. Iron Age turf-stripping was noted at Farmoor, and it was suggested that the material had been used in house-construction (Lambrick and Robinson 1979).

The compacted gravel surfaces observed at Milton Common (Rowley 1973) and Langford Down (Williams 1946) may have resulted from wear after the removal of topsoil or turf, though there was no indication at either of these sites of the use of such material. Mass walls may be revetted internally as at Hod Hill (Richmond 1968) with a ring of postholes, though these were not necessarily evenly spaced or uniform in size and shape.

At Mingies Ditch, Hardwick House 1 (Fig. 4.7) consisted of an oval of widely-spaced postholes sur-

rounded by a drainage gully and the settlement's enclosure ditch. These postholes corresponded with the edge of a darkened floor area. There was no trace of any wall-foundation penetrating the ground, and the posts seem too slight to be the principal roof-supports. Outside this oval building upcast from the enclosure ditch had been thrown into the half-silted drainage gully and along the east side of the house, stopping about 0.9 m from the floor and parallel to it. It is possible that this upcast had been thrown against the side of the house and that its edges represent the limit of a mass wall. Although nothing survived of the wall *in situ*, there were spreads of clay loam and gravel overlying several of the Mingies Ditch houses, which may be the remains of decomposed cob walls.

House 3 at Mingies Ditch (Fig. 4.7) was also indicated by an oval of postholes set within a circular drainage gully. A large entrance lay to the south-east and a narrower one to the north-west. Ash raked from an internal hearth spread beyond the post-ring and indicated that the posts did not represent the wall-line. A line of gravel outside the post-ring ran in an arc concentric to the surrounding gully, and is interpreted as scuffed up against the inside of the wall, while a soil change on the south probably reflected the differing wear between the floor and the area outside. The building was therefore aisled with a circular outer wall. The internal posts were irregularly spaced and of varying sizes: it is doubtful whether they were intended to support the roof by themselves. It is possible therefore that the thrust of the roof was carried in part on a mass wall of turf.

The implication of the Mingies Ditch houses are significant. The post/ring which is all that would remain on a plough-eroded site, would not be readily recognised as an aisled building — or even as a circular structure. The evidence here also suggests that irregular widely-spaced post-rings may result from a type of construction fundamentally different to regular post-rings, and one which normally leaves no trace below ground.

Internal Features in Round Houses

Most Upper Thames structures, even well-preserved ones, contain disappointingly few internal features and are relatively meagre in artefacts. Circular clay-lined pits were a recurrent feature at Claydon Pike. These possibly acted as water-containers or cooking-holes. The burnt stones found within them may have been secondary refuse, as such material is ubiquitous on this mid-Iron Age site. These pits appear to be a local phenomenon and have not been found on other Thames Valley sites, but they do occur intermittently throughout southern England.

Traces of hearths are occasionally found within round houses but cannot always be definitely associated with the structure. At Mingies Ditch, where the preservation allows us to be certain, one house contained a central hearth made of gravel conglomerate, which had replaced a posthole. A patch of laid clay floor survived in this

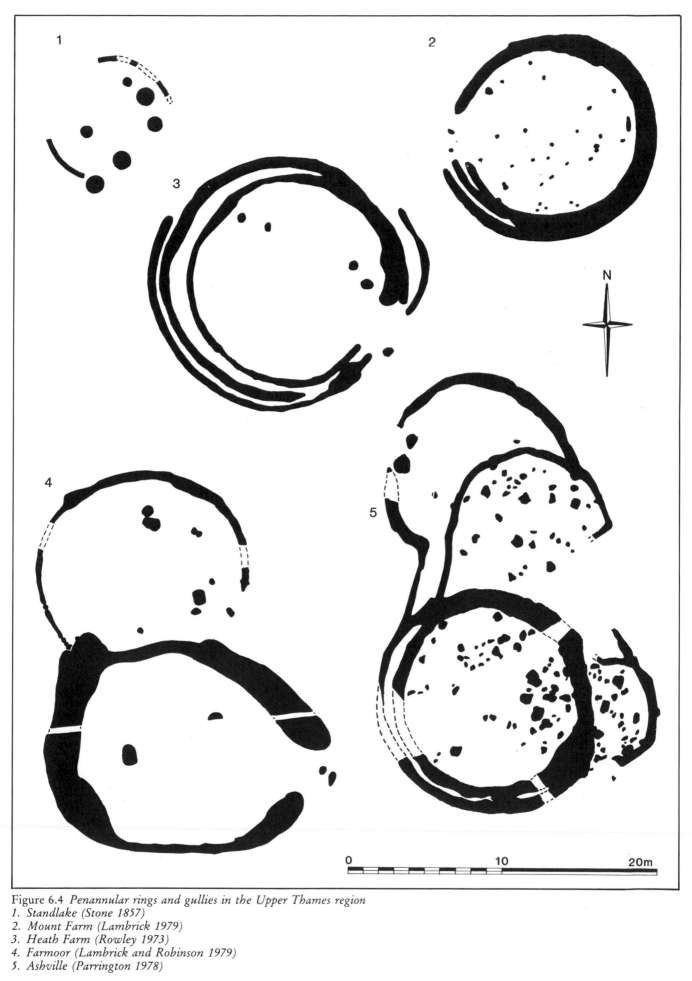

Figure 6.4 *Penannular rings and gullies in the Upper Thames region*
1. *Standlake (Stone 1857)*
2. *Mount Farm (Lambrick 1979)*
3. *Heath Farm (Rowley 1973)*
4. *Farmoor (Lambrick and Robinson 1979)*
5. *Ashville (Parrington 1978)*

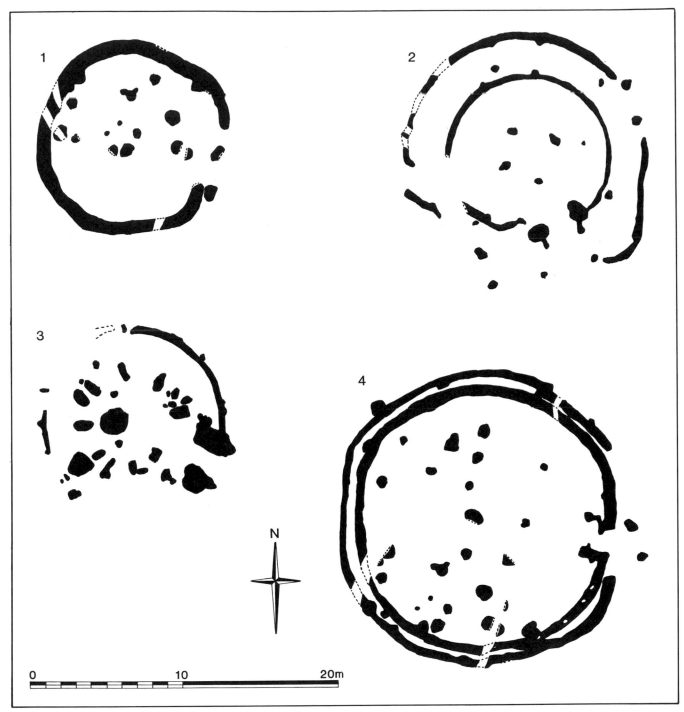

Figure 6.5 *Structures at Groundwell Farm, Wilts (Gingell 1981)*

house. Another house, House 4 (Fig. 4.7) also had a hearth made of clay and limestone slabs. If this site had been extensively ploughed the hearths would have left no trace.

Flooring material was also found at Claydon Pike. One round house had limestone cobbling laid in its northern half, to the right of the doorway. A similar feature has been noted at Port Meadow, Oxford (Atkinson 1942) and possibly at Farmoor (Lambrick and Robinson 1979). Round houses cannot be so conveniently divided as rectangular structures. Internal structural post-rings may have served to divide some houses concentrically and also into bays. The stone floors suggest subdivisions into two halves, perhaps with

animal kept on the more substantial surface (cf Fleming 1979, 124).

Rectangular Structures

Harding's survey of Upper Thames house types discussed the possibility of rectangular buildings (Harding 1972, 34–35). He was most positive about the compacted rubble floor outside the Wittenham Clumps hillfort, although only a corner less than 3 × 2 m was uncovered (Rhodes 1948). Other possibilities were: the shallow depression at Wigbald's Farm which the excavator regarded as a rubbish-pit (Savory 1937); Langford Down's irregular 'floor' area (Williams 1946) and

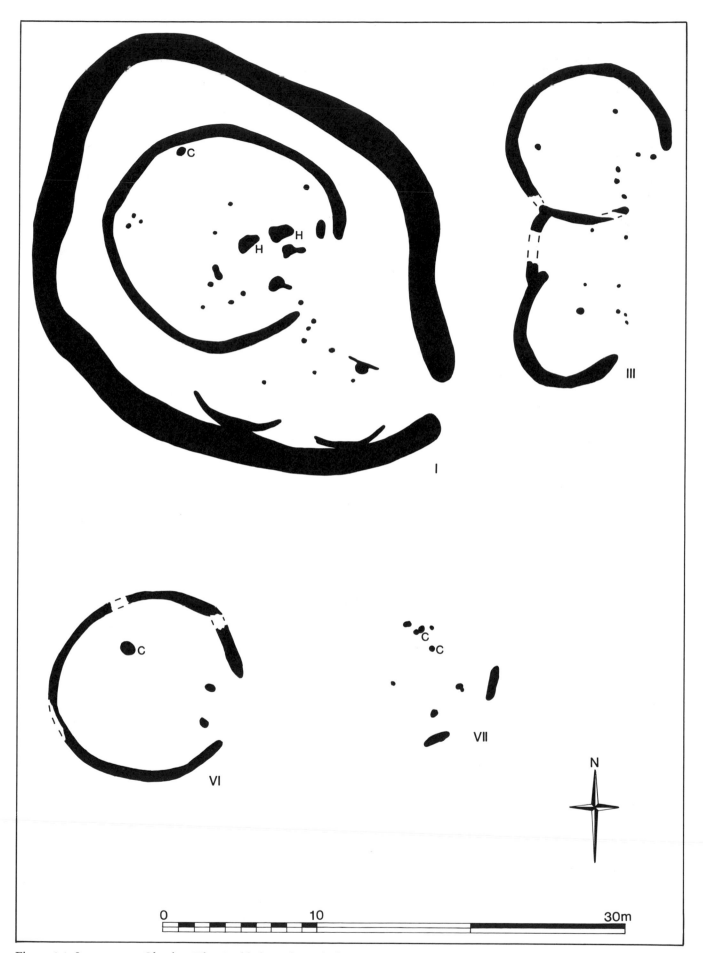

Figure 6.6 *Structures at Claydon Pike, Lechlade (Miles and Plamer 1983)*
C — clay lined pit; H — Hearth

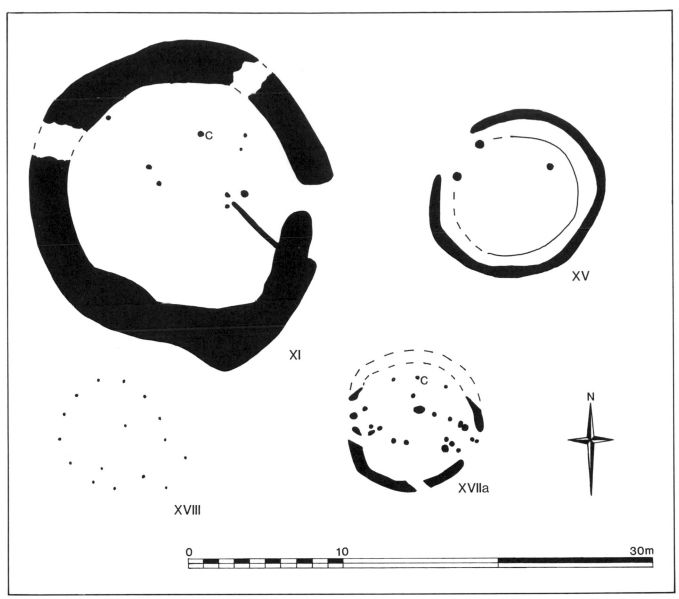

Figure 6.7 *Structures at Claydon Pike, Lechlade (Miles and Palmer 1983)*
C — clay line pit

Standlake Down's gully which formed three sides of a rectangle 3 × 2.5 m. Most of these features were only partially excavated, so that their interpretation is at best speculative. Harding did, however, utilise this evidence in support of his theory that the northern part of the valley was a conservative backwater.

Harding expanded his discussion of possible rectangular buildings in a wider context (Harding 1973; 1974), and others have also contributed to the discussion (Stanford 1970; 1974) Dixon 1973; 1976) Rodwell 1978). Since Harding summarised the evidence in the Upper Thames Valley several sites have produced relevant information. At Claydon Pike, Lechlade, seven stone-packed postholes formed a rectangle 7 × 2 m. Such a narrow setting may indicate a small aisled building. However the dating of this structure is not at present conclusive and its form is in marked contrast to the circularity of the middle Iron Age houses on the site. Another possibility is an unusual wedge-shaped ar-

rangement of postholes at Mingies Ditch, one side of which was backed by a wall-trench. Settings of four and six posts have been much discussed since Bersu (1940, 97–98) suggested that they represented above-ground storage units (for example Ellison and Drewitt 1971).

No Upper Thames Valley open sites have thus shown the linear arrangements of four and six posters so apparent in densely-occupied hillforts such as Danebury (Hants.), Moel-Y-Gaer (Clwyd) (Guilbert 1975, 207–8) or in Crickley Hill (Gloucs.) and Croft Ambrey (Hereford) where these rectangular settings are interpreted as longhouses (Dixon 1973) and less convincingly as small 'squarish' dwellings (Stanford 1974, 230).

Upper Thames examples have appeared in small numbers on a variety of sites on the floodplain and on the first and second gravel terraces. Variations both in settlement context and in the size of the postholes themselves suggest that we have in fact a variety of building-types and functions. Both at Mingies Ditch,

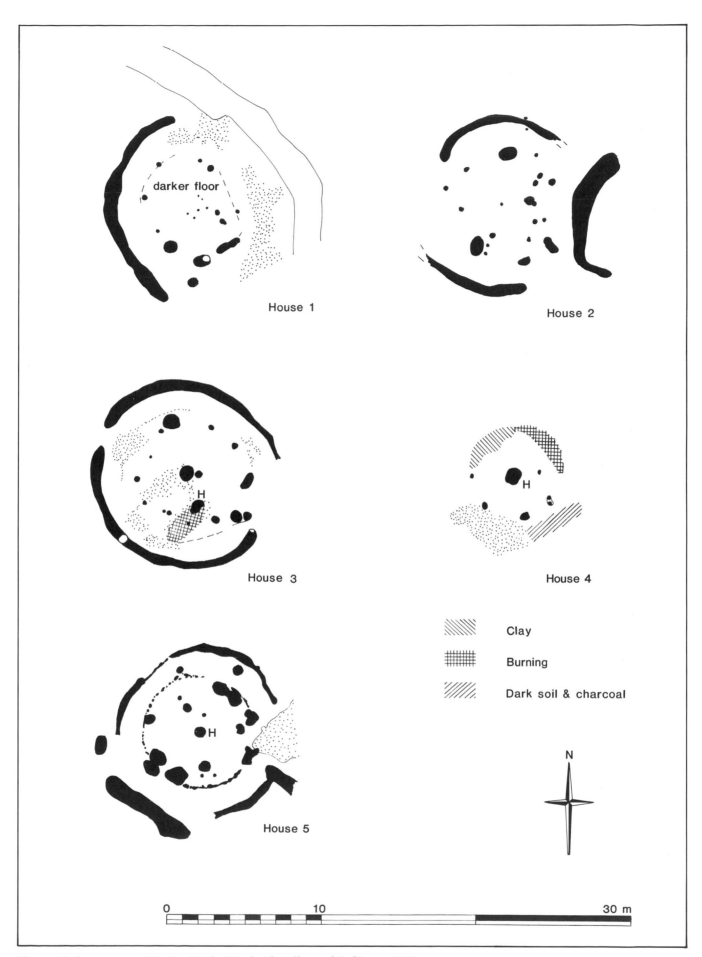

darker floor

House 1

House 2

House 3

House 4

H

H

H

House 5

Clay

Burning

Dark soil & charcoal

N

0   10   30 m

Figure 6.8 *Structures at Mingies Ditch, Hardwick (Allen and Robinson 1979)*
H — hearth

99

Hardwick and at Claydon Pike, Lechlade substantial pairs of posts have been found linked by shallow slots. At Danebury Cunliffe has suggested (pers. comm.) that this slot simply represents a method of digging the postholes. Alternatively the slot might indicate a bracing timber in the ground to help support a structure required to bear a heavy weight. This type of four or six poster is the most convincing as a storage unit.

An unusual four-post arrangement, surrounded by a circular ditch, was excavated at Appleford (Hinchliffe and Thomas 1980, 44). This was rather isolated from the rest of the contemporary settlement. The authors suggest a possible funerary or religious function, noting the presence of a similar though larger six-post structure at Frilford (Bradford and Goodchild 1939, fig. 5). Equally the structure might be a storage unit, protected from grazing animals, of the kind still in use in contemporary Europe. Another unusual small four-poster was found set within a rectangular trench, possibly a wall-slot, at Smith's Field, Hardwick. The presence of a complete animal burial and the structure's similarity to examples at Danebury suggest that this may have had a ritual function.

Unfortunately such formal analogies around which present interpretations revolve are extremely weak. Similar discussion, for example about Saxon sunken-featured buildings, has been advanced by the discovery of burnt structures.

Rodwell (1978) has proposed that the rectangular building, probably of timber-frame construction, became the norm in the south-east in the century preceding the Roman conquest. Possible houses of this date in the Upper Thames region are rare. These are: two post circles at Langford Downs (Williams 1946); another at Shakenoak (Brodribb et al. 1971) and two at Barton Court Farm (Miles forthcoming). The excavator doubted whether the larger of the two at Langford Downs, at 15 m diameter, had ever been roofed. Reynolds has reconstructed a similar post-ring, excavated at Balksbury, as an animal pen. The date of the Shakenoak structure is uncertain, and the excavator has suggested that the small Barton Court post-rings may belong to ancillary structures.

No convincing late Iron Age rectangular structures have been found in the region. As in the middle Iron Age, however, house sites may be indicated by small enclosures whose ditches contain significant quantities of domestic debris. In the Stanton Harcourt area enclosures of the mid (and later) first century AD have been found at Linch Hill Corner (Grimes 1943), Vicarage Field (Case and Whittle 1982), and Smith's Field, Hardwick (Allen and Robinson 1979). These were all of similar internal area of middle Iron Age house-enclosures (6 to 13 m across — generally 6 to 9 m). Most were subrectangular, but some were oval. This evidence might suggest that rectangular or subrectangular buildings were appearing early in the first century AD but

were so constructed that they left no physical trace. Other extensively-excavated settlements of this period have failed to produce clear structural evidence. At both Barton Court Farm, Abingdon and Claydon Pike, Fairford the earliest rectangular buildings were dated to the later part of the first century AD.

Chronological Summary

Later Bronze Age: Although houses of the post-ring type, either single or double, are well-attested from Sussex Downs sites such as Shearplace Hill, Ilford Hill and Black Patch (Drewett 1982) evidence is sparse from the Upper Thames region. On the edge of the region such structures have been excavated at Rams Hill (Bradley and Ellison 1975), and in the Upper Thames Valley a possible example was found at Corporation Farm, Abingdon (Henderson pers. comm.); (Barrett and Bradley 1980, fig. 4).

Early Iron Age: Again house plans are not abundant but the house forms are still of the post-ring type e.g. Rough Ground Farm, Lechlade (Harding 1972, fig. 3).

Middle Iron Age: Drainage gullies became common and stake-built houses without post-rings appear. Post-ring construction continues usually but not invariably for houses of larger diameter. Factors such as the better management of decreasing woodland might explain the use of stakes rather than larger timbers. Other forms of construction such as mass walls are also becoming apparent.

Late Iron Age: Examples of excavated buildings are again scarce though settlements are not. Post-ring houses continue: one is known at Langford Downs, and there are two possible structures at Barton Court Farm. Rectangular buildings cannot be discounted.

Summary

It is clear that the study of vernacular architecture in the Iron Age has barely begun. Despite the Upper Thames region's varied landscape, houses have mainly been excavated on the gravel terraces. Here buildings of timber construction and, on the better-preserved flood-plain sites, buildings of mass-wall construction (be it cob or turf) have been discovered. It is difficult to comment on the possible use of other materials in other areas, for example, stone on the Cotswold slopes.

Excavation is needed in a wider variety of settlements and geographical locations before the full range of building-types can be appreciated. The number of complete settlement-plans is still relatively small and a precise chronology is not yet available (see Lambrick this volume). More large-scale excavation will be needed before the patterns of regional variability emerge.

References

ALLEN, T. and ROBINSON, M. 1979: Mingies Ditch, Hardwick. *CBA Group 9 Newsletter* 9, 116.

ATKINSON, R.J.C. 1942: Archaeological sites at Port Meadow, Oxford. *Oxoniensia* 7, 24–36.

BENSON, D. and MILES, D. 1974: *The Upper Thames Valley: an archaeological survey of the river gravels.*

BERSU, G. 1940: Excavations at Little Woodbury, Wiltshire. Part I: the settlement as revealed by excavation. *Proc. Prehist. Soc.* 6, 30–111.

BRADFORD, J.S.P. 1940: The Excavations at Cherbury Camp, 1939. *Oxoniensia* 5, 13–20.

BRADFORD, J.S.P. and GOODCHILD, R.G. 1931: Excavations at Frilford, Berks, 1937–8. *Oxoniensia* 4, 1–80.

BRADLEY, R. and ELLISON, A. 1975: *Rams Hill* (Oxford, BAR 19).

BRODRIBB, A.C.C., HANDS, A.R. and WALKER, D.R. 1971: *Excavations at Shakenoak* II (Oxford).

BULLEID, A.H. and GRAY, H.ST.G. 1911 and 1917: *The Glastonbury Lake Village* Vols I and II.

CARR, R.D. 1972: Wallingford. In *Archaeological Excavations* (HMSO).

CLOSE-BROOKS, J. and GIBSON, S. 1966: A Round Hut near Rome. *Proc. Prehist. Soc.* 32, 349–52.

CUNLIFFE, B. 1984: *Danebury: an Iron Age hillfort in Hampshire. Vol. 1 The excavations, 1969–1978: the site* (CBA Res. Rep. 52).

DENYER, S. 1978: *African traditional architecture* (London).

DIXON, P. 1973: Longhouse and round house at Crickley Hill. *Antiquity* 47, 56–9.

DIXON, P. 1976: Crickley Hill, 1969–72. In Harding, D.W. (editor), *Hillforts: Later Prehistoric earthworks in Britain and Ireland* (London), 161–75, 424–9.

DREWETT, P.L. 1982: Excavations at Black Patch, Sussex. *Proc. Prehist. Soc.* 48, 321–400.

DUDLEY, D. 1957: An excavation at Bodrifty, Mulfa Hill, near Penzance, Cornwall. *Archaeol. Journ.* 113, 1–32.

DUNNING, G.C. 1976: Salmonsbury, Bourton-on-the-Water, Gloucestershire. In Harding, D.W. (editor), *Hillforts: Later prehistoric earthworks in Britain and Ireland* (London), 75–118, 373–401.

ELLISON, A. and DREWETT, P. 1971: Pits and post-holes in the British Early Iron Age; some alternative explanations. *Proc. Prehist. Soc.* 37, 183–94.

FLEMING, A. 1979: The Dartmoor Reaves: Boundary Patterns and Behaviour Patterns in the second millennium BC. In *Prehistoric Dartmoor in its context, Proc. Devon Archaeol. Soc.* 37.

GINGELL, C. 1981: Excavation of an Iron Age enclosure at Groundwell Farm, Blunsdon St. Andrew, 1976–7. *Wilts. Archaeol. and Nat. Hist. Mag.* 76, 33–75.

GUILBERT, G. 1975: Planned hillfort interiors. *Proc. Prehist. Soc.* 41, 203–21.

GUILBERT, G. 1976: Moel y Gaer (Rhosesmor) 1972–1973: an area excavation in the interior. In Harding, D.W. (editor), *Hillforts: Later prehistoric earthworks in Britain and Ireland* (London), 303–317.

GUILBERT, G. 1981: Double ring roundhouses, probable and possible, in Prehistoric Britain. *Proc. Prehist. Soc.* 47, 299–317.

GUILBERT, G. 1982: Post-ring symmetry in roundhouses at Moel y Gaer and some other sites in Prehistoric Britain. In Drury, P.J. (editor), *Structural Reconstruction* (Oxford, BAR 110), 67–86.

HALL, E.T. 1973: *The Silent Language* (New York).

HARDING, D.W. 1972: *The Iron Age in the Upper Thames Basin.*

HARDING, D.W. 1973: Round and Rectangular: Iron Age houses, British and Foreign. In Hawkes, C.F.C. and S.C. (editors), *Greeks, Celts and Romans.* 43–62.

HARDING, D.W. 1974: *The Iron Age in Lowland Britain.*

HARDING, D.W. (editor) 1976: *Hillforts: Later prehistoric earthworks in Britain and Ireland* (London).

HILL, P.H. 1982: Towards a new classification of prehistoric houses. *Scottish Archaeol. Rev.* 1, 24–37.

HINCHLIFFE, J. and THOMAS, R. 1980: Archaeological Investigations at Appleford. *Oxoniensia* 45, 9–111.

HODDER, I. 1983: *The Present Past* (London).

LAMBRICK, G. 1979: Mount Farm, Berinsfield. *CBA Group 9 Newsletter* 9, 113.

LAMBRICK, G. and ROBINSON, M. 1979: *Iron Age and Roman riverside settlements at Farmoor, Oxfordshire* (London, CBA Res. Rep. 32).

MILES, D. 1983: An integrated approach to the study of ancient landscapes: the Claydon Pike project. In Maxwell, G.S. (editor), *The Impact of Aerial Reconnaissance on Archaeology* (London, CBA Res. Rep. 49), 74–84.

MILES, D. forthcoming: *Archaeology at Barton Court Farm, Abingdon* (London, CBA Res. Rep.).

MILES, D. and PALMER, S. 1983a: *Figures in a Landscape* (Oxford).

MILES, D. and PALMER, S. 1983b: Claydon Pike. *Current Archaeology* 86, 88–92.

MUSSON, C. 1970: House plans and prehistory. *Current Archaeology* 2, 267–75.

OLIVER, P. (editor) 1971: *Shelter in Africa* (London).

PARRINGTON, M. 1978: *The excavations at Ashville, Abingdon (Oxon) 1974–76* (London, CBA Res. Rep. 28).

PRYOR, F. 1983: Gone, but still respected: some evidence for Iron Age house platforms in lowland England. *Oxford Journ. Archaeol.* 2(2), 189–98.

REYNOLDS, P.J. 1979: *Iron Age Farm. The Butser Experiment* (London).

REYNOLDS, P.J. 1982: Substructure to Superstructure. In Drury, P.J. (editor), *Structural Reconstruction* (Oxford, BAR 110), 173–198.

RHODES, P.P. 1948: A Prehistoric and Roman site at Wittenham Clumps, Berks. *Oxoniensia* 13, 18–31.

RICHMOND, I. 1968: *Hod Hill* (Vol. 2) (London).

RODWELL, W. 1978: Buildings and Settlements in South-East Britain in the late Iron Age. In Cunliffe, B. and Rowley, T. (editors), *Lowland Iron Age Communities in Europe* (Oxford, BAR S48), 25–41.

ROWLEY, T. 1973: An Iron Age Settlement Site at Heath Farm, Milton Common. *Oxoniensia* 38, 23–40.

SAVILLE, A. 1983: Hazleton. *Current Archaeology* 87, 107–12.

SAVORY, H.N. 1937: An Early Iron Age site at Long Wittenham, Berks. *Oxoniensia* 2, 1–11.

STANFORD, S.C. 1970: Credenhill Camp — an Iron Age Hillfort Capital. *Archaeol. Journ.* 127, 82–129.

STANFORD, S.C. 1974: *Croft Ambrey* (Hereford).

WHEELER, R.E.M. 1943: *Maiden Castle, Dorset* (Rep. Res. Comm. Soc. Antiq. London).

WHORF, B.L. 1940: Science and Linguistics. *Technology Review* April 1940.

WILIAMS, A. 1946: Excavations at Langford Downs, Oxon. *Oxoniensia* 11, 44–64.

Animal Husbandry in Wessex and the Thames Valley

Annie Grant

The evidence

Published studies of animal-bone remains recovered during the excavation of British Iron Age sites date from as far back as the late nineteenth century, and include many from sites in central southern England as this area has in the past been the focus of a great deal of archaeological attention. However, when reviewing the available evidence for this area, it became clear that the information contained in all but a few of the studies was neither of the detail nor the quality to allow any real assessment of the man–animal relationships which animal bones studies should be designed to explore. This was partly a function of the small scale of many of the early excavations, partly because recovery-techniques were not rigorous enough, partly because of the absence of a rational and standardised method for animal-bone analysis and partly through a failure to realise the potential of animal-bone studies.

In the report by Boyd Dawkins and Jackson (1917) on the large and important collection of animal bones recovered from the Glastonbury lake village, the authors comment:

> 'Remains were so numerous that it is impossible to indicate the total number of individuals represented. Several hundredweights of bones were gone through . . . and a selection made of the more striking varieties in the different species.'

We are not told what makes a bone 'more striking'.

Watson (1932), who examined large numbers of bones recovered from excavations at Lydney Park in Gloucestershire, gave only a list of species found, mentioned two possible breeds of ox and concluded:

> 'The bones as a whole do not call for further comment.'

A preoccupation with the description and definition of breeds, to the exclusion of many of the other aspects of animal husbandry was current throughout the first part of this century. This was particularly unfortunate, for it was during this period that many key Iron Age sites, such as Little Woodbury (Bersu 1948) and All Cannings Cross (Cunnington 1923) were excavated. Wilfred Jackson reported on the faunal remains recovered from a large number of sites excavated during this period and his work undoubtedly stimulated interest in animal-bone studies. However, although his reports may give a great deal of information on bone measurements, even including inter-site comparisons, many do not give a clear indication of the relative proportions of species represented, information which we would consider to be essential today.

The small number of animal bones recovered from the vast majority of excavations was a result not only of the small scale of many of the excavations but also of a lack of widespread interest in the study of faunal remains.

This is illustrated in Fig. 7.1, which shows the numbers of identified fragments recovered, compiled from a survey of published animal-bone reports from all areas of Britain (excluding Ireland). At a very large number of sites, it was not even clear how many bones were recovered, and other detail was similarly lacking. At only a handful of sites were there large enough numbers of animal bones recovered for detailed analysis to be possible, and it is to these few sites that we must turn for a discussion of animal husbandry. The present writer makes no apology for frequent reference to a few sites: it should now be clear why this is unavoidable.

Comparisons of animal-bone evidence from sites excavated at different times and analysed by different workers will always be problematic. Varying standards of excavation and recovery, differential preservation, different levels of expertise in identification and methodological approach will produce results that will not be strictly comparable from site to site. The present writer is well aware of the problems and pitfalls involved in inter-site comparisons of animal-bone evidence: it is hoped that the reader will also consider these problems.

The sites

Fig. 7.2 gives the locations of the sites that form the basis of the following discussion. Details of the sites are given in Appendix A. All are settlement sites, but a range of settlement types is represented. Some are large hillforts (for example, Danebury and Balksbury), while others are small settlements or farmsteads (for example Ashville and Old Down Farm). Even within these broad groups there are differences; contrast for example the dense occupation at the hillfort at Danebury with the very sparse occupation at the hillfort at Balksbury. Discussion of settlement typology and distribution is included elsewhere in this volume (Cunliffe, Miles and Hingley).

Landscape and environment (discussed in detail by Robinson, this volume) are likely to have had a large influence on the nature of animal husbandry. The settlements are found in a range of environments, but two main environments can be defined. The first is the chalk downland, where sites such as Danebury, Old Down Farm, Meon Hill and Gussage are located, and the second is the valley gravel areas where, for example, Ashville, Farmoor and Odell are situated. The majority of the sites discussed are located within a fairly small area; those that lie outside the main concentration (for example, Odell, Gussage, Eldon's seat) are included because they have particular relevance for the following discussion.

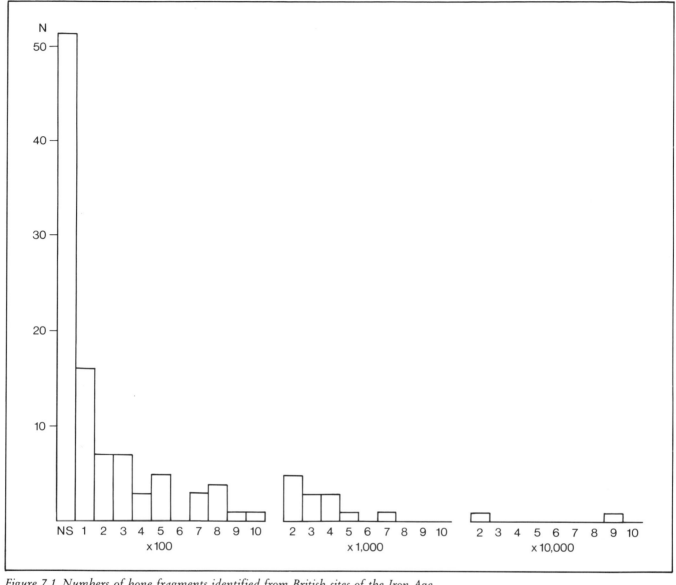

Figure 7.1 Numbers of bone fragments identified from British sites of the Iron Age.
N.S. Sites where the numbers of bones recovered was not specified.

Animal husbandry: general considerations

At all sites discussed in this paper, as at all but a few sites in the Iron Age, the majority of the bones found are those of cattle, sheep and pigs. If environmental conditions are affecting the nature of the animal husbandry, this may be reflected in the relative proportions of the main domestic species found at different sites. In Fig. 7.3, the relative percentages of cattle, sheep and pig bones are shown for the sites given in Fig.7.2 and listed in Appendix A. The sites have been divided into two groups on the basis of their height above sea-level, 250 feet (76 m) having been chosen as the dividing line. This clearly separates the main downland sites from the Thames Valley sites, but there are inevitably some that lie at around 250 ft where their allocation to one or other of the groups may seem to be arbitrary. At some sites, where distinct differences between the relative proportions of the species have been observed in different phases of occupation, these have been shown on the figure.

Broadly speaking, those sites that lie on the higher ground have higher percentages of sheep bones than those on the lower ground. If we consider the first group, we should not be surprised to discover that sheep husbandry was apparently the mainstay of the animal-based economy, with generally high percentages of sheep bones recovered. Historical evidence shows the traditional association between sheep and the chalk downland, which was only broken when, with the agricultural improvements in the eighteenth century and the wide availability of root crops for supplementary feeding, cattle could be kept on the downland in large numbers (Jones 1960). Without extensive supplementary feeding, much of the downland is unsuitable for large-scale cattle-rearing, as the grass is of relatively poor quality, and access to water is limited. For sheep, neither of these factors is a particular problem. The nutritional requirements of sheep are much lower than those of cattle, and sheep may obtain their required intake of water from the grass they eat, without direct access to

could cattle really be kept in Danebury?

103

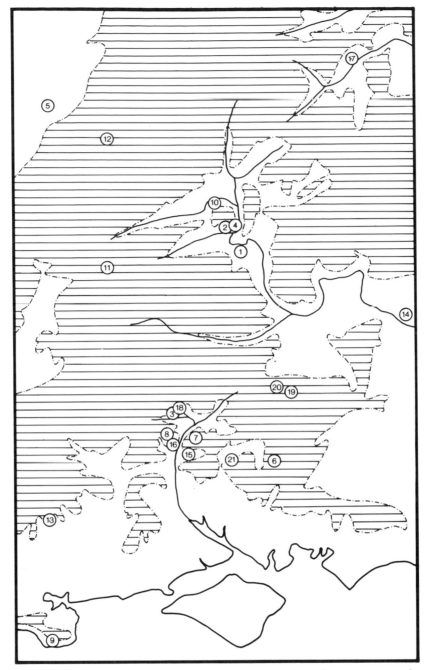

Figure 7.2 *The location of Iron Age sites in central southern Britain with evidence for animal husbandry. The numbers refer to the listing of the sites given in Appendix A.*

water-supplies. Cattle, on the other hand, have higher nutritional requirements and they need regular access to water. A heavy milking cow, such as a modern Friesian, may drink as much as 12 or 14 gallons of water per day, and although a small Iron Age cow could certainly survive on a great deal less than this, access to water must have been a major factor in cattle-rearing.

The lowland areas of the Thames Valley gravels provide a much more suitable environment for cattle-raising, with heavier soils providing lusher grass and plentiful water. This seems to be reflected in the generally higher percentages of cattle bones found on the lowland sites. These lower-lying areas may be considered far less suitable for the raising of sheep, as in

damp conditions sheep are more likely to contract foot-rot and liver-fluke than when they are kept on well-drained land. The identification of the remains of the gastropod that is the intermediate host for the liver fluke at Appleford (Robinson 1980, 94) is interesting in this context.

However, even though there is evidence for a greater emphasis on the keeping of sheep on downland sites and on the keeping of cattle on valley sites, it is clear that in all environments cattle, sheep and pigs were exploited. Even on downland sites such as Danebury, significant numbers of cattle and pig bones were found, and at none of the lowland sites was the percentage of sheep bones lower than 30%, and at some more than 50% of the

Could have been kept.

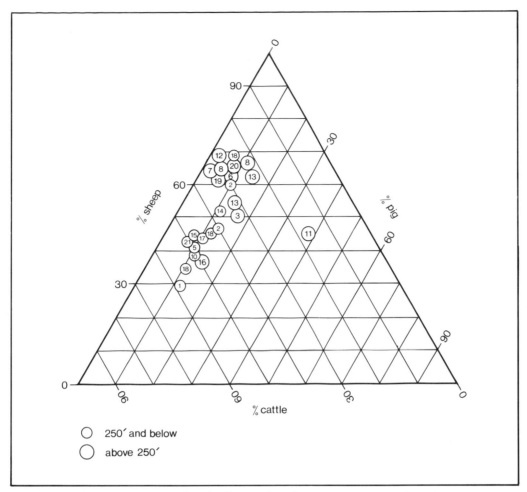

Figure 7.3 *Relative proportions of cattle, sheep and pig bones at sites in central southern Britain. For key see Appendix A.*

bones were from sheep. It is clear that the husbandry systems were fairly complex, suggesting perhaps the exploitation of a range of environments by the inhabitants of these settlements.

It should be pointed out that animal bones found during the excavation of habitation sites seem almost always to be the remains of meals eaten within or near to the habitation areas. The relative proportions of the bones from different species therefore suggest primarily the relative proportions of the animals consumed as meat. This may not be the same as the relative proportions of species kept in live herds. More detailed analysis of the bone material can be informative in this matter. If, for example, cattle were traded between communities as deadstock, specifically for consumption, one might expect to find in the bone debris a high proportion of the main meat-bearing bones at the consuming site, and a high proportion of 'waste' areas of the anatomy at the supplying site. However, at none of the sites discussed here, where such detailed analysis was available, was there any evidence for trade in deadstock.

Animals can, of course, be traded live, and then slaughtered, in which case bone from all parts of the body would be found; but one would not expect to find the bones of very young animals at sites where the inhabitants were not breeding the animals they exploited.

To examine the nature of the exploitation of the animals we must now turn to a more detailed look at the individual animal species.

The individual species considered

Sheep

Perhaps one of the most informative aspects of animal-bone analysis lies in the determination of the age at death of the animals. Analysis of this information suggests the nature of the animal exploitation more clearly that any other aspect of the animal-bone evidence. The age at death of animals whose remains are found in archaeological contexts can be deduced from the state of fusion of the long bones and from the eruption and wear of the teeth, the most useful evidence being provided by the eruption and wear of the mandibular teeth, particularly when different sites are to be compared (but see Grant 1978). Fig. 7.4 shows the sheep mandible wear stages (**MWS**) (Grant 1983) from five sites. Such information was not available for the other sites. Examination of the evidence presented in this figure suggests that although the vast majority of the animal bones recovered on all sites appear to be food refuse, many of the animals represented were not primarily raised to provide meat.

If a community were raising animals mainly for meat

105

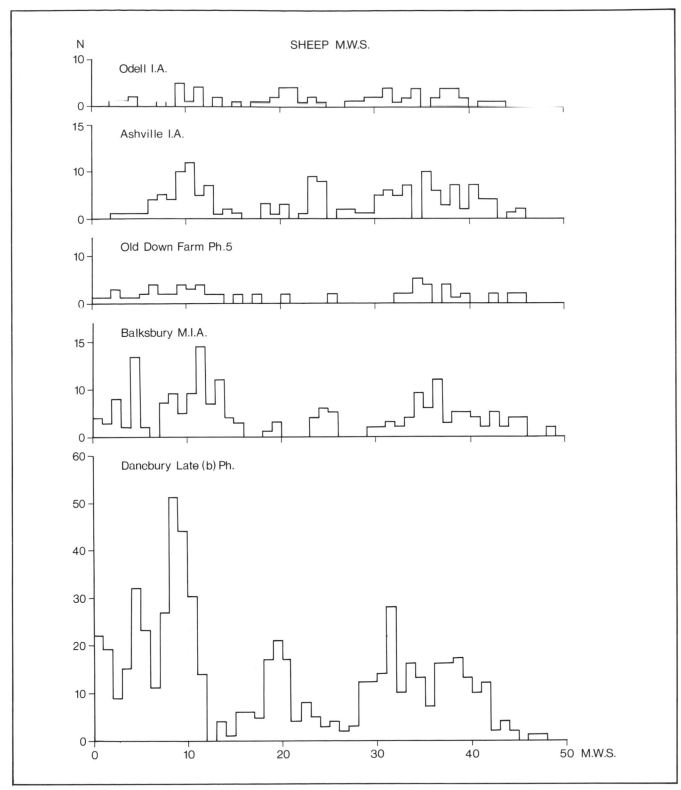

Figure 7.4 *Sheep mandible wear stage (MWS) distribution.*

production, one would expect a particular pattern of exploitation to be revealed by an analysis of age at death. One would expect a relatively large proportion of the animals to have been killed when they were around 18 months to three years of age, the aim of the animal-management being to balance expenditure — food consumed and time and effort expended — against the amount of meat produced. This model does not fit the evidence presented here. If we take the Danebury MWS distribution (although only the evidence for the latest phase of occupation is shown, this is typical of all phases of occupation at the site) we can see that approximately one third of the animals represented, died when they were mature (MWS 30+) and past the optimum age for meat production. At the other sites too, a relatively high proportion of the animals seem to have been mature at death. These mature animals may best be interpreted as mainly comprising ewes kept for breeding purposes and wethers and ewes kept for wool. A very small proportion of males would be needed for breeding. Finds of the artefacts associated with spinning and weaving — spindlewhorls and loomweights — support a view that wool may have been an important commodity at both the downland and the valley sites.

Only a relatively small proportion of the sheep appear to have been at an age for optimum meat production. The mandibles with MWS falling between 17 and 27 may represent animals killed for meat, but overall, at Danebury for example, only 17% of the mandibles fell within this group.

At Danebury, a particularly large proportion of the sheep seem to have been no more than about one year old at death (MWS 1–9) and a significant proportion of these were neonatal mortalities (MWS 1 and 2). The presence of the bones of so many very young animals suggests that lambing may have taken place within the hillfort. Pregnant and nursing ewes and their lambs are, if kept on open downland, easy prey for such predators as wolves and foxes. If the pregnant ewes were brought into the hillfort for lambing, the risk of loss of young animals, whether from predation or difficult unattended births, would have been reduced. Nonetheless, one would expect natural mortalities to have been high. Studies of feral Soay sheep in the Hebrides (Grubb 1974) show neonatal mortalities as high as 20 to 40% and medieval records too suggest high neonatal losses (Trow-Smith 1957). Even on a modern hill farm, neonatal loss may be as high as 20% (G. Davies, pers. comm.). Thus if lambing were taking place within the hillfort, a significant proportion of bone from neonatal animals would be expected.

There may of course have been some deliberate killing of young animals, although we may speculate that any deliberate killing can only have been of male animals. The prime object of any stable animal-management system, whether the livestock were required primarily for meat, wool, milk or any other product, must be at least to maintain the size of the flock. Since a ewe may be expected to have produced only four to five lambs in her lifetime, and since 50% of these are likely to have been male, in order to ensure that each ewe at least replaced herself it would seem unlikely that any healthy female lamb would be deliberately killed. Preliminary investigation of the sexual structure of the Danebury sheep suggests that the majority of the mature sheep were indeed female. Wilson (1978, 115) suggests an overall preponderance of female sheep at Ashville, Barton Court, Guiting Power and Appleford.

Any deliberate killing is thus likely to have been predominantly of male lambs. It seems possible that the milk produced by the mothers both of lambs that died of natural causes and of any that were deliberately killed may have been an important resource.

Mandibles of young animals were found at Balksbury and Old Down Farm, but were less common at Ashville and Odell. Comparisons are inevitably hampered by differing conditions of preservation which may account for the scarcity of the fragile small bones of young

animals at some sites. We cannot rule out differential preservation and indeed differential recovery as a factor in explaining the different age-structures seen at the chalk and gravel sites; but at both Ashville and Odell the bones seem to have been fairly well-preserved. The scarcity of the bones of young animals at these sites may then suggest that the inhabitants of the settlements in the river valleys were not as involved in sheep-breeding as those who lived on the downlands.

At all sites there is a peak in the MWS distribution at around 10+, which may represent animals little more than a year old, killed perhaps in the spring or possibly the autumn. These animals seem likely to have been predominantly male (and further research on the sexing of the bones may confirm this). They were presumably killed for meat; but if we assume that growth-rate was very much slower in these primitive sheep than in modern improved breeds, one-year-old sheep may still have been rather small. This perhaps indicates that a shortage of food led to meat animals being killed off before they had reached optimum size.

Although the idea of autumn killing has been criticised (Higgs and White 1963) as an interpretation of mortality patterns, the peaks in the MWS distribution, seen particularly at Danebury, suggest that mortality, whether natural or as a result of man's intervention, was not random. There may have been some deliberate culling of animals at particular times of the year. Thomas Tusser (Hartley 1931) a medieval writer on agricultural matters, advocated a strict regime of culling the weakest members of a flock at regular times of the year, including spring and autumn. We may speculate that the hillfort sites in particular may have served in some way as a centre for the gathering together of sheep, for lambing and for the culling of the weak. Males and castrates that had lost too much condition in the winter, and barren ewes and even lambs may have been eaten at such times. The rationalisation of the flocks may even have been followed by a redistribution of some animals to other settlements.

Cattle

The available evidence for the exploitation of cattle as revealed by analysis of the tooth wear is shown in Fig. 7.5. The MWS distribution for cattle shows perhaps even more clearly than for sheep a contrast between the upland chalk sites and the lowland gravel sites. At Danebury, the majority of the cattle seem to have either been very young (MWS 1 to 10) or mature (MWS 30+) with relatively few juvenile animals represented. Thus the cattle age-structure shown for this site is not consistent with the production of meat as the main aim of cattle husbandry. Many of the animals were kept until they were mature or even quite old. We may suggest that these animals may have been mainly cows and a few bulls kept for breeding and cows and oxen kept to provide traction, particularly for agricultural purposes. The pattern of mortality at Balksbury is broadly similar to that shown for Danebury, although the remains of very young animals were not found as quite such a large

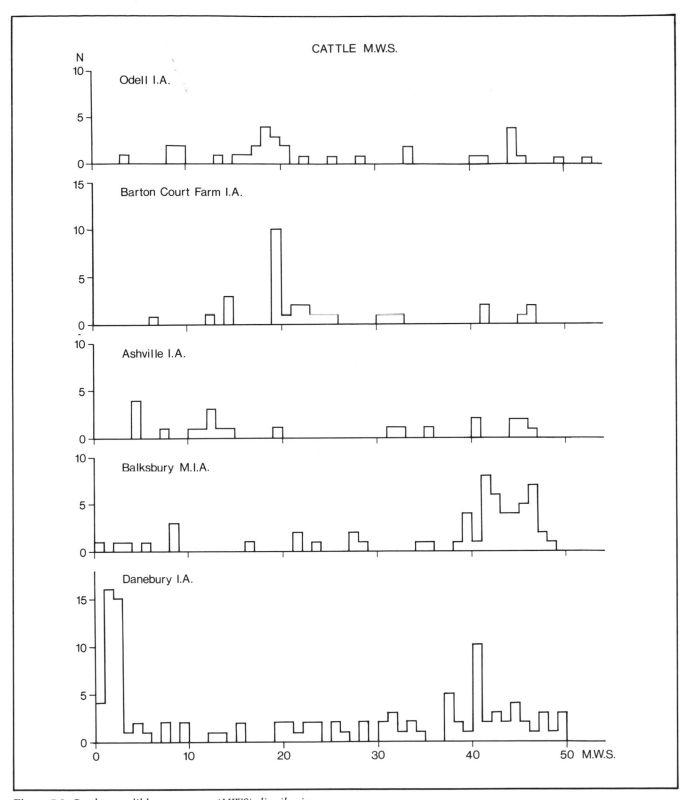

Figure 7.5 *Cattle mandible wear stage (MWS) distribution.*

proportion, and a slightly higher percentage of the mandibles came from animals that were fully mature at death. However, at the lowland settlement-sites of Ashville, Odell and Barton Court Farm, while the bones of very young animals were very rare, those of juvenile animals were far better represented than at either of the upland sites.

The high percentage of mandibles from very young calves found at Danebury suggests that calving, like

lambing, may have taken place within or close to the hillfort; but there is little evidence for calving having been a frequent occurrence at the lowland sites. For cattle kept on the chalk downlands, enclosed sites such as Danebury would not only have provided a protected environment for calving, but may also have been used for stalling animals during the winter months. Although small cows can survive on grass for much of the year, during the winter pregnant cows and even oxen and

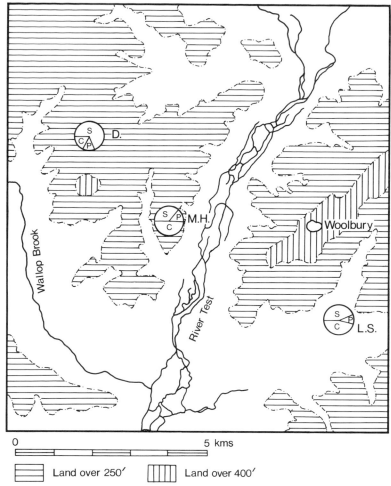

0   5 kms

▭ Land over 250′   ▥ Land over 400′

thus no middle aged cows at Danebury

Figure 7.6 *Relative proportion of domestic species at Danebury and sites in the Test Valley.*
D — Danebury; MH — Meon Hill; LS — Little Somborne. S — sheep; C — cattle; P — pig.

bulls would almost certainly have required supplementary feeding. This may have been provided by the waste products of agricultural activities or even by crops grown specifically for animal fodder and kept stored within the settlements. The exploitation of milk resources would have been facilitated if the cows were stalled or confined in some way in the spring months, although when assessing the possible importance of milk in the economy, it should be remembered that primitive cattle will generally not produce milk beyond the time when the calf is weaned. Milk would thus have only been available, from animals whose calves had died or were deliberately killed, for a relatively short season in the spring each year.

For those living in settlements in the river valleys, lush pasture may have been available for grazing by cattle in the spring and summer months; however, any river flooding in the autumn and winter may have necessitated the movement of cattle to higher ground. The particular seasonal advantages of settlements situated in different environments suggest the possibility of cooperative relationships existing between sites. We may further examine this possibility by looking in more detail at two areas. Fig. 7.6 gives the location of three sites in the Test Valley, and shows the relative percentages of cattle,

sheep and pig bones found at each. At Danebury, sited on a hilltop in the middle of the downland, cattle bones accounted for only a relatively small proportion of the animal-bone remains. Few of the bones were from juvenile animals and yet many of the bones were from very young calves. In the Test Valley itself evidence from two sites, Little Somborne and Meon Hill, suggests that rather higher percentages of cattle were kept at these sites than at Danebury.

Both Meon Hill and Little Somborne lie quite close to water; even though Meon Hill is actually situated on quite high ground (see Fig. 7.3), it is less than one kilometer from the Test, and the tributary of the Test probably ran even closer to Little Somborne in the Iron Age than it does at the present day. Both sites are thus in excellent positions for raising cattle. We may suggest that cattle bred at Danebury may have been fed during the warm months on the grasslands bordering the Test or its tributaries, and these cattle may have been tended by people living at settlements such as Meon Hill. The cattle-management system could have involved reverse transhumance or close ties between separate permanent communities living within the same area. If, as has been suggested, the cattle were not bred for meat but were more important for their role in agricultural activities, a cow or an ox would be little use to an agricultural community until it was old enough to be trained for pulling ploughs and carts, or old enough to bear calves. Medieval records (Trow-Smith 1957) suggest that a castrated male may be trained for drawing the plough when around two or three years of age, and cows should not be served until of a similar age. During the two or three years when a young cow was of little use to the community, it may have been more practical to keep them where there were sufficient natural resources to minimise the necessity for supplementary feeding, the lower-lying areas of the downlands being the obvious choice.

Deaths would have occurred of juvenile animals — both natural deaths and the deliberate culling of weak animals and of animals that were surplus to agricultural and breeding requirements. The presence of the bones of juvenile animals at the lowland sites would thus be expected. Unfortunately there were not sufficient numbers of bones recovered at either Meon Hill or Little Somborne for an analysis of the age-structure of the animal bones found at these sites to be undertaken; but we may speculate that the age-structure of the cattle found at these sites is likely to be more like that seen at Odell than that of Danebury.

This is not to suggest that Little Somborne, Meon Hill and other sites like them existed only to raise juvenile cattle. In fact the animal-bone evidence suggests that they kept all the main domestic animals, and the remains of older cattle were certainly present among the animal bones from these sites. They may have been partly or even largely self-sufficient but this would not have precluded a close relationship with other sites and a mutual cooperation in the raising of domestic animals. It is of course possible, however, that some sites were occupied only seasonally, but we have no evidence for this in the downland area. Historical evidence shows us that the typical chalkland parishes established before the Norman Conquest of Britain were long and narrow, encompassing a strip of land that ran from the valley bottom to the down pastures. The whole area was exploited as a single farming system, with cattle kept predominantly in the valleys, although occasionally grazed on the down — the 'cow down'. Sheep were folded in pens on the arable by day and turned onto the downs at night. Here the centre of the farming system was a village in the valley. In the Iron Age a group of interrelated settlements, perhaps controlled from a hilltop site, may have exploited a similar strip of land.

In the Thames valley area shown in Fig. 7.7 there is animal-bone evidence from four sites. None of these sites lies on the higher ground of the region, so we do not have a situation that is directly comparable to the chalkland area just considered. At Farmoor and Appleford, on the floodplain and the first gravel terrace, fairly high percentages of cattle bones were recovered, and their immediate environment is certainly more suitable for the raising of cattle than for the raising of sheep. At Farmoor, the occupation area included both the floodplain and the gravel terrace, and since the lower

farmsteads were subject to flooding from the river, the use of this area must have been seasonal. The farmsteads on higher ground were protected from flooding; but it is not clear when, and for how long, they were occupied. Botanical evidence suggests that the predominant economy was a pastoral one, and Lambrick and Robinson (1979, 134) conclude that 'these seasonal, self-contained units must have been established for the primary purpose of minding the grazing herds'. Unfortunately, the numbers of bones recovered at both Farmoor and Appleford were low, and we do not have a detailed age-distribution for these sites.

Ashville lies on slightly higher ground, and the proportion of cattle bones found here was rather lower than at the first gravel terrace sites. The situation of Asvhille is ideal for the exploitation of both the lusher soils of the valley and the better-drained areas of higher ground. This is shown in Fig. 7.8, which emphasises the contrast between the situations of Danebury and Ashville. There is a more limited range of environments within a short distance of Danebury, particularly in relation to access to water. The main excavation report for Barton Court Farm has not yet been published, but the distribution of the MWS for the cattle mandibles (Fig. 7.5) suggests that the cattle husbandry here may have been similar to that at Ashville.

If the animal husbandry were organised in the Thames Valley in a similar way to that suggested for the chalk downlands, one should expect to find sites on higher ground with higher percentages of sheep bones, and a larger proportion of the bones of young sheep and cattle, than are found at the sites on the lower ground. The suggestion of seasonal occupation at Farmoor presupposes the existence of more permanent sites on higher ground. However, there are no large hillforts in the area immediately to the north of the Thames Valley, and the different settlement-pattern in this area may reflect important differences in economic and social organisation.

Pigs

Pigs are adaptable animals, surviving and breeding in a wide range of environments. They are omnivorous, and can thus be fed on a wide range of foodstuffs. However, if they are not to compete with man for food, they ideally require access to forested or wooded areas for autumn and winter feeding. One would thus expect to find pig remains more commonly in areas where heavier soils were able to support woodland growth. From the evidence presented in Fig. 7.3 it would seem that in general slightly higher percentages of pig bones were found at sites in the lowland regions than at sites on the downlands, although the proportions of pig bones overall vary rather less than the proportions of sheep and cattle bones. Perhaps surprisingly, there were comparatively high percentages of pig bones found at Danebury in the early and middle phases of occupation. However, Cunliffe (1984) has shown that there are areas of heavy clay-with-flints on the downs near the site, and these may have supported woodland in the Iron Age.

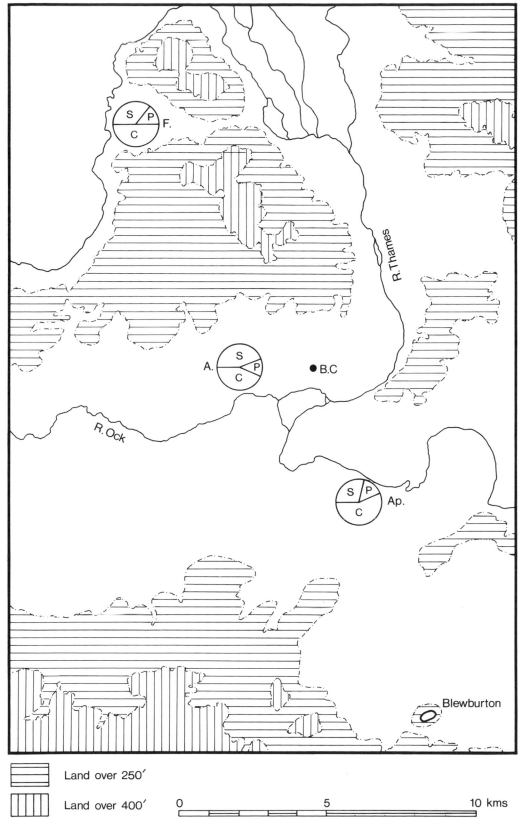

Figure 7.7 *Relative proportions of domestic animals at sites in the Upper Thames Valley.*
A — Ashville; Ap — Appleford; BC — Barton Court; F — Farmoor. S — sheep; C — cattle; P — pig.

At one site, a particularly large proportion of the bones recovered were pig bones. Between 30 and 40% of the bones found at Groundwell Farm were identified as pig bones. Coy, discussing this unusual situation noted that much of the bone from this site was in eroded condition. However, since pig bone is rather more prone to decay than that of sheep or cattle, taphonomic processes are likely to cause the under-representation rather than over-representation of pig bone. Coy also notes that most of the bone from this site was recovered

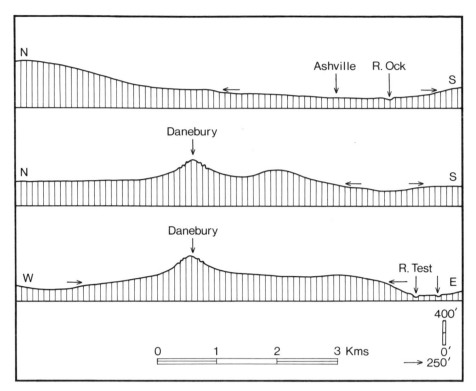

Figure 7.8 *The location of Danebury and Ashville.*

from the excavation of two houses, and not from pits and ditches which are the usual provenance of Iron Age bone remains. However, it is nonetheless possible that we have at this site an example of a community that chose to exploit a particular enviroment by an unusual concentration on pig-keeping.

Interpretation of the economic value of pigs is generally more straightforward than for cattle and sheep. The main value of a pig lies in its ability to transform a wide variety of normally inedible organic matter, including fruits such as acorns that are poisonous for most creatures, into first-class protein. As they are doing this, they produce manure of the highest quality. Thus any husbandry system for pigs is likely to have two main aims — to ensure that there are sufficient breeding animals to maintain the size of the herd at the required level, and to rear the rest of the pigs to an age when there is maximum yield of meat and fat for the minimum expenditure of food.

The only site where pig mandibles were recovered in sufficient numbers for an analysis of the age-structure to be made was Danebury; the pig MWS distribution for this site is shown in Fig. 7.9. In the large proportion of bones from young animals, the pig age-distribution is like that of the cattle and sheep, and suggests that pigs too were being bred at the site. In other respects, however, the pig age-distribution is in marked contrast to that of the other animals from this site. Many of the pigs were juveniles and suggest, as expected, animals kept and killed for consumption. A relatively small proportion of mature animals were represented, and we may suggest that these were mainly sows, killed at the end of their useful breeding life.

Pigs are much less easy to move around than either cattle or sheep, although they can be driven quite long distances if necessary. Pig-management would seem to be more likely to have been carried out on a local basis than to have involved any large-scale movement of animals, although they may have been driven into local woods for feeding at some times of the year. Even where pigs are kept for a great deal of the year in semi-wild conditions, they are likely to be confined at least for farrowing. If pig-rearing is undertaken by individual settlements, we may expect to find the bones of very young pigs at most sites. At Gussage, the epiphyseal fusion data suggest that a higher percentage of the bones of pigs were from very young animals than was the case for either sheep and cattle, and Maltby records finds of very young pig bones at Old Down Farm. However, there was rather less evidence for the presence of very young pig at Ashville. This is perhaps surprising and raises the possibility of poor survival of very young bone at this site.

The relatively small proportion of pig bones found at the majority of sites in this area is further evidence for the suggestion that meat production was by no means the only aim of the animal husbandry; but the fact that pigs were kept, and the evidence that almost all animals (whether young or old) were eventually eaten, show that meat was a significant component of the diet. It is interesting to compare these fairly typical southern British sites with some of the sites in continental Europe in the Iron Age, where frequently very much higher percentages of pig bones were found. Poulain (1958; 1971; 1973; 1974) showed pig bones to predominate at sites in the Moselle, Haute Saône, Haute Garonne and Charente. Pigs predominated in the domestic fauna from Vix (Joffoy 1960), and at Manching (Boessneck 1971)

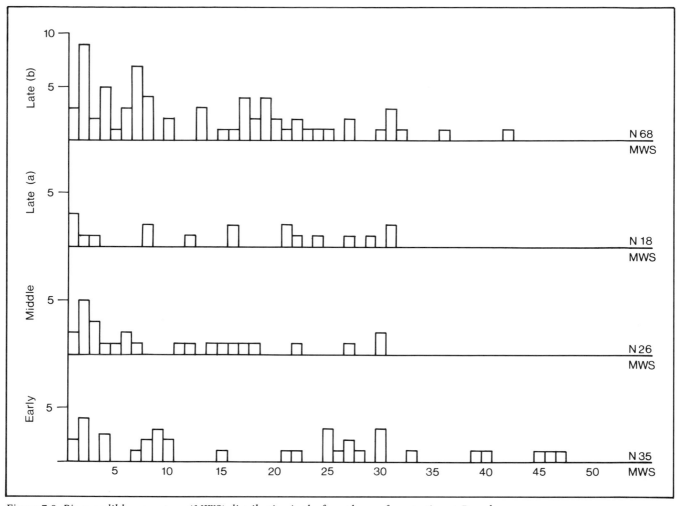

Figure 7.9 Pig mandible wear stage (MWS) distribution in the four phases of occupation at Danebury.

approximately 30% of the domestic animal bones were identified as pig bones. Clearly a detailed comparison between British and continental sites would be profitable. The higher percentages of pig bones and the larger numbers of bones from wild animals also found at many continental sites may suggest that meat was a more important part of the diet there.

Goats

Goats have not been mentioned so far in this discussion although, as is well known, there can be difficulty in separating the sheep from the goats. At least some of the bones identified as sheep bones may in fact have been from goats; however, the evidence is that in Britain generally at this period goats were kept in very small numbers. At Danebury, a very small number of goat bones were identified, and the proportion of goat remains may have decreased over the period of occupation. Wilson also assumes that goat was present in 'minimal quantities' at Ashville.

As several sites, the most common evidence for the presence of goats were finds of horn cores, many of which seemed to have been chopped from the skull. Goats may have been kept specifically to supply horn; or, where goat horn cores were found in disproportionate numbers, we may have evidence for trade with some communities specialising in the raising of these

animals. At one site, not within the area considered here, very large numbers of goat bones were found. Eighty % of the very large number of animal bones found at the Iron Age and Roman temple site at Uley (Ellison 1980) were identified as goat bones. These bones seem to be largely from sacrificial animals, but it is not yet clear, without the publication of the full bone analysis, whether or not the goats were being raised at the site.

Goats are animals that are, in fact, rather better adapted to rough mountainous country in temperate regions than to cold, wet English winters; and their temperament makes them less easy to keep in herds than sheep (Ryder 1981). Small numbers of goats may have been kept tethered, perhaps to supply milk. Since they can eat a wider range of foodstuffs than sheep, they may have been kept successfully this way, perhaps within or near to the settlement sites.

Horses

Horse bones have been found in the domestic refuse at all the sites discussed here, accounting for between 3 and 15% of the animal bones. They thus appear to have had some importance in the Iron Age. The most striking differences observed between the horse bone remains and the remains of all the animals so far discussed lies in the remarkable scarcity of the bones of very young horses, even on sites like Danebury, where the bones of very young animals were so common.

Harcourt was the first writer really to draw attention to this fact. In his analysis of the bone from Gussage, he suggested that horses were not bred but 'were rounded up periodically and selected animals caught and trained'. This theory is supported further by evidence from Danebury which shows that a high proportion of the horses are likely to have been male. It is perhaps important to note that in the latest phase of occupation at Danebury, there were among the horse bones a very small number of bones from young animals, suggesting that horse-breeding might have been beginning here in the late middle Iron Age.

Horses are likely to have been required to provide a few limited, but specialised, functions. Clear evidence of butchery-marks on horse bones has been reported at some sites (for example, Danbury and Ashville) although at Danebury at least, the incidence of butchery-marks was much lower on horse bones than on the similarly-sized bones of cattle. A higher proportion of the horse bones than of the cattle bones at both Danebury and Gussage were complete and unbroken.

Horses seem likely to have been kept mainly for riding and traction, although until the development of improved harnesses in the Saxon period it seems that horses would only have been able to pull light loads (Trow-Smith 1957). Cattle may have provided all the heavy traction needed for pulling ploughs and heavy carts. The only real advantage that a horse had over a cow at this period was its speed and ability to be trained and ridden. In many other respects a cow is a superior animal, and perhaps less costly to feed.

Horses seem to have enjoyed some sort of special status in man's eyes in many periods of history. This is demonstrated for the Iron Age by the craftsmanship and expertise expended in the production of chariot and harness fittings and bridle bits. Complete, apparently unbutchered horse skeletons are not uncommon finds on British Iron Age sites and may be further evidence of the special importance attached to horses (see Grant 1984).

Although, at most sites, horse bones were found in rather low proportions — figures of 3–6% are typical — at a few sites horse bones were rather more common. Relatively high percentages of horse bones could be a reflection of the status of a site, as the keeping of animals that were of severely limited economic value and relatively costly to feed might seem a luxury. In the downland area, the highest percentages of horse bones were found at Old Down Farm, Winall Down, Gussage and Chilbolton Down and not at the large hillfort sites such as Danebury. In the Thames Valley, there were fairly high proportions of horse bones at Appleford and Farmoor. It would therefore seem unwise to equate high percentage of horse bones with high status.

Dogs

Dog bones were found at almost all the sites discussed and are generally assumed to have been kept as guard dogs, sheep dogs and perhaps hunting dogs (but see below). Butchery marks are recorded on the bones of dogs from several sites, but they are relatively rare, and, like horse bones, dog bones are frequently found complete and unbutchered. Dog bones are also found as complete skeletons, and there is the possibility that dogs, like horses, may have had some special status. It is of course possible that a distaste for dog meat meant that these animals were only used as food in exceptional circumstances.

Although at Danebury no neonatal dog bones have been found, young, juvenile and adult animals were represented. At Ashville the complete skeleton of a puppy of around five months was found, and the other dog remains included bones of very young puppies. There is thus no evidence to suggest that dogs were not breeding on these sites, although the extent of human intervention need not have been great.

Percentages of dog bones at most sites ranged from 1 to 4%, but at Little Somborne and in some phases of occupation at Old Down Farm, rather higher percentages of the bones were from dogs. At Old Down Farm the relatively large number of dog bones from Phase 3 included five fairly complete dog skeletons.

One of the problems of small-scale excavations is that the relative proportions of species can be distorted if in the area chosen for excavation there happened to be a particular concentration of the bones of a species that was otherwise not well-represented at the site. The problems arising from small sample sizes will always hamper inter-site comparisons, particularly when comparisons are made between the proportions of the generally less well-represented animals.

Keeping a relatively small number of dogs on an occupation site may not have provided any very serious feeding problems. The dogs themselves may have provided much of their own food by scavenging. Many of the animal bones found on these settlement-sites had clearly been gnawed by dogs, and dog coprolites found at Danebury included a large amount of tiny bone fragments.

Birds

Bird bones have been found at many of the sites, but because of their small size inter-site comparisons of the relative proportions of the bones of bird species are not possible. Many of the bird bones found are those of wild species, and their presence in archaeological deposits may not always be due to any deliberate exploitation of wild birds by man. However, bones of domestic birds — fowl, geese and ducks — have also been found, suggesting at some settlements the keeping of these birds. There is some evidence to suggest that the keeping of domestic fowl was a relatively late phenomenon in the Iron Age. At Danebury and at Ashville, Coy (1984) and Bramwell (1978) have identified fowl bones only in the late Iron Age occupation-material. At Gussage, fowl bones were dated to the second and third phases of occupation.

The significance of these bird remains is not clear. Rivet (1964) quotes Caesar's belief that the Britons kept chicken and geese for amusement but regarded their consumption as tabu. We do not have to assume that Caesar's information was correct for all Britons, and it is possible that the economic significance of fowl as suppliers of eggs, meat and even feathers was being exploited by the late Iron Age. Butchery-marks on the bones of birds are very rare, but they have been recorded (Coy 1984) and suggest that bird meat may indeed have been eaten at least occasionally.

Wild animals

The bones of wild animal species are very rare on the majority of Iron Age sites in Britain. Occasional bones from red and roe deer are found, and the presence of small numbers of bones from other wild species such as fox, badger and the smaller mice and voles has been recorded. It seems clear that, even though the animal husbandry in this area of Britain does not seem to have concentrated on meat production, sufficient meat must have been available to supply the needs of the communities without the necessity to supplement the diet by hunting for food. The relationship between hunting and farming is discussed in more detail elsewhere (Grant 1981).

Animal husbandry and agriculture

It is rightly or wrongly becoming accepted that growing of cereals and other foodstuffs was more important in supplying the food needs of the Iron Age population than the rearing of animals for meat. The evidence to support this viewpoint lies not only in the strong suggestion that meat production was not the focus of the animal husbandry, but also in anthropological studies of modern, so-called 'primitive' peoples, many of whom eat a mainly vegetable diet. Eating vegetable products makes sound economic sense since at every successive level in the food chain there is a considerable loss of energy.

Clearly it is not possible to evaluate the precise relative contributions of meat and vegetable matter — this can only be a subject for speculation. However, whatever the importance of meat, the efficiency of the agricultural system must have been vitally linked to the animal husbandry. Cultivation of the same area of land for more than a few years will lead to a considerable loss of fertility unless the essential nutrients for plant growth are returned to the soil. Many of the settlements discussed here were occupied, apparently continuously, for hundreds of years. The obvious solution to the problem of soil depletion is to use animal manure. Manure from stalled animals can be carted out to the fields, and animals put to graze on the stubble will, while utilising food that is of no other value to humans, manure the soil for the next crop.

A mixed farming and animal-husbandry system has enormous advantages, making it possible to maximise the use of all available resources. For example, surplus milk (or at least the by-products of cheese and butter-making) can be fed to pigs, and the waste products of

cereal cultivation can be used as animal fodder.

Animals may have played a more active role in the agricultural system too. Cattle are almost certain to have been used to pull ploughs and carts, and even pigs may have some practical value. If a pig is turned out onto a stubble field that has already been grazed by cattle and sheep, it will turn over the soil so effectively in its search for roots that the ground may be used for crop growing with little further preparation.

Change through time

The discussion so far has to some extent assumed that all sites were contemporary and occupied throughout the Iron Age. In fact, of course, this is not true. In Appendix A the approximate dates for the Iron Age occupation for each site are given, and the same information is shown graphically for some of the main sites in Fig. 7.10. At some sites there is a long period of occupation throughout most of the Iron Age and even into the Roman period, but at others the occupation ceases in the Iron Age or is discontinuous.

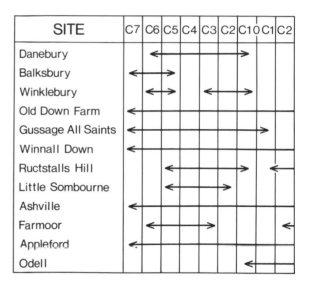

SITE	C7	C6	C5	C4	C3	C2	C10	C1	C2
Danebury		←				→			
Balksbury	←	→							
Winklebury		←	→		←	→			
Old Down Farm	←								
Gussage All Saints	←						→		
Winnall Down	←								
Ructstalls Hill				←		→		←	
Little Sombourne				←		→			
Ashville	←								
Farmoor			←		→				←
Appleford	←								
Odell								←	

Figure 7.10 *Occupation of selected sites.* (C = century).

Clearly the long occupation by man of the same area will have an effect on the local environment. The problems associated with continuous cultivation have already been mentioned as one example; the keeping of animals may also have a direct environmental impact. Grazing animals can in fact improve grassland areas (Goudie 1981). The vigour and growth of some plants may be increased by grazing — this is comparable to the regular mowing of a lawn. However, if an area is overgrazed, considerable damage may be done by animals. Trampling in dry conditions leads to soil erosion and in wet conditions turns grassland into a mud bath. Pigs, by eating nuts and acorns and rooting up young seedlings, may, unless carefully controlled, have a detrimental effect on the regeneration of woodland.

From the admittedly small amount of evidence available, there seem to be two main trends in the animal husbandry in this area, which may be at least partly related to changing environmental conditions. At the downland sites, the changes seem to be towards a greater emphasis on sheep rearing, relative to both cattle and pig keeping. Increased proportions of sheep bones and reduced proportions of cattle and pig bones have been reported in the later phases of Iron Age occupation at Winnall Down, Old Down Farm and Danebury. At Gussage, there was a slight increase in the proportion of sheep bones in the second phase of occupation, and a decrease in the proportion of pigs in the third phase. An increased emphasis on sheep may reflect a general impoverishment of the soil in the region through over-exploitation, which made cattle, with their higher nutritional requirements, more difficult to keep. The reduction in the proportion of pig bones at these downland sites may well reflect a reduction in the amount of woodland, which may have been due not only to exploitation for animal food but also to the heavy demands made on woodlands as a source of raw material for building.

In contrast, in the lowland areas, the evidence for economic change seems to point to an increased emphasis on cattle rearing. At Ashville, in the latest phases of Iron Age occupation, an increased proportion of cattle bones were found. At Odell, whose earliest Iron Age phase is broadly contemporary with the latest Iron Age phase at Ashville, the relatively high percentage of cattle bones that characterised the husbandry from the outset was increased over the period of Roman occupation. At both these sites there is also evidence for a decline in pig keeping.

The admittedly small amount of evidence that we have suggests that the differences between the two areas were increased over time, with the downland concentrating more on sheep rearing and the valleys on cattle rearing. These changes may well be related to environmental factors but may also reflect changing social patterns and inter-site relationships.

The situation does not, however, seem to be simply one of increased specialisation. It may be that sites that were in the most restricted environments and had the most specialised economies were those that were least able to survive environmental and social pressures. If one compares sites that have a long and continuous occupation which lasts into the Roman period with those that have shorter or discontinuous occupation, there is some suggestion that those settlements in the most restricted environments were those where the occupation did not continue as long. Occupation at the hilltop sites of Danebury and Winklebury had ceased by the end of the first century BC and Balksbury was only occupied in the early Iron Age. We have already discussed the fact that occupation at Farmoor, in the very restricted environment of a floodplain, may have been seasonal and shortlived. Ashville, Old Down Farm and Gussage, which were all better sited to exploit a wider range of environments, had a rather longer period of occupation, which at Ashville and Old Down Farm continued well into the Roman period (but see Jones p.

121). Some sites that are also, in these terms, well sited do not, however, have a long period of occupation — Little Somborne is one example.

Looking at Danebury in more detail, we have here some evidence that, by the latest phases of occupation, the fairly stable economy that seems to have supported the settlement for a considerable period was beginning to show signs of stress. This is seen in an increased incidence of diseases that may have been caused by overgrazing and in a possible increase in the absolute numbers of animals kept, which again may have resulted in overgrazing. Although a smaller proportion of pigs were kept in the later phases of occupation, they were killed off at slightly younger ages than in the earlier periods (Fig. 7.9). This may suggest that there was less food to feed them than there had been previously, and that there was also less meat available for human consumption. Because Danebury was situated where it was, it may have been less able than some of the other sites to adapt to environmental and social change. Any population increase may have particularly pressured the settlement. We may speculate that environmental pressures and population pressures, perhaps together with the breakdown of the social relationships that had enabled the site to exploit the more distant valley resources led to its ultimate abandonment in the first century BC (see Cunliffe, this volume).

It has not been possible or appropriate to discuss all the complexities of animal husbandry. Many of its aspects have not even been mentioned — for example — the size and the form of the animals themselves and the important animal secondary products of hides, hair, sinew, fat and bone. Although the possible ritual importance of animals in the Iron Age is perhaps not strictly speaking part of the animal husbandry, any special significance attached to animals may well have influenced the management of animals and their uses. There is evidence from several sites, notably Danebury and Ashville, that some of the animal bone found at these sites may be interpreted as ritual deposits and not food refuse. However, this aspect of man's animal relationships has been discussed elsewhere (Grant 1984a, 1984b) and will not further be mentioned here.

Conclusions

A general picture of the animal husbandry of central southern Britain has been offered which suggests that the raising of sheep was of prime importance, particularly on the chalk downlands. Cattle were also raised on the downlands, but these animals seem to have been more important at sites on the heavier soils of the valleys. Sheep may have been especially prized for their wool and the cattle may have been used extensively in agriculture, but both sheep and cattle were eaten and must have made significant contributions to the diet. Pigs, kept primarily for consumption, were raised in relatively small numbers, but in all areas.

A range of animal products will have been utilised, not the least important being manure, which was vital to an efficient agricultural system. Other animal by-products such as milk, skins, hides, horns, sinews, fat and bones are likely to have been utilised even though their use leaves little trace in the archaeological record.

It has been suggested that the animal-husbandry system may not have been simply one where each individual settlement looked after its own animals from birth to death. It is clear that at no site do we have evidence for intensive specialisation in any single aspect of animal husbandry: at all sites the resources of the community seem to have been directed to a range of farming activities. However, there are signs of smaller-scale specialisations that allow speculation about the nature of the relationships that existed between settlements of different types and in different locations.

Some sites, and Danebury is the obvious example, may have been centres for animal-breeding and others such as Ashville and Odell may have been particularly involved in the raising of juvenile cattle. Each site may thus have taken advantage of its own particular environmental position. Movements of animals and of animal products may have taken place within small local territories, as for example between Danebury and the smaller sites between the Test and the Bourne.

It is also possible that wider-scale movements of animals and animal products may have occurred, perhaps between settlements in very different environments. Each area may have had an animal-husbandry system that satisfied the majority of its own needs, but which produced some surpluses which could be traded to communities in different regions.

This paper does not attempt to offer the final word on animal husbandry in this area of Britain. Many of the ideas and interpretations put forward are, and with the small amount of evidence available have to be, speculative. Other interpretations of the evidence that exists are possible. It is, however, hoped that the paper will stimulate discussion, argument and perhaps most importantly, the better integration of the many different facets of archaeology. As more sites are excavated and the quality of the analysis of excavated material improves, some of the hypotheses put forward here may be tested on a much more extensive body of evidence.

Appendix A

Site, phase		Reference	Date	C	S	P	H	D	N
			BC	%	%	%	%	%	
1	Appleford	Wilson 1980b		49	25	11	13	2	403
2	Ashville 1	Wilson 1978		33	51	10	4	1	472
	2			29	58	9	4	1	1259
	3			41	48	5	5	1	700
3	Balksbury	Harcourt 1969 Maltby 1981 *2	C7–C6	24	35	12	12	18	17 *1
4	Barton Ct. Farm	Hamilton 1978 *3							
5	Beckford	Gilmore 1974	LIA	31	27	6	36		432
6	Bramdean	Clutton-Brock 1982 *4	LIA	26	58	8	7	1	678
7	Chilbolton	Maltby p.c.		27	54	4	15	1	423
8	Danebury E	Grant 1984a	C6–C5	24	58	16	1	1	11446
	M		C5–C4	17	58	18	4	2	6774
	La		C4–C3	17	59	14	4	6	7779
	Lb		C3–C1	21	66	8	3	2	26522
9	Eldon's seat	Philipson 1968	C5–C3	29	62	6	3	1	491
10	Farmoor	Wilson 1979		40	31	9	16	3	220
11	Groundwell Farm	Coy 1982 *5	C5–C3	15	45	37	3	1	2269
12	Guiting Power	Wilson 1980a	C3–C1	27	66	2	5	1	288
13	Gussage 1	Harcourt 1979	C8–C5	29	48	14	9	?	96 *6
	All 2		C5–C2	21	60	14	5	?	131 *6
	Saints 3		C1–C1A	27	54	11	8	?	207 *6
14	Heathrow	Sutton 1978	C6–C4	32	47	12	9		34 *7
15	Little Somborne	Locker 1981	C5–C2	34	35	6	6	16	736
16	Meon Hill	*8		44	33	12	10		228
17	Odell	Grant 1984c	C1–C1A	41	39	10	6	3	2867
18	Old Down 3	Maltby 1981	C7	24	27	7	13	28	1250
	Farm 4	*9	C6–C4	48	31	10	8	2	513
	5		C3–C1	20	53	4	13	9	1965
	6		C1–C1A	34	50	8	6	2	448
19	Rucstalls Hill	Gregory 1979	C5–C1	30	60	6	3	1	779
20	Winklebury	Jones 1977	C6–C1	24	57	8	6	5	3171
21	Winall Down	Maltby 1981 *10	C7–C3	44	37	8	11		1576

Abbreviations
C — cattle; S — sheep; P — pig; H — horse; D — dog; N — number of fragments identified. C — century; A — A.D.; LIA — Late Iron Age; E — early; M — middle; L — late.

Notes

* 1. The proportions of species used in Figure 7.4 and in this table are those given by Harcourt. The age distributions given in Figures 7.5 and 7.6 are from Maltby 1981. These bones are from a later, as yet unpublished excavation at the same site.
* 2. N and all percentages based on a MNI and not a fragment count. Goat MNI figures have not been included.
* 3. Age information only. Full site report not yet published.
* 4. The figures for cattle, pigs and dogs exclude finds of skeletons. Some material from this excavation known to have been mislaid before analysis.
* 5. Bone fragments from two Iron Age houses only — numbers of eroded bone from general Iron Age features not given.
* 6. see * 2.
* 7. see * 2.
* 8. Percentages based on a re-examination by the present writer of the bone material from this site.
* 9. The high percentage of dog bones recorded for Phase 3 incudes five dog skeletons.
* 10. Figures given for phase 3 of this site only. Main report not yet published.

The figures given in this appendix are mostly based on what the individual authors have described as fragment counts. Different authors have different ways of counting fragments (c.f. Grant 1983 and Wilson 1978) and some do not record what they have counted. Thus percentages of species from sites where the bones have been analysed by different authors are not strictly comparable. Where MNI counts have been used, comparisons are even more problematic. For a fuller discussion of the problems of determining the relative proportions of species represented and intersite comparison see Grant, (1975 and 1983) and Maltby (1981).

References

BERSU, G. 1940: Excavations at Little Woodbury, Wiltshire, part I. *Proc. Prehist. Soc.* 6, 30–111.

BOESSNECK, J., VON DEN DRIESCH, A., MEYER-LEMPPENAU, V. and WECHSLER VON OHLEN, E. 1971: Die Tierknochenfunde aus dem Oppidum von Manching. *Die Ausgrabunger in Manching 6* (Wiesbaden).

BOYD DAWKINS, W. and JACKSON, W. 1917: Animal bones. In Bulleid, A. and Gray, H.St.G., *The Glastonbury Lake Village 2* (Glastonbury Antiquarian Society).

BRAMWELL, D. 1978: The bird bones. In Parrington, M., *The excavation of an Iron Age settlement, Bronze Age ring-ditches and Roman features at Ashville Trading Estate, Abingdon (Oxfordshire) 1974–76* (London, CBA Res.Rep. 28), 133.

CLUTTON-BROCK, J. 1982: Animal Bones. In Perry, B.T., Excavations at Bramdean, 1973–77. *Proc. Hants. Field Club and Archaeol. Soc.* 38, microfiche.

COY, J. 1982: The animal bones. In Gingell, G., The excavation of an Iron Age enclosure at Groundwell Farm. *Wilts. Archaeol. Mag.* 76, 68–73.

COY, J. 1984: The bird bones. In Cunliffe 1984.

CUNLIFFE, B.W. 1984: *Danebury, an Iron Age hillfort in Hampshire* (London, CBA Res. Rep. 52).

CUNNINGTON, M.E. 1923: *The early Iron Age inhabited site at All Cannings Cross Farm, Wiltshire* (Devizes).

ELLISON, A. 1980: Natives, Romans and Christians on West Hill, Uley: an interim report on the excavation of a ritual complex of the first millennium AD. In Rodwell, W., *Temples, churches and religion: recent research in Roman Britain* (Oxford, BAR 77), 305–320.

GILMORE, F. 1974: Animal remains. In Oswald, A., Excavations at Beckford. *Trans. Worcs. Archaeol. Soc.* 3, 18–28.

GOUDIE, A. 1981: *The human impact* (Oxford).

GRANT, A. 1975: The animal bones. In Cunliffe, B.W., *Excavations at Portchester Castle. Volume I; Roman* (London, Society of Antiquaries), 378–408.

GRANT, A. 1978: Variation in dental attrition in mammals and its relevance to age estimation. In Brothwell, D.R., Thomas, K.D. and Clutton-Brock, J. (editors), *Research problems in zooarchaeology* (London, Institute of Archaeology Occasional Paper), 103–106.

GRANT, A. 1981: The significance of deer remains at occupation sites of the Iron Age to the Anglo-Saxon Period. In Jones, M. and Dimbleby, G. (editors), *The environment of man: the Iron Age to the Anglo-Saxon period* (Oxford, BAR 87), 205–213.

GRANT, A. 1983: The use of tooth wear as a guide to the age of domestic ungulates. In Wilson, B., Grigson, C. and Payne, S. (editors), *Ageing and sexing animal bones from archaeological sites* (Oxford, BAR 109), 91–108.

GRANT, A. 1984a: The animal husbandry. In Cunliffe 1984.

GRANT, A. 1984b: Survival or Sacrifice: a critical appraisal of animal burials in Britain in the Iron Age. In Clutton-Brock, J. and Grigson, C. (editors), *Animals and Archaeology* 4 (Oxford, BAR).

GRANT, A. 1984c: The animal bones. In Dix, B., Excavations at Harrold Pit, Odell, Bedfordshire 1974–1978. *Bedfordshire Archaeological Journal* 17.

GREGORY, I. 1979: Animal bones. In Oliver, M. and Applin, B., Excavation of an Iron Age and Romano-British Settlement at Ructstalls Hill, Basingstoke, Hampshire, 1972–5. *Proc. Hants. Field Club and Archaeol. Soc.* 35, 82–86.

GRUBB, P. 1974: Population dynamics of the Soay sheep. In Boyd, J.M. and Jewell, P. (editors), *Island survivors: the ecology of the Soay sheep at St. Kilda* (London), 242–272.

HAMILTON, J. 1978: A comparison of the age structure at mortality of some Iron Age and Romano-British sheep and cattle populations. In Parrington, M., *The excavation of an Iron Age settlement, Bronze Age ring-ditches and Roman features at Ashville Trading Estate, Abingdon (Oxfordshire) 1974–76* (London, CBA Res. Rep. 28), 126–133.

HARCOURT, R. 1969: The animal remains from Balksbury Camp. In Wainwright, G., The excavation of Balksbury Camp, Andover, Hampshire. *Proc. Hant. Field Club and Archaeol. Soc.* 26, 21–55.

HARCOURT, R. 1979: The animal bones. In Wainwright, G., *Gussage All Saints. An Iron Age settlement in Dorset* (London, Department of the Environment Archaeological Reports, 10), 150–160.

HARTLEY, D. 1931 (editor): *Thomas Tusser: His Good Points of Husbandry* (London, Country Life).

HIGGS, E. and WHITE, P. 1963: Autumn killing. *Antiquity* 37, 282–9.

JACKSON, W. 1935: Report on animal remains found at Meon Hill. In Liddell, D., Report of excavations at Meon Hill, second season, 1935. *Proc. Hant. Field Club and Archaeol. Soc.* 13, 39–42.

JOFFROY, R. 1960: *L'Oppidum de Vix et la civilization hallstattienne* (Paris).

JONES, E.C. 1960: Eighteenth-century changes in Hampshire chalkland farming. *Agricultural Hist. Rev.* 8, 5–19.

JONES, R. 1977: Animal bones. In Smith, K., The excavation of Winklebury Camp, Basingstoke, Hants. *Proc. Prehist. Soc.* 43, 58–69.

LAMBRICK, G. and ROBINSON, M. 1974: *Iron Age and Roman riverside settlements at Farmoor, Oxford* (London, CBA Res. Res. 32).

LOCKER, A. 1981: Animal bones. In Neal, D.S., Bronze Age, Iron Age and Roman settlement sites at Little Somborne and Ashley, Hampshire. *Proc. Hants. Field Club and Archaeol. Soc.* 36, 122–4.

MALTBY, J.M. 1981a: Animal bone. In Davies, S.M., Excavations at Old Down Farm, Andover. *Proc. Hants. Field Club and Archaeol. Soc.* 37, 81–163.

MALTBY, M. 1981b: Iron Age, Romano-British and Anglo-Saxon animal husbandry — a review of the faunal evidence. In Jones, M. and Dimbleby, G., *The environment of man: the Iron Age to the Anglo-Saxon period* (Oxford, BAR 87), 155–203.

PHILIPSON, D.W. 1968: The animal bones. In Cunliffe, B.W. and Philipson, D.W., Excavations at Eldon's Seat, Encombe, Dorset. *Proc. Prehist. Soc.* 34, 266–9.

POULAIN, T. 1958: Faune du puits de Vielle Toulouse. In Fouet, G., Puits Funeraires d'Aquitaine: Vielle Toulouse, Montmaurin. *Gallia* 16, 154–57.

POULAIN, T. 1971: Etude de la faune. In Burnez, C., Le site Gauloise de la Croix des Sables a Mainxe (Charente). *Bulletin de la Societe Prehistorique Francaise* 68, 469–71.

POULAIN, T. 1973: La faune. In Morin, Y. and D., Sondage au camp protohistorique de Cita. *Revue Archaeologique de l'Est* 24, 285–287.

POULAIN, T. 1974: La faune du site de Koenigsmacher (Moselle). *Revue Archaeologique de l'Est* 2, 186–00.

RIVET, A.L.F. 1964: *Town and country in Roman Britain* (London).

ROBINSON, M. 1980: Roman waterlogged plant and invertebrate evidence. In Hinchliffe, J. and Thomas, R., Archaeological Investiagtions at Appleford. *Oxoniensia* 45, 90–106.

RYDER, M.L. 1981: Livestock. In Piggott, S. (editor), *The agrarian history of England and Wales, Volume I.I: Prehistory* (Cambridge), 301–408.

SUTTON, M. 1978: The bone evidence. In Canham, R., Excavations at London (Heathrow) airport. *Trans. London and Middlesex Archaeol. Soc.* 29, 38–43.

TROW-SMITH, R. 1957: *A history of British livestock husbandry to 1700* (London).

WATSON, D.M. 1932: Bones. In Wheeler, R.E.M. and Wheeler, T.V., *Report on the excavation of the prehistoric site at Lydney Park, Gloucester* (London, Society of Antiquaries Research Report), 131.

WILSON, B. 1978: The animal bones. In Parrington, M., *The excavation of an Iron Age settlement, Bronze Age ring-ditches and Roman features at Ashville Trading Estate, Abingdon, Oxfordshire, 1974–6* (London, CBA Res. Rep. 28), 110–137.

WILSON, B. 1979: The vertebrates. In Lambrick, G. and Robinson, M., *Iron Age and Roman riverside settlements at Farmoor, Oxfordshire* (London, CBA Res. Rep. 32), 128–133.

WILSON, B. 1980a: The bone report. In Saville, A., *Excavations at Guiting Power Iron Age site, Gloucestershire 1974* (CRAAGS Occasional Paper 7), 142–4.

WILSON, B. 1980b: Bone and shell report. In Hinchliffe, J. and Thomas, R., Archaeological investigations at Appleford. *Oxoniensia* 45, 84–89.

Postscript

An apicultural Postscript: the Honey Bee in the Iron Age
by Mark Robinson

The discovery of the head of a worker honey bee (*Apis mellifera* L.) preserved in peat at the bottom of an Iron Age sump at Mingies Ditch, Hardwick, Oxon., on the floodplain of the lower Windrush (Robinson, unpublished) raises the interesting possibility that apiculture was practised in Southern England during the Iron Age. A radiocarbon date of 220 ± 90 bc was obtained on waterlogged wood from the primary silting of the enclosure ditch-system to which the sump was related. At present, this single specimen represents the earliest and the only Iron Age find of honey-bee remains, although fragments of two individuals were recovered from a 1st century AD Roman context at Caldecotte, Milton Keynes (Robinson, unpublished).

Limbrey (1982, 285) believes that it is probable that the honey bee had become a natural member of the British insect fauna at least by 6000 bc, with the spread of the small-leaved lime (*Tilia cordata*), and possibly earlier. Northover (this volume), however, points out that there is only evidence for lost wax casting of bronze in Britain from about 300 bc onwards, whereas this innovation occurred much earlier in continental Europe. If the honey bee did not arrive in Britain until the Iron Age, this would imply the introduction of skeps of bees. Unlike most flying insects, colonisation cannot be achieved by a single fertilized female carried a long distance on the wind. By this date, the English Channel would have been too wide for bees to cross by swarming (Limbrey 1982, 281).

Bee-keeping was well known in the Mediterranean region throughout the classical period (Crane 1975, Ransome 1937, 75–90) but the presence of a single honey bee need not imply that the Iron Age occupants of the settlement at Mingies Ditch kept bees. It shows that the various products of honey bees — propolis (a resinous adhesive), honey and beeswax — were available

locally during the later Iron Age. They are all sufficiently valuable commodities as certainly to have been exploited. Apiculture of the sort where bees are kept in hollow log or woven skep hives and individual colonies are asphyxiated with smoke when their products are to be extracted seems plausible for Iron Age Britain. It required an ability to catch swarms, but otherwise the hives only need to be protected against the weather and damage by animals. At the end of each summer, some hives would be harvested while other colonies would be left for the next season to swarm or to increase in size. The Romans, however, had hives that could be opened so that comb could be cut away without the destruction of the colony (Varro III, xvi) and it is possible that this more advanced method of apiculture occurred in Iron Age Britain. Occurring either alongside or instead of beekeeping would have been the exploitation of wild colonies nesting, for example, in hollow trees. There is documentary evidence that in medieval England wild honey was a valued resource and the right to exploit bee trees in a wood, like the hunting rights, was sometimes separate from the tenure of the land (Ransome 1937, 197–8).

The honey bee can now take its place in considerations of the Iron Age eocnomy. The evidence from bronze-casting might hint at a deliberate introduction and therefore at beekeeping, but unless identifiable hive remains are discovered, apiculture must stay a hypothetical aspect of Iron Age animal husbandry in England.

References

CRANE, E. 1975: *Honey, a comprehensive survey* (London).

LIMBREY, S. 1982: The honeybee and woodland resources. In Bell, M. and Limbrey, S. (editors), *Archaeological aspects of woodland ecology* (Oxford, British Archaeological Reports S146), 279–286.

RANSOME, H.M. 1937: *The sacred bee in ancient times and folklore* (London).

VARRO, M.T. 1967: *On agriculture* (translated), Hooper, W.D. and Ash, H.B. (London).

Regional Patterns in Crop production

Martin Jones

Introduction

As the techniques of environmental archaeology diversify, so our perception of the agrarian base of early societies gains clarity. We are ever less dependent on the passing remarks of ancient historians and geographers such as Tacitus and Strabo, and ever more able to examine the actual soils cultivated, and harvests taken by the prehistoric farmer. A series of papers published in 1981 assembled the evidence derived from pollen, macro-fossils and sediments relating to crop production in later prehistory (Jones and Dimbleby 1981). At the time that volume was published, the regional coverage of each form of evidence was extremely patchy. Iron Age crop-records were virtually nonexistent north of the Severn-Wash line. The contrasting bias of pollen records away from the south and east was as true for the Iron Age as for any other period. The kind of integrated study of waterlogged Iron Age farmsteads described by Robinson (1981) was virtually unique in Britain as a whole.

By focussing its attention on a particular region, central southern Britain, this volume finds itself in direct confrontation with the spatial patchiness of the database. There have however, been some improvements: Paul Watson's (1982) analysis of pollen-bearing deposits, sought out from within the predominantly alkaline environment of central southern Britain, have gone a long way to compensate for the regional biases in pollen evidence. The southerly bias of crop records has also been alleviated by the work of Murphy, Hillman, and Van der Veen. Nevertheless an attempt to examine regional patterns in the crop production of Iron Age Britain is still hampered by the paucity and regional discontinuity of the data-base. Any inferences on this matter must be preceded by a clear appraisal of the state of the evidence.

The Data-Base

A wide range of evidence, environmental, artefactual and structural, may be brought to bear on the study of Iron Age crop-production, and evidence of the general environment and of settlement structure are dealt with in some detail in other papers in this volume. In addition to these aspects, our understanding of crop-production has rested on the direct evidence of agricultural implements, and of the crops cultivated.

Rees (1979) has conducted the most recent survey of agricultural implements in Britain, and readers are referred to that publication for a most useful gazeteer and catalogue. The wooden parts of Iron Age ards have been recovered from a few sites in Scotland, Wales and Ireland, but none from central southern Britain, though a wooden share of Donnerupland type ard has been recovered from a third- century AD context at Abingdon, Oxon (Fowler 1978). In this part of Britain, the evidence comes from the iron parts of agricultural implements, in particular reaping-sickles and the small iron cappings with which some wooden shares were tipped. The former are widely distributed, but the latter have a distinctly southern distribution in Britain. While it is difficult to assess the importance of metal implements relative to wooden implements in crop-production as a whole, the first millennium BC is clearly a period which sees a far greater adoption of metal in the techniques of crop-production than the previous millennium. No share-tips of bronze are known, and while a large number of sickles exist, doubt has been cast on the agricultural function of many of them. Rees (1979) comments that many were too flimsy to have been practical for hard everyday use as reaping-hooks. The vertically socketed bronze sickles, which Rees considers are most likely to have functioned as reaping-hooks, do not appear until the late Bronze Age.

Cultivation traces in pre-Roman Britain as a whole reflect the use of ards and manual implements on easily tractable soils (Fowler and Evans 1967; Rees 1979). In addition a number of poorly-dated traces suggest changes in practice predating Roman levels. Ard traces have appeared below Roman levels on heavy clay soil in Avon (Everton and Fowler 1978) and at various places along Hadrian's Wall (Julian Bennett pers. comm.). Uniaxial cultivation-traces have appeared beneath the Roman fort at Rudchester (Rees 1979), at Iron Age levels at Mount Farm, Dorchester-on-Thames (Lambrick forthcoming), and beneath Roman roads at Stratton Park, Hants., and Stane Street, Surrey (Fasham and Hanworth 1978). However, the last two examples may have more to do with the plough as a constructional implement than as a cultivation tool, and as such, they may be Roman in date.

Each survey that has been conducted on the remains of Iron Age crops has focussed on preservation by carbonisation. Thus, while the important survey of early crops in southern Britain conducted by Helbaek (1952) places a greater reliance on impressions in pottery for the prehistoric period as a whole, for the Iron Age only 42 individual impressions are listed in contrast to eleven fairly plentiful assemblages of carbonised material. Since this publication, the widespread use of flotation techniques has suggested that the carbonised remains of cereal grain, weeds, and chaff were as customary a part of the archaeological debris of at least the Iron Age and Roman periods as were pottery and animal bones (Jones 1978).

Carbonised remains have therefore continued to constitute the central focus of discussions of crop-production. However, it should be remembered that carbonised material is almost invariably biased towards certain crops, in particular the cereal crops. While we may reasonably assume that cereals were the principal crops of Iron Age Britain, the importance of complementing this picture with evidence of ancilliary economic plants from the rare contemporary waterlogged deposits must be remembered.

A number of surveys relevant to Iron Age central southern Britain have been conducted since Helbaek's classic work. Peter Murphy's M. Phil Thesis covers the Hampshire chalklands from circa 800 BC to 400 AD and includes evidence from a number of recently-excavated farmsteads (Murphy 1977). Green (1981) has drawn together Iron Age, Roman and Saxon evidence from Wessex. In the same volume Jones (1981) attempts a synthesis of evidence of crop-husbandry from the Iron Age to the Anglo-Saxon period for Britain as a whole. Readers are referred to this paper for a gazeteer and catalogue of crop records.

The data-base outlined above cannot be defined simply in terms of findspots of either artefacts or ecofacts. The findspots vary considerably in terms of the associated contextual information. On the one hand, we may have an iron sickle or grain impression that is unprovenanced, on the other we may have a variety of evidence collected from well-excavated sites where much is known about settlement-structures and the contemporary environment. While the latter category constitutes a small minority, it will dominate any discussion of crop-production purely on the basis of the quality of information produced. It should therefore be borne in mind that, regardless of the number of 'findspots', our ideas of Iron Age agriculture are based on a rather small number of individual sites against the background of a much larger body of data that is less well-understood. The Iron Age sites in central southern Britain from which both carbonised seeds and animal bones have been systematically collected and analysed in detail alongside other forms of environmental analysis include, in the Upper Thames Valley, the sites at the Ashville Trading Estate (Parrington 1978), Barton Court Farm (Miles in press), Farmoor (Lambrick and Robinson 1979), Mount Farm (Lambrick forthcoming) and Hardwick (Robinson and Allen forthcoming). In Wessex they include Micheldever Wood and Winnal Down (Fasham 1983; Monk and Fasham 1980), Old Down Farm (Davies 1981), Portway and Owselbury (Murphy 1977), Gussage All Saints (Wainwright 1979) and the hillfort at Danebury (Cunliffe 1984).

Drawing on these and all other sources of data, it is possible to discern various themes which seem to characterise crop-production in the period under study. These themes are expanded in the following sections.

Diversification

On the basis of data available to him in 1952, Helbaek observed that the Iron Age in Britain was marked by an increase in the number of crop species encountered in the archaeological record, and in general terms this observation seems to hold true. Thus a 'traditional' combination is of 6-row barley (*Hordeum* spp.) spelt (*T. spelta*), bread wheat (*T. aestivum/compactum*), beans (*Vicia faba*), and possibly oats (*Avena* spp.) and rye (*Secale cereale*). I have argued elsewhere that each of the crop species involved in this increase is suited to adverse conditions in one form or another, (Jones 1981). The trend may reflect the attempts of individual farmers to expand the area of soils under cultivation in the face of declining fertility and worsening climate.

This may be illustrated by Iron Age evidence from the Ashville site at Abingdon. This is located on an island of second-terrace river-gravels approximately 29 ha. in extent. Beyond this area to the north lies a ridge of Corallian limestone, to the west an expanse of Kimmeridge clay, and to the south the damp lowlying floodplain and lower gravel terrace along the river Ock. Bearing in mind what is known of contemporary agricultural method, a minimal arable strategy would confine cultivation to the second gravel terrace, and an intermediate strategy might take in the Corallian limestone to the north. By contrast, the wide range of weed seeds recovered suggested that each of the land units cited above was at least in part brought under cultivation, from the earliest phase of the Iron Age.

It may be possible to draw a similar inference from the evidence of Micheldever Wood in Hampshire. The site is located at the edge of a deposit of clay-with-flints overlying upper chalk (Monk and Fasham 1980: site R27). Adopting a minimal arable strategy from this position, it would certainly be possible to avoid soils that were sufficiently poor to bear the acidophile *Chrysanthemum segetum* whose seeds were recovered from Iron Age levels, again suggesting that even the poorer soils around the site were cultivated.

In a similar vein, it is hardly surprising that the weeds of damp ground that are commonly found in the Upper Thames Valley assemblages are far less common in the assemblages from Danebury, situated as it is within an expanse of free-draining chalkland. However, the mere presence of such a plant as *Eleocharis palustris* among the weeds at this site would again suggest that poorer soils were brought into cultivation from the early Iron Age.

As mentioned above, this extension of cultivation onto less favourable land may be associated with the decreasing fertility of the traditional soils, a point reflected in the behaviour of leguminous weeds at the Ashville site. An increase through time of these weeds has been related to decreasing levels of soil nitrogen, in other words to a progressive decline in soil-nutrient status. It is interesting to note that such an increase has been observed on other sites in central southern Britain. In the Upper Thames Valley the nearby site of Mount Farm, and in Wessex Gussage All Saints and Winnall Down each show a numerical increase in leguminous weeds (Lambrick forthcoming; Evans and Jones 1979; Monk and Fasham 1980). While the published section of the Old Down Farm report excludes detailed figures, Green (in Davies 1981) comments on 'the great quantity of small *Vicia* species' in the richest late Iron Age deposit on the site. Such a pattern, if extensive, could reflect a widespread ecological stress related to the diversification of crops and an extension onto less favourable soils.

The expansion of the data-base since Helbaek's first observation of this diversification has raised a number of other points. First, the phenomenon is not confined to Britain. The extensive body of data from Germany and the Low Countries collated by Körber-Grohe (1981) reveals a similar pattern. Any explanation of this diversification must therefore be applicable on a larger scale than that of Britain alone.

Secondly, the actual timing of this diversification is not clearcut. Indeed changing ideas on pottery chronology have undermined Helbaek's 'early Iron Age' category. The phase of Maiden Castle from which spelt wheat, rye, and the two cultivated oats *Avena sativa* and *A. strigosa* were recorded could now be placed anywhere between the eighth and fifth centuries BC on ceramic grounds. In addition a series of new records of the crops in question is associated with pre-Iron age dates. An important assemblage from Black Patch in East Sussex includes spelt wheat and Celtic bean in association with ninth century bc radiocarbon dates. This complements the less reliable record of spelt wheat from Godmanchester, Cambridge, in association with a radiocarbon date of 930 ± 80 bc (H.J.M. Green, unpublished typescript). Small *Vicia faba* seeds of the Celtic bean type are now recorded from as early as the late Neolithic as a single pottery impression from Glamorgan (Hillman pers. comm.). An assemblage of such beans in the carbonised state has been recovered from the Bronze Age settlement on Holne Moor, Dartmoor, associated with radiocarbon dates of c. 1200 bc (Jones forthcoming), and late Bronze Age records have been made in the Isle of Wight (Scaife, pers. comm.). The apparent hiatus between the early Neolithic and Iron Age occurrences of bread wheat has largely disappeared, and various late Neolithic and middle Bronze Age records are now known from the Upper Thames Valley. The cultivated oat, *Avena sativa*, has been recovered from late Bronze Age/Iron Age transitional levels at Cowdery's Down near Basingstoke (Millet and Green pers. comm.). This evidence is less consistent with a wholesale Iron Age introduction than with a general adoption some time in the first half of the first millennium BC of a range of crops, some of which had been individually utilised for some time in particular parts of Britain in response to particular agricultural conditions.

There is also some broad variation between the Upper Thames Valley and Wessex. In the former the more traditional crops, emmer wheat and naked barley, go into a marked decline, the latter disappearing entirely, whereas in Wessex they retain a significant presence. The two areas vary in terms of their emphasis on new crops, with a greater presence of bread wheat but lesser occurrence of the legume crops and Brassicas in the Upper Thames Valley than in Wessex.

This diversification in field crops contrasts with the changing occurrence of other possible food plants. In those pre-Iron Age assemblages that exist, the remains of field crops are usualy accompanied by other plant resources. Thus, hazelnut fragments and wild apple pips may be found in substantial numbers in Neolithic assemblages, (Jones 1980; Murphy 1982) and edible grass tubers may be found in Neolithic and Bronze Age assemblages (Godwin 1975; Jones 1978; van der Veen forthcoming). This is in contrast to Iron Age assemblages, in which such remains are infrequent. Indeed the whole character of these carbonised assemblages differs from earlier assemblages. It would seem that during the first half of the first millennium BC, the typical scatter of carbonised seeds of wild and cultivated food plants is replaced by larger concentrations of grains, chaff and a wide range of arable weeds which appear with monotonous regularity and consistency throughout Iron Age debris.

We may be seeing a change of behaviour as much as a change in the plants actually used. It is tentively suggested that the earlier assemblages are more consistent with the waste from small-scale subsistence use, and that the later assemblages are more consistent with spillage from larger-scale agricultural production and distribution.

Specialisation and Interdependence

While the first half of the first millennium BC has been identified as a period in which the arable use of soils diversifies, there are certain signs of specialisation as the Iron Age progresses. In Wessex, Green (1981) has observed that, during this period, individual sites come to contain a smaller range of crops. In the Upper Thames Valley, Robinson's environmental studies of Iron Age settlements point to the marked degree of variation in farming-strategy between co-existing sites over a very short distance (Robinson 1981; 1983; this volume). A necessary corollary of specialisation is interdependence; it is not possible to examine one without an understanding of the operation of the other.

Straightforward lists of crops present may illuminate some aspects of agricultural specialisation, but they cannot demonstrate interdependence between sites. If a series of sites is linked in terms of the production, distribution and consumption of a particular crop, one would expect to recover remains of that crop on each type of site. In order to determine the nature of the linkage between sites, it is not sufficient to detect the crops involved; the activities to which those crops were subjected must be identified. This entails a detailed analysis of the waste secondary products, weeds and chaff, as well as of the grain. Hillman (1981) has derived a useful framework for such analysis from ethnographic parallels, and I have attempted to apply the general approach to Iron Age sites in the Upper Thames Valley, and to the hillfort at Danebury, (Jones 1984a and b). In the Upper Thames Valley a distinction may be drawn between sites on the free-draining second gravel terrace, such as the Ashville site and Mount Farm, in which carbonised assemblages are relatively rich in cereal grain, and sites on the first terrace and floodplain such as Claydon Pike and Hardwick, in which the sparse carbonised assemblages are dominated by weeds and chaff. In the light of the qualitative composition of these assemblages, the general layout of each site, and Robinson's environmental analysis of the area, this difference may be explained in terms of the difference between waste generated during the initial processes and the final consumption of cereals. The hillfort at Danebury produced a very diverse series of carbonised assemblages, varying greatly from context to context in composition and quantity, and including weeds reflecting a wide range of ecological conditions. These variations could be accommodated by a model in which crops were brought to the hillfort from throughout its 'territory' and communally processed and stored.

The activities indicated above of production, consumption and communal processing of crops do not provide a model for the whole of central southern Britain, but they do give some idea of the scale of interdependance between sites, and the folly of treating such sites as self-contained subsistence units. In order to understand the nature and development of Iron Age agriculture it is vital to view Iron Age farmers in the context of their community, as well as of their environment.

This theme of specialisation may be developed by looking at a single crop species, bread wheat (*Triticum aestivocompactum*), whose frequency in assemblages from central southern Britain was beginning to grow in the Iron Age.

The increasing frequency of bread wheat (Triticum aestivocompactum)

In the historical period, bread wheat has become the single most important species in terms of kilocalories of food consumed by the human race. It was in existence in the Near East by the sixth millennium BC (Kislev 1981) and subsequently became a common, if minor, component of crop assemblages in prehistoric Europe. However, with the exception of an assemblage from Vlaaringen in the Netherlands dated to 2350 bc (Van Zeist 1970) and an assemblage from Forchheim, southern Germany of the Hallstatt A period (Schultz 1917), it is not until the late Iron Age and Roman periods that crop assemblages are found in northern Europe that are dominated by large numbers of bread wheat grains.

In many parts of Britain, the increased use of bread wheat may be reasonably associated with the contemporary expansion of agricultural settlement into clay areas, and the deep ploughing of these soils, and both of these trends may be seen within the Iron Age and Roman periods (Jones 1981). Indeed the original extension of cultivation onto these soils may be seen as part of the general diversification of soil-types used for agriculture which has been outlined above. The actual occurrence of bread wheat in British assemblages appears to increase at a relatively late stage in this process, and in most places not until the Roman, or even the post-Roman period. However, the earliest assemblages in which bread wheat is the major component are of late Iron Age date.

At the multi-period site of Bierton in Buckinghamshire, bread wheat is the most abundant component of the carbonised assemblages in every phase, from the site's late Iron Age inception through into the Roman and mediaeval phases (Jones forthcoming b). The Iron Age origins of a settlement that continued in use into the historical and modern period is thus paralleled by the contemporary origins and similar persistence of a system of agriculture in which bread wheat cultivation was a major component.

Bread wheat also formed a substantial part of the late Iron Age crop remains from Barton Court Farm in Oxfordshire (Miles in press). This enclosed farmstead also continued in use, at least into the late Roman period, by which time it was recognisable as a villa. Barton Court Farm is situated 3 km to the east of the Ashville site discussed above, and an interesting comparison may be drawn between the two settlements. Although a trace of bread wheat was found in the early and middle Iron Age phases of the Ashville site, none was found in late Iron Age or Roman levels. In contrast to the novel and successful format of the nearby enclosed farmstead, the Ashville site may well have been going into decline in the late Iron Age and Roman periods, and have ceased to exist by the fourth century. The depletion of soil-nitrogen suggested by the leguminous weeds continued, and the occurrence of a Donnerupland-type ard share in the latest levels on the site, by then a very traditional form of tillage equipment, may reflect the conservative nature of agriculture on this declining site.

This fragmentary picture of the origins of modern bread-wheat-based agriculture does indicate something of the complexity of the adoption of new agricultural methods. Settlements within an hour's walking distance of one another are responding to the new possibilities in different ways. It is these patterns within and between regions that may give some indication of how the changes took place. This is considered in the following, final, section.

Regional Patterns in Crop Production

The above discussion has drawn attention to patterns within the data at two levels. On the one hand, the different fates of two nearby sites in the Upper Thames Valley reflect diversity at a local level. On the other hand, it has been implied that the general trends that may be seen in Iron Age crop production have an overall consistency applicable not only to central southern Britain, or even Britain, but to northern Europe as a whole. In other words there seems to be a consistent direction of change in the long term, but the details of that change vary from place to place, leading to a mosaic of agricultural practices at any one time.

The consistent direction of change may be summarised in two stages; an increase in the scale of arable production, involving a diversification of soils under cultivation and field crops in use, followed by a specialisation in particular crops that become the major crops in the historical period. For central southern Britain attention has been drawn in this later context to the growing use of bread wheat. Other parts of northern Europe saw a more or less contemporary growth in the use of rye and oats (cf. Körber-Grohne 1981).

The first stage may, in general terms, be associated with the first half of the first millennium BC, though the spread of dates within this period, discussed above, underlines the very variable response to the potential of adopting new crops. While many farmsteads continued with traditional methods into the Roman period, the origins of the second stage may be found in certain sites that were newly established in the late Iron Age.

Both in the Upper Thames Valley and in Wessex, the diversity of response to these trends between nearby farming settlements may be observed, and for western Europe as a whole the adoption of new crops may be seen to have a substantial chronological spread.

There are various ways in which such patterns of adoption may be examined. Diffusionists may separate individual farms along a continuum between 'early adopters' and 'laggards' (cf. Grigg 1982): but such an approach is more descriptive than explanatory.

It may be interesting to compare these Iron Age data with data reflecting regional patterns in more recent periods of agricultural change. In an influential contribution on agrarian development in Europe in the historical period, Brenner (1976) lays great stress on regional variations in the adoption of capital-intensive farming methods in the late medieval and early modern periods. This regional patterning, in particular the differences between northern France and England and between east and west Europe, is taken to demonstrate the insufficiency of demographic pressure alone to explain these agricultural changes, and the importance of social factors that may introduce variation at both the regional and local level.

An analogy may be drawn with the study by Griffen (1979) of the twentieth century 'Green Revolution', in which newly-bred cultivars were made available to Third World countries. Here, too, Griffen observed that the response of Third World farmers to the new crops has varied from place to place, and from farmstead to farmstead. Dealing with a 'living' data-base, he was also able to observe that this varied response has depended on such things as access to land, capital, water and technical knowledge, which in turn have depended on literacy, social status, and political influence at the local levels.

Griffen has been able to observe these social factors directly. Brenner has speculated on the social factors responsible for regional patterning in his data-base and has related it to agrarian class structure, but his speculations have been the subject of much comment and criticism (numerous replies are published in subsequent volumes of *Past and Present*). The grounds for such speculation in prehistory are even more shaky, but it is interesting to note that the two newly-established late Iron Age farmsteads that have been described as innovative, Bierton and Barton Court Farm, have produced imported bronze objects and coinage. It may be that Iron Age farmsteads can yield material evidence of the kinds of social distinction observed by Griffen among modern farmers.

The points raised in this final section deal less with the evidence so far collected than with the possible direction that future work could take. It has been suggested that a general outline exists for the Iron Age crop record for northern Europe, and that central southern Britain has constituted a significant part of that data-base. It is now the time to explore, within this outline, the diversity of strategies adopted by contemporary farming groups, and to relate that diversity to the material evidence for the social context of those groups. This entails not only a continuation of the scale of comprehensive environmental analysis on the model of the sites discussed, but also an integrated approach to the study of biological and artefactual remains within those excavated farmsteads.

References

BRENNER, R. 1976: Agrarian class structure and economic development. *Past and Present* 70, 30–74.

CUNLIFFE, B.W. 1984: *Danebury: an Iron Age Hillfort in Hampshire* (London, CBA Res. Rep.).

DAVIES, S.M. 1981: Excavations at Old Down Farm, Andover, Part II: Prehistoric and Roman. *Proc. Hants. Field Club and Archaeol. Soc.* 37, 81–163.

EVANS, A. and JONES, M. 1979: The plant remains. In Wainwright, G. (editor), *Gussage All Saints: An Iron Age Settlement in Dorset* (London, HMSO), 172–175.

EVERTON, A. and FOWLER, P.J. 1978: Pre-Roman and marks at Lodge Farm, Falfield, Avon: a method of analysis. In Bowen, H.C. and Fowler, P.J. (editors), *Early Land Allotment* (Oxford, BAR 48), 179–185.

FASHAM, P.J. 1983: Fieldwork in and around Micheldever Wood, Hampshire, 1973–80. *Proc. Hants. Field Club and Archaeol. Soc.* 39, 5–45.

FASHAM, P.J. and HANWORTH, R. 1978: Plough-marks, Roman Roads and Motorways. In Bowen, H.C. and Fowler, P.J. (editors), *Early Land Allotment* (Oxford, BAR 48), 175–177.

FOWLER, P.J. 1978: The Abingdon ard-share. In Parrington, M., *The excavation of an Iron Age settlement, Bronze Age ring-ditches and Roman features at Ashville Trading Estate, Abingdon (Oxfordshire) 1974–76* (London, CBA Res. Rep. 28), 83–88.

FOWLER, P.J. and EVANS, J.G. 1967: Plough-marks, lynchets and early fields. *Antiquity* 41, 289–301.

GODWIN, H. 1975: *History of the British Flora* (Cambridge), 2nd edition.

GREEN, F.G. 1981a: Iron Age, Roman and Saxon Crops: The archaeological and evidence from Wessex. In Jones, M. and Dimbleby, G. (editors), *The environment of man: The Iron Age to the Anglo-Saxon period* (Oxford, BAR 87), 129–153.

GRIFFEN, K. 1979: *The political economy of agrarian change* (London), 2nd edition.

GRIGG, D. 1982: *The dynamics of agricultural change* (London).

HELBAEK, H. 1952: Early crops in Southern Britain. *Proc. Prehist. Soc.* 18, 194–233.

HILLMAN, G. 1981: Reconstructing crop husbandry practices from charred remains of crops. In Mercer, R.J. (editor), *Farming practice in British Prehistory* (Edinburgh), 123–162.

JONES, M. 1978: The plant remains. In Parrington, M., *The excavation of an Iron Age settlement, Bronze Age ring-ditches and Roman features at Ashville Trading Estate, Abingdon (Oxfordshire) 1974–79* (London, CBA Res. Rep. 28), 83–88.

JONES, M. 1980: Carbonised cereals from Grooved-Ware Contexts. *Proc. Prehist. Soc.* 46.

JONES, M. 1981: The development of crop husbandry. In Jones, M. and Dimbleby, G. (editors), *The environment of man: the Iron Age to the Anglo-Saxon period* (Oxford, BAR 87), 95–127.

JONES, M. 1984a: Archaeobotany beyond subsistence reconstruction. In Barker, G. and Gamble, C. (editors), *Beyond Domestication: Subsistence archaeology and social complexity in prehistoric Europe* (London).

JONES, M. 1984b: The plant remains. In Cunliffe, B.W. *Danebury: an Iron Age Hillfort in Hampshire* (London, CBA Res. Rep.).

JONES, M. forthcoming a: The Plant remains. In Fleming, A. (editor), *Excavations on Holme Moor, Dartmoor.*

JONES, M. forthcoming b: The plant remains. In Allen, D., Excavations at Bierton, *Records of Buckinghamshire.*

JONES, M. and DIMBLEBY, G. (editors) 1981: *The environment of man: the Iron Age to the Anglo-Saxon period* (Oxford, BAR 87).

KISLEV, M. 1981: The history and evolution of naked wheats. *Zeitschrift fur Archaologie* 15, 57–64.

KÖRBER-GROHNE, U. 1981: Pflanzliche abdrucke in eisenzeitlicher Keramic-Spiegelbild damaliger Nutzpflauze? *Fundberichte aus Baden-Wurttemburg* 6, 165–211.

LAMBRICK, G. forthcoming: *Excavations at Mount Farm, Berinsfield, Oxon 1977–78.*

LAMBRICK, G. and ROBINSON, M. 1979: *Iron Age and Roman riverside settlements at Farmoor, Oxfordshire* (London, CBA Res. Rep.).

MILES, D. (editor) in press: *Archaeology at Barton Court Farm, Radley, Oxon* (London, CBA Res. Rep.).

MONK, M.A. and FASHAM, P.J. 1980: Carbonised plant remains from two Iron Age sites in Central Hampshire. *Proc. Prehist. Soc.* 46, 321–344.

MURPHY, P.L. 1977: *Early agriculture and environment on the Hampshire Chalklands, circa 800 B.C.–A.D. 400* (M. Phil. Thesis, University of Southampton).

MURPHY, P.L.: Plant impressions on local Neolithic and Bronze Age pottery and daub. In Case, H.J. and Whittle, A.W.R. (editors), *Settlement patterns in the Oxford Region: Excavations at the Abingdon Causewayed Enclosure and other sites* (London, CBA Res. Rep.), 152.

PARRINGTON, M. 1978: *The excavation of an Iron Age settlement, Bronze Age ring-ditches and Roman features at Ashville Trading Estate, Abingdon (Oxfordshire) 1974–76* (London, CBA Res. Rep. 28).

REES, S. 1979: *Agricultural implements in prehistoric and Roman Britain* (Oxford, BAR 69).

ROBINSON, M. 1981: The Iron Age to Early Saxon environment of the Upper Thames Terraces. In Jones, M. and Dimbleby, G. (editors), *The environment of man: the Iron Age to the Anglo-Saxon period* (Oxford, BAR 87), 251–286.

ROBINSON, M. 1983: Arable/pastoral ratio from insects? In Jones, M. (editor), *Integrating the subsistence economy* (Oxford, BAR Supplementary Series 181), 19–55.

ROBINSON, M. and ALLEN, T. forthcoming: *Excavations at Hardwick, Oxon.*

SCHULTZ, A. 1917: Uber prahistoriche Reste des Einkorns (Triticum monococcum L.) und des Spelzes (*T. spelta L.*) aus Suddeutschland. *Berichte Deutsche Botanische Geschichte* 35, 726–731.

VAN DER VEEN, M. in press: Evidence for crop plants from North-East England: an interim overview with a discussion of new results. In Gilbertson, D. and Ralph, N. (editors), *5th Symposium of the Association for Environmental Archaeology* (Oxford, BAR).

VAN ZEIST, W. 1970: Prehistoric and early Historic food plants in the Netherlands. *Palaeohistoria* 14, 71–173.

WAINWRIGHT, G.J. 1979: *Gussage All Saints. An Iron Age settlement in Dorset* (London, HMSO).

WATON, P. 1982: Man's impact on the chalklands: some new pollen evidence. In Bell, M. and Limbrey, S. (editors), *Archaeological aspects of woodland ecology* (Oxford, BAR Supplementary Series 146), 75–91.

Iron Age Bronze Metallurgy in Central Southern England

Peter Northover

Several categories of bronze artefact from the Iron Age have been studied in considerable detail by archaeologists, but the results have never been incorporated in any systematic exploration of the structure of Iron Age bronze-working or its relationship to the society supporting it. Neither has there been a corresponding study of the metals and techniques used, although some progress has been made on specific topics such as decoration and refractories. As a result there is not the large body of quantitative typological, distributional or metallurgical data that should form the foundation of any such work. A paper such as this must therefore rely heavily on extrapolation from other periods and areas in prehistoric metallurgy to achieve anything approaching a coherent picture of the manufacture and use of bronze products in the Iron Age of our area. This paper will consider the metal resources available to Iron Age bronze-workers in relation to those actually used, developments in technique and the typical products of Iron Age bronze industries and their association with particular types of site, in order to suggest an outline of the status and structure of such industries in the area surveyed. Inevitably it must draw heavily on the new understanding which metallurgical research has given us of metal-working in the late Bronze Age; but it must also contain some estimation of the impact of spreading Romanisation in the last years of the Iron Age.

Resources

For any conceivable level of metallurgical activity obtaining in pre-Roman Britain the British Isles are equipped with abundant non-ferrous metal-ore deposits. However, these resources are located, almost without exception, in areas of the Highland Zone remote from many of the centres of population and economic activity. It is clear that in the Bronze Age production from these sources was largely distributed within the Highland Zone, and an exceptional economic climate was required to stimulate a wider distribution in any significant quantity. In lowland Britain the usual source of metal was bronze imported from the Continent, either as finished objects or, more often, as scrap for immediate re-use. Wherever metal was coming from, whether primary production in the Highland Zone or secondary sources of whatever type, there is a continual shift in the metal sources used, giving in turn a chronological sequence of alloy types and impurity patterns (Northover 1980). At the same time the areas of distribution of individual metal types are clearly defined, and they show their own cycles of expansion and contraction. The changes in all these patterns can be either gradual and evolutionary, or abrupt and revolu-

tionary. The more abrupt changes in particular can be associated with major shifts in typological or other developments and, with luck, with other important changes in the archaeological record. As will be seen, these observations have an equal validity in the Iron Age and provide a powerful case for a thorough and systematic investigation of Iron Age bronze-working to clothe the skeleton hinted at by existing analysis.

The area of central southern England contains virtually no indigenous deposits of ore suitable for the manufacture of bronze; Somerset has small deposits of copper, but there is no reason to suspect their use in prehistory. The lead deposits of the Mendips may, however, have come into production in the later Iron Age for the extraction of lead for alloying, for lead objects as found at a number of sites, and for making materials for craft use. The area was in a position to have reasonably close relations with two important sources of non-ferrous metal ores: the Welsh Marches, in particular the Shropshire/Montgomeryshire area, for copper, lead and, perhaps by the end of the Iron age copper-zinc alloys, and the SW peninsula, both Devon and Cornwall, for those metals and for tin. Both Wales and the SW could also be expected to be potential sources of precious metals. As suggested above, it seems that the copper deposits of these areas were of limited significance in lowland Britain in most periods of the Bronze Age (Northover 1980; 1984). The assumption has frequently been made that the abundant deposits of alluvial tin in the SW must have been heavily exploited in prehistory, particularly because of the ambiguous references in classical sources. As far as the Bronze Age was concerned this was not so, and the principal source of tin in the bronze in circulation in southern Britain was in the bronze imported from the Continent. The only exception was in rare periods, principally the first part of the middle Bronze Age, when the metal needs of southern Britain were satisfied from the Highland Zone. There is evidence of some change in this pattern in the Iron Age, but its dating and extent require further study. In the Bronze Age the principal movements of tin would have been to Highland Zone copper producers without their own local supplies and, probably, to Ireland. There is no evidence to suggest that alloys were manufactured from their individual components at locations remote from British copper resources with a consequent movement of pure metals in ingot form. The ingot copper characteristic of late Bronze Age hoards of the Carp's Tongue group almost certainly represents a copper surplus dumped from the Continent. A small amount of tin achieved a wider circulation for technical purposes such as plating or soldering.

Well-defined local typologies and distributions show

that metal was imported as scrap for immediate re-use rather than as finished or semifinished products; in Britain it would join scrap already in circulation as the principal metal resource. With the late Bronze Age the evidence for the collection and movement of large quantities of scrap becomes considerable. The sources of this scrap and the sources and proportion of newly-mined metal used in the late Bronze Age are beginning to be understood. A brief discussion of this will provide a basis for understanding the exploitation of non-ferrous metal resources in the Iron Age.

At the beginning of the late Bronze Age (LBA I, contemporary with BF II in France and Ha B1 in central Europe) a new industrial tradition was established in southern Britain, named after the Wilburton, Cambridgeshire hoard (Savory 1958; Northover 1982). At the time it is likely that the production of copper from British sources was on a very small scale and the metal economy of southern Britain was dependent upon imports from the Continent and, to a lesser extent, from Ireland. One feature of the early LBA I period is the sequence in the development of the manufacture of swords based on imported prototypes. The metal of these swords has a distinctive impurity-pattern which has been traced to an Alpine or Central European source, reaching Britain by a number of routes. These changes were also associated with the establishment in Britain of a highly sophisticated casting technology, which excelled in the manufacture of objects with thin-walled hollow sections using clay bi-valve and piece moulds and newly developed leaded alloys. The comprehensive nature of these changes suggests the arrival of a group expressing its wealth in this material way and having established trading contacts for the supply of metal. The production most typical of 'Wilburton' metal-working was of fine weapons and weapon accessories, and the spread of this material outside its base area was extremely limited. It was possible therefore for an intrusive grouping to establish itself in southern Britain and maintain a varied production of bronze goods initially independently of British resources except, maybe, for the absorption of some of the extant metal circulation. There was very limited exchange with surrounding areas, although as the industry developed an increasing amount of lead from British sources was incorporated. It is not so clear how the production of utilitarian metalwork was organised. It may have had a firmer basis in existing traditions, reacting to a variable degree with Wilburton influences, and combining some continuation of existing metal-supplies with an increasing interchange with metal from the high 'level' system via locally-collected scrap.

It seems increasingly likely that the sector of society that supported the manufacture of what, in terms of the labour and skill involved, must have been extremely expensive and prestigious metalwork had a relatively short life in Britain, perhaps less than a century, and retreated very quickly. It is possible that this process meant the abandonment of workshops and metal stocks, resulting in the concentration of 'late' Wilburton hoards that led Burgess and Coombs to explore the 'bunching' in time of hoard depositions. The demands of the society left behind were noticeably different and, in part reacting to major re-alignments of metal distribution in Europe, the pattern of metal production and distribution was much changed. Because much of the metalwork of this period has been investigated primarily from a typological viewpoint, the quantitive data necessary for the development of sound economic arguments is lacking. Another difficulty occurs because this period of the late Bronze Age as defined by the metalwork (LBA II, usually called the Ewart Park phase after the type site for the swords of this period (Burgess 1968), contemporary with BF III in France, HA B2/B3 further east) is very long, perhaps two centuries or a little more. There is as yet only a limited degree of chronological arrangement of the material within it. Certain generalisations can be made which are also relevant to later periods.

The most striking aspect of Ewart Park metalwork in southern Britain is the sheer quantity that survives, particularly in hoards. This quantity is, however, unevenly distributed. In some areas, notably the south-west and parts of the south coast and central southern England, the quantity of metalwork is not significantly different from that surviving from the most productive years of the middle Bronze Age. In some areas, such as the Isle of Wight, the quantity is in fact far less. On the other hand, in south-east England, the London basin and East Anglia the quantity is significantly increased, to the extent that it can be said that there was a surplus of bronze in relation to the needs of the time. A number of reasons could be advanced to account for this surplus. First, a substantial proportion of the metal is clearly imported scrap yet to be used; more is ingot copper or bronze scrap in a condition through an excess of oxygen or lead that caused it to be disregarded for large-scale direct use. Both types of metal could be incorporated at a limited rate with the more regular supplies in circulation. As these supplies were usually available in sufficient quantity from a number of sources, it is reasonable to accept that a proportion of the less-useful surplus was simply abandoned. In fact it is possible that this metal, along with the many recognisable products of Carp's Tongue metal-working, represents the export of a surplus from France with only a limited prospect of its being absorbed into the British system. The presence of such metal in France is, in turn, possibly the result of a surplus, expecially of copper, being dumped from elsewhere, especially Iberia. At the same time bronze of a useful quality was being imported from elsewhere into Britain, especially the east coast, and was also being produced from British resources, although we have yet to understand how this was organised.

The metalwork of southern Britain, incorporating perhaps some elements of the Carp's Tongue tradition, is one of many regional groupings apparent in the Ewart Park period. These groups can be identified typologically, for instance in terms of axe form or variations in the detail of the standard Ewart Park sword, or in terms of the mix of metal that they used. Distinctive compositions can now be associated with Carp's Tongue metalwork; one contains some proportion of central European metal and can be matched with end-winged axes, while the other is Atlantic in orientation and is associated with some of the socketed axes typical of the industry and, especially, with high-lead examples. The Atlantic connection is perhaps underlined by an increasing penetration of metal from Ireland: these changes were part of a cyclical process that lasted throughout the Bronze Age and continued into the Iron Age. At the same time metal from central or Alpine Europe was still entering Britain via the east coast. It is also possible to recognise some production of metal from British resources, at least in the south-west, possibly also in Wales and Scotland. A final, but declining component would be residual scrap in circulation from the preceding industries. Although these types can be recognised, the use of metal in the Ewart Park period was such that they were frequently mixed, and a rather uniform composition typical of much metalwork was the result. It is interesting to note that some of the patterns detected in the distribution of implement and composition types can approach the pattern of tribal divisions in the later Iron Age (Burgess and Northover, forthcoming).

The way these resources were used in the Ewart Park period contrasts with that of the Wilburton period. There is considerable evidence that, in southern Britain at least, the presence of an element in society willing and able to support production of the more sophisticated products that were typical of Wilburton metal-working effectively ceased. Other types, such as swords and spearheads, became simpler and often smaller, making fewer demands on labour, fuel and skill. The general aspect of Ewart Park metalworking, when the interference of imported typologies is removed, is much plainer, with an emphasis on tools and simple weapons and personal items. In comparison with earlier periods there is a greater range and survival of craft tools, partly because of changes in the organisation of production and partly, perhaps, because of a growing importance of other crafts such as wood and leather-working. There were still some fine products, such as some of the barbed spearheads, locally made; but their overall importance and production-life are not clear. Other examples, usually identified as typical of the Ewart Park phase and especially associated with Carp's Tongue traditions, were surely made outside lowland Britain and imported, frequently as scrap.

Another contrast is that in the Wilburton areas it is clear that fine metalwork was an expression of wealth, and that there was a mechanism for the disposal of such wealth, perhaps of a ceremonial or ritual nature, particularly in rivers such as the Thames. The decline in elaboration, size and finish of Ewart Park equivalents suggests that metal was no longer regarded in the same way, and there is far less deposition of metalwork in rivers and other special sites. The absence of this mechanism for the abstraction of a quantity of metal from the sum of metal resources would also have tended to increase a surplus. Wealth and prestige would have

found some other expression, perhaps agriculturally based, and metal resources would have retained a value only in as much as they satisfied everyday demands. This depression in the value of metal may have had its origin in basic changes in society and the use it made of its metal; but at the same time, as we have suggested above, there was an increasing surplus of metal in southern Britain. The generation of such a surplus, especially as it may not have been under the control of the metal industry in Britain, could also have depressed the value of metal as an expression of wealth. There is a modern word for this process — inflation.

The nature of this surplus deserves some further consideration as there may be some elements of comparison with the rapid increase in the amount of metal surviving from the last centuries of the Iron Age (say from 200 BC onwards). The suggestion has been made (e.g. Burgess 1979) that much of the metal represented by the hoards of southern Britain was dumped or abandoned under pressure from the changed conditions resulting from the spread of Hallstatt C (Ha C) metalworking, in particular an expansion of iron production. On this view the large quantity of metal represented by these hoards is simply a large proportion of the metal in circulation at the end of the Ewart Park period. It is possible that some metal was removed from circulation in this way at this time; but there are difficulties with such an interpretation, arising from a misunderstanding of the nature of the Ewart Park/Ha C transition. We have suggested earlier that the concentration of hoards associated with the production of high-quality/high-value metalwork at the end of the Wilburton period was caused by the rapid withdrawal of the element of society supporting it. As will be explained later, the arrival of Ha C metalwork in Britain corresponds with the arrival or emergence of a group with similar characteristics to that which supported the highest levels of metalworking in the Wilburton industry. New types of bronze goods were introduced, and new versions of existing types which could have either influenced or replaced them. If a comparison is made with earlier transitions that have been described (Northover 1984a) it will be seen that the replacement of one metal-supply system by another was generally a gradual process. Provided the compositions are sufficiently different this process can be followed and mathematically described. The evidence so far available suggests that change generally became first apparent at the highest 'levels' of metalworking. This would be emphasised if the new grouping was introduced in an abrupt and violent manner, because it would be the higher levels of society, for instance a warrior class, that would be the instruments of such a change, because they supported and/or controlled most directly those levels of production.

On the other hand, the very large hoards, say above 10 kg, have a restricted distribution and a remarkably uniform pattern of contents. These contents suggest that many of these hoards relate to the large-scale manufacture of axes and tools, a process that could turn over very large quantities of metal in a short time. If there was a surplus of metal available in some areas, and it is likely to have occurred in those areas closest to the Continent where these hoards are distributed, the need for careful conservation of metal and multiple re-use would be avoided. For a given number of axes a larger weight of metal would be involved and a greater probability of survival. The converse is true of the Penard period of the end of the middle Bronze Age where the number of surviving axes is very low. This need not mean that demand was necessarily smaller or that fewer axes were made, but just that the quantity of metal available was less and each piece was more likely to be re-cycled many times. This effect would be strengthened if, as in the Penard and Wilburton periods, metal was being removed from circulation by the special deposition of high-status goods. This relationship between the weight of metal being put into circulation at a given time, the number of products made from it before it disappeared from circulation, and the number of those products surviving to be recovered today is of the utmost importance in understanding the use of metal resources in any early industry.

A further consideration with Ewart Park metalwork is that, as described above, the surplus of bronze in southern Britain was probably not generated in Britain. Although much of the metal so imported was of a useful standard, a substantial proportion, yet to be determined quantitatively, was either ingot copper or high-lead bronze which would be regarded as a nuisance by the bronze founders. There is some evidence to support this, as in two deposits (Petters' Sports Field, Egham, Surrey (Needham, pers. comm.) and Gilmonby, Co. Durham (Coggins 1983)) metal in these classes has been separated from the bulk of the hoard. If the surplus represented by this material is a product of events outside Britain, then events outside Britain could be expected to account for the reduction of that surplus. It is then possible to suggest that changes within the Carp's Tongue area of France, both in its way of dealing with a metal surplus and in its probable geographical extent, were seriously restricting the import of metal into Britain, and leading to the disappearance of a current surplus. The Ewart Park hoards in southern Britain can then be seen as being deposited in relation to local fluctuations in demand for the production of the industry handling that metal. Some further suggestions about the reduction of metal imports will be made below.

The change from Ewart Park to Ha C metal-working traditions signalled a reversal of some of the Ewart Park trends in the use of metal, which would have an impact on the metal available and the use made of it. The character of Ha C metalwork in southern Britain has much in common with Wilburton production, which is perhaps not surprising in view of the similar European connections of both. During the Ha C period there is a renewal of the special deposition of fine metalwork, particularly in wet sites; and teh standard of that metalwork in terms of alloy, complexity, size and finish improves markedly. At the same time some continuity is maintained, as can be seen in the groups of metalwork found in settlement-excavations which span the two eras.

As in the Ewart Park period, there was a variety of metal available. In general Ha C metal had a reduced level of impurities; this could have arisen from a number of causes. The few analyses from central Europe for this period (Northover 1984a) indicate that similar changes were taking place there. The work of Rychner (1981; 1983) suggests that in Ha B2/B3 tin contents had sunk to a very low level and some attempt had been made to substitute antimony for tin. The impact of these events is seen as far away as Britain. There was clearly a hiatus in the supply of tin, and the inauguration of new supplies suggested by the markedly increased tin contents of Ha C in central Europe is associated with a change in copper source to one producing a purer metal. This effect is seen, albeit in reduced form, in southern Britain; so it is reasonable to assume that the import of metal from central Europe, directly or indirectly, was continuing and possibly expanding. This would be matched by a decline in imports of metal with higher levels of impurity, either from central Europe or Atlantic France, while continuing British production would, as far as the evidence permits, appear to be of reasonable purity and alloy standard. The combined effects of these trends would be to submerge the residual effects of typical Ewart Park compositions fairly quickly, to produce the pattern of compositions observed for Ha C metalwork in Britain (Northover 1984b).

It is worth looking at the origins of the metal in use in the Ha C period in a little more detail, as this period is very much the bridge between the Bronze and Iron Ages. In Britain analyses are basically restricted to a small number of hoards (e.g. Danebury, Llynfawr, Eggardon, Thorney Down) and the metal-working site at Mount Batten. They suggest that there must have been some residual Ewart Park scrap in circulation. This composition is especially marked in the Llynfawr and Cardiff hoards (Savory 1980; Northover 1980). This is not surprising in view of the evolutionary nature of change in axe production. A possible course of such evolution is seen in the hoard from Roseberry Topping, Cleveland (Schmidt and Burgess 1981), which combines a Yorkshire ribbed socketed axe and a bronze mould for a Sompting-type socketed axe which Schmidt and Burgess describe as the typical form of the Ha C period. There is also an example of the Roseberry Topping variant which they see as intermediate between the Ewart Park phase ribbed axes and the Sompting axes.

There is some evidence also to suggest that bronze was still being produced from copper and tin mined in the south-west, but many more analyses are needed to confirm this. There could also have been continuing production in Wales, but this is harder to detect. It is also not possible to detect any specifically Irish contribution in Britain; but analyses in Ireland suggest a continuing use of the copper sources in production in the Irish equivalent of the Ewart Park phase, named the Dowris phase by Eogan (1965).

Besides the import of metal from central Europe indicated above, there was clearly still an import from Atlantic and northern France but its nature had changed. The most characteristic fossil of this process is the distribution of Armorican socketed axes in Britain (Dunning 1959; Briard 1965). Besides their physical presence, Schmidt and Burgess (1981) see them as influencing the shape of other Ha C axes. The purpose of Armorican socketed axes has been argued on a number of occasions, but a slightly different approach is suggested here. The characteristic features of this very large group of axes is their poor quality, their standardised, non-utilitarian form with little solid metal behind the 'cutting-edge', their very high lead contents (usually above 20%) and their frequent occurrence in carefully-arranged cylindrical stacks indicating some special function in their deposition. Compositionally they seem to have their roots in some of the highly-leaded metal found in Carp's Tongue contexts in France from the end of BF II onwards (*Analyses Spectrographiques* 1–4). Recent analysis of highly-leaded late Bronze Age metalwork from Iberia (Harrison, Craddock and Hughes 1981) raises the possibility that Iberia was the source of such metal in the Carp's Tongue era along with some of the many copper ingots. Both these groups might be the result of a surplus of metal from an expansion of production in Iberian (and perhaps southern French) mines that could not be or was not balanced by a corresponding increase in the production of tin. This surplus was therefore exported and included haphazardly in the regular distribution of bronze. The development and specialised use of some such metal in Armorican socketed axes began in the Carp's Tongue era (O'Connor 1980) and suggests that an increasing discipline was brought to the handling of this metal, just possibly for use as some form of currency. Whatever its purpose, the manufacture of these objects certainly isolated a very large quantity of metal and this process could have been a prime cause of the reduction in the cross-Channel flow of metal which we have suggested for the Ewart Park/Ha C transition. Associated economic and social changes could have provided the opportunity for the expansion of Ha C metalworking and its patronage group.

Armorican axes did reach southern Britain, but there was no appreciation of their specialised purpose across the Channel. At Mount Batten, Plymouth (Clarke, P.J. 1971) one has been cut down for use as a hammer, while some bronze cakes, left as they had solidified in the crucible, almost certainly derive from the re-melting of Armorican axes. It is possible that some were made into a possible English equivalent in the linear-faceted axe as seen in the Eggardon and Portland hoards (Northover and Pearce, forthcoming). Some of these differ, however, in having higher tin contents as well, and have been cast in such a way as to produce a well-defined silver surface from the segregation of a high tin phase to the surface. This process of inverse segregation has been observed to be particularly marked in axes that have been cooled very fast from the melt (Northover,

unpublished). The tin-rich metal might be locally produced, but further compositional and lead-isotope analyses might go some way to sorting out locally produced and imported metal in this group.

As yet there is no quantitative corpus of Ha C metalwork available, although a thesis on this topic is in preparation (Turnbull, forthcoming); so it is not possible to test these ideas further at present. It is apparent from the above that the changes associated with Ha C metalworking had an impact on the nature of the metal in circulation and on increased demand for more sophisticated products. It is possible that the amount of bronze *in circulation* as everyday objects at any given time was not very different from that in the Ewart Park phase, at least in the earlier stages of Ha C. What may have begun to decline steadily was the cross-Channel movement of bronze, especially for the more sophisticated products where iron was beginning too be substituted. It can be assumed that this trade was controlled by the group supporting the manufacture of such metalwork, and as iron came to be preferred there would have been a declining incentive for the import of bronze by the same group. What is not clear yet is whether the cross-Channel movement of metal for the manufacture of basic tools was controlled by the same group or at the level at which axes were produced. If bronze entered circulation mainly via the higher level, the decline in bronze movement was more likely to be accelerated. This is still very much an area for speculation. Certainly, if the introduction of iron was initially restricted to the products of the 'prestige' industry, the demand for basic products would have necessitated a continued exploitation of non-ferrous resources on a scale to satisfy them. The substantial diversion of iron to basic needs would indicate the end of this demand, and this can be associated with the rapid disappearance of basic bronze products by the beginning of Hallstatt D. The rate at which this change took place, as well as the supplanting of Ewart Park products by Ha C equivalents, also needs further study. At the basic level it could well be that the rates varied considerably across Britain and that in some areas, such as North Wales, where Ha C products are scarce, the transition at that level may have been effectively from a developed, late Ewart Park to an Ha D mix of iron and bronze-working. This idea may be a little unfashionable at present but it is still worthy of considerable attention.

As far as we can tell, in the period conventionally defined as Hallstatt D, the use of bronze for major products (for instance axes, swords and other tools and weapons) had effectively ceased. The only very large bronze products remaining were some vessels, but in the south at least they were imported (O'Connor 1980). An immediate problem in assessing the use of metal resources in this period is that equally little bronze and iron survive. The bronze and one or two iron Ha C swords were replaced by iron daggers and short swords; the iron in these might have been imported, but it is clear that their sheaths were fabricated in Britain (Jope 1961). Iron spearheads would also have been used. It is not clear which iron tools are contemporary; but some axes and knives must be, and there is a sickle from ceramic phase 3 from Danebury which dates roughly to this period (Salter and Ehrenreich, this volume). There is no evidence of the continued use of bronze for these or for more specialised craft tools, although some personal items such as pins, rings and bracelets remained in bronze. This apparently sharp drop in the demand for bronze would have severely restricted the need for the primary exploitation of British non-ferrous metal-resources although, as we shall see, it is likely that this never ceased entirely, even if their use may have had only a local significance. There was a continued import of bronze products as shown by the vessels, brooches and some braceletes. This and residual Ha C metalwork could have satisfied the bronze demands of our area very easily. As we shall see matters were a little more complicated than this.

The lack of surviving metalwork from this period could have the same causes as in the Bronze Age cases cited earlier, and be the result of the physical disappearance of early iron through corrosion (cf Burgess 1979); it is not clear why it should be assumed that the earliest iron should suffer such a severe differential in its survival. If neither bronze nor iron were in surplus and demand was satisfied by restricted imports and by very limited local production (Salter and Ehrenreich, this volume), extensive re-cycling would have been essential; and normally only very small fragments would escape this process, unless there was some special deposition mechanism as with the daggers and their sheaths. The problems of re-cycling wrought iron are by no means as great as implied by earlier discussions (e.g. Burgess 1979); Bronze Age models for re-cycling could apply. In fact the re-cycling process could have been to the advantage of iron. In terms of hardness and wear-resistance early ironwork could do no better than compete on equal terms with bronze; but it was considerably tougher than bronze and therefore less prone to fracture, a common failure in bronze axes. It is much simpler to re-work and re-harden a bent iron cutting-edge than re-melt a bronze axe to repair a broken one; there would also be a corresponding fuel economy, as a wood fire might be sufficient for heating the iron whereas charcoal is required to melt bronze, besides the necessity of providing mould and crucible. This property could have been of major importance in meeting the demand for tools at a time when the provision of bronze tools was fast coming to an end, and when domestic iron production was still at a very low level.

As we have seen in a number of cases already, the use of British resources for non-ferrous metal production could have reached a very low level or even have ceased in some areas, despite the potential abundance of such metal in Britain. As implied above, it is possible that iron production found itself in the same state. The exploration of the social, political and economic causes of such a situation will be a fruitful subject of future research. With apparently so low a domestic metal stock the

organisation of a surplus for export would be rather unlikely. The Ha D period coincides with the establishment of Greek trading colonies in the western Mediterranean, such as Marseilles in c 600 BC. These colonies and, perhaps, Phoenician ones have been associated with export of Cornish tin to the Mediterranean from this time. In view of the above discussion of the minimal use of British resources, it is hard to envisage a structure that could support such an export trade at the time, apart from a direct colonial-style exploitation; and there is no evidence for that.

There are very few analyses for this period. One group, from sheet-bronze dagger sheaths from the Thames (Northover, unpublished), shows that essentially the same types of bronze were available in the Thames Valley area as in Ha C. The only exception is heavily-leaded bronze of French origin. The few analyses for Atlantic France (Mohen 1980) show a similar drop in the use of leaded bronze in France.

It is possible that one or two rings and pins from the Breiddin date to this period (Musson, forthcoming). These have zinc and arsenic as their principal impurities, and the metal can probably be associated with ores to be found within 6 km of the site. Two fragments of bronze strip from Danebury, Hampshire, have a composition that potentially can be associated with a source in SW Britain and are datable to ceramic phase 3, perhaps late in Ha D. If this metal is not residual from an earlier period — and the Breiddin metal being of a type not seen at an earlier date suggests that it is not — then some exploitation of ores in these two areas is confirmed. The manufacture of bronze of course implies the production and transport of tin. The Breiddin metal has a significant lead content, but so does the ore deposit probably used. Examination of the debris from the working of copper alloys at Dinorben, sealed by material with a C14 date-range centering on 465 bc might be of some assistance in increasing our understanding of bronze use at this time. But we must always beware of a continuing divergence in metalworking practice and organisation between Highland and Lowland Britain.

The change from Hallstatt D to La Tène metalworking traditions, even though the nature of the change in Britain still has many obscurities, is again associated with a change of styles, in types of product, in techniques, but not necessarily in the types of metal exploited. In technical respects it does represent a marked division in the British archaeological record. The quantity of metal involved in both ferrous and non-ferrous production begins to increase, in the latter part of the La Tène period with increasing rapidity right through to the Roman period. Within the La Tène period itself change tends to be evolutionary rather than revolutionary, although new types of artefact, such as mirrors, are added. We have suggested above that the Hallstatt D period saw minimal exploitation of British ore resources, certainly of copper and probably of iron. The debris of copper-working at, say, Dinorben is very slight, and the one or two possible iron-extraction sites (such as Brooklands, Surrey; see Salter and Ehrenreich, this volume for discussion) are similarly very small. Analysis, limited at present, shows an increasing quantity of metal that can be associated with British resources, but possibly only in roughly constant proportion to the total quantity of bronze. There is also an expanding product range, especially from the second century on. Specialised uses of metal, particularly currency, appear. As most of the metallurgical evidence dates to the later La Tène period this is what must be considered here. However it is likely that the seeds of developments described here were sown earlier in the La Tène period.

As so often, there are both discretely identifiable impurity-patterns and some general ones suggesting some mixing of metals — evidence for the use of British metal resources and for continuing imports of bronze.

There are two impurity-patterns securely identified so far. The first was recognised at Danebury (Class I of Northover, in Cunliffe 1984); it has varying amounts of As, Fe, Ag with 0.05–0.25% Co and Ni, Co usually greater than Ni. This is particularly to be associated with sheet bronze from ceramic phase 7; elsewhere it is seen in the Standlake sword scabbard (Northover, unpublished). Comparison with certain Bronze Age compositions (Northover and Pearce, forthcoming) indicate that this metal is to be associated with source areas in south-west England. Inevitably this demands the contemporary extraction of tin in the SW, but the metal is largely lead-free. The other metal at Danebury (Class II) differs little from earlier bronze compositions in the area except, perhaps, for a lower lead content and it probably contains its share of scrap and imported material. This nondescript metal is seen at other sites where Iron Age bronze has been analysed.

The second characteristic group as yet only marginally affects our area; but possible examples do exist (one piece from Danebury and a mirror handle from the SW). It can, however, be closely associated with La Tène metalwork in north and mid Wales and the Marches but might have had its origins in Ha D. The principal impurities are As and Zn with Zn up to 1.25%. In the later La Tène period it is seen in sheet-bronze products from Tal-y-llyn and Llyn Cerrig Bach, Gwynedd and Cerrig-y-Drudion (Stead 1983) and Moel Hiraddug, Powys. It has also been detected in crude copper from a late Iron Age furnace at Llanymynech, Powys (Northover, forthcoming) and possibly in other metal from sites in the Marches such as Croft Ambrey (Stanford 1976). The group has so far been seen mainly in sheet products or working-debris but was used for castings as well. There are too few analyses to confirm any product-specialisation, but some of the metalwork involved is of the highest standard.

The Moel Hiraddug site has also produced, in the metal from the shield fittings, bronze with impurities similar to those in Irish late Bronze Age metalwork. If this metal is an import from Ireland it must have been reworked, as the shield is of a specifically British type. Moel Hiraddug is in an area where Irish metal is seen periodically from the earliest periods of the Bronze Age.

This is as far as bronze analysis can take us at present. Clearly more impurity-patterns will be confirmed, and probably some guess made about their origins. In the exploitation of resources there must be parallels with periods in the Bronze Age when the use of British resources was increasing. The coming of the Romans and increasing Romanisation is probably paralleled by those periods where new elements in society emerge or migrate, at the same time supporting the production of new types and styles of metalwork which gradually modify or replace local production. This is of especial importance in the Roman period, as there is a much greater range of non-ferrous metal products. Further, the Roman system, with its much greater separation of military and civilian functions and the greatly increased demands on resources made by the former, might have effectively supported two separate metal-supply and distribution systems. The same can be paralleled today where whole ranges of products and materials essentially have only a defence application, overt or disguised.

One difference between the Bronze and earlier Iron Age and the later part of the Iron Age is that in the later period there was, to judge by the evidence from many sites, a demand for the distribution of tin and lead as separate commodities. This must have been for a variety of craft uses other than alloying, as there is no evidence to hint at the manufacture of bronze alloys from their individual components at sites remote from copper deposits at this time. The large-scale transport of copper, tin and lead in ingot form for this purpose, at least in NW Europe, appears to be a product of Roman metallurgical organisation.

The lead and tin sources are very much larger than any potential demands from the British Iron age on its own, so there was never any fundamental cause for a shortage of these commodities. By the late La Tène period the minimal production of the Ha D period had been left behind, and it is possible that a surplus was beginning to develop. Such a surplus would give a potential for export. This brings us to the classical view of the abundance of British metal resources, if indeed the identification with Britain is correct in all cases. From the archaeological record it is hard to see how British metal, except in special circumstances at the beginning of the middle Bronze Age (Northover 1980; 1984a), had any appreciable impact overseas until this late La Tène period. There was often a two-way circulation of metal across the Channel; but this was confined to areas sharing a common industrial tradition and would have had no impact outside it.

The export of iron mentioned by Caesar is a more realistic proposition. Salter and Ehrenreich (this volume) suggest that the iron resources of the chalklands were not significant in terms of the production of the later Iron Age, and were probably used for other purposes. In this case it is reasonable to think of an export of iron from productive areas such as the Weald, probably active at the time, to the vast chalklands of northern France and perhaps to a wider market than that. With a substantial cross-Channel movement of metal in that direction it would not be surprising if the non-ferrous resources of Britain achieved prominence as well. This would be reinforced by the cross-Channel political and economic links, also recorded by Caesar, which effectively covered the whole south coast of Britain and would have used sites such as Mount Batten, Portland and Hengistbury which would have been ports in this trade. The classical view of Britain as an important source of metal may have been correct in Caesar's day, but this position was quite possibly not of long standing.

Techniques

Alloying

Throughout the Bronze Age there was a continuous pattern of change in the bronze-alloy compositions used in Britain. These changes were ultimately a function of the properties of the raw copper, the availability of alloying elements and the tradition in which the founders were working. Once the metal was distributed there was no subsequent *deliberate* modification of the tin content. Groups dependent on secondary resources therefore had to adapt themselves to the preferences of the primary source areas; there was considerable variety among these with 6–9% in the EBA in southern Ireland, 13–16% in parts of MBA France, 11–12% in Wales in MBA I/II and 3–6% in Ha B2/B3 in Alpine Europe. There would of course be some gradual modification of these levels through mixing of different varieties of scrap and evaporation losses during melting. Often, however, a secondary metal industry would be obtaining its scrap from one principal source area which would minimise variations in composition from mixing.

In the late Bronze Age, however, at least in Britain, there was considerable local modification of the lead content of imported metal and primary production of leaded bronze. This was often a cumulative process with low lead contents being increased at each successive melting. There is little hint of any attempt to preserve particular compositions, and the founders would notice little difference between, say, 5% and 10% lead alloys with 10–12% tin. It seems that as with tin there were regional preferences in lead use, with some industries making a high initial addition. In areas where there was a cumulative addition of lead the lead content will also be a function of the number of times an object has been recycled, which could emphasise differences between weapon and tool production. It is likely that not all industries systematically added lead, and that much of the lead in late Bronze Age metal is effectively residual.

Before looking at alloying practice in the Iron Age it is as well to look at what purpose might be served by careful control of alloy content downstream from the primary producers. The answer is that within fairly broad limits there is very little point. The behaviour of a plain tin bronze within the range 7–13% is not going to vary sufficiently to cause problems within the context of Bronze Age metalworking, and the founder could easily adapt to many sorts of scrap. An excess of a particular component in the scrap mixture such as ingot copper would be a different matter, and there is clear evidence that this was understood and controlled. In this respect it can be argued that there was secondary control of alloy content but, again, the permissible limits of variation were broad: the founder would not have a set composition in mind and, in fact, would probably not know how to achieve it from its individual components of copper, tin and lead without considerable trial and error. Rather, he would know what would or would not take him outside an acceptable range of properties with the types of metal he regularly received. The temperature-control of casting and working processes has a far greater effect in modifying mechanical properties and the response to heat treatment and cold work.

A small amount of lead considerably reduces the viscosity of a melt; further lead additions depress the liquidus temperature still more. Both effects materially assist the production of complex castings and ease the problems of mass production. Provided lead contents remain below about 12%, mechanical properties are not severely affected, given proper control of casting conditions. Higher lead contents were used in some cases but not generally for utilitarian products. It is clear that difficulties were occasionally encountered in the use of heavily-leaded alloys, but there are some high-lead sword blades where temperature-control during casting has produced a distribution of the lead which minimises its overall effect (Hughes *et al.* 1982).

The one area where alloy selection always seems to have occurred in the late Bronze Age is in the manufacture of wrought sheet bronze, which is almost always lead-free. The use of lead-free bronze is not strictly necessary, as experiment has shown that leaded bronze can be reduced to sheet thickness with 10% lead or more (Staniaszek 1982) and the lead content is not significantly reduced in the process; indeed 1–2% lead would help to improve the formability of the metal. Two possible explanations exist for this: either low-lead bronze was deliberately manufactured for sheet purposes in Britain or was imported, and the sector of the industry which used it was organised in such a way that lead was not added. One way of ensuring this would be to import the metal as sheet; however the Worth (Devon) hoard (Northover and Pearce, forthcoming) of the Late Penard period has a partly worked sheet-blank which suggests the manufacture of sheet in Britain. The manufacture or import and use of sheet bronze in late Bronze Age Britain was clearly a highly specialised business, but its organisation is still obscure.

There is no need here to review the alloying history of the late Bronze Age as a whole, and this discussion can be begun with Ha C. For the majority of cast and wrought products alloy standards were improving, with tin contents rising back towards the 9–12% Sn range and lead contents falling, generally to the 1–5% range. Although, as stated above, a broader range of alloy contents is not particularly disadvantageous, the ranges of tin and lead seen in the best Ha C bronze provide the optimum combination of properties. A few analyses (Northover 1984a) show that this might also be typical of Ha C metal on the Continent. If this is so there was an even more remarkable change there, as tin contents has sunk as low as 3–6% in Ha B2/B3 with some compensation from antimony (Rychner 1981, 1983).

It is possible that the lead levels of Ha C bronze in Britain were largely residual, deriving from Ewart Park scrap and some addition of heavily-leaded metal, as from Armorican socketed axes, although this would usually have been used with caution. A consequence would have been a severe reduction in demand for lead from British sources; and it is possible that the production of lead as a separate commodity ceased. As we have already seen, high-lead metal was still imported in the form of Armorican axes; but these did not serve the specialised purposes that they did in France. Such metal was certainly re-melted in Britain as the evidence from Mount Batten shows and, possibly, incorporated into local axes of non-utilitarian type such as linear-faceted axes.

Unfortunately there are too few analyses to give an overall picture of Iron Age alloying practices, particularly with regard to chronological and regional variations. The few available Ha D analyses suggest that bronze types remained much the same but, at least in our area, with a further decline in the use of lead. The main series of analyses, apart from brooches, is from Danebury (Northover 1984b). For both sheet and other products, tin contents are in the range 7–14%; but there is some variation within this. Of the two basic impurity-patterns Class I (p. 132, Co greater than Ni) is associated with a lower range of tin contents than the remainder (largely Class II):

	Class I		Class II
% Sn:	5 *	5	
	6	6	
	7 **	7	*
	8 **	8	**
	9 *	9	***
	10 *****	10	*****
	11 **	11	*****
	12 ***	12	***
	13	13	**
	14	14	*
	15	15	

As we have suggested that these two groups have widely differing sources, the continued existence of regional alloying traditions is confirmed. This is further emphasised by a comparison of the results from the Breiddin (Musson, forthcoming) with those from Danebury. There are difficulties because the product ranage analysed at the Breiddin is very limited (pins and rings), and few of the items have a really secure stratigraphy; but, in general, the Breiddin material has significantly higher lead contents (4–14% as opposed to less than 3%). These lead contents are associated with a variety of impurity-patterns, although some may be locally produced in an area where lead ores are common in association with copper. It is unfortunate that Iron Age leaded bronze at the Breiddin does not have a secure chronology, because it is impossible at present to determine whether the contrast with Danebury has a greater significance chronologically or geographically. Other Iron Age metalwork so far analysed from North Wales is sheet and predominantly low-lead, but is also later than at least some of the metalwork from the Breiddin. It certainly appears that the use of lead-free bronze for sheet bronze was continued. The Breiddin metal may be tenuous evidence for the continued use of lead in alloys, but the occurrence of lead objects at several Iron Age sites shows that lead was being produced in the latter part of our period, perhaps in the Mendips. Its use seems to be for some specific objects such as weights, and for craft uses like enamelling and, perhaps, soldering. Glastonbury and Meare also demonstrate the production of tin for similar purposes. Tin must also have been distributed to Highland Zone and Irish copper producers as in the Bronze Age. We have already speculated on how much further it might have been taken.

Copper alloys also feature in three other aspects of Iron Age metallurgy. One, which will not be discussed further in this paper, is coinage. A second is the use of bronze in composite products with iron; this will be discussed in the section on working and finishing, but such products have only ever received a small amount of metallographic attention.

The third topic is brass. We have seen how a group of bronzes in Wales and the Marches is associated with the exploitation of Zn-rich copper ores and this leads to speculation about the possible Iron Age use of brass. Cu-Pb-Sn-Zn alloys certainly occur in Britain in pre-AD 43 contexts. A long series of brooches from SE Britain has been analysed (Bailey, pers. comm.) and it is clear that such metal does appear in first-century BC/first century AD contexts. At present these can be attributed to the import of brass from France, which had been in close contact with Roman metal-working traditions. A more difficult problem is presented by the find from Tal-y-llyn, Gwynedd (Savory 1964, 1966), where a number of sheet-metal objects in the native La Tène tradition were associated with what has been identified as a Roman lock escutcheon. This argues for a late date for the deposition but, conversely, Savory argued on stylistic grounds for a La Tène II date for some of the shield fittings. Jope (pers. comm.), however, suggests that these early features are illusory and that the hoard is probably no earlier than the first century BC. What is undeniable is that the hoard associates the bronze group with a Zn impurity with other, apparently contemporary, items of a high-zinc brass (about 20% Zn). This has also been assumed to argue for a late date as well, and this may well be true. It is therefore interesting to note that the analysis of furnace remains from Llanymynech, Powys (Northover, forthcoming) showed corroded droplets of metal which suggest the presence of high-zinc brass on the site. These remains are associated with C14 dates the latest of which is centred on 65 bc, which gives a possibility of brass being present at Llanymynech in the second century BC (it should be pointed out that metallurgical charcoal in such a furnace would almost certainly be made of young wood, 10–20 years old). The evidence is inconclusive as the copper ores in the area are associated with a considerable amount of zinc, and high-zinc levels were found in all parts of the furnace linings. Nevertheless we must not ignore the possibility of an indigenous discovery of brass-making in Britain in the Iron Age; so we cannot now automatically regard brass from pre-Roman Iron Age contexts in Britain as being late and imported. It is planned to explore this problem more thoroughly in the near future.

Casting

The late Bronze Age in Britain exhibits a very sophisticated casting technology that shows a sound appreciation of the variables involved in the production of castings of the highest quality. This is only part of the story, and surviving metalwork shows a wide range of skill and carefulness.

Stone, bronze and clay moulds were used; these were all of bivalve or piece-mould types and there is no evidence at all for the use of investment casting methods at any stage in the British Bronze Age. Stone and bronze moulds were used for tools, principally axes; but examples are also known for gouges. Recent experiments (Staniaszek 1982; Staniaszek and Northover 1982) show that there were important advantages deriving from this choice of mould material. It was found that both stone and bronze could give roughly similar cooling rates; crude tests suggested that the initial cooling rate was in excess of 500°C/min. The microstructure created by this very rapid cooling rate permits substantial cold-work without the need for an initial homogenisation anneal. This last would have to be at a temperature of the order of 700°C; the ability to avoid this effort and possible damage to the casting would be highly regarded. The rest of the late Bronze Age repertoire was cast in clay moulds, usually with high-quality, well-finished mould surfaces and coarser wrappers. The moulds would be carefully dried and fired to avoid distortion and to avoid any suspicion of dampness. The distribution of alloying elements is different following the much slower cooling obtained in clay moulds, and homogenisation is required before significant cold-work can be carried out. Many products would not require this, but swords for example, where the cutting edges were substantially cold-worked, would. There is evidence that in some cases this was achieved by pre-heating the mould to a high temperature and then furnace-cooling the casting. The outer layers of the casting would then be at a high temperature long enough to permit sufficient homogenisation. One example, with a microstructure indicating very slow cooling, has been recently published (Hughes *et al.* 1982); the pre-heating of the mould was also used to assist the filling of thin sections, but the other advantages were clearly realised. Despite the differentiation between axe and other production in this way, clay moulds exist for axes (e.g. at Jarlshof and at Fimber

(Schmidt and Burgess 1981)); they were probably made by founders working with clay moulds to cast their own tools. Similar objects might have formed the masters for the manufacture of bronze moulds although wooden patterns could have been used as well. Some late Bronze Age moulds, particularly bronze tool moulds, show that considerable thought had been given to the problems of registration and venting.

There is sufficient evidence surviving from moulds (e.g. Roseberry Topping and Rosskeen (Schmidt and Burgess 1981)) that stone and bronze moulds survived into Ha C for the manufacture of axes, and the number of mould-linked examples of the Sompting type (e.g. Coombs 1979; Curwen 1948) confirms this. The increasing elegance of other bronze products, such as the Ha C cheek-pieces from Liynfawr and elsewhere, demonstrate a continued skill with clay-mould technology. There is no clear evidence for the use of investment casting in Britain and late Bronze Age techniques persisted to the end of Ha C bronze types.

The transition to the use of iron for tools, which we must assume to be largely complete early in Ha D at the latest, removed the need for the production of sophisticated bronze and stone moulds, and cored castings possibly also disappeared. Possibly a majority of bronze products made in Britain during Ha D were fabricated from sheet. Casting skills of a sort would have been retained for the making of billets and blanks for strip and sheet. It is hard to identify other bronze castings as specifically belonging to this period, but it is probable that at least some pins and bracelets were made in Britain and, depending on type, stone or clay moulds would have been used. Stone moulds would have been used for billet and blank production, and the survival of this sort of technology is suggested by a piece of sheet in ceramic phase 3 at Danebury (Northover 1984b) with a probable origin in southwest England. The simplified product-range with an emphasis on sheet would have reduced the need for careful control of casting conditions. Outside southern Britain other objects might have been cast, such as vessel and harness fittings; but the major Ha D vessels in our area, both from the Thames Valley, are imported (O'Connor 1980).

It is still difficult to resolve the way in which the bronze-casting industry may have been reduced and, in some places, lost at this time. In a later section of this paper it will be suggested that iron was introduced during Ha C at a high structural 'level' in the industry, gradually substituting for bronze in the manufacture of weapons and prestige- and ornamental metalwork, i.e. those objects produced with a clay-mould technology. The same workshops produced tools for their own use, and the substitution of iron for bronze here would have been a first step in the spread of iron tools. If, because of the moulding-skill required, these same workshops had controlled the casting of bronze axe-moulds, the cessation of this type of work could have been a further step in the replacement of bronze tools. This could have caused a significant reduction in the amount of bronze in circulation or, equally, could have resulted from such a reduction. The use of stone moulds was largely a Highland Zone tradition and there their use for tools might have lasted longer. Eventually these too were replaced, a result perhaps of a general reduction in the amount of bronze available and of the spread of iron. Clearly there was no incentive to step up Highland Zone bronze production to compete with iron. It would appear from the evidence available to us that there was not a significant survival of bronze tool manufacture in the Highland Zone. Whatever the cause of the reductions in the range of casting, it is clear that by the end of Ha D bronze casting occupied a very much smaller place in Britain metallurgy than in earlier periods. It is to be hoped that continued work on the finds from settlement-excavations may enable us to follow this process better.

There are some major changes in casting-practice during the La Tène period in Britain. There is a continuation of stone-mould technology, both for ornamental items as shown by a stone mould from Worms Head in South Wales (Savory 1976), and for the casting of blanks for sheet-working (for example from Dinorben (Guilbert 1979)). All clay mould fragments that have survived from the later Iron Age are for lost-wax casting. There is no reason to suspect the appearance of this technique in Britain before La Tène I.

The bringing of lost-wax casting must have been a deliberate process. Although there are native wild bees in Britain which would have made honey of a sort for human consumption, the highly-structured hive of the honey-bee is necessary for the manufacture of significant quantities of clean beeswax suitable for the lost-wax process. There is as yet no evidence that the honey-bee arrived in Britain before the destruction of the land-bridge to the Continent. Honey-bees will only migrate in swarms, such migrations being in annual steps of no more than 1–2 km; clearly if they were to cross the Channel hives had to be brought. At present the earliest datable remains of honey-bees from environmental samples are no earlier than 300 BC (p. 119). It is tempting therefore to see the introduction of lost-wax casting and of the honey-bee as part of the package of changes that accompanied the introduction of La Tène metalworking traditions. It is of course possible that the introduction of the honey-bee itself was later than that of lost-wax casting and that beeswax was imported for a time. It must be re-emphasised that there is no firm evidence for lost-wax casting in Britain earlier than La Tène. (I am indebted to Dr M.A. Robinson for the entomological information used in this discussion see p. 119).

The technique was already highly developed when introduced into Britain and it was presumably first used for high-status material. Although surviving moulds are generally dated towards the end of this period they are all designed for such products, usually for horse-harness (e.g. Gussage All Saints, Dorset (Foster 1980); Weelsby Avenue, Grimsby (Howard 1983). Although no moulds have been found for vessel, weapon and scabbard fittings they would have been made in the same way. One of the earlier examples is the chape of an early La Tène dagger-scabbard from Minster Ditch (Jope 1961 and pers. comm.), again compatible with an early La Tène date for the introduction of lost-wax casting.

Working and finishing

Within the space of this paper it is not feasible to give a full description of Iron Age bronze-working and finishing techniques; to do so would be to undertake an exploration of the whole range of Iron Age bronzework to determine a great variety of beating, embossing, engraving, joining, plating and enamelling techniques to say the least. The principal outlines are given here.

The division of late Bronze Age metal-working in terms of status and casting technology is continued into the area of finishing. Bronze and stone moulds could give a casting a good finish but this would tend to deteriorate as the mould aged. When an axe or other tool was removed from the mould the runners would be knocked off and any flash removed by hammering and grinding, although this was not always done. The cutting edge was then formed by working and annealing. Leaded bronze is extremely hot-short, so cold work only was possible. The area of the blade worked in the late Bronze Age was very limited, extending only a short distance from the cutting edge. It is possible that the concept of toughness had some meaning to the smiths, as the final working in some cases was designed to harden the surface layers only, leaving them backed by a tougher, fine-grained annealed structure towards the centre. The working process would tend also to heal any porosity in the cutting edge. Even so, fractures of the cutting-edge were probably the commonest form of failure in the Bronze Age and it is in this area that iron tools would show to greatest advantage. There would often be some further finishing and sharpening by grinding, and maintenance of the cutting edge in use would be by both working and grinding. The finishing and re-working processes (where the cutting edge is blunt and not broken) would only involve low temperatures and wood would have been the appropriate fuel. Axe-smithing therefore need not be tied to a particular site and to a charcoal supply for any length of time. The content of 'trade' hoards shows that this type of finishing was almost certainly done at the point of exchange.

Finishing of higher-status metalwork was a lengthier process. The use of clay moulds of the right composition and structure could give a very high standard of finish, but it is likely that many items received a further polishing. Other pieces, such as swords, that required working as well, demanded a more complicated series of heat treatments as described in the section on casting. Even so the evidence of hoards such as Isleham (Northover 1982) indicates that a large number of grinding and polishing steps were involved as well. The consequent demand for abrasives and polishing media is a topic that has hardly ever been considered.

A third class of metalwork is sheet and wire. Both would have involved multiple working and annealing cycles, the working being with a set of hammers for sheet and, in some cases at least, by drawing through a die for wire. The range of sheet and wire products, apart from vessels, shields and a small amount of decorative metalwork, is not clear, for this class of metalwork is most affected by corrosion. Joining in bronze-work was either by riveting, with a variety of styles of rivets and washers, or by casting-on of extra metal. The use of low-melting alloys for joining was known in gold-work. There appears to be no evidence for it in bronze-work but very little attention has been paid to this question. Decorative techniques would have included a number of styles of engraving and embossing using bronze, wood, stone and bone tools. In some cases the pattern of hammer-marks left in the making of sheet was retained as a decorative feature (Gerloff, pers. comm.). The finishing and decoration of high-status metalwork were clearly labour-intensive operations.

This discussion of late Bronze Age working methods applies equally to the Ha C period. There is some evidence of products using both bronze and iron (Gingell 1979), but the techniques involved were simple. The great reduction in bronze-casting during Ha D would have restricted the range of techniques needed for finishing castings, but there was a corresponding expansion in capabilities for sheet-bronze working, particularly for small and intricate work as in the components for Ha D dagger-sheaths (Jope 1961). This more detailed work possibly involved some transfer of techniques from goldsmithing and a more varied range of tools. The finishing of fine sheet metalwork requires some care in preventing the working in of oxide formed during the annealing process; if the metal is quenched after each anneal and then dipped in an acid pickle, the metal is kept clean although polishing with a fine abrasive like jeweller's rouge was also required. Although a much later find, the partially-worked blank in the Ringstead, Norfolk hoard (Clarke, R.R. 1951) is a good demonstration of the way in which a sheet was worked up from a blank. In the opposite direction from the forming of small items from sheet the size of sheets handled increased until a cauldron could be formed from a single sheet, exceeding in size those produced for late Bronze Age shields. A blank of the size that would be cast in the Dinorben mould (Guilbert 1979) would have been required for the largest of these vessels.

The La Tène period brought a new and wider repertoire for the bronzesmith. Existing techniques were retained, but would have been added to because of the new types of product such as fibulae and, later, mirrors, made in Britain for the first time.

Lost-wax casting has the potential to produce an object with a high degree of finish; but this was not always achieved and tool-marks can be seen on a number of articles. Certainly the majority of the effort in investment casting would have been in the preparation of the wax model and the mould; but cleaning and polishing would still have been required although not always carried out.

Working-techniques would also have become more specialised. A new element would have been introduced by the finishing of pins and springs in fibulae and the polishing of mirror faces. The greater variety of sheet products and their increasing decoration would have promoted the development of larger ranges of tools, and these would have been made from a variety of materials as such tools are today.

Joining-techniques still seem to have been based on riveting and casting-on. The use of solders is possible as lead and tin were available for this purpose. Other metal-to-metal bonding-techniques were developed. There was a continued growth in the manufacture of bronze/iron composites. These can be particularly associated with horse harness and vehicle fittings, and there is a complete spectrum from bronze types through bronze and iron to all iron. It is possible that the value of the object varied accordingly, at least by the time that iron had become abundant. It appears that bronze might have been cast-on or formed into a coat by hot dipping with or without an intermediate tinning operation. The metalwork in the Llyn Cerrig Bach deposit suggests that bronze claddings were added mechanically to wood and iron. Such mechanically-formed composites are seen in dagger-hilts as early as Ha D (Jope 1961). A further coating process is gilding. Gold leaf had been applied to objects in the Bronze Age purely mechanically. The evidence for the Iron Age is equivocal, but one of the shield fittings anlaysed from Moel Hiraddug, Powys showed an abnormal gold level in its analysis (North-over, unpublished); if this arises from gilding, a thermal process involving diffusion is indicated (e.g. cement-ation). Other decorative finishes might include tinning and enamelling, involving the tin and lead found at sites such as Glastonbury and Meare (Bulleid and Gray 1911; 1917; 1948; 1953).

There is clearly a very wide range of decorative techniques for the manufacture of high-grade metalwork and a considerable amount of specialisation can be envisaged; but we have no significant site evidence for many of the processes although there are some important finds of tools (e.g. Bredon Hill (Hencken 1938) and South Cadbury (Alcock 1972)). As opposed to the history of casting where some techniques, particularly for tools and very large castings, were effectively lost, the history of working-techniques shows a continually expanding range of skills.

Refractories

The study of the refractories involved in bronze-working has recently made considerable progress, especially through the work of Hilary Howard; I am indebted to Dr Howard for the information contained in this section (see also Howard 1983).

There are considerable variations in both the style and fabrics of refractory artifacts and these variations have considerable chronological importance. In the late Bronze Age crucibles are invariably thick-walled, large with capacities up to 3 kg of bronze and either bowl-shaped with legs or pear-shaped with a marked pouring lip. They have frequently been relined and heightened. Fabrics show roughly 50–60% inclusions of uniform grain-size in a matrix of selected and carefully prepared clay. There is a wide range of recipes suggesting that the makers selected material from close to the metal-working site to give the necessary refractory properties. This in turn argues considerable knowledge and experience of refractory technology to permit this type of exploitation. The sample of material is, however, biased toward sites working with a clay-mould technology, for it is only those sites which have produced refractory remains. Practice at axe-production sites is unknown.

Clay moulds are all of the bivalve type and consist of an inner layer in which the matrix is formed and an outer wrapper. The inner part is almost always of fine texture and well worked with a high finish on the mould faces. The outer wrapper is always more porous with a lower inclusion density and less careful preparation. Apart from that difference the recipe is usually the same for both inner and outer parts. The principal exception is the site at Fimber (Howard 1983), where different materials are present and a source at some distance is suggested for one of them. Apart from that, mould material was generally chosen as locally as for crucibles.

Other refractory components are tuyères, generally of the same clay as for crucibles, and cores. Examples so far analysed show a mixture of granitic sand with a clay binder or a micaceous clay with a similar sand and some quartz. There are examples known from the Bronze Age where a bronze core was used, or bronze incorporated into a core, to act as a chill.

There is no evidence so far from the earlier part of the Iron Age. Apart from the introduction of lost-wax casting it is possible that carbon-filled crucibles were a La Tène innovation in Britain (there is one possible LBA example, from Beeston Castle, Cheshire (Howard 1983)). Graphite and clay crucibles are in common use at the present time, but it is interesting to note that in the Iron Age they eventually went out of fashion. Dr Howard identifies three basic fabrics: carbon, carbon/sand and sand with a clay binder. As far as the limited dating evidence permits the first two can be roughly associated with La Tène I/II and the third with La Tène III, although there is some overlap between the two. In contrast with Bronze Age practice the crucibles are almost always small, generally triangular in form; typical capacities are of the order of 0.25 kg.

All clay mould fragments surviving are for the lost-wax process. In general they are sand-filled and finer-grained than the crucibles. The fabrics range from fully oxidised to fully reduced. Some moulds show a layer structure, each layer having been dried before the next was applied.

An important difference between Bronze and Iron Age refractories is that the former are usually carefully selected from resources local to a working site to give the best set of properties, while in the Iron Age a standard recipe was applied and the makers made a wider search for the materials to fit it.

Other skills

Two other areas to be considered briefly are fuel and abrasives. To reach the temperatures required to melt copper and bronze, charcoal was essential as a fuel. It is best made from young wood, as old wood is too dense and would not give suitable characteristics for burning. A forced draught would also be required, volume of air being more important than pressure. The preparation of this fuel is demanding of both time and labour. A mass-production run of axes might consume up to 50 kg in a working day so the problems in fuel supply could be significant.

For all other bronze-working processes, except, perhaps, homogenisation, wood provides sufficient temperature and so the organisation of those processes will not have been so constrained by fuel demands. It is hoped that experiment will provide a measure of the fuel consumption required for these processes.

As already mentioned, abrasives were of great importance in finishing bronze. A number of sandstones, whetstones and sands would be suitable for the coarser abrasives. For fine work a substance such as jeweller's rouge would be ideal. This could be obtained by the roasting of the iron sulphide nodules common in the chalk to give haematite, which is the mineral forming jeweller's rouge. Its application would have been improved by mixing in a suitable medium; beeswax and egg-white are examples.

When considering the organisation of a prehistoric metal-working it is important to consider the demands made by the need to provide all these materials. Presumably the necessary knowledge belonged to the bronze-workers who would have had to provide the labour for preparing them. In recent times charcoal-burning was a specialised activity that occupied its labour force full-time for a large part of the year. It is not clear whether or not this was so in prehistoric times.

Products and Organisation

The end of the Bronze Age and the impact of iron

It is evident that a structured, probably hierarchical society existed in Britain in the late Bronze Age. The organisation of bronze-working was also structured on a number of levels, each level effectively supported by different levels or sectors of that society. The division was reinforced by the differing demands on resources — metal, fuel and refractories on the one hand and labour, skill and space on the other — of the different levels of the industry. A further factor relating to this differentiation is a constrast in the modes of finishing, distributing and exchanging the products and the relationship of these processes to the location and nature of bronze-working sites.

The two major divisions are the manufacture of tools (axes and other) on the one hand, and of weapons, ornaments and other prestige- and personal items on the other. Some of the distinguishing features of each are listed below:

Tools

1) Permanent moulds — stone or bronze, perhaps supplied by specialists in exchange for tools.

138

2) Many items from the same mould.

3) Single hearth for melting; limited space required.

4) Casting process simple; potential of high turnover of metal with small labour force; relatively insensitive to alloy content and furnace conditions provided certain minimum standards are met; relatively low level of skill.

5) Hoards/sites relative to production:

    a) 'Founders' containing scrap (either exchanged locally at same 'level' (tools), with higher 'levels' (e.g. swords, vessels), or imported through an exchange system at own 'level' or via patronage or trading group at a higher 'level'; smith's tools either new or used; casting-debris; failed castings — this grouping constitutes a metal stock although sorting might be required before use. Some of these hoards might actually be abandoned at a metal-working site.

    b) 'Craft' possibly a subset of (a) but with an emphasis on craft tools, moulds, etc. — this grouping describes the smith's tool-kits.

    c) 'Trade', containing mould-linked unfinished and semi-finished products, smith's tools and, perhaps, minor debris of production and smithing; linked to distribution rather than basic production.

6) Goods finished as part of the distribution process, perhaps at the point of exchange (several models are possible for this); simple fuel-requirements, wood rather than charcoal; not tied to a single site.

7) Production not usually directly linked to settlement-sites; probably peripatetic and operated in short campaigns, possibly linked to but not on a group of settlements; furnace-remains ephemeral. Some hoards are sorted by content and probably relate directly to production-sites.

Weapons and ornaments

1) Ephemeral moulds — clay; high degree of skill required for manufacture; clay source, space and fuel required for forming, drying and firing; possible high failure rate.

2) Single casts from each mould for large objects, multiple moulds possible for small items.

3) Hearths required for pre-heating moulds/melting/homogenisation/annealing as it is likely that in this case all these were carried out on the same site; probably only melting required charcoal as fuel; much greater demands on space.

4) Casting process complex; high level of skill required; potentially highly labour-intensive with low turn-over of metal (individual items generally lighter, lower production rate unless more labour employed); greater need for temperature control; alloy content still unimportant but low liquidus points offer advantages as do low viscosity melts.

5) Hoards/sites relative to production:

    a) 'Founders' similar to those for tool production but dominated by scrap exchanged at the weapon 'level' (weapons and accessories); likewise some

tools, low-level scrap, failed castings etc.

    b) 'Craft', probable in this context but not identified; but some hillfort collections might be relevant.

    c) 'Trade' hoards are not apparent, at least in southern Britain — production and finishing carried out on same site; possible exchange at point of production.

    d) Metal-working sites are characterised by moulds, refractory debris, worn or broken tools, and small quantities of scrap or mis-cast products. Intact finished products typical of sites' own production generally not found. Possible local production of tools using the clay-mould technology available on site; these tools would be for the smith's own use.

6) Goods finished (as far as we can tell) at point of manufacture.

7) Production directly associated with settlement or similar sites either open (Dainton, Runnymede, Mucking) or fortified (Breiddin, Cadbury, Ivinghoe, Beeston Castle); associated settlements show some metalwork probably made on site (e.g. at the Breiddin, (Musson, forthcoming). Distribution presumably to supporting settlement and area controlled by particular patronage group and beyond that by other processes of exchange. Majority of sites show mould debris relating to the casting of weapons and weapon accessories which would be a major user of metal in this category of production; personal items were sometimes produced on the same type of site but might also have been a specialised activity.

This two-fold division effectively accounts for production in southern Britain in the Ewart Park period. There is some variation in the pattern, such as in the size and content of hoards, the relative importance of the two classes of production and the control of their metal resources.

It is possible to see two further 'levels' in the industry. One, a third, higher 'level' was concerned with the manufacture of elaborate articles with very high inputs of skill and labour, such as vessels and musical instruments. In southern Britain in the Ewart Park period, because of the reduced value of metalwork described earlier, it is not clear that this type of manufacture was supported in the area. Such products, or remains of them, do occur in the area and were perhaps only acquired as scrap or at the highest level of gift exchange. On the other hand Ireland shows a number of intact examples, often in sites suggesting special deposition; so it is possible that society there retained an element willing and able to support such production.

The other possible 'level' of bronze-working is at the opposite end of the scale. Provided bronze implements are not seriously damaged (e.g. fractured) it is possible to re-work them, although the process would always be easier with iron. It is possible to envisage the establishment of settled part-time semi-skilled workers in an agricultural community who could, with some simple tools, effect minor repairs, re-haft axes, perhaps even re-work broken pieces into other objects. This would obviate the need to make contact with a professional bronze-worker except for the exchange of scrap or other goods for new tools. The existence of such a level of organisation, once the properties of iron were understood, would provide facilities for the similar treatment of iron tools.

As we have seen earlier in the Ewart Park period, in our area metal was not seen as the most important expression of wealth with special demands in terms of curation and deposition. It is possible that there were exceptions of regional significance. This is not to deny the relative value added to, say, swords by the complexities of their production and the cost of supporting it; but it is clear that these objects did not have the importance and associations that they did in, say, the Wilburton period. This then is an outline of the structure of metalworking in southern Britain at the beginning of the Ha C period; the distribution of metal-resources and the demands made on them have been discussed in an earlier section. The arrival of Ha C metal-working presents, as in other periods, a mixture of continuity and change.

One noticeable feature is a sharp decline in the number of large hoards of scrap, changed circumstances on the Continent having removed the conditions that generated the surplus of bronze that permitted the deposition or abandonment of such hoards in the Ewart Park period. Nevertheless there are finds indicative of the continued use or availability of scrap metal (Sompting, Danebury, Mount Batten). There is an increase in the number of trade hoards with mould-linked axes in an unfinished or semi-finished state. This is comparable with other periods in the Bronze Age in central southern Britain; the best parallel is, perhaps, the palstave hoards and associated finds of MBA II in the area (Rowlands 1976). This reflects a different balance between the demand for bronze products and the availability of bronze.

In no way is it possible to see the majority of hoards of the Ewart Park period being dumped because of the effects of the spread of Ha C bronze- and iron-working. Rather the reverse may be true, that Ha C metal-working may have spread into Britain because its expansion, with associated changes in metal supply, met a declining resistance from the existing industry as the metal-supply arrangements typical of the Ewart Park period in southern Britain went into decline. The deposit or abandonment of the Ewart Park hoards probably took place throughout the period when metal was in surplus, in response to local fluctuations in supply and demand and the success or otherwise of individual metal-working groups. We have also suggested that some of that surplus was unsuited for immediate use. If this model is correct, metal in circulation at the start of Ha C would certainly have been used, especially if the rate of addition of new metal was declining. Such new metal would have been from new imports associated with the Ha C metal-supply system and from Atlantic France and some new production from British and Irish sources. This situation differs from the Wilburton/

Ewart Park transition when the sector of society that supported the highest 'levels' of production, and for whom such production formed a feature of their wealth, was no longer able to support such work.

The Ha C period can be regarded as part of the full Bronze Age, at least in Britain. There are distinctive bronze products of all categories associated with this period, particularly axes, swords, chapes, razors, sickles, ornaments, pins, harness and vehicle fittings. Some items continued relatively unchanged such as some types of spearhead, razor and craft tools, all perhaps showing some continued evolution during this period. In some areas, especially in the Highland Zone, there may have been a carry-over of Ewart Park style axe-production, but this is a very debatable point. The non-uniformity of the distribution of Ha C axes which gives rise to this suggestion may rather be due to local shortages of metal depressing the survival rate. An interesting comparison may be made with the EBA/MBA transition in North Wales. There the last stage of early Bronze Age metalworking is poorly represented (Burgess and Northover, forthcoming) and it appears that there was both an extension of the life of the previous stage and an accelerated development of new axe types linked to a concentrated exploitation of new copper resources. The stimulus to this development was, perhaps, partly the declining vigour of surrounding industries. The new industry is characterised by large-scale production and a healthy export trade. This is in marked contrast to the Ewart Park/Ha C/Ha D and bronze/iron transitions in the same area where, although the earlier industry may have had its life extended, there was no corresponding development of new metal resources and new types, although the resources were there. The supply of metal, both bronze and iron, to the area was kept extremely restricted, presumably through external rather than internal causes. It is therefore rather difficult to argue that the absence of very late Bronze Age metalwork implies an early, large-scale development of iron. All that can be said is that, for whatever reason, metal was very scarce.

It can be imagined that the division of bronze production obtaining in the Ewart Park period continued into Ha C but with a different pattern of high- and low-'level' production arising from changes in patronage and the availability of metal. An important change is a renewed interest in the highest-status bronze-work in southern Britain, shown both in the finds themselves and by an increase in special deposition in rivers and similar types of site. There is also an elaboration of decoration seen in the axes and in the cross-sections of sword-blades. Where metal-working with an Ha C context is suspected on an occupation site, as at Mount Batten, there is no evidence for axe production; Mount Batten itself is probably concerned with the manufacture of sheet bronze and, perhaps, bracelets, among other items, and perhaps was also involved in the reception of bronze from across the Channel. Axes are still associated with founders' and trade hoards although the former have been found on hillfort sites (Danebury). The hoards are smaller, but moulds are still either single finds or in hoards and not associated directly with occupation. This is probably one of the best signs of continuity in the organisation of tool production.

It is within this context that iron made its first impact. As has been hinted earlier, it has become popular in recent years to see a very rapid expansion of the use of iron at this time with a correspondingly rapid abandonment of the use of bronze for most major products (e.g. Champion 1975). Burgess (1979) modifies this view to include the impact of Ha C metal-working as a whole leading to the replacement of Ewart Park practices and the large-scale dumping of unwanted bronze, but he still sees the Ha C period as showing a rapid build up of iron. The reasons cited for the expansion of iron-working are the greater availability of iron resources and their proximity to centres of economic activity, and iron's supposed superior mechanical properties, notably hardness, in relation to contemporary bronze. Both these views are fallacious. As Salter and Ehrenreich show elsewhere in this volume, by no means all available sources of ore were exploited for iron, especially in the earlier Iron Age; indeed by no means all were suitable in terms of contemporary technology. At the present time there is no evidence for the development of British iron resources during Ha C — presence of a small amount of iron, some certainly imported, is not evidence for this. This is but one example of a recurring illusion in the archaeological literature, especially with respect to metallurgy: that because a resource was available and usable it was necessarily exploited. Now that the fallacy of this has been recognised, to explore the reasons why particular resources were not exploited in prehistory should prove a fruitful line of research.

The review of hardness made by Champion was, in effect, made with the wrong data. It is true that the typical hardness of Ewart Park cutting-edges was in the range 140–170 VPN whereas the highest hardnesses likely with early iron, in the absence of quenching and tempering, were of the order of 200 VPN. However, hardness measurements from Ha C bronze axes and sickles are in the range 190–210 VPN and we have as yet no identifiable Ha C iron axes; the hardness of the iron sickle blade is of the order of 140–150 VPN. This is certainly an indication of the improvements in Ha C bronze-working; but hardness is not the only property to consider when assessing the usefulness of an axe for a particular purpose.

It is very difficult to see the iron objects with a certain Ha C dating as either a dominant component of Ha C metal-working or as evidence of the extraction of iron in Britain. There is certainly evidence from the earliest phases at Danebury (ceramic phase 3) (Salter and Ehrenreich, this volume) that iron could be moved for long distances. The piece in question is rather later in date and attributable to a British source, but the principle of long-distance movement of iron remains. There is indeed a good case for seeing a number of Ha C iron objects as direct imports, notably the swords (O'Connor 1980) and, perhaps, some of the pins. Admittedly the Llynfawr iron sickle is an excellent copy of a native cast bronze type, but it does not imply that the iron was produced in Britain. It is evidence of a considerable ability in ironsmithing being available in Britain. This smithing ability is largely foreign to an area where metalworking was dominated by casting, and when smithing skills outside specialist industries (i.e. sheet) were generally limited. The skills must have been largely imported and perhaps taught to local metalworkers. It is surely significant that the majority of datable Ha C iron finds are what in bronze terms would be the product of a 'high-level' industry. This in fact provides a possible context for the Llynfawr sickle, which is rather an oddity among the swords and spearheads and pins. The bronze-working debris from Mucking contains among its mould fragments some which are possibly for a sickle. If iron was gradually being substituted for bronze in the higher 'level' of the metal industry, as most iron finds would suggest, and at least some sickles were being made within that level, the extension of the use of iron to such implements is reasonably explained: the iron, the smithing skill and the demand for the tool would all coincide on such a site. It may be significant that perhaps the best candidate for an Ha C socketed axe is at Traprain Law (Burley 1955–6), a site with considerable indications of higher-level Ha C metalworking.

In previous transitions, when typological changes are accompanied by a change in metal type, the new metal type is generally associated with products made at the higher level. One possible exception is the early middle Bronze Age industry in Wales mentioned earlier, but this is because it is likely that the whole product-range was made by the same group of bronze-workers. This is not the context in which we first find iron, so that there is no reason to suspect that the introduction of iron differs from previous 'high-level' introductions of new metal.

By the time Ha D metalworking traditions were fully developed bronze was no longer the dominant metal, and it appears that metal of all types was in short supply. The reasons for this are not clear. If it is assumed that most of the bronze and iron used in southern England during Ha D is either imported or residual, it must also be assumed that the availability of metal was controlled by events outside the control of British metal-workers. Residual metal would eventually be used up, and we have already suggested that there was limited incentive to develop British metal resources. In the Bronze Age the bulk of metal, however it was supplied, was finally handled at the axe level. It is possible to see a situation where the knowledge and use of iron was disseminated downwards from the high-level smiths under the patronage of a group that controlled both the supply of metal, now largely iron, and the work of the high-level smiths. There could then come a time where the supply of metal was rationed from above and the workers at the axe level, although adapted to the smithing of iron, had no knowledge of how to extract iron for themselves or to put bronze alloys together as a substitute. Those few workers, say some associated with the hillforts of the Marches, who knew how to extract copper and make bronze castings would find at last that bronze could no longer compete for tools because too few people knew how to use it. This model is still very imperfect; but it does attempt, perhaps for the first time, to describe conditions at the end of the Bronze Age from the point of view of the metalworkers themselves.

We have no evidence of a metalworking site definitely dated to Ha D; but a careful review of the results of excavations at sites such as Dinorben may tell us a little about bronze-working at the time. Iron is identifiably the dominant metal for weapons and, by impication, for tools. There remain three categories of bronze products. It is possible that large bronze vessels were still imported to our area, but the evidence from Danebury shows that sheet bronze was produced in Britain at this time. The dagger sheaths from the Thames, generally sheet bronze or bronze and wood or iron fabrications, were certainly made in Britain as idiosyncrasies of their manufacture suggest (Jope 1961). Their association with iron daggers, and the mixing of bronze and iron in the sheaths and in the dagger-hilts, show that their making must have been intimately linked with that of the dagger. The highly-developed smithing skills and the need for special iron tools underlines this link. The bronze-casting industry would have been confined to the making of blanks for the sheet industry (they may not have been cast at fabrication sites) and the casting of simple bracelets, rings and pins. In Ha D it is likely that any more complicated objects such as brooches were imported to southern England. Thus, even with the restricted bronze industry there is a specialisation in Ha D. The casting industry retained traditional technologies while the smithing industry was closely related to the manufacture of high-status iron objects, and the smiths for both may have been the same people who possibly knew little of the melting and casting of bronze.

La Tène and the coming of Rome

The development of La Tène metalworking traditions brought an increasing variety of bronze products, new casting and fabrication techniques, a new repertoire of decoration and decorative finishes and, ultimately, an expanding metal supply. In some ways what did not change was the basic pattern of organisation. Although the number and variety of metal-working sites increased, the division implicit in the discussion of Ha D bronze-working into sheet and cast bronze remained. Basically this is again a reflection in organisation of the different demands on skills and resources of the two branches.

The new techniques and products, it would be reasonable to assume, were again introduced at a high 'level' of metal-working, particularly as they would involve a considerable degree of skill. Let us also assume that by the beginning of the La Tène period the manufacture and distribution of ironwork had become organised in much the same way as it had for bronze, perhaps with an increase in the lowest level of smithing

for the repair and re-furbishment of iron tools in everyday use. Salter and Ehrenreich in their contribution to this volume also indicate the development of a hierarchy within the iron industry. It is clear that as the La Tène period progressed, especially in the second and first centuries BC, there was a rapid build-up of metal in circulation. The facts that scrapmetal begins to become an increasing component of the metal recovered from excavations and that the size of the pieces abandoned also increases, suggest that for the first time since the late Bronze Age metal was in surplus. This surplus was probably also accessible to all levels of the metal-working industry. This can be contrasted with the Wilburton period, when it appears that a very substantial proportion of the metal available was concentrated in the hands of the 'high level' industry and not accessible at lower levels. To a part of society accustomed to expressing its wealth in material terms, this might have been interpreted as an abundance of wealth which permitted its use for display and for ostentatious consumption by special means of deposition (Bradley 1980). The number of very high-value finds of La Tène metalwork (swords, shields, armour etc) from river-contexts suggests that there was again an element of society which was able to express its wealth in this way and which chose to do so (see Fitzpatrick, this volume). The Ha D daggers are an interesting aspect of this phenomenon. There are in fact very few of them (barely half a dozen surviving) and in view of the apparent contemporary scarcity and value of metal products, the deposition of these pieces in the Thames must have been a remarkable act.

Perhaps the most characteristic product of the La Tène period is the fibula, and this was certainly a La Tène introduction. It combined lost-wax casting and some intricate smithing and incised decorations. Insular variants soon appeared. There is only one site, Caistor-by-Norwich (Tylecote 1969) which has produced any evidence for their manufacture and this dates to the first century BC. The fibula-production is associated there with the manufacture of other items of personal ornament. By this time such brooches were extremely common and must have penetrated a long way down through society. Even if bronze, by virtue of the remoteness of its sources and the increasing abundance of iron, was now a metal with high value, there was sufficient available to make fibulae a product available to a wide cross-section of the population. The evidence from Caistor-by-Norwich would suggest a considerable degree of product-specialisation in their manufacture.

The major products by lost-wax casting throughout the La Tène period were horse-harness and vehicle-fittings, terrets, bits, linch pins strap unions and many others. Again their quantity increases rapidly towards the end of the period as does their elaboration and combination of decorative techniques. Their production was a specialised business. It is concentrated on a number of open settlements (e.g. Gussage All Saints, Dorset; Weelsby Avenue, Grimsby; Beckford, Gloucestershire, although at the last it is not clear what form the settlement took in relation to all periods of metallurgical activity (Howard 1983)). The evidence so far suggests that the production of such material on any given site had a limited life of a few years at most. However, until the metallurgical material from these sites is fully interpreted it must remain unclear how the debris of other casting campaigns on each site might have been disposed of — we may be looking at only part of the metallurgical activity on each site. It is possible that these sites were also associated with some iron-working, for many pieces of horse-harness are of composite type.

A bridge between sheet and cast production is suggested by the manufacture of chapes for sword- and dagger-scabbards and vessel-fittings. It must be assumed that the manufacture of the sheet and cast components was closely linked. However we have no evidence.

Sheet bronze itself was used as indicated for scabbards and vessels for shield-fittings, for armour, for musical instruments, for decorative metalwork of many types and a variety of strips and bindings. The production of this type of metalwork was associated with a different group of sites from the casting industry. In particular it appears to be associated with hillforts (e.g. South Cadbury, Alcock 1972; Bredon Hill, Hencken 1939) and with other settlements of major economic importance such as Glastonbury and Meare. There would be some associated casting, for the production of blanks and crucibles has been found at the sites mentioned while there were no significant traces of clay moulds. Stone moulds have been found at Meare and Dinorben and sheet-working tools at South Cadbury and Bredon Hill. This begins to suggest that this type of production, highly skilful and labour-intensive, was to some extent tied to such important sites of economic activity as hillforts. The work of Salter and Ehrenreich may be beginning to suggest some similar associations in the iron industry.

There is not space here to go further into the manufacture of the many forms of La Tène bronze-work, but this discussion should serve to indicate the general form of its organisation. We have said nothing here about the control and distribution of metal resources. Any sensible discussion of this must await many more analyses. The few analyses available have established the importance of British sources, and that metal of several different origins may be found on one site, a marked change from the Bronze Age. The relationship of the hillfort as Llanymynech to the copper resources underneath and the recently discovered furnaces by its ramparts indicate one way in which such resources might have been controlled. Investigation of such sites as Hengistbury and Mount Batten might show the way in which the import of bronze into Britain was controlled. We still need to know a lot more about the possible contemporary export of metal.

The first century BC and the years leading up to the Roman conquest in 43 AD saw an accelerating pattern of change and had an important impact on the use of metal in Britain. The time of the Belgic settlement saw an important change in the pattern of settlement, with a move beginning from hillforts to the lower-lying oppida. Oppida can have important metal-working remains as at Bagendon (Clifford 1961) and were sites for the manufacture of coinage. Whether the product-specialisation of earlier years persisted is not clear, but it would seem likely that it did. The Roman conquest of the adjacent parts of France was complete by the middle of the first century BC and this led to an increasing Romanisation of the metal imported into Britain with the appearance of new types of, say, brooches and of the new alloy, brass (although a small amount may have already been made in Britain). There was probably a corresponding export of iron and, perhaps, of tin and bronze from Britain. A thorough review of all the relevant material would be needed to determine whether the pattern of organisation was changing or whether the making and distribution of metalwork was still carried on within the framework already described for Iron age metalworking. The Roman conquest and its accompanying military and social changes did have a very large effect on the metal industry in Britain. Society became more complex and there was a marked division into military and civilian sectors, each with its own organisation. The demand for metal of all kinds increased greatly; a much greater range of objects was made from non-ferrous metal, and to suit the demands of the Roman towns in particular the balance of production changed. For example there was a notable increase in the use of lead, for plumbing, roofs and so on. The scale of Roman metalworking in Britain has so far deterred the type of survey already carried out for Bronze Age metalwork and attempted here for the Iron Age. Many questions present themselves: at what stage was metal-extraction reorganised so that long-distance movement of copper, lead and tin ingots became normal? How did native and Roman traditions overlap in the early years? Despite the different society, was Roman civilian metal-working essentially still structured in the same way, by the status of the objects produced and the classes of society supporting their manufacture? How important was governmental intervention in the use of non-ferrous metal? The list is endless.

Conclusions

The conclusion of this survey is very brief. The production and use of bronze metalwork in the Iron Age shows many parallels with the Bronze Age. There was a very considerable degree of specialisation dependent on the status of the object being made and the methods by which it was made, and these were in turn related to the sector of society supporting the manufacture, the type of site on which it was made and the way in which production and distribution were controlled. The patterns of change and regional preference in the use of alloys and metal resources seen in the Bronze Age also continued. The introduction of new products and techniques also seems to have followed the same routes as before. This includes the introduction of iron. We have advanced some reasons that possibly explain the success of iron and the end of the use of bronze for weapon- and tool-production. What has been observed but not accounted for is the great fluctuation in the availability of metal for use despite the abundant metal resources of Britain which should have been able to satisfy the needs of prehistoric society manyfold. The apparent great shortage of metal in the early Iron Age still defies explanation. It is a little easier to see the causes of the surpluses of the late Bronze Age and the later Iron Age. This area should be one of the priorities for future research in prehistoric metalworking. The economics are just as important as the technology.

References

ALCOCK, L. 1972: *By South Cadbury is that Camelot . . . Excavations at Cadbury Castle, 1966–1970* (London).

Analyses spectrographiques d'objets préhistoriques et antiques, première à quatrième serie, 1966–1981, Rennes, Travaux du Laboratoire d'Anthropologie Préhistorique de Rennes.

BRADLEY, R.J. 1980: Subsistence, Exchange and Technology — a social framework for the Bronze Age in southern England, c. 144–700 bc. In Barrett, J. and Bradley, R.J. (editors), *The British later Bronze Age* (Oxford, BAR 83(i)), 57–75.

BRIARD, J. 1965: *Les Depots Bretons et L'age du Bronze Atlantique* (Rennes).

BULLEID, A. and GRAY, H.ST.G. 1911: *The Glastonbury Lake Village, Vol. I* (Glastonbury).

BULLEID, A. and GRAY, H.ST.G. 1917: *The Glastonbury Lake Village, Vol. II* (Glastonbury).

BULLEID, A. and GRAY, H.ST.G. 1948: *The Meare Lake Village, Vol. I* (Taunton).

BULLEID, A. and GRAY, H.ST.G. 1953: *The Meare Lake Village, Vol. II* (Taunton).

BURGESS, C.B. 1968: The later Bronze Age in the British Isles and north-western France. *Archaeol. Journ.* 125, 1–45.

BURGESS, C.B. 1979: A find from Boyton, Suffolk and the end of the Bronze Age in Britain and Ireland. In Burgess, C.B. and Coombs, D. (editors), *Bronze Age hoards, some finds old and new* (Oxford, BAR 67), 269–282.

BURGESS, C.B. and NORTHOVER, J.P. forthcoming: Welsh Bronze Age metallurgy (Cardiff).

BURLEY, E. 1955–6: A catalogue and survey of the metalwork from Traprain Law. *Proc. Soc. Antiq. of Scotland* 89, 1–46.

CHAMPION, T. 1975: Britain in the European Iron Age. *Archaeologia Atlantica* 1(2), 127–45.

CLARKE, P.J. 1971: The Neolithic, Bronze and Iron Age and Romano-British finds from Mount Batten, Plymouth, 1832–1939. *Proc. Devon Archaeol. Soc.* 29, 137–161.

CLARKE, R.R. 1951: A hoard of metalwork of the Early Iron Age from Ringstead, Norfolk. *Proc. Prehist. Soc.* 17, 214–225.

CLIFFORD, E.M. 1961: *Bagendon, a Belgic oppidum* (London).

COGGINS, D. 1983: A hoard of late bronze age metalwork from Gilmonby. *The Bowes Museum Archaeological Reports* 2 (Barnard Castle).

COOMBS, D. 1979: The Figheldean Down hoard, Wiltshire. In Burgess, C.B. and Coombs, D. (editors), *Bronze Age hoards, some finds old and new* (Oxford, BAR 67), 253–268.

CURWEN, E.C. 1948: A bronze cauldron from Sompting, Sussex. *Antiq. Journ.* 28, 157–163.

DUNNING, G.C. 1959: The distribution of socketed axes of Breton type. *Ulster Journ. Archaeol.* 22, 53–5.

EOGAN, G. 1965: *Catalogue of Irish Bronze Swords* (Dublin).

FOSTER, J. 1980: *The Iron Age moulds from Gussage All Saints* (London, British Museum Occasional Papers 12).

GINGELL, C. 1979: The bronze and iron hoard from Melksham and another Wiltshire find. In Burgess, C.B. and Coombs, D. (editors), *Bronze Age hoards, some finds old and new* (Oxford, BAR 67), 245–51.

GUILBERT, G.C. 1979: Dinorben, 1977–8. *Current Archaeology* 6, 182–88.

HARRISON, R.J., CRODDOCK, P.T. and HUGHES, M.J. 1981: A study of the Bronze Age metalwork from the Iberian Peninsula in the British Museum. *Ampurias* 43, 113–70.

HENCKEN, T.C. 1938: The excavation of the Iron Age camp on Bredon Hill, Gloucestershire, 1935–7. *Archaeol. Journ.* 95, 1–111.

HOWARD, H. 1983: *The bronze casting industry in later prehistoric southern Britain: a study based on refractory debris* (Ph.D. thesis, University of Southampton).

HUGHES, M.J., NORTHOVER, J.P. and STANIASZEK, B.E.P. 1982: Problems in the analysis of leaded bronze alloys in ancient artefacts. *Oxford Journ. Archaeol.* 1(3), 359–63.

JOPE, E.M. 1961: Daggers of the early Iron Age in Britain. *Proc. Prehist. Soc.* 27, 307–43.

MOHEN, J.-P. 1980: *L'age du fer en Aquitaine* (Memoires de la Société Préhistorique Française 14), 31–35.

MUSSON, C.R. forthcoming: *The excavations at the Breiddin* (Cambrian Archaeological Association Collections and Monographs).

NORTHOVER, J.P. 1980: Analysis of Welsh Bronze Age metalwork, appendix to Savory, H.N. 1980.

NORTHOVER, J.P. 1982: The metallurgy of the Wilburton hoards. *Oxford Journ. Archaeol.* 1(1), 69–109.

NORTHOVER, J.P. 1984a: The exploration of the long-distance movement of bronze in Bronze and Early Iron Age Europe. *Bull. University of London Inst. Archaeol.*, 45–72.

NORTHOVER, J.P. 1984b: Analysis of the bronze metalwork. In Cunliffe, B.W., *Danebury, an Iron Age hillfort in Hampshire II* (CBA Res. Rep.).

NORTHOVER, J.P. forthcoming: *Analysis of vitrified material from Llanymynech hillfort*. Report for Clwy-Powys Archaeological Trust.

NORTHOVER, J.P. and PEARCE, S.M. forthcoming: *The Bronze Age metalwork and metallurgy of south-west England*.

O'CONNOR, B. 1980: *Cross-Channel relations in the later Bronze Age* (Oxford, BAR International Series 91).

ROWLANDS, M.J. 1976: *The organisation of Middle Bronze Age metalworking* (Oxford, BAR 31).

RYCHNER, V. 1981: Le cuivre et les alliages du Bronze Final en Suisse occidentale. Premières analyses spectrographiques à Auvernier Nord/Le Cret. *Musee neuchatelois* 13, 97–124.

RYCHNER, V. 1983: Le cuivre et les alliages du Bronze final en Suisse Occidentale, II: Corclettes VD. *Jahrbuch der Schweizerischen gesellschaft für Ur- und Frühgeschichte* 66, 75–85.

SAVORY, H.N. 1958: The Late Bronze Age in Wales: some new discoveries and interpretations. *Archaeologia Cambrensis* 107, 3–63.

SAVORY, H.N. 1964: A new hoard of La Tène metalwork from Merionethshire. *Bull. Board of Celtic Studies* 20, 449–75.

SAVORY, H.N. 1966: Further notes on the Tal-y-llyn (Mer.) hoard of La Tène metalwork. *Bull. Board of Celtic Studies* 22, 88–101.

SAVORY, H.N. 1976: *Guide Catalogue to the Iron Age collections* (Cardiff, National Museum of Wales).

SAVORY, H.N. 1980: *Guide Catalogue to the Iron Age collections* (Cardiff, National Museum of Wales).

SCHMIDT, P.K. and BURGESS, C.B. 1981: *The axes of Scotland and northern England* (München, Prähistorische Bronzefunde, IX (7)).

STANIASZEK, B.E.P. 1982: *An investigation of the use of leaded bronze in Bronze Age castings* (B.A. dissertation, Department of Metallurgy and Science of Materials, University of Oxford).

STANIASZEK, B.E.P. and NORTHOVER, J.P. 1982: The properties of leaded bronze alloys. In Aspinall, A. and Warren, S.E. (editors). *Proc. 22nd International Symposium on Archaeometry* (Bradford), 262–272.

STEAD, I.M. 1983: The Cerrig-y-Drudion 'hanging bowl'. *Antiq. Journ.* 62, 221–34.

TURNBULL, A. forthcoming: *The Bronze Age to Iron Age transition* (Ph.D. thesis, University of Edinburgh).

TYLECOTE, R.F. 1969: Bronze-melting remains and artifacts from Caistor-by-Norwich. *Bull. Historical Metallurgy Group* 3(2), 46–7.

145

Iron Age iron metallurgy in central southern Britain

Chris Salter and Robert Ehrenreich

Introduction

Although the period we are considering is called the Iron Age, iron is almost the least-studied part of the archaeological record. This is in part the result of the need to know a considerable amount of iron metallurgy and production technology, which may not necessarily be readily accessible to the average archaeologist. It is, also in part the result of the unappealing visual nature of iron and the fragility of the corroded material. It has, however, proved possible to sample ancient iron artefacts without destroying or causing excessive damage to the artefact. From such samples useful information has been obtained, but unfortunatly the present studies are hampered by the lack of comparative data with which to work. However, a data-base is slowly being built up, (Haldane 1970, 53–66; Hedges and Salter 1979, 171; Salter 1984), but the detailed study of the metallurgy and chemistry of iron and iron slags is only in its infancy. It is not yet clear to which archaeological problems the modern techniques will provide the answers but the following discussion will outline some of the problems associated with Iron Age iron.

Iron Production

The change from the copper-based matallurgy of the Bronze Age to one based on iron required a change in the techniques needed to smelt the metal and to produce the finished artefacts. These changes were necessary because of the relatively low temperatures obtainable in the furnaces of the period. The working temperatures of these furnaces would have been in the range 1100 to 1300 degrees Celsius. These temperatures are below the melting point of pure iron, which melts at 1534°C, but are above that of the copper alloys, which have melting points up to that of pure copper at 1083°C. It was not until the medieval period that the water-powered blast-furnace capable of melting iron was developed in Europe.

This inability to reach high temperatures under reducing conditions had a number of consequences.

a. The iron remained solid during the smelting operation and therefore the physical separation of the metal from the slag was poor. The entrapped slag was carried through all the subsequent processes, and it is found in the final artefact in the form of characteristic lines of slag inclusions. In some of the Danebury artefacts these inclusions represent up to 5% of the total area of the metallurgical cross-section. Such an inclusion-density probably would not have any detrimental effect on the mechanical properties of the metal. However, above a certain level such inclusions would make the metal brittle during cold working.

b. Rich iron ores had to be used, as refractory elements such as calcium, which increases the melting point of the slag, could not be added to replace the iron in the slag. When an iron ore with a high silica content was smelted, much of the iron was used up in forming the low melting-point (about 1250°C) slag-phase fayalite (Fe_2SiO_4). Thus, for any ore to be useable in the primitive bloomery smelting furnace, it had to have at least four times as much iron as silicon by weight. This would make some of the commercially-used iron ores unsuitable for bloomery smelting, as some of these ores have iron contents as low as 25%.

c. All artefacts made from iron had to be forged, all joins had to be rivetted or hammer-welded. Usually forging an object is more time-consuming and difficult than casting it. However, this did not stop the early blacksmiths from producing exact copies of tools previously cast in bronze. This is shown by the iron sickle and its bronze counterparts in the Llyn Fawr Hallstatt C hoard (Fox 1939, 367–78).

Factors influencing Bloomery Siting and Production-Capacity

There are a number of factors which control the siting of bloomeries and their ability to produce iron, other than those directly related to the furnace design. These constraints become apparent if one studies Fig. 10.1 which illustrates the iron production-cycle. The estimates of the quantity of input-materials required and output-material produced at each stage are based on the use of a simple bowl furnace of the type found at Kestor, Devon (Fox 1954, 18–77) and West Brandon, County Durham (Jobey 1962, 1–34), and the experimental work by one of the authors and others (Wynne and Tylecote 1958, 339–348; Salter 1983). It should be emphasised that the weights of the input- and output-materials given in Fig. 10.1 are only an order-of-magnitude estimate for a single run of this type of furnace. These early furnaces did not have facilities to tap the slag, so that the quantity of iron that could be produced in a single run was limited by the time it took to fill the lower part of the furnace with slag. Probably in the last century BC or certainly in the first century AD, a more advanced type of furnace was introduced, as is shown by the presence of slag-tapping furnaces at Wakerley (Jackson et al. 1978, 151–66) and at Dellfield, Berkhamsted (Thompson and Holland 1977, 137–48). Such furnaces would have been more efficient and would have produced greater quantities of metallic iron per run. This, in turn, would have reduced the quantity of fuel required to produce each unit of iron but would have increased the quantity of charcoal required for each run.

Typically, the early Iron Age smelter would require

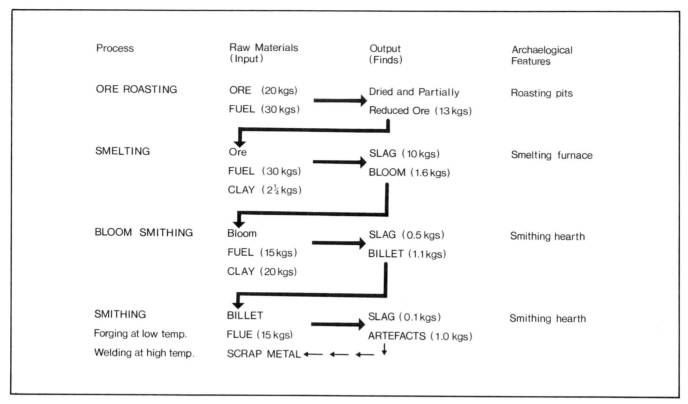

Process	Raw Materials (Input)	Output (Finds)	Archaeological Features
ORE ROASTING	ORE (20 kgs) FUEL (30 kgs)	Dried and Partially Reduced Ore (13 kgs)	Roasting pits
SMELTING	Ore FUEL (30 kgs) CLAY (2¼ kgs)	SLAG (10 kgs) BLOOM (1.6 kgs)	Smelting furnace
BLOOM SMITHING	Bloom FUEL (15 kgs) CLAY (20 kgs)	SLAG (0.5 kgs) BILLET (1.1 kgs)	Smithing hearth
SMITHING Forging at low temp. Welding at high temp.	BILLET FLUE (15 kgs) SCRAP METAL	SLAG (0.1 kgs) ARTEFACTS (1.0 kgs)	Smithing hearth

Figure 10.1 *The iron production cycle.*

the following to produce every kilogram of finished metallic iron:

a. About 20 kg of iron ore, assuming that a sideritic ore was used. This figure would be less for other ores, but the exact quantity would depend on the ore's purity

b. About 90 kg of fuel, not all of which had to be charcoal. However, charcoal had to be used for the smelting stage. Dried wood could have been used in the ore-roasting process. Charcoal or coal could have been used for the smithing stages. It should be remembered that the process of converting wood into charcoal would have been fairly inefficient, so that 90 kg of charcoal represent a much larger quantity of wood. Cleere (Cleere 1976, 240) gives the wood-to-charcoal conversion-factor as seven to one; thus, if all the fuel were charcoal, 630 kg of timber would have been required. On the other hand, the amount of wood required for the smelting stage alone would have been only 210 kg. Collecting and converting this amount of wood to charcoal must have required much more in the way of man-power than was required to mine 20 kg of iron ore.

c. About 40 kg of clay would be required to line the furnaces. This quantity would depend on the furnace-design and the local geology, as some sandstones can make suitable refractories.

Iron Resources

Of the inputs discussed above, the iron resources have the most restricted distribution, and hence are likely to be the most important as far as the siting of iron-smelting sites were concerned. Fig. 10.2 shows the distribution of the regions in which iron ores can be found. Although iron ores are widely distributed throughout central southern England, there are areas in which there would be no immediate access to a supply of iron ore. Even within the areas marked, each settlement would not necessarily have its own ore supply, as the ores occur only within restricted horizons of the formations marked. Also, the geology of the area may make access to a thin ironstone bed impossible to the shallow mining techniques available in the Iron Age. The regions with possible ore supplies are:

1. The Tertiary Basins of Hampshire, and the Lower Thames Valley. In these areas, the rocks consist of mixed beds of clays and sands. The sands often have a high iron content, but not usually high enough to be classed as iron ores. Occasionally there are bands of ironstone, such as those found at Hengistbury Head, Dorset; but generally, the iron needs to be concentrated by the chemical action of the ground water before usable ores are found. These are found either as hardpans or as bog iron ores, and thus, occur in restricted deposits.

2. The chalklands. This rock is not noted as an iron-bearing formation, but it does contain iron sulphide nodules which can be weathered out of the surrounding rock to accumulate on the surface. When oxidised, either naturally or artificially by roasting, they can form a very high-quality iron ore. It is still possible to collect several kilogrammes of nodules from ploughed chalklands today in a few hours (Clough 1982). Iron sulphide nodules have been recorded on the hillforts of Danebury (Cunliffe 1984) and Hambledon Hill (Turnbull 1982); however, it is not clear why the nodules were collected. It has been proposed that the smaller nodules were used as slingstones as they are about the right size. This would not explain the use of the larger nodules, some of

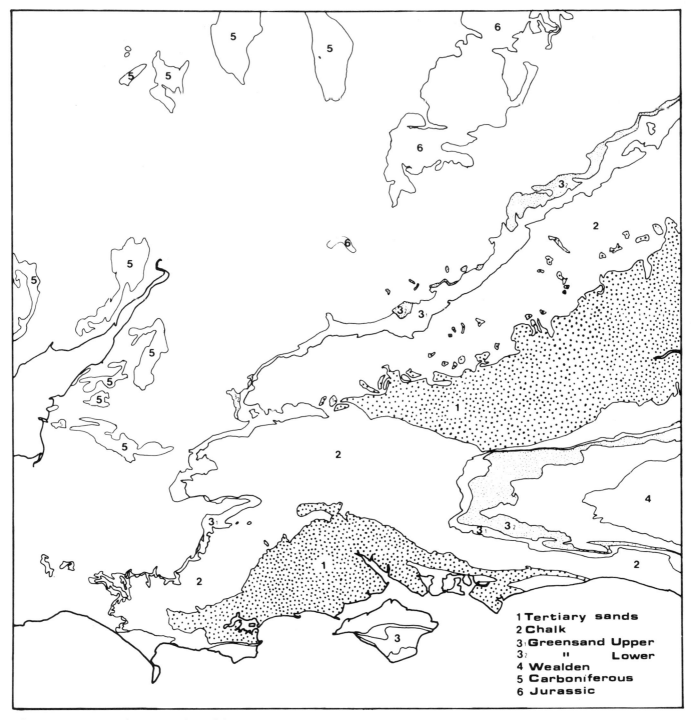

Figure 10.2 *Iron ore bearing geological formations.*

1 Tertiary sands
2 Chalk
3₁ Greensand Upper
3₂   "   Lower
4 Wealden
5 Carboniferous
6 Jurassic

which at Danebury show signs of having been roasted. Another explanation could be that they were being used as a source of a red pigment when roasted to haematite.

It has been argued that the sulphur content of these nodules was too high for them to have been used for smelting; but experimental work (Clough 1982) has shown that as long as the nodules are well-roasted to remove the sulphur, they are an excellent iron ore.

3. The Greensands. Ore-quality ironstone is found in the Lower Greensands at a number of places, for example Westbury and Seend in Wiltshire. The Upper Greensands consist of iron-rich sands which can

produce bog iron ores by natural concentration of the iron.

4. The Wealden ores. These ores occur mainly within the Wadhurst Clay formation in the centre of the Weald. It was these beds that provided the ore for the extensive Roman iron industry of the first and second centuries AD (Cleere 1970; Straker 1931).

5. The Carboniferous iron ores. These really include two types of ore which occur on the western fringes of the region shown on Fig. 10.2. The ores are: the nodular ironstone associated with the Coal Measures; and the limestone-replacement haematite and limonite deposits

of the Carboniferous Limestone of the Forest of Dean and of the Bristol–Mendip area.

6. The Jurassic ores of the Midlands. These Lias ores were used commercially until recently, and outcrop extensively in the northern part of the region. Material derived from these beds occurs mixed with the gravels of the Upper Thames Valley, but there is no evidence that these gravel pebbles were used as an ore in ancient times.

Clay and Charcoal

For most areas charcoal would not have been much of a problem. There would have been sufficient to supply the smelter as long as the scale of iron-production remained small — that is, with the occasional use of a single furnace. Conflicting demands on woodland-resources might develop in the heavily-populated chalk-land areas around a large-scale smelting or metalworking site. It is likely that even on the chalk there would have been sufficient woodland left on the areas of clay-with-flints to provide the fuel needs of the local population for cooking and heating and to supply the needs of a small-scale metallurgical industry (Robinson 1983). Typically, the wood required for conversion to metallurgical charcoal would have been coppice wood rather than timber. Ideally, the final charcoal particle-size should be between 1 cm and 3 cm across. This is required to maintain an even airflow through the fuel and hence to produce even heating within the furnace. If the woodland was managed properly, the time between 'crops' of charcoal could have been relatively short, between five and seven years. Thus, for most of central southern England fuel should not have been much of a problem.

The same is true of clay; most sites would be able to find a suitable source of clay within a few kilometres. Thus, it is unlikely that charcoal or clay resources would have had an undue influence on the positioning of the smelting sites.

Distribution and Scale of Iron-Production

The locations of the smelting sites within the region are shown on Fig. 10.3, together with the locations of a number of other sites which have produced smithing slags. Also indicated on the map are the locations of the sites from which the iron artefacts have been examined metallurgically by the authors. It should be noted that this list is almost certainly not complete. All the sites where it was uncertain whether or not the smelting activity took place during the Iron Age have been rejected. It is possible that some of the Romano-British smelting sites began during the late Iron Age. Also, it is possible that the extensive Roman activity in the Weald has destroyed the evidence of earlier periods.

It is often very difficult to judge from the excavation report whether the ironworking activity on a site was the result of smithing or smelting. All too often the report only indicates the presence of slag with some such statement as 'a large quantity of slag was noted'. The only way to be sure one is dealing with a smelting site is to examine *all* the slag from the site, but it is rare for anything but a small sample of the slag to be stored. The weight of slag from a site gives a clue to the type of activity involved, as is shown in Fig. 10.1. The quantities of slag coming from the various processes were estimated as 10 kg from the smelting stage, 0.5 kg from the bloom-smithing stage, and about 100 gm from the final artefact-smithing processes. Clearly the vast majority of the slag was produced during smelting. Thus, it is unlikely that a site that produced only a few lumps of slag, weighing a kilogram or so in total, can be realistically classified as a smelting site. Danebury, for example, has produced about 8 kilograms of material classified as slag. Over half of this material (58.1%) proved to be smithing slags, with oxidised iron-sulphide nodules making up the majority of the remainder (25.4%). The rest of the material was fuel-ash slag (9.6%) and slagged furnace-lining material. The largest single piece of slag weighed under 500 gm, and most of the other complete or almost complete samples had weights below 300 gm. As each one of these plano-convex 'buns' represents the slag accumulated between each cleaning of the furnace, it seems very unlikely that these slags could have been produced by a smelting operation.

Given these difficulties in the interpretation of the data, it is noticeable that the majority of the smelting sites are situated within 5 to 10 km of a viable iron-ore source. Iron-smelting sites do occur on the chalklands, but they are mostly situated near the boundaries of the chalk, and surrounding geological formations are known ore sources. At Swallowcliffe Down (Clay 1927, 59–93), a sample of the nearby Greensand ironstone was found, and it was suggested that this was the ore being used. Even at Dellfield, near Berkhamsted, the ore used appears to have come from a band of ironstone found in an isolated patch of Reading Beds on the adjacent hilltop. The one exception to the trend that the smelting site occurs close to its ore supply is Bagendon, where a sample of haematite iron ore was found, together with a large quantity of iron slag (Clifford 1961, 8–21). The nearest sources of this type of ore would have been either the Forest of Dean or the Bristol–Mendip area. However, the other metallurgical debris, such as the coin moulds, indicates that this oppidum was a rather more complex and important industrial site than the majority of Iron Age smelting sites.

Dating of iron-smelting sites is often difficult, but all the earliest furnaces seem to have been of the bowl type. It is probable, as Cleere (1972, 8–11) points out from Wynne and Tylecote's experiments (1958, 339–48), that these furnaces would have had some form of superstructure of clay to exclude oxygen and to retain the heat. However, such structures rarely survive. The furnaces at Brooklands at Weybridge, Surrey (Hanworth and Tomalin, 1977) are of the A2 type, the non-slag-tapping shaft-furnace. O'Connor (1980, 306) suggested that the metal-working site was in operation during the Hallstatt D stage.

The Brookland site also illustrates the problems

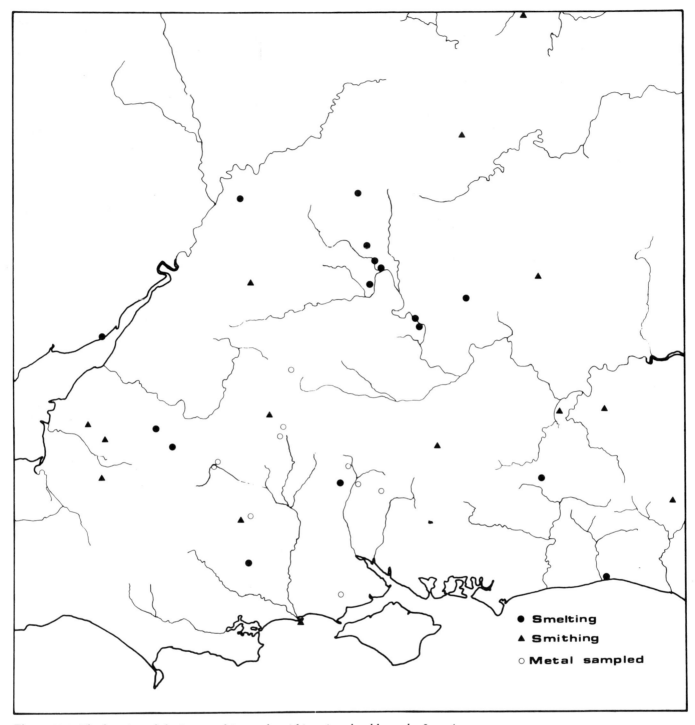

Figure 10.3 *The location of the iron smelting and smithing sites datable to the Iron Age.*

associated with the estimation of the production from early iron-smelting sites. The excavations revealed a handful of smelting furnaces, which the excavators estimated as being capable of producing about 200 kg of metallic iron. This estimate was based on the number of furnaces, the number of times they could have been reused, and on the fact that each run would have produced between 5 and 10 kg of metallic iron. This would have made it a major production-site, as 200 kg of iron could have been made into a very large number of swords, spearheads, axes and other iron artefacts.

On the other hand, if one bases the estimate of the iron-production on the published weight of slag found and on the analyses of the local ironstone, the theoretical maximum iron-production from the site falls to 16 kg. When the same calculations are performed using the composition of the slag found at the site, the yield drops still further to about 2 kg of metallic iron. This last figure is unreasonably low and could have been caused by the analyses given being unrepresentative, or by poor recovery of the virtually indestructible slag.

The production of 200 kg of metal would have resulted in the production of over 600 kg of smelting slag, that is over twelve times the amount actually discovered. As slags are of little use, they are not usually moved far from the production site. There are, however, situations where iron slag was moved appreciable distances. One was during the Roman period, when the material was used for road-metalling in the Weald. The other was after the introduction of the blast-furnace, when earlier iron slags were resmelted. However, it is not obvious that either of these events would have occurred at the Brooklands site. It is difficult to use the furnace evidence to determine the scale of production, the use to which a metallurgical hearth was put, or how many times it had been used. Thus, slags should provide a better indication of the scale of production than the number of furnaces. This is especially true if there are any ore samples present on the site, as one can then obtain a more accurate estimate of the efficiency of the smelting operation.

At the Brooklands site, a more realistic estimation of the iron-production might be between 20 and 50 kg of metallic iron. This would still represent a large-scale production compared with the majority of the sites using the 'bowl' (Cleere type A) furnaces. Only a kilogram or so of slag was recovered from Kestor, and this is typical of many of the other smelting sites from the earlier parts of the Iron Age.

The middle to late Iron Age seems to have witnessed an increase in iron-production, as illustrated by the gradual increase of use of iron at Danebury (Fig. 10.4). A number of smelting sites appear to have produced a considerable quantity of iron. The unpublished site at Trevelgue Head, Cornwall, produced several hundred kilograms of slag using type A furnaces, sometime

between 300 and 200 BC (Woolf 1982). At Ructstalls Hill, Basingstoke (Oliver and Applin 1978, 41–92) a single pit dating to sometime between 300 and 55 BC yielded 32 kg of slag. In the late Iron Age the more efficient slag-tapping furnaces (Cleere's type B) were introduced on sites such as Dellfield (Thompson and Holland 1977, 137–48). The introduction of the new type of furnace is likely to have led to a further expansion of the production-capacity of the industry. By the late Iron Age, there was sufficient capacity in the south east of England to supply the domestic demand and to export the surplus to the Continent, as is shown by Caesar's statement that iron was among the exports from Britain.

However, there appears to be a gap between the demand for iron during the whole of the Iron Age and the smelting capacity at present recorded by archaeology. The losses of iron per year per settlement-unit through wear, non-recoverable use (structural nails etc.), forging and welding during tool-repair, and deliberate deposition could be estimated at about 200 gm. This figure is only equivalent to the loss of a sickle or to the use of a few large nails. If there were a settlement-density of one unit every ten square kilometres, then in the area covered by Fig. 10.1, the annual iron demand would have been about one tonne. In turn, this would have entailed the annual production of between four and ten tonnes of slag, the exact figure depending on the quality of the ore used. At present, the total amount of slag recorded from all the Iron Age contexts in England

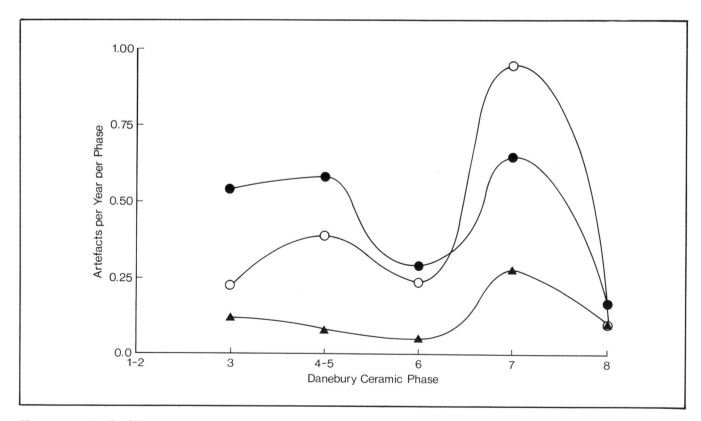

Figure 10.4 *Graph of the total number of artefacts per year per phase versus phase*
o = *Iron*
● = *Bone*
▲ = *Bronze.*

outside the Weald might amount to one tonne. During the late Iron Age, the Wealden smelting sites might have filled this gap, as there was a great deal of early smelting activity in the area which has not been dated. The intensive Roman activity will have obscured the evidence of the earlier phases; however, at Saxonbury Camp (Winbolt 1930, 223–36) Straker dated the smelting-slag to the Belgic period. Other Iron Age sites in the area such as Hascombe Camp (Winbolt 1932, 86), and Piper's Copse (Winbolt 1936, 246) can only be classified as smithing sites, when the limited amounts of slag found is considered.

At Danebury, the iron used on the hillfort came from a number of different sources (Salter 1984). The chemical characteristics of one of the compositional groups suggests that the iron was coming from the southwest of England. This group does not represent a very large proportion of the iron used at Danebury, but it does indicate that metal was being brought to the site during ceramic phases 3–7 (550 to 100 BC) from over 120 km away. Metal of the same composition has been recorded in the Standlake sword from Oxfordshire and at Glastonbury (Haldane 1970, 53–62). This group has not yet been recorded from the other Hampshire sites from which metal has been examined. More work is required, especially in the South West, before we will be able to locate the exact source of the metal and to follow its distribution. Thus it is apparent that the Tertiary Basin ore sources were not supplying all the needs of the Danebury hillfort. As the sword-shaped currency bars seem to have a distribution centred on the Jurassic ridge (Allen 1967, 307–35), it could be argued that their presence at Danebury indicates that metal was also coming into the region from the iron-ore fields of the Midlands. Then there are the double-pyramidal iron ingots of continental type found at Portland, Dorset (Tylecote 1962, 205), which would indicate that there was some movement of iron from across the Channel. In the early Iron Age, the Lynn Fawr sword shows that metal was being imported. It would be interesting to know how much of the other iron from this phase of the Iron Age was of continental origin.

Smithing Slags

This activity would almost certainly have been carried out wherever iron tools were used. Thus, most settlement-sites might be expected to show evidence of smithing. The evidence can be very difficult to detect, for when an object was shaped by hot forging the temperatures involved are relatively low and the heating could have been carried out in a domestic hearth. It would only be the presence of tuyères and bellow-protectors, or the presence of the small quantities of magnetic hammer scale which fall from the artefact, that indicate that smithing had been carried out. Welding involved rather higher temperatures, and this results in the production of larger quantities of hammer scale. This scale then reacts with the fuel and the furnace lining to produce the characteristic smithing-slag plano-convex

'buns'. Occasionally spheres of slag, a few millimetres in diameter, have been found on carefully excavated sites such as Bryn-y-Castell, Snowdonia (Crew 1983). These spheres were created by the rapid cooling of the slag formed by the flux added during welding. The higher temperatures required for the welding operation also result in the furnace-lining becoming highly vitrified in a manner similar to that found in smelting furnaces. Thus, the sites in the Upper Thames Valley where the presence of smithing slags has been recorded indicate the extensive use of iron, even though the archaeology of these gravel-terrace sites does not produce much in the way of iron artefacts.

Smithing Technology

To assess the degree of control which the Iron Age smith had over the properties of the metal and how this skill varied through the Iron Age, it is necessary to be able to study a large collection of well-stratified artefacts.

The Danebury hillfort in Hampshire has provided the most extensive, well-stratified iron assemblage published. Three hundred and six iron artefacts were recovered during the first ten years of excavation. One hundred and forty-one of these have been sampled. An additional 111 iron artefacts from settlements and other hillforts within the Danebury vicinity have also been metallurgically examined (Fig. 10.3).

Of the 306 iron artefacts discovered at Danebury, 262 could be accurately assigned to specific ceramic phases. The fraction of the total iron assemblage found per phase is:

cp 1–3 (550–450 BC) — 7%
cp 4–5 (450–400 BC) — 6%
cp 6 (400–300 BC) — 8%
cp 7 (300–100 BC) — 62%
cp 8 (100BC–10AD) — 3%

The variation in the quantity of iron artefacts per phase may reflect the acceptance of iron technology and the growth of the iron industry in the Hampshire-Wiltshire region from 550 BC to 10 AD. A study of this nature, though, is only valid if the trends revealed can be shown to be independent of such external factors as variations in the duration of the ceramic phases and fluctuations in the size of the resident community of the site.

The different lengths of each phase may be compensated for by dividing the variable to be examined (i.e. number of artefacts or weight of material) by the duration of its phase in years. If reliable population-indicators are present on the site, the adjustments for fluctuations in the population may be calculated for in the same manner (by division of the number of artefacts or weight of material by the number of people per phase). Danebury, however, did not produce sufficiently suitable indicators of the size of the resident community of each phase for this calculation to be performed. An alternative method to determine if the quantity of iron discovered per phase is dependent on population-changes is to compare iron's fluctuations with those of other artefacts of similar utility.

The diagram of the total number of artefacts of iron, bronze and bone per year per phase versus phase (Fig. 10.4) suggests that the factors controlling loss (or deposition) had the same general effect on all three materials. However, when the total weight of each material discovered per year per phase is plotted similarly (Fig. 10.5), it becomes clear that the trend for iron deviates from those of bronze and bone. The quantity of iron lost increased drastically with time, while the weights of bone and bronze rose and fell in the same manner as shown in Fig. 10.4.

Another deviation of interest in Fig. 10.4 and 10.5 is the large decrease in the quantity of bronze discovered from phases 1–3 to phases 4–5. This drop is more dramatically revealed in a graph of tools per year per phase versus phase (Fig. 10.6). All of the bronze tools associated with phases 1–3 were from a single Hallstatt C hoard. Thus, there was only a small number of bronze tools being used and lost at Danebury from its initial occupation in the mid sixth century BC to the abandonment of the site, while iron tools were becoming increasingly common in the archaeological record. This may reflect two trends occurring during the Iron Age: the decrease in use of bronze for tools with the increased use of iron, and the increasing availability of iron with the growth of the iron industry, which eliminated the need to recycle all iron scrap.

The determination of the sophistication of iron technology during the Iron age requires three levels of examination: first, the macro-analysis of each artefact to discern the forging expertise available; second, the microscopic examination of the grain structure of each artefact to determine the utilisation of hardening techniques; finally, the trace element analysis of the iron to reveal extenuating criteria which may affect the production and function of the finished article.

The spearheads discovered at Danebury exemplify the different levels of iron-forging expertise available during the Iron Age. The first spearhead (772) (Fig. 10.7, no. 1) was fashioned from a poorly-produced saw. The teeth of the saw are mere indentations. After the saw broke, or became too dull to be effective, a blacksmith hammered the base of the saw around a wooden shaft to form a socketed spearhead. No attempt was made to weld the socket together, or in any other way to finish the weapon. Spearhead 1297 (Fig. 10.7, no. 2) is another crudely formed artefact. The blade is a flat, leaf-shaped configuration with no midrib visible. Again, the blacksmith simply hammered the two flanges directly around the shaft of the spear. Artefact 1303 (Fig. 10.7, no. 3) is a much finer product. The socket is completely welded, and the blade possesses a midrib for added strength. The fourth spearhead (Fig. 10.7, no. 5) discovered at Danebury is artefact 1300. Not only is the socket of this spearhead welded shut, but an additional ring was also

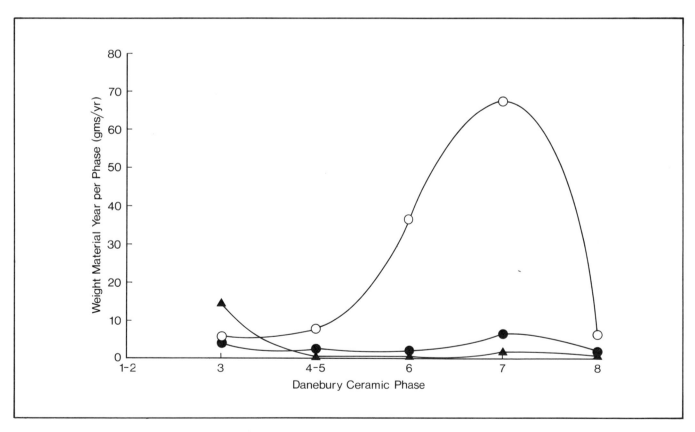

Figure 10.5 *Graph of the total weight of material per year per phase versus phase*
 ○ = *Iron*
 ● = *Bone*
 ▲ = *Bronze.*

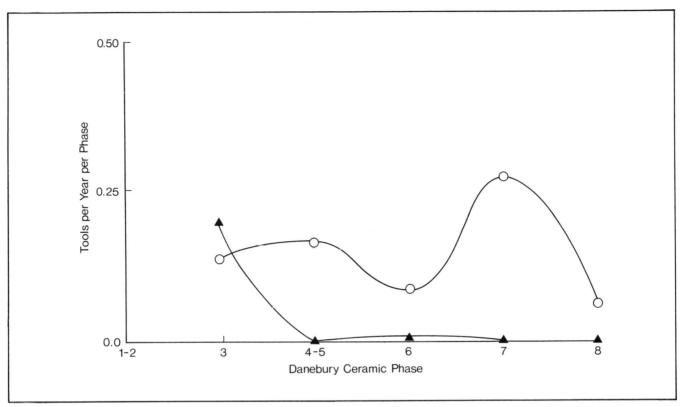

Figure 10.6 *Graph of the total number of tools per year per phase versus phase*
o = *Iron*
▲ = *Bronze.*

welded around the base of the socket for added strength. The blade is an extended leaf-shaped configuration with a midrib. Two bronze rivets are also present, one on each side of the midrib approximately half way up the blade. The addition of the bronze rivets was purely decorative. It may safely be assumed that spearhead 1300 was produced by a seasoned blacksmith.

A second example of the different forging skills present during the Iron Age is saw 1396 (Fig. 10.7, no. 4). The saw itself is finely manufactured with the teeth aligned to cut on the pull stroke. It had broken across the blade during the Iron Age and in an attempt to repair the saw, a blacksmith had overlapped the two halves and welded these together, producing an area of double thickness. The weld should have been hammered to the width of the original blade, since the increased thickness of the lapweld would have prevented the saw from functioning efficiently. Either the work was unfinished or the skill of the smith was limited.

Though the differences in both the complexity of the four spearheads and the saw and its repair would indicate a variation of forging capabilities and expertise during the Iron age, it is difficult to say whether these differences were due to an established hierarchy of blacksmiths, or merely to the amount of time and effort a blacksmith devoted to each endeavour. More extensive analysis of the grain structure of the tools and the trace-element concentration of the iron is required before a valid hypothesis may be formulated.

The concentration of carbon in iron and the use of hardening techniques may be learnt from the examin-ation of the tool's grain structure. The addition of carbon to iron, even without quenching, produces an alloy with significantly altered characteristics: the higher the concentration of carbon, the harder the alloy. The increased hardness of high-carbon iron (unquenched steel) allows the metal to be honed to a sharper edge, and is more resistant to wear. The increased hardness of steel also makes it less resilient and more brittle than wrought iron.

Carburization is the technique for increasing the carbon concentration in iron. The simplest carburizing process involves heating iron in a forge to a temperature of above 900°C in contact with a carbon source (for instance organic matter or charcoal) for an extended period of time (Lang and Williams 1975, 199). Unoxi-dized carbon is absorbed slowly from the surface. If the duration of the carburization process is not sufficient, the concentration of carbon near the edges will be higher than at the centre of the iron bar (Fig. 10.8A compared to 8B which is an extensively carburized sample).

A blade forged from high-carbon steel is very hard and sharp, but also brittle. A more desirable carbon-distribution for a knife is a layer of high carbon steel situated between two layers of low carbon iron (Fig. 10.9A). This allows the high-carbon steel blade to be honed to a sharp edge, yet cushioned in a casing of more resilient iron. Such a carbon configuration can be manufactured in two ways: either a piece of steel is welded between two pieces of low-carbon iron, or an evenly-distributed high-carbon steel is placed in a forge at a temperature above 900°C with an oxidizing atmos-

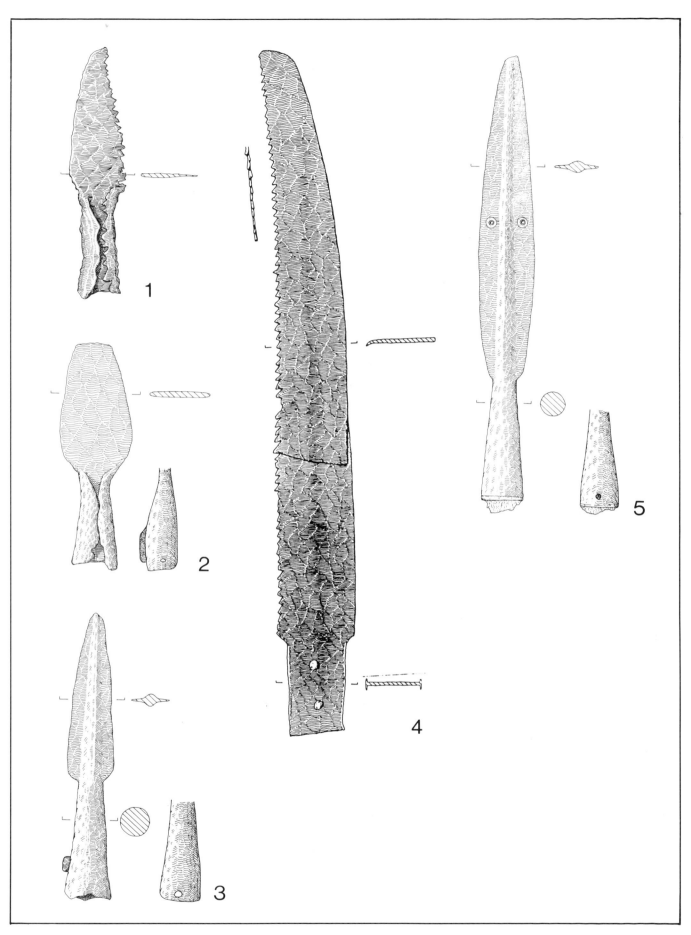

Figure 10.7 *1. Spearhead fashioned from saw — Danebury small find 722 (3/4). 2. Spearhead — Danebury small find 1297 (3/4). 3. Spearhead — Danebury small find 1303 (3/4). 4. Spearhead — Danebury small find 1300 (3/4). 5. Saw with unreduced lapweld — Danebury small find 1396 (1/2).*

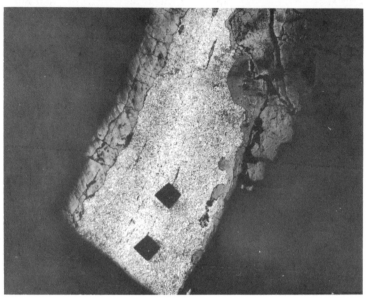

Figure 10.8 *A. Socketed object exhibiting partial and uneven carburization — Danebury small find 774 (Magnification 20X). B. Awl possessing even carburization — Barbury Castle, Wiltshire small find 19 (Magnification 20X).*

phere for a shorter period of time than required to carburize the piece. This will eliminate the carbon on the surface, leaving a high-carbon strip in the middle.

Poorly carburized iron may result for two reasons:
a. Incorrect placement of an iron bar in a forge will cause an uneven carbon distribution (Fig. 10.8A);
b. Impurity-bands high in phosphorus slow the diffusion of carbon in iron. A layered effect of high-carbon, low-carbon and high-phosphorus iron areas will result when phosphoritic iron is carburized (Boylston 1928, 446; and Fig. 10.9B).

Sixty-five percent of the artefacts sampled contained carbon concentrations of below 0.1%. Twenty-eight percent were mild steels (0.1–0.5% carbon). The remaining 7% were high-carbon steels (0.5–0.8% carbon). It is difficult to determine whether the artefacts possessing carbon were intentionally carburized, or whether they were accidents of forging or smelting.

Piaskowski (1974, 325) states that the evenly-carburized artefacts could be the result of conscious selection by the blacksmiths of those areas of iron blooms naturally high in carbon; the poorly-carburized iron was caused by forging. According to Piaskowski (1974, 324), a metallurgist may conclude that blacksmiths were conscious of naturally-carburized materials and carburizing if tools are regularly discovered with low- and high-carbon iron welded together; if a certain tool or

weapon is consistently found possessing a high carbon concentration; if a blade has the structure similar to that exhibited in Fig. 10.9A; or if those areas of a tool requiring an increased hardness have a higher carbon content than the rest of the artefact.

At present, no consistent selection of carburized material for the production of specific tools has been discovered in the Hampshire-Wiltshire region. However, a number of tools satisfying Piaskowski's requirements indicate that some understanding of carburization or bloom selection was present during the Iron Age.

Steel possessing a carbon concentration of above 0.3% may be hardened significantly by quenching. Quenching is the process of rapidly cooling steel from a temperature of approximately 990°C to room-temperature or colder by dipping in a liquid bath (Lang and Williams 1975, 199). Quenched steel is also more brittle than unquenched high-carbon iron. By heating the quenched material a second time to a temperature of between 230°C and 650°C and letting it cool slowly, a high hardness is maintained, but not as extreme (Rollason 1973, 187). The tool is then harder than unquenched iron, but also less brittle than just quenched steel. This second heating process is tempering.

Only three of the 252 artefacts sampled were quenched and tempered: two chisels from Danebury (ceramic phases 5 and 7), and one wedge from Worthy

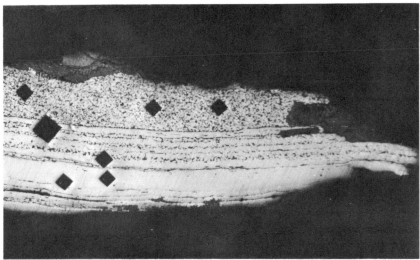

Figure 10.9 *A. Wedge with high carbon, quenched and tempered blade embedded in low carbon body — Worthy Down small find 321.17 (Magnification 20X). B. Spearhead exhibition uneven carburization due to bands of high phosphorus — Barbury Castle, Wiltshire small find 10 (Magnification 20X).*

Down (equivalent to Danebury ceramic phase 7). The trace-element concentrations of the wedge and the currency bars discovered at Worthy Down are comparable. This similarity in trace-element concentrations would imply that the wedge was produced from one of the currency bars on the site. Although slag was only discovered in the later pits (Hooley 1929, 192), the presence of 13 currency bars, 6 of which are incomplete, implies that forging was also performed in the vicinity during the earlier phases.

The wedge was not quenched and tempered accidentally. The blade (Fig. 10.9A) is composed of a high-carbon strip embedded in a low-carbon body. This, as explained earlier, is the most desirable configuration for a knife. The wedge was quenched and tempered to a hardness of 333 VPN. Thus, the technique of quenching and tempering was understood by the local prehistoric blacksmiths of Britain.

There are three explanations for the limited use of quenching and tempering during the Iron Age:

a. The carbon content of most artefacts was too low for quenching to be effective. Seventy percent of the iron artefacts sampled contained carbon concentrations of below 0.3%. Thus, the blacksmiths of the Iron Age may have attempted to quench and temper ironwork earlier, but the low carbon concentration did not permit any noticeable effects. The technique was then disregarded.

b. Quenching and tempering may have been generally understood, but were considered undesirable. During the expansion period in United States history, some tools were not quenched and tempered so as to be sufficiently tough not to break. The density of the population was so low that opportunities to obtain new tools or repair old tools were rare. Therefore, it was safer to have tools that needed constant sharpening and were tough, than to have sharper, brittle tools whose loss could cause severe hardship for the owner (Manning, pers. comm.).

c. Finally, metallurgical techniques have been closely-guarded secrets throughout history. Ironworking litera-

157

ture from the eleventh to the sixteenth century (Agricola 1950; Biringuccio 1942; Theophilus 1847) discusses numerous tricks utilized by different blacksmiths. One recent example was recounted by Professor Max Black of Cornell University. Professor Black told of the time he visited a local blacksmith in a small village in Great Britain. When he inquired of the blacksmith how the smith knew how much iron was required to rim a wheel, the blacksmith replied that he had a secret: if he multipled the diameter of the wheel by 22/7 (π), the smith could determine exactly how long the strip of metal should be. The techniques of quenching and tempering may have been similar secrets during the Iron Age, with only a few blacksmiths knowing of the processes. Quenched and tempered tools would then have been limited products, and traded only to those who could afford them. If so, quenched and tempered tools would rarely be discovered in the archaeological record.

Trace-element analysis reveals the concentration of impurities which affect the properties of iron. Phosphoritic iron has significantly different characteristics to the carbon-iron alloy. The presence of minute quantities of phosphorus both hardens iron, and makes it excessively cold-short, or brittle at 0°C and colder (Piaskowski 1974, 327). The ASTM handbook and the *Smithells Metals Reference Book* both state that the phosphorus concentration in iron, on average, should not exceed 0.080% (ASTM, 1983; Brandes 1983).

Metallurgy texts published circa 1900 debate the extent of the effects of phosphorus in iron. J.M. Camp and C.B. Francis, in the *The Making, Shaping and Treating of Steel* (1920, 573), assert that phosphorus 'is another element that has been painted a little blacker, perhaps, than it should'. Camp and Francis conducted experiments on iron samples containing phosphorus concentrations of between 0.018% and 0.110%. Their conclusion was that high-phosphorus iron withstood cold working tests as well as low-phosphorus iron. They later warn of the detrimental effects of phosphorus, but still state that it is difficult to determine a definite concentration above which phosphoritic iron should be discarded.

F.W. Harbord (1904, 604) points out that in his experience phosphorus concentrations of up to 0.25% in iron showed no ill effects in rolling-mills. However, he writes: 'cold bending tests with a falling weight (not in a press) are probably among the most practical tests for high-phosphorus material, but here again we find the influence of phophorus is very capricious, some extraordinarily good results being obtained with material which would be distinctly dangerous, to say the least, for use in structural work' (Harbord, 1904, 605).

Karsten, however, (*Handb. d. Eisenhuttenkunde,*, 1841; reiterated in: Percy 1864, 64; Greenwood 1884, 207) believed that concentrations of phosphorus in iron of up to 0.3% showed only an increase in hardness without any rise in cold-shortness. This iron, he states, is of the best quality. At 0.5% phosphorus, 'there is still little cause for apprehension respecting the quality of the iron' (Percy 1864, 64). It is not until the phosphorus concentration reaches 0.75% and above that Karsten believed the metal became cold-short and not of general use (Greenwood 1884, 207).

The discrepancies between the phosphorus concentrations considered permissible are considerable. There are three possible explanations for this deviation in theories. First, the method of producing phosphoritic iron may not have been very accurate earlier. Thus, tests were not actually performed on iron samples with the phosphorus concentrations designated. Secondly, testing has become more sophisticated and accurate recently. Thirdly, the requirements for iron have slowly become more stringent since the Industrial Revolution. Iron and steel have had to withstand more abusive treatment within the last two centuries than ever before. Also, the failure of iron and steel parts had not previously led to such disastrous consequences. If a hand tool breaks, the amount of time required to fix it, make a new one or just switch tools is negligible compared to the disruption or catastrophe caused if one part of an engine, boiler or train-rail fractures. Therefore, what is considered seriously detrimental must be seen from the perspective of the period questioned, and not by the standards of another era.

Predominantly, the phosphorus concentration for prehistoric iron remains below the 0.5% mark which Karsten (1841, 420) still designated as good-quality iron (Fig. 10.10). The artefacts with phosphorus concentrations of below 0.080% and hardness values of above 180 VPN are all high-carbon steels. Ninety-three percent of the samples with a VPN hardness below 180 and a phosphorus concentration of below 0.080% are low-carbon iron. The average VPN hardnesses for the low-phosphorus, high-carbon and low-carbon artefacts are 235 VPN and 135 VPN respectively. Ninety-five percent of the artefacts with phosphorus concentrations of above 0.080% are low-carbon samples. The average hardness for high-phosphorus, low-carbon samples is 180 VPN. The phosphorus concentration of 0.080% was selected as the boundary because phosphoritic iron within this limit still possesses certain properties considered beneficial by present standards. Thus, 0.080% phosphorus is the maximum concentration to be found at present in any iron products.

These data indicate that the hardness of phosphoritic iron, on average, was midway between that of low-carbon and high-carbon iron. As stated earlier, only 7% of the iron artefacts sampled possessed a high-carbon concentration. Thus, for a society which may not have completely understood the processes of carburization, quenching and tempering, the only readily-available source of harder iron would have been high-phosphorus iron.

Eighteen socketed hooked blades have been sampled from Danebury, All Cannings Cross, Battery Hill and Barbury Castle. Of the 18 sickles sampled, 10 were large blades (socket-widths of above 3.0 cm; Fig. 10.11, no. 1) and eight were small blades (socket-widths of below 2.5 cm; Fig. 10.11, no. 2). Remarkably, 80% of the large

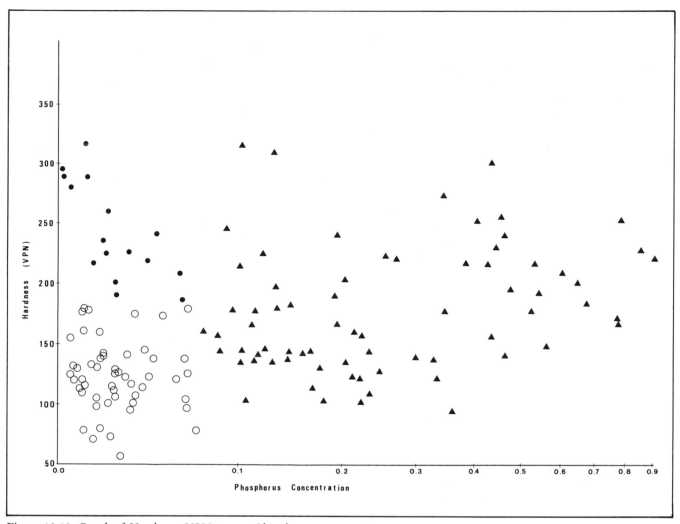

Figure 10.10 *Graph of Hardness (VPN) versus Phosphorus concentration*
○ = *low carbon, low phosphorus artefact*
● = *high carbon, low phosphorus artefact*
▲ = *low carbon, high phosphorus artefact.*

sickles had phosphorus concentrations of over 0.080%; and 75% of the small sickles possessed phosphorus concentrations of below 0.080%.

The sickles sampled from Danebury phase 7 divide exactly along these boundaries. Three of the six blades examined were large sickles and contained phosphorus concentrations of above 0.080%. The remaining three were small hooked blades with low phosphorus concentrations.

This correlation of socket-width against phosphorus concentration is the first indication of a conscious selection by prehistoric blacksmiths of a specific alloy for the production of a specialized tool. It is still difficult to be sure, however, whether this was because of the higher hardness of phosphoritic iron or not. No other correlations have been discovered which would lend more support to this hypothesis. More comprehensive research of other tools which should yield similar results, and tests with reconstructions of Iron Age tools of low- and high-phosphorus iron may assist in the resolution of this dilemma.

High-phosphorus iron was produced by the smelting of iron ore naturally rich in phosphorus. With time, blacksmiths realised that the iron smelted from certain sources possessed special properties. Each source was then exploited for its unique characteristic and the iron was traded as different-quality stock.

Piaskowski (1974, 327) also states that prehistoric blacksmiths could recognise phosphoritic iron by its 'bright and brilliant' luster. Thus, phosphoritic iron and wrought iron could be distinguished readily in the late Iron Age and exploited in any manner desired.

The data presented in this paper would imply that the hardness and nature of an artefact was determined by the type of iron selected. The two forms most generally available were wrought iron and phosphoritic iron. The reason why each was chosen for certain tools or purposes cannot yet be assessed. Iron high in phosphorus may have been selected because it was harder than wrought iron; or phosphoritic iron may have been avoided since it was cold-short. All that may be concluded at present with any conviction is that the Iron

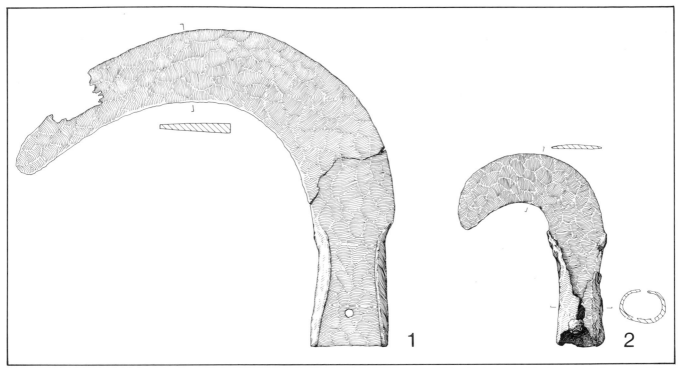

Figure 10.11 *1. Large hooked cutting blade — Danebury small find 866 (3/4). 2. Small hooked cutting blade — Danebury small find 211 (3/4).*

Age blacksmiths could distinguish between the two alloys, and definitely did so.

The range of forging expertise available, the predominant use of wrought iron and phosphoritic iron by most blacksmiths instead of gradations of carburization, and the limited use of quenching and tempering during the Iron Age imply the existence of a hierarchy of blacksmiths. Most blacksmiths were restricted to the simple techniques of metal selection for the alteration of a tool's characteristics. Some smiths, however, knew the finer techniques of carburization, quenching and tempering, and could produce superior tools. The nature of this ranking, though, must be carefully approached. Some smiths may have possessed greater knowledge of the metal they were working with as the result of a family heritage. However, the distribution of knowledge was probably uneven and flexible. As Vannoccio Biringuccio (1942) stated in *The Pirotechnia*: 'When, finally, I consider what this act (blacksmithing) is, it seems to me that everything in all kinds depends only on experience, since these craftsmen are people without plan, and most of them are crude country people, and if they know how to do one thing they do not know how to do another.' The existence of an established hierarchy of blacksmiths in the Iron Age is probably not an accurate description of the state of iron technology. A broad distribution of blacksmiths each with his own secrets and specialities is probably more apt.

Summary

Iron technology was in a dynamic state throughout the Iron Age. The availability of iron was increasing steadily from 700 BC. Numerous small groups of blacksmiths were experimenting with the new material in an attempt to discover innovative forging styles and techniques. Predominantly, the properties of a tool could only be altered by the selection of the particular iron stock from which the tool could be manufactured. Occasional settlements with more advanced blacksmiths who understood any number of such closely-guarded secrets as bloom selection, carburization or quenching and tempering, were in existence. However, the transfer of ironworking technology appears to have been restricted. Thus, the distribution of knowledge was limited and anomalous.

Acknowledgements

We wish to acknowledge the help of the following and to express our thanks to Professor Barry Cunliffe, Professor Peter Wells, Professor C.C. Lamberg-Karlovsky, Mrs Victoria Swerdlow and Mrs Melissa Banta of the Harvard University Peabody Museum for the use of the PHIND computer system, Mr Stephen Nickels of the Saugus Ironworks, Professor William Manning, Lyn Sellwood, Sarah Pollard, Morris and Mary Hasnas, Mr F.K. Annable and Dr P.H. Robinson of the Wiltshire Museum, Mr P. Drury and Mr N. Wickenden of the Chelmsford Archaeological Trust, Ms E. Lewis and Mr G.T. Denford of the Winchester City Museum, Dr A.J.N.W. Prag of the Manchester Museum, and finally to Professor Sir Peter Hirsch for allowing us access to laboratory facilities.

References

AGRICOLA, G.1950: *De Re Metallica* (New York).

ALLEN, D. 1967: Iron Currency Bars in Britain. *Proc. Prehist. Soc.* 33, 397–335.

AMERICAN SOCIETY FOR TESTING AND MATERIALS 1983: *1983 Annual Book of ASTM Standards* (Philadelphia).

BIRINGUCCI, V. 1942: *The Pirotechnia* (New York, The American Institute of Mining and Engineers).

BOYLSTON, H.M. 1928: *An Introduction to the Metallurgy of Iron and Steel* (New York).

BRANDES, E.D. (editor) 1983: *Smithells Metals Reference Book* (Sixth edition: London).

CAMP, J.M. and FRANCIS, C.B. 1920: *The Making, Shaping and Treating of Steel* (Second edition: Pittsburgh).

CLAY, R.C.C. 1927: An inhabited site of La Tène date on Swallowcliffe Down. *Wilts. Archaeol. Mag.* 43, 59–93.

CLEERE, H.F. 1970: *The Romano-British Industrial Settlement at Bardown Wadhurst* (Sussex Archaeol. Soc. Occasional Papers 1).

CLEERE, H.F. 1972: The Classification of Early Iron-Smelting Furnaces. *Antiq. Journ.* 52, 8–23.

CLEERE, H.F. 1976: Some operating parameters for Roman ironworks. *Bull. Instit. Archaeol. London* 13, 233–46.

CLIFFORD, E.M. 1961: *Bagendon, a Belgic Oppidum* (Cambridge).

CLOUGH, R. 1982: pers. comm.

CUNLIFFE, B.W. 1984: *Danebury: an Iron Age hillfort in Hampshire* (London, CBA Res. Rep. 52).

FOX, A. 1954: Excavations at Kestor. *Trans. Devon. Ass.* 86, 21–62.

FOX, C. 1939: A second Cauldron and an Iron Sword from the Llyn Fawr Hoard, Rhigos, Glamorganshire. *Antiq. Journ.* 19, 369–404.

GREENWOOD, W.H. 1884: *Steel and Iron* (New York).

HALDANE, W. 1970: A study of the chemical composition of Pre-Roman ironwork from Somerset. *Bull. Historical Metallurgy Soc.* 4, 53–66.

HANWORTH, R. and TOMALIN, D.J. 1977: *Brooklands, Weybridge: The excavation of an Iron Age and Medieval site 1964–5 and 1970–1* (Research Volume of the Surrey Archaeological Society 4).

HARBORD, F.W. 1904: *The Metallurgy of Steel* (London).

HEDGES, R.E.M. and SALTER, C.J. 1979: Source determination of iron currency bars through analysis of the slag inclusions. *Archaeometry* 21, 161–175.

HOOLEY, R.W. 1929: Excavation of an Early Iron Age Village on Worthy Down, Winchester. *Proc. Hants. Field Club and Archaeol. Soc.* 10, 178–192.

JACKSON, D.A., AMBROSE, T.M., PACITTO, A.L. and WOODS, P.J. 1978: Excavations at Wakerley, Northants., 1972–75. *Britannia* 9, 115–242.

JOBEY, G. 1962: An Early Iron Age homestead at West Brandon, County Durham. *Arachaeol. Aeliana* 40, 1–34.

KARSTEN, K.J.B. 1841: *Handbuch der Eisenhüttenkunde* (Berlin).

LANG, J. and WILLIAMS, A.R. 1975: The Hardening of Iron Swords. *Journ. Archaeol. Science* 2, 199–207.

O'CONNOR, B. 1980: *Cross-Channel Relations in the Later Bronze Age* (Oxford, BAR S91).

OLIVER, M. and APPLIN, B. 1978: Excavation of an Iron Age and Romano-British settlement at Ructstalls Hill, Basingstoke, Hampshire, 1972–5. *Proc. Hants. Field Club and Archaeol. Soc.* 35, 41–92.

PERCY, J.P. 1864: *Metallurgy* (London).

PIASKOWSKI, J. 1974: Metallographic Examinations of Ancient Iron Objects. In Gosh, A.K. (editor), *Perspectives in Paleoanthropology* (Calcutta), 321–329.

ROBINSON, M. 1983: pers. comm.

ROLLASON, E.C. 1973: *Metallurgy for Engineers* (Fourth edition: London).

SALTER, C.J. 1983: An investigation into the Nature of the Slags and slag inclusions produced during the smithing of Ancient wrought iron. (Presented at the 23rd Symposium on Archaeometry, Naples Arpil 1983).

SALTER, C.J. 1984: In Cunliffe 1984.

STRAKER, E. 1931: *Wealden Iron* (London).

THEOPHILUS, R. 1847: *De Diversis Artibus* (London).

THOMPSON, A. and HOLLAND, E. 1977: Excavation of an Iron Age site at Dellfield, Berkhamsted. *Herts. Archaeol.* 4, 137–148.

TURNBULL, A. 1982: pers. comm.

TYLECOTE, R.F. 1962: *Metallurgy in Archaeology* (London).

WINBOLT, S.E. 1930: Excavations at Saxonbury Camp. *Sussex Archaeol. Coll.* 71, 223–236.

WINBOLT, S.E. 1932: Excavations at Hascombe Camp, Godalming, June–July 1930. *Surrey Archaeol. Coll.* 40, 86–96.

WINBOLT, S.E. 1936: An Early Iron Age Camp in Piper's Copse, Kirdford. *Sussex Archaeol. Coll.* 77, 246–249.

WYNNE, E.J. and TYLECOTE, R.F. 1958: An experimental investigation into primitive iron smelting techniques. *Journ. Iron Steel Institute* 190, 339–348.

Pitfalls and possibilities in Iron Age pottery studies — experiences in the Upper Thames Valley

George Lambrick

Introduction

The impressive progress made over the last few years in Iron Age ceramic studies in Wessex (Cunliffe, this volume) may well be envied by excavators and pottery specialists in other regions. In the Upper Thames Valley various factors have conspired to hinder the testing or refinement of Harding's (1972) assessment of the pottery. There are still no good stratified sequences of large assemblages, let alone ones containing all the more distinctive types of pottery; the only petrological analysis to date (Williams unpublished) suggested that the results were likely to be inconclusive in an area so dominated by the reworked materials of glacial drift; and the analysis of any regional styles is complicated by the possibility that the Thames and Cherwell represented important tribal boundaries (Harding 1972; Sellwood this volume). In addition only a limited amount of work has been done outside the confines of rescue archaeology which has inevitably been concentrated on the gravels, leaving other parts of the region under-represented. In particular no high-status site comparable with Danebury has been examined on a sufficient scale or in adequate detail to provide a basic framework.

Attempts to establish a more securely-founded ceramic typology, however, have both revealed various pitfalls of interpretation, and have suggested some new lines of productive enquiry. This paper is an attempt to rationalise and illustrate these somewhat miscellaneous observations; many of its considerations may have a wider relevance.

The Life-Cycle of Pottery: Implications for Interpretation

In a paper given at the conference Dr T.C. Champion drew attention to the need to consider the nature of Iron Age currency and the way in which coinage was used, hoarded, and lost, if what it can tell us about Iron Age economics and social interaction is to be fully understood. Both the need for such considerations and their relative neglect in the past is closely paralleled in the field of pottery studies. There is widespread acknowledgement of the complex interrelationships of characteristics within pottery assemblages and the wide range of information that their analysis can provide (Renfrew 1977); but most studies emphasise the various possibilities of exploiting these to provide different lines of evidence rather than the complications of interpreting data created by such a range of interacting variables. Schiffer (1976) has drawn attention to these problems in

his discussion of 'cultural formation-processes' but his relative neglect of some important formation-processes, most notably the effects of redeposition, has left an incomplete assessment and one which in any case needs specific application to Iron Age pottery studies in Britain.

Every stage in the life-cycle of pottery contributes something to the final characteristics of excavated assemblages. They may be classified as follows:
1. Manufacture
2. Distribution
3. Usage
4. Breakage and discard
5. Post-depositional disturbance and redeposition
6. Post-depositional deterioration
7. Archaeological recovery.

What complicates the interpretation of pottery assemblages is first that several of these stages are both subjects of study in themselves and are capable of biasing the other aspects, and secondly that observed characteristics in the pottery — say the proportion of fineware — may be the product of more than one influence. What follows is not a systematic analysis of all the complexities involved, but an illustration of some of them in the hope that it may result in better appreciation of the practicalities of interpreting pottery assemblages, particularly the less spectacular ones which account for the vast majority of excavated pottery.

The cultural formation-processes inherent in the life-cycle of pottery are obviously cumulative, and our analysis should perhaps be like the excavation of similarly cumulative stratified soil-deposits, working backwards through the stages of formation, removing the accretions of new characteristics and the disturbance of old ones. We thus begin with the final stage.

Archaeological recovery

General Consideration

Archaeological excavation is invariably selective. Sites are rarely completely excavated and the characteristics of pottery assemblages may often be influenced by which areas are examined. On a regional scale differences may result from which sites are examined.

Actual recovery from the ground is affected by the competence of individual excavators, methods of excavation, weather, lighting and soil-conditions — all familiar considerations in the analysis of surface collections from field-walking, but seldom recorded or considered for excavated material. Apart from quantitative biases, differential recovery may be evident from the size and recognisability of sherds and in their finishing and colour (Levitan 1982). In the Upper Thames area checks on recovery have included sieving at Mount Farm (Jones 1978) and spoil-sifting at Claydon Pike (S. Palmer pers. comm.).

At Mount Farm one objective was to provide general qualitative checks. Recovery from sieving, both with and without water, using a 6 mm mesh was compared with manual collection. The results (Table 1) show that the average size of sherds from both types of sieving was about half that of those recovered manually. Up to about 13% of the sieved sherds were too small even for fabric identification. This also explains the lower figures for oxidised surfaces: these smallest sherds usually lacked their surfaces, leaving only scraps of normally reduced core. If the core scraps are excluded, the occurrence of the oxidised sherds is almost the same for sieving and manual recovery. The generally smaller size of sieved sherds must also partly account for the more substantial differences in the occurrence of distinctive forms and burnishing: obviously smaller sherds are less likely to include some recognisable part of a pot's form, while the frequent patchiness of burnishing also renders it less likely to occur on small sherds.

The comparison of wet and dry sieving, for ditches 200/203 and 206, suggests that the two produce similar results, though the smallness of the wet sieved sample leaves room for doubt. The difference in average weight of sherd is largely explicable in the much lower number of unidentifiable scraps in the water-sieved sample. If the scraps are excluded the other figures are again fairly comparable (identifiable forms 8.9% and 11.9%; burnishing 16.6% and 16.1%; oxidised surfaces 46.4% and 51.8%).

Although there are shortcomings in the quality of the data (for instance the mixture of random and non-random samples, and more particularly the lack of control data on the figures for manual recovery), some further observations are possible. There is no indication that surface colour was a significant factor in biasing any of the recovery methods. There may be a bias towards identifiable forms and towards burnished sherds in the manual recovery, but it may be entirely explicable by the very evident bias towards larger sherds. This could be checked by using a mesh size which would catch sherds close in size to those recovered manually. It is worth noting here the other advantages of a larger mesh size: on many sites sorting would be greatly aided by letting more gravel and stones through the sieves, analysis and recording would benefit by not having to deal with unidentifiable scraps, and the viability of using dry sieving rather than wet sieving would be further enhanced since the biases likely to occur would be reduced as larger sherds are less likely to be missed.

The combination of using larger mesh sizes and dry rather than wet sieving is very attractive both in reducing processing times and in obviating the logistical problems of organising an adequate water-supply for large-scale sieving. Provided that it is remembered that sieving for pottery should be used to provide a quantitative and

Table 1 Comparison of Wet sieving, Dry sieving and Manual Collection at Mount Farm, Dorchester, Oxon.

A. Comparison of wet sieving and manual collection over whole site, pits and ditches random and non-random samples.

	No Sherds recovered	Weight of sherds	Av. weight of sherds	No sherds of unidentifiable fabric. (+%)	No sherds of identifiable form. (+%)	No of burnished sherds. (+%)	No sherds with part or wholly oxidized surface (+%)
Manual Recovery	686	13079g	19.1g	0(0%)	172(25.0%)	105(15.3%)	375(54.7%)
Wet Seiving	591	6126g	8.7g	63(10.7%)	82(13.9%)	33(5.6%)	283(47.9%)

B. Comparison of wet sieving, dry sieving and manual collection for two ditches, F200/203 and F206 randon and non-random samples.

	No Sherds recovered	Weight of sherds	Av. weight of sherds	No sherds of unidentifiable fabric. (+%)	No sherds of identifiable form. (+%)	No of burnished sherds. (+%)	No sherds with part or wholly oxidized surface (+%)
Manual Recovery	624	7450g	11.9g	3(0.5%)	124(19.9%)	125(20.0%)	304(48.7%)
Dry Sieving	627	3432g	5.5g	84(13.4%)	65(10.4%)	90(14.4%)	252(40.2%)
Wet Sieving	116	826g	7.1g	4(3.4%)	10(8.6%)	18(15.5%)	58(50.0%)

qualitative check on recovery, not actually to recover every last scrap of fired clay, these advantages will be appreciated and it is to be hoped that simple sieving programmes will be more widely used to provide controls on ceramic data.

Influence on other lines of evidence

The ways in which recovery may affect pottery data are diverse. At the regional level trading-patterns may be distorted if the variety and status of different types of site are not properly represented by those excavated. The absence of excavated material from the relatively high-status sites of a region may result in artificially-restricted ranges for some widely-traded wares, while an over-abundance of material from higher-status sites might equally underestimate the general importance of domestic production or very local trade in pottery. The general strategies of excavation in Wessex and the Upper Thames (see Cunliffe this volume and Miles this volume) may well have resulted in such differences between the two areas.

Within settlements, partial excavation may lead to over-representation of particular activities or social distinctions, giving a misleading impression of the general character of the pottery. At present it is unclear how far such differentiation is evident on Iron Age sites in the two regions; but it could affect interpretations of usage, status and trade, and also the value of the pottery as dating evidence since finewares tend to be more diagnostic.

In the actual recovery of sherds quantitative biases affect assessment of the density of occupation-refuse and the abundance and therefore reliability of readily-datable sherds. Qualitative biases affect a whole range of variables: sherd size is relevant to the problem of redeposition and to discard patterns, burnished pottery affects assessments of function, status and trade, and colour of pottery is relevant to the proportion of different fabrics or wares and to any consideration of firing and manufacture.

Recovery can thus affect almost every aspect of pottery analysis. What is unclear is the actual degree of bias that does occur. Even if it cannot be quantified precisely, better assessment of its effects is necessary if the reliability of ceramic evidence is to be established.

Post-Depositional Deterioration

General Considerations

Apart from further breakage because of disturbance (see below), pottery in the ground may undergo various changes. It is well recognised that fabric-identification can be affected by secondary leaching of shell or limestone fragments in the body of pottery, and this is usually taken into consideration by the identification of voids (Peacock 1977). At Mount Farm (Lambrick in prep) one vessel exhibited greater leaching on the inside than the outside, and this was considered as possible evidence for vessel-usage (perhaps suggesting processes involving relatively acidic liquids). However, this was not systematically analysed, and the possible effect of post-depositional leaching is unclear. Another source of direct evidence for usage, the occurrence of lime-scale on pottery, may be difficult to interpret where secondary calcium carbonate deposits occur (see below), or will not survive at all in acidic soils.

On some low-lying sites in the region, particularly those on the floodplain or first gravel terrace, where clay soils are common, the problem of losing burnished surfaces has been noted. Nevertheless relatively high proportions of burnished pottery were recorded at Farmoor (see below p. 170) on the floodplain where clayey soils predominated, and it seems that traces of burnishing may be less obvious but are not necessarily entirely obliterated by this problem. A further factor affecting this may be how well-fired the pottery is.

Influence on other lines of evidence

Post-depositional changes again affect various types of evidence. Differential survival of particular fabric-types could exaggerate differences in the origins of pottery at neighbouring sites. Interpretations of usage, status and trade as expressed in the quality of pottery may be affected by the survival of burnishing. The interpretation of pottery-usage may be complicated by post-depositional factors affecting the condition of the pottery itself and the disappearance or addition of deposits on its surface. On the whole these problems can be allowed for as analysis proceeds, often by only regarding gross differences as significant.

Post-Depositional Disturbance and Redeposition

General Considerations

For the most part pottery-analysts work from the assumption that assemblages are not seriously contaminated by redeposited material unless there are obvious anomalies in them. This is mistaken: it would be more realistic, at least on relatively densely-occupied sites, to assume that most assemblages have more or less redeposited material in them, and that much of it is not easily distinguished. Certainly in the Thames Valley very few deposits can be shown to have accumulated by purely natural processes, and repeated soil-moving (inevitable in digging and backfilling pits and ditches) is obviously likely to result in redeposition of earlier artifacts in the soil.

The proportion of redeposited sherds which can be recognised specifically is highly variable and depends largely on the extent to which the pottery of the periods concerned can be distinguished. Redeposited early or middle Iron Age sherds in Roman assemblages are easily recognised because of fundamental technical and stylistic differences. For periods where these differences are too slight to be evident in every sherd it is more difficult to quantify proportions of redeposited material, since distinctions may be revealed only by a limited range of stylistic characteristics. The introduction of new styles may be more obvious than their demise, and the proportion of sherds which are chronologically diagnostic further depends on the distinctiveness of the styles current in different periods.

Where the proportion of specifically recognisable redeposited material is low, the degree of redeposition has to be assessed by reference to more general trends. These include less clear-cut technical and stylistic changes (such as changing fabric-proportions); the tendency for pottery to break into smaller pieces down to relatively unbreakable small sherds; the tendency for once-discreet types of refuse to be mixed into homogeneous assemblages lacking distinctive characteristics, and similarly the tendency for soil containing old refuse to be relatively homogeneous.

How these trends are used to assess the degree of redeposition, however, depends on a proper appreciation of the mechanisms of the process and the potential complexity of resulting patterns. The character of assemblages contaminated by redeposited objects depends not only on how much earlier material has been disturbed and on the number and character of the disturbed deposits represented, but also on how much and what type of contemporary refuse reaches the new deposit.

Some of the main points can be illustrated from post-Iron Age examples, where the amount of redeposited material is readily recognisable and the scale of the problem can be assessed. At Mount Farm, for instance, as much as 75% Iron Age pottery occurred in Roman contexts, and an even more extreme example was encountered on a Roman and later site at Towcester, Northants (Lambrick 1980). Here a pit which was stratigraphically later than a good post-medieval assemblage contained 185 Roman sherds, 68 medieval and only 9 post-medieval sherds along with a few clay pipes. Yet in spite of the huge proportions of redeposited Roman pottery in medieval and later deposits on this site, it was notable the the animal-bone assemblages differed significantly from the Roman ones.

These examples show how redeposition may occur at very high levels, even 100%, how more than one period may be represented in the disturbed material, and how the proportion of redeposited material need not be the same for all types of refuse. The character of redeposited material will also vary with the degree of disturbance: it may retain its original character as fresh refuse if it is immediately incorporated into a new deposit, or may become lost in the homogeneity of other material through constant recycling.

The general trends mentioned above — the occurrence of outmoded but not necessarily obsolete pottery, highly-fragmented sherds and generally homogeneous refuse-characteristics and soil-deposits — may be indicators of assemblages with large redeposited components. The reverse of these trends, however, should not be taken to demonstrate the absence of redeposited material. The quantification of such indicators is thus not a measure of redeposition itself but of the strength of warning available to the analyst. Furthermore, because of the potential variability in the character of both redeposited and fresh refuse, it would also be wrong to expect any close correlation between the indicators when applied to a number of assemblages: the character of each assemblage will have been determined by a unique and probably complex set of circumstances. It seems likely that the various indicators will be clearest for material that has spent a good deal of time on the surface, or in topsoil subject to constant disturbance, before being incorporated in a sealed deposit. This will apply to contemporary as well as to redeposited refuse, and the indicators of redeposited material could thus be exaggerated.

The application of these considerations can be illustrated from the analysis of pottery and other refuse at Mount Farm (Fig. 11.1). The problem arose from difficulties with dating evidence: there was very little useful stratigraphy, and it was unclear whether the occurrence of earlier Iron Age forms in contexts with middle Iron Age sherds was due to continued use or to redeposition, though the latter was suspected. It was also clear that expected changes in fabric-proportions, as at Ashville (De Roche 1978) or Farmoor (Lambrick 1979), were not as marked as on these sites. The rate of occurrence of diagnostically middle Iron Age sherds, where they were present, was mostly around 2% to 6%, whereas diagnostically early IA sherds occurred at levels of 10% to 25% and sometimes more. Since most assemblages contained under 100 sherds, it was clear that even with fairly moderate rates of redeposition (c. 30%) it was likely that middle Iron Age assemblages would occur in which all the diagnostic sherds were early Iron Age. This was indeed the case in some ditches which on spatial and stratigraphic grounds were clearly of the middle Iron Age or later.

Since the extent of the problem was thus unclear, some consideration was given to the indirect indicators of redeposition described above. Fig. 11.1 gives the broad characteristics of forms, fabrics and the size of sherds for the main pottery assemblages. The homogeneity of the refuse and of the soil-deposits are also indicated.

The assemblages have been ranged by broad fabric-proportion, the shelly wares tending to be more common in the earlier Iron Age (De Roche 1978; Lambrick 1979). The general fall in the proportion of early sherds and increased occurrence of mid Iron Age ones from about F615 downwards in the diagram seems broadly to agree with this.

The evidence for redeposited material given by these figures is not clear-cut. The trends used as possible indicators of its presence do not correlate well; but, as discussed above, this is not surprising given the variability of redeposition-processes. The use of the figures is therefore highly interpretive. This is not the place to discuss them in detail, but a few points are worth mentioning.

Among the supposedly earlier contexts F303, F531, F541, F115, F257 and F656 contain middle Iron Age sherds, and the relatively high proportions of shelly fabrics might be suspected to reflect the presence of much redeposited material. In the case of F115 the other

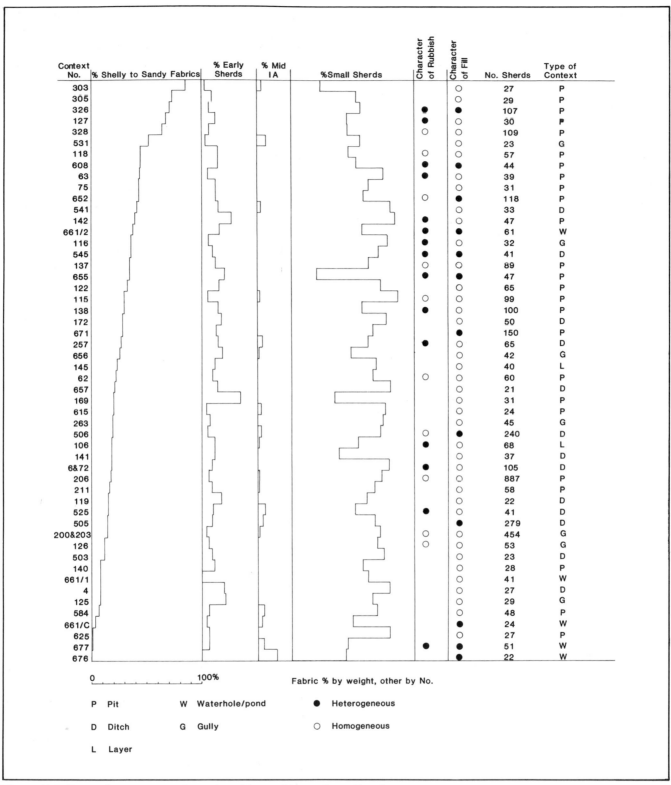

Figure 11.1 *Data relevant to assessing redeposition at Mount Farm, Dorchester.*

indicators would seem to support this (low occurrence of early sherds, highly-fragmented sherds and homogeneous rubbish and backfill). With the rest, however, these indicators do not follow the same pattern and, in the case of F303 at least, one might suspect that the late sherd was intrusive through animal burrowing. In some other contexts such as F116, which on spatial and stratigraphic grounds is probably middle Iron Age, the presence of early sherds but absence of later ones and the

relatively high proportion of shelly fabrics seem misleading; only the high proportion of small sherds would indicate a problem of redeposition.

It is uncertain how long early styles lasted; but the continued presence of early sherds in the supposedly later contexts is good reason at least to suspect redeposition. Many though not all of these contexts have small sherds. Some such as F4 and F125 contain substantial proportions of early sherds and no middle Iron Age ones, but there are again spatial and stratigraphic grounds for believing them to belong to the later period, apart from the predominance of sandy fabrics.

At Appleford (De Roche and Lambrick 1980) another example of the possible effects of redeposition was noted. Figures on sherd-size suggested that an apparent reversal of the usual chronological development in fabrics might have resulted from relatively higher rates of redeposited pottery caused by a fall off in the amount of contemporary refuse away from a habitation site.

These examples illustrate how awkward and elusive the assessment of redeposition can be. The major conclusion is that it is seldom measurable except in periods in which the pottery is totally different from preceding ones. Otherwise assessment of the problem may only give a vague impression of how serious the biases might be. There is seldom any firm evidence for the proportion or identity of redeposited material. The possible indicators do not correlate well and none of them seems reliable by itself.

Influence on other lines of evidence

The problem of redeposition affects most of the lines of evidence sought by pottery analysts. Dating is made more difficult because the distortions in the expected rates of occurrence of diagnostic types and/or very high rates of redeposition may result in all the datable sherds being redeposited ones: the higher the rates of redeposition the larger the size of assemblages in which this may be a problem. Pottery typologies based on stratified sequences of assemblages are prone to difficulties in distinguishing between the continuation of older styles and their occurrence as redeposited items.

Where redeposition is common or suspected in most assemblages, as at Mount Farm, analysis phase by phase of different aspects of pottery and (importantly) other, undatable materials such as animal bone or carbonised remains is hindered. However the bias will tend towards suggesting continuity: where differences are evident (and as at Towcester, this may only be one type of refuse) the effect of redeposition will have been to mask the true degree of difference. In these circumstances relatively slender evidence for chronological developments may be more significant than is immediately apparent, while apparently strong evidence of continuity would be less significant.

Finally there is a more positive aspect of redeposition in the possibility of detecting shifts in density or location of domestic activity. High rates of redeposition may indicate a shift away from an area formerly used intensively or over a long period. Where this is evident in the pottery but not in other types of refuse, a change in discard patterns resulting from different usage of an area may be indicated.

The problem of redeposition has been discussed at some length because it is seldom adequately considered. The tendency to underestimate the potential effects of the problem even at a relatively simple level can lead to basic misinterpretations. This may be the case in the rather implausible phasing of Ructstalls Hill (Oliver and Applin 1979). If it were acknowledged that 100% redeposition may well occur, especially in small assemblages when intensity of occupation-activity is low, a more straightforward interpretation, which did not involve alternate switching between two very different lay-outs, would be reasonable.

Breakage and Discard

General Considerations

From what has already been said it is clear that the life of pottery as sherds, from its breakage to its recovery, can be complicated. Most attention, particularly in the United States, however, has been paid only to the initial stage, its breakage and discard. The literature on the subject in the last decade has become voluminous (e.g. Schiffer 1976; Plog 1980). For the Iron Age in this country much less detailed attention has been paid to the subject, though both Bradley and Fulford (1980) and Halstead et al. (1978) have used models of the breakage and discard of pottery to provide information about internal site-organisation and usage. In neither case, however, were the complexities of these mechanisms fully considered in the published accounts.

With the exception of a few rare sites where occupation-layers survive, as at Danebury in Wessex (Cunliffe 1981) or Mingies Ditch in the Upper Thames (Allen and Robinson 1980), the British Iron Age is represented almost entirely by 'secondary refuse' in Schiffer's definition. Even where the absence of earlier occupation excludes the complication of redeposited material, however, depositional processes are not simple and no one model applies to all cases. Secondary refuse may be the rubbish from a specific operation deliberately discarded nearby; it could also be primary in situ rubbish cleared up and thrown out elsewhere; it could represent burial of rubbish which had accumulated on a midden having been generated by a variety of activities; or it may be scattered refuse accidentally incorporated in the backfill of pits, ditches and other holes in the ground. None of these models need involve the processes of redeposition already discussed, and all of them could be represented within a single settlement. Each is likely to lead to different characteristics in breakage and the recognisable identity of rubbish.

Patterns of breakage have already been touched on in the previous section. Patterns of discard were also examined at Mount Farm. The first approach was to examine the character of individual refuse-assemblages by correlating the characteristics of three types of rubbish which often occur together in reasonable abundance (animal bones, pottery and carbonised seeds). The animal bones were divided between those parts of the skeleton more likely to represent butchery waste and those characteristic of consumption refuse. For the pottery, burnishing was used to distinguish fine from coarse wares, which were shown by analysis of cooking residues to have distinct functions, though lime-scale on the finewares suggested that they did have some 'kitchen' uses (see below, 'Usage'). The carbonised remains were characterised on the basis of the proportion of grain in the samples. The percentages of butchery bones, fineware and grain were then plotted against each other as shown in Fig. 11.2.

At Wendon's Ambo (Halstead *et al.* 1978) significant correlations between pottery and bone refuse were claimed, but the characterisation of the bone was so suspect as to invalidate the study. At Mount Farm no simple association between different activities is suggested by the refuse characteristics examined.

If anything the predicted variability in the factors influencing the overall character of the rubbish is apparent. In each graph the central group of points represents assemblages with average characteristics in the types of refuse plotted; these assemblages are more or less the same in each case, suggesting that they contain thoroughly mixed homogeneous refuse reflecting no particular activity. Around these contexts other points on the graphs indicate assemblages with more distinctive types of refuse, suggesting the input of rubbish from specific activities. The absence of clear correlations between these distinctive types of refuse seems to suggest that in some cases other rubbish was already homogenised, and in others that the activities generating distinctive refuse were not themselves closely correlated, or that an intermediate stage of discard (perhaps reflecting the distinction between primary and secondary refuse) meant that any correlations were broken down by rubbish being collected up from different areas to be disposed of in one place. It is also unclear how far

some of the homogeneity of refuse is the result of redeposition and mixing of earlier rubbish (see above p. 165).

Although there was thus no clear correlation between these characteristics in individual refuse-assemblages, a second less specific approach, examining the character of finds from two main concentrations of settlement-features on the site suggested that differences were detectable. In the middle Iron Age the northern part of the site produced more loomweights and more slag but fewer bone tools. Slightly less burnished pottery but more sherds with cooking residues, and slightly fewer cattle bones were found, but this could partly result from greater redeposition of early Iron Age material. No distinction in the proportion of skeletal elements in the animal bones was apparent.

Influence on other lines of evidence

The effect that patterns of breakage and discard have on the wider analysis of pottery is relatively restricted, being mainly confined to questions of intra-site variability, particularly the identification and relationship between activity areas and social organisation. Breakage also affects how far the problem of redeposition can be assessed (see above). The Mount Farm study indicates that over-simple models of breakage and discard should be avoided, and that tight correlations in the characteristics of different types of refuse in single deposits should not necessarily be expected. The evidence for some spatial variation in the character of finds across the

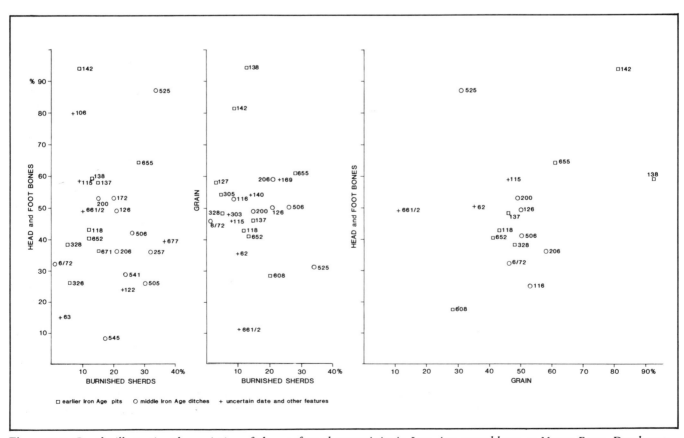

Figure 11.2 *Graphs illustrating the variation of three refuse-characteristics in Iron Age assemblages at Mount Farm, Dorchester.*

site, however, suggests that factors affecting the character of different types of refuse may still be apparent through more general discard patterns.

Usage

General Considerations

The function of pottery vessels has for the most part been interpreted from characteristics of form, fabric and finishing. Apart from burial, the main uses usually considered are storage, cooking, and consumption of food and drink. More specialised uses may be indicated by particular characteristics, as with crucibles and strainers; but in addition to these many uses may not be directly evident at all, or are so only in characteristics which are capable of other interpretations, such as decoration. Multiple uses are also to be expected. Hodder (1981a, 1981b) has drawn attention to the social and symbolic functions of pottery, which in ethnographic contexts can vary considerably in their manifestations between different settlements and tribes. Other ethnographical studies have observed the use of pottery trade in the development of political or diplomatic relationships (Plog 1980, 21–22).

The archaeologist, lacking the directly observable context in which pottery is made and used, may feel somewhat daunted by this variety of possible functions and uses and by the frequent lack of evidence for them. Nevertheless direct evidence for function is obtainable from residues and other traces on some sherds. This may at least show that different types of pottery had distinct practical functions, in which case unsupported social interpretations might be invalid.

This question has been examined in a limited way at Mount Farm. No microscopic or chemical investigation has yet been undertaken. The main concern was to establish whether different usage was broadly discernible rather than to identify precisely what had been stored or cooked in different vessels. It is fairly common to find both carbonised residues and lime-scaling on Iron Age pottery. On this site they occurred on about 6% of the sherds. It was sometimes difficult to distinguish burnt food residues from sooting (either from cooking or the original firing of the pottery), especially on the external surfaces; similarly it was not always easy to distinguish lime-scale from secondary calcium carbonate deposition.

The analysis showed that only 7.5% of the carbonised residues occurred on fineware sherds, whereas 49% of the lime-scale occurred on fineware. This strongly suggests different usage of coarse-ware and fineware pottery, but also an overlap between them with fine wares having a more restricted role in cooking (presumably involving heating water), rather than being used purely for consumption.

The analysis of superficial residues could be applied to a more tightly-defined range of pottery types — different forms, decorated wares etc; but at Mount Farm in common with most other sites in the Upper Thames Valley, the pottery is too fragmented, and the occurrence of decorated sherds is too sparse (c. 1% at Mount Farm) for this to be possible.

The slight spatial differences in the occurrence of burnished pottery and cooking-residues at Mount Farm noted in the previous section may reflect different emphasis in usage of the two areas or possibly some social distinction. Apart from this doubtful case, no evidence for social distinctions within settlements has emerged from pottery studies in the region. Decoration, which is potentially most useful for this, occurs too sparsely to be much use. Even where internal settlement-layout is sufficiently clear and has been extensively excavated, as at Claydon Pike (Miles and Palmer 1982) and Mingies Ditch (Allen and Robinson 1980), the pottery has been insufficient in quantity or variety for such distinctions to be reliably evident even if they existed.

Influence on other lines of evidence

The function of pottery has a bearing on various aspects of pottery analysis. The complex interaction of the evidence for actual use and social function are relevant to the spatial organisation and use of settlements. Evidence for how far high-quality wares were used in cooking etc. may have a bearing on assessments of the relative wealth or status of settlements or households. If usage is reflected in discard patterns (see above) the presence or absence of finewares may affect how well assemblages can be dated.

Distribution

General considerations

The term 'distribution' in archaeology all too often means the static spatial patterns revealed by the occurrence of particular artifacts. However, some element of the mobility of artifacts — of distribution in its true sense — is often revealed by the physical origins of pottery from outside a region (Peacock 1968, 1969a) or the fall-off curves of particular types away from their production centres. It is much rarer that studies of distribution and trade attempt to examine the fluid complexities of a region's total trading pattern, still less the economic interaction of supply and demand, resources and communications which actually determine distribution. These are often unapproachable within the constraints of archaeological evidence, but they require consideration even in the study of purely stylistic distributions.

The difficulty of identifying Iron Age pottery-producing sites (see below) makes it almost impossible to recognise the full range of wares produced at any centre, or their relative distributions. Nevertheless, assuming a multiplicity of producers working at different levels of output, we might expect highly variable sizes of market for different products. Such variability almost certainly occurred within areas displaying the same cultural affinities, and there are obvious dangers in conflating petrological evidence and stylistic characteristics in the consideration of ceramic distributions, as in

Ellison's (1981) wide-ranging consideration of pre-historic trade in Britain.

The supply of pottery to markets should not be viewed in isolation from other traded commodities which may substantially affect distributions. At Claydon Pike the range and sources of the fabrics suggest very local origins for well over 95% of the pottery. A small number of sherds of Malvernian ware, however, indicates more distant exchange, which the presence of Droitwich briquetage suggests was intimately bound up with the salt trade (Morris 1981). This type of piggy-back commerce may have been a not uncommon means by which markets for some pottery-products were artificially extended, by exploiting long-distance trans-port of scarce commodities from the same area. Perhaps similar associations might be identified with other traded minerals such as iron or quernstones.

The physical production sources, stylistic affinities and trading associations of pottery are obviously all useful in studying the supply side of ceramic trade. The demand side is less often considered in analysing pottery distribution, though the status and availability of markets is of obvious importance.

Market status may be evident from site typology or artifact studies. Pottery may be useful not only as direct evidence for trade, but also as a possible indicator of economic or social status through the proportion of fineware or decorated vessels. In employing these characters as indicators of status the possible biases of usage must be borne in mind (see above).

In the Upper Thames region there are hints of a pattern emerging from the quantification of finewares in middle Iron Age settlement-assemblages. On the higher second-terrace sites, mainly associated with arable or mixed agriculture, fairly high proportions of burnished pottery occur (Ashville 49%, Mount Farm 21%, Gravelly Guy 33%). On two lower-lying sites, associ-ated more with pastoralism, lower proportions occur (Claydon Pike 1.75%; Mingies Ditch 0.6%). At Far-moor, where the floodplain farmsteads were shown by biological evidence to be seasonal short-lived specialised pastoral units (Lambrick and Robinson 1979), the proportion of burnished pottery was 29%, comparable to the second-terrace sites. Possibly this might be because the Farmoor farmsteads were dependent on a parent settlement perhaps of the Ashville type, rather than being more permanent, independent economic units like Claydon Pike and Mingies Ditch. Further work may overturn or change this pattern, or perhaps show the problems of survival of burnishing to be too great; but for the moment it is an area of study which deserves more attention.

Other possible indications from pottery of the econ-omic status of sites may be the diversity of fabric-types and of decorative motifs. At Rams Hill, for example, diversity of fabrics was taken as evidence for a func-tioning market (Bradley and Ellison 1975). Some Upper Thames sites, such as Blewburton or Allen's Pit exhibit much stylistic variation in the pottery. With both fabric and styles, however, the variability may reflect the

settlements' status as consumers rather than an active role in exchange.

Some insight into the general character of pottery-distribution on the Upper Thames has been gained in a preliminary analysis of the occurrence of decorative motifs recorded for different parts of the region (Figs. 11.3 to 11.5). In general a greater variety of decoration is recorded for the southern part of the region than for the northern part. To some extent this may result from inequalities in the status of the sites, but it could also reflect the influence of more highly-developed pottery-production in Wessex.

There is much variation in how widely particular motifs are found. Some of the early Iron Age motifs are found virtually throughout the region, others have more or less restricted distributions, including a few which occur repeatedly on single sites. Some of these may represent the output of single potters — stylistically this is most likely in the Chinnor material (Richardson and Young 1951).

In the middle Iron Age the pattern seems to be similar but with fewer clear examples. The most interesting point is the different distributions of the two main types of swag decoration. The tooled-lines version is concen-trated around Stanton Harcourt and Cassington (Area b) but is found as far south as Blewburton (Area e). The tooled-bands version is more tightly restricted to the Frilford area and the Corallian ridge (Area c).

In both periods some of the apparently-restricted distributions reflect much wider areas beyond the study area. The middle Iron Age scoring or combing at Madmarston (Area a), which occurs only sporadically further south, represents the edge of its wide distri-bution in the Midlands (Cunliffe 1974).

In both periods there is some indication of more general differences in the distributions. In the earlier Iron Age the use of stabbing is particularly characteristic of the southern part of the region, mainly on the chalk, while cross-hatching and multiple linear decoration is more characteristic of the Thames gravels, in particular round Dorchester. In the middle Iron Age, apart from the division in the type of swag design, there is a more general distinction between the Cassington/Frilford area, in which curvilinear designs are dominant, and the Dorchester/Blewburton area where geometrical designs occur as frequently as curvilinear ones.

This analysis is obviously crude; it is limited in the size of area covered, and quantification based on data from old excavation-reports has inevitable short-comings. In addition the grouping of the sites and the classification of motifs is somewhat arbitrary, while form was not considered at all. Some allowance for settlement-status was made by grouping the lesser sites for comparison with the higher-status ones, but some bias must remain. Despite these limitations, this rapid preliminary analysis does convey quite a useful im-pression of some of the different levels of style-variation over the region. Some may reflect different cultural influences and others may map the products of indivi-dual potters or small local groups, whose market-range

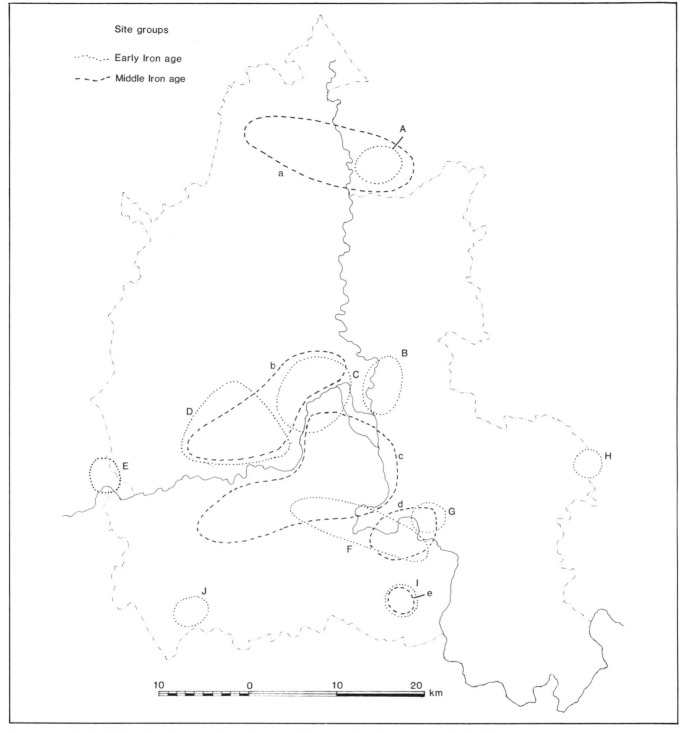

Figure 11.3 *Oxfordshire, showing groupings of sites used in recording decorative motifs for Figs. 11. 4–5.*

EARLY IRON AGE Group A: *Rainsborough (Avery* et al. *1967)*; Group B: *Woodeaton (Bradford 1942a), Old Marston (Harding 1972)*; Group C: *City Farm (Case* et al. *1964), Foxley Farm (Bradford 1942a), Purwell Farm (Dawson 1962), Yarnton (Bradford 1942a), Wytham (Bradford 1942a)*; Group D: *Beard Mill (Williams 1951), Stanton Harcourt (Bradford 1942a, Hamlin 1963), Standlake (Harding 1972)*; Group E: *Loders (Hingley in prep.), Roughground Farm (Hingley in prep.)*; Group F: *Ashville (De Roche 1978), Frilford (Bradford and Goodchild 1939), Appleford (Hinchliffe and Thomas 1980), Long Wittenham (Savory 1937), Wittenham Clumps (Rhodes 1948, Hingley 1983)*; Group G: *Allen's Pit (Bradford 1942a), Mount Farm (Myres 1937, Lambrick in prep.)*; Group H: *Chinnor (Bradford 1942a, Richardson and Young 1951)*; Group I: *Blewburton (Bradford 1942b, Collins 1947, 1952, Collins and Collins 1959, Harding 1972, 1976)*; Group J: *Ram's Hill (Bradley and Ellison 1975)*.

MIDDLE IRON AGE Group a: *Rainsborough (Avery* et al. *1967); Madmarston (Fowler 1960)*; Group b: *Yarnton (Bradford 1942a), Foxley Farm (Bradford 1942a), City Farm (Case* et al. *1964), Cassington (Harding 1972), Calais Farm (Bradford 1942a), Gravelly Guy (Lambrick excavation in progress)*; Group c: *Frilford (Bradford and Goodchild 1939, Harding 1972), Cherbury (Harding 1972), Hatford (Harding 1972), Farmoor (Lambrick 1979), Ashville (De Roche 1978)*; Group d: *Appleford (Hinchliffe and Thomas 1980), Mount Farm (Lambrick in prep.)*; Group e: *Blewburton (Bradford 1942b, Collins 1947, 1952, Collins and Collins 1959, Harding 1972, 1976)*.

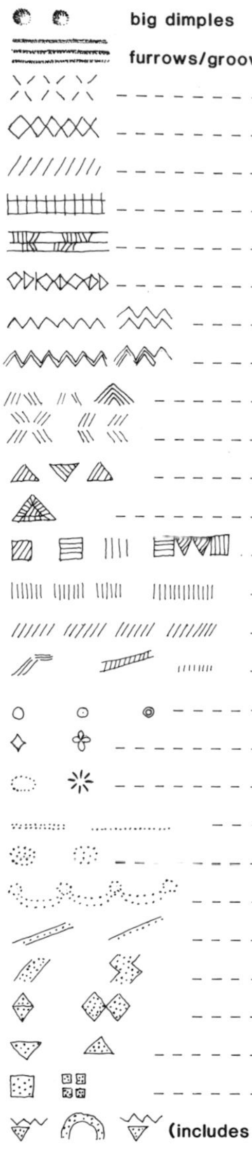

EARLY IRON AGE

#	Motif	A	B	C	D	E	F	G	H	I	J
1	big dimples							3			
2	furrows/grooves	2		4	6		5	3	1	2	1
3		2									
4		3									
5		1			1						
6								1	1		
7									1		
8									2		
9		1			1	1	2	2	11	5	
10			1				2	1	3	3	
11			1	2	5	3	7	8	5	3	
12				1	2	1	2	2			
13			1		1	5	2	4		1	1
14			1		2			1			
15			1			1	1	1			
16							1	4	6		
17				1		7	6	4	2	3	3
18				1	4	1		1			3
19					1		1	3	3	2	
20								1		1	
21									3	9	
22				1	1		2	2	1	4	4
23									3		
24									3		
25			2	1	2				8	3	1
26					4	2			1	2	1
27					1				2		
28							3		11	2	
29									1		1
30	(includes 9,25–29)								9		

SUMMARY (includes unclassified)

	A	B	C	D	E	F	G	H	I	J
Cross-hatching		3		3	9	9	9		1	2
Stabbed infilling			1	4	4	6		16	5	6
Multiple linear	7	6	5	12	30	33	31	30	11	10
Spotty motifs		1	1		3	2	1	7	18	
No. of motifs represented	5	7	8	11	9	13	17	16	15	9

Figure 11.4 The occurrence of decorative motifs in the Upper Thames region in the earlier Iron Age.

varied from regional to very local level. These make it difficult to detect a clear-cut style for the Upper Thames (cf. Cunliffe 1974, 38–9, 46) or alternatively any clear boundaries between different style-zones meeting in the region. For example, what is the significance of the swagged globular bowls which have been taken as so characteristic of the region's middle Iron Age pottery? As Harding (1972; 1974, 196–9) pointed out, both bowls and swags occur outside the Upper Thames. Within the region the use of geometrical designs on similar bowls has tended to be overlooked, as has the difference of technique in the execution of the swags. These variations have different spatial distributions and clearly complicate the overall picture. They emphasise how different levels of variation and distribution occur even within what is supposedly a highly distinctive style of pottery. If the distribution of the full range of contemporary pottery were considered, the pattern would become a good deal more complicated. Any interpretation must take into account how the interlocking facets of stylistic

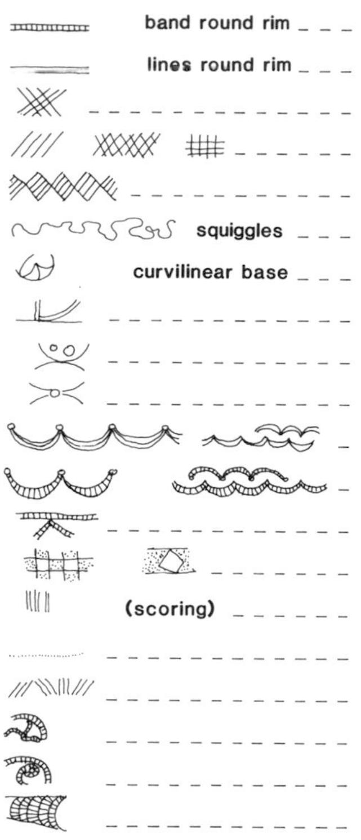

MIDDLE IRON AGE		a	b	c	d	e
1	band round rim		1	3	5	5
2	lines round rim	1	2	2	2	7
3					1	1
4				1	1	4
5			1	1	3	1
6	squiggles	1				2
7	curvilinear base		1	3		2
8						1
9					1	
10				3		
11			10	4	3	
12				13	1	
13			1		1	4
14			1		2	1
15	(scoring)	5		1	1	1
16						1
17			1			
18			1			
19				1		
20						1
SUMMARY						
Geometric tooled lines			1	2	5	5
Geometric bands & infills		2			2	5
Curvilinear tooled lines		2	12	9	6	5
Curvilinear bands			1	13	2	2
Scoring		5		1	1	1
No. of motifs represented		6	7	10	10	13

Figure 11.5 *The occurrence of decorative motifs in the Upper Thames region in the middle Iron Age.*

variation and distribution are the product of many different influences.

Influence on other lines of evidence

The patterns of distribution that can be detected provide much of the evidence for the organisation of manufacturing (see below). Distribution also has an influence on dating through the presence or absence of many of the more diagnostic types of vessel. As we have seen, the interaction of supply and demand which controls distribution may reflect various points about the economic or social status of settlements.

Manufacture

General Considerations

It is extremely difficult to be specific about the organisation and location of Iron Age pottery-production. It used traditionally to be assumed that all prehistoric pottery-manufacture was essentially a domestic craft, and indeed this is still believed to have been an important type of production. On some sites virtually all the pottery seems to have been made within the settlement. In the Upper Thames Valley this may be true at Claydon Pike and Mingies Ditch. These sites display a limited range of forms, rather crude manufacture and finishing, and a high preponderance of very locally-derived fabrics (S. Palmer, D. Wilson pers. comms.).

It has now long been established that Iron Age pottery was also produced for trade over large areas and was often highly specialised in quality and design. This was most clearly demonstrated by Peacock's (1968, 1969a) petrological analysis for south-west Britain. In the Upper Thames Valley the occurrence of the few Malvernian sherds at Claydon Pike reminds us of more distant production-centres. The work of specialist potters may also be reflected in the higher-quality wares at sites such as Blewburton, Ashville and Mount Farm. The possible existence of particular pottery-producers in the region has already been mentioned in connection with the distribution of some of the decoration motifs.

In Wessex there are hints that another form of production, involving itinerant specialist potters, may be evident from the variety of fabrics in which some of the strikingly similar, highly-finished and technically accomplished haematite bowls occur (Davies 1981, 146). Given that no fixed plant such as kilns and workshops was necessary in Iron Age pottery production, this is perfectly plausible.

Three radically different modes of production may thus have contributed to the output of Iron Age pottery. Their relative importance varies from site to site depending, as we have seen, on factors controlling distribution.

The identification of the three types of manufacture is unlikely to be easy, especially as there may well have been intermediate producers, local semi-mobile, semi-specialist craftsmen, whose products may obscure any clear distinctions.

There may have been chronological changes in production-methods; but it would be over-simple to suggest a progression from domestic to semi-mobile, and then to itinerant and ultimately to fixed specialist production with fully-developed marketing. Specialist production and trade is also evident in earlier prehistoric ceramics (Peacock 1969b; Howard 1981).

Other chronological changes in manufacture, most notably in styles, have always been recognised as providing invaluable dating evidence. Technical changes in the character of clay body used for potting and in forming-techniques are also well recognised. In both cases, however, their use for the purpose of dating assemblages has been inadequately quantified.

In the absence of a good stratified sequence, the age of the latest pottery in an assemblage is normally taken as dating evidence. But in fact this relies on the absence of still later sherds, and the significance of that absence needs to be assessed in terms of the rate of occurrence of diagnostic sherds. We have already seen how this may be influenced by redeposition, breakage, usage and distribution factors. It will also depend on how many vessels of different types were manufactured. Thus archaeological refinements based on rarely-occurring attributes, such as footrings on angular bowls (Barrett 1978, 286–7) or different types of decoration on globular bowls (Harding 1972, 107) tend to be of limited value in practice.

De Roche (1977) calculated that under 10% or Iron Age sherds from the Upper Thames region were chronologically diagnostic on the basis of form and decoration. At Mount Farm we have seen that c. 10 to 25% of early Iron Age sherds were diagnostic, whereas only 2 to 6% of those in middle Iron Age assemblages were. The difference in the figures in the latter case is partly explicable by the change of pottery styles itself: there is a much greater chance of a sherd from the distinctive angular profiles of the early Iron Age being recognisable than there is for one from the relatively formless rounded profiles of the middle Iron Age.

Fabric proportions are now more commonly quantified, but usually on the basis of already-established chronologies rather than as an independent or primary chronological indicator. The preponderance of shelly wares in the earlier Iron Age compared with sandy wares in the middle Iron Age in the Upper Thames was noted by Harding (1972, 98). At Farmoor, where the two phases of occupation were physically separate, the change in fabric-proportions was dramatic, and in the absence of more diagnostic forms was used as the primary chronological indicator (Lambrick and Robinson 1979).

At Ashville the same trend was evident (De Roche 1978). The data for this site are worth re-examining by presenting De Roche's Table II and other information in diagrammatic form (Fig. 11.6). The assemblages are arranged by proportion of shelly wares, the order being adjusted to be acceptable within the stratigraphic sequence. The occurrence of form types was expressed as a percentage of total assemblages, and the stratigraphy and radiocarbon dates were also added. De Roche's period divisions and form and fabric classifications were retained. The order in which the assemblages appear is not of course a precise chronological sequence, but the diagram does show that the changing fabric-proportions are generally consistent with the stratigraphy and the occurrence of forms. It should be noted that the trend is based on a very generalised fabric division.

The pattern revealed by the occurrence of forms is also instructive. Their presence in individual assemblages is somewhat haphazard, and in the case of the expanded rims is too irregular to be much use in dating. The various angular forms occur regularly up to the middle of Period II and then become more sporadic. The barrel

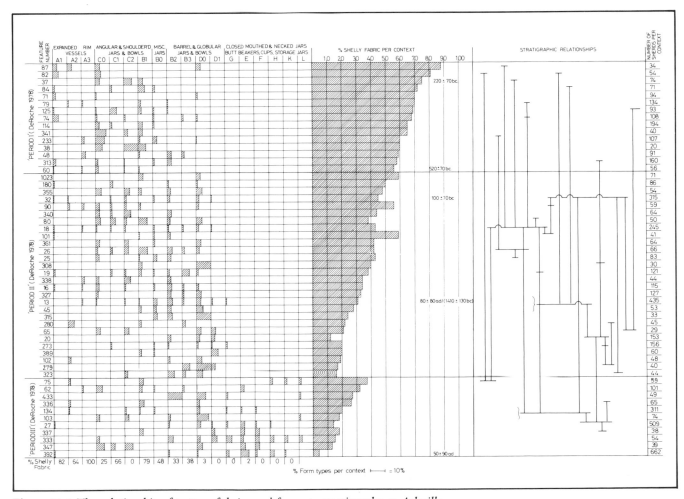

Figure 11.6 *The relationship of pottery fabrics and forms to stratigraphy at Ashville.*

174

jars and more globular forms of the middle Iron Age begin to occur regularly in Period II. Most interestingly the fineware globular bowls (form D1) are characteristic of contexts in the later part of Period II, apparently replacing the fineware angular bowls (form C2), which seem to occur less regularly in these assemblages. The sporadic occurrence of the early forms in later contexts is presumably an indication of redeposition. This is directly comparable with a similar exercise carried out by Carver on much more closely-stratified medieval pottery from Worcester (Carver 1980, fig. 52, 222). De Roche had suggested in the original report that there was an overlap between the early angular styles and the middle Iron Age rounded forms. This is now more clearly evident and can be seen as representing the first part of Period II, separated on grounds of fabrics, stratigraphy and forms from the later part, which should perhaps now be regarded as a separate phase.

Fabric-proportions have also proved useful for the identification of late Bronze Age pottery at least in the lower part of the Upper Thames where, in common with many other areas, vessels are characteristically flint-tempered (De Roche and Lambrick 1980; Hingley 1983). At Roughground Farm, Lechlade, however, late Bronze Age pottery was mainly in shelly fabrics (Hingley in prep.). Some of the late Bronze Age forms and decoration clearly continued into the early Iron Age, and Barrett's original (1978) suggestion that sites such as Mount Farm, Allen's Pit and Long Wittenham should be regarded as belonging to the late Bronze Age horizon must be regarded with scepticism. It remains to be seen how useful the chronological distinction between his decorated phase and plainware phase (Barrett 1980) will prove: in view of the potential biases of use and status already discussed, problems may well arise. Ideally all possible chronological indicators should be used and the value of each carefully assessed.

In the past the importance of technical change in the development of Iron Age pottery has probably been underestimated as well as under-used. Changes in form could also indicate technical developments, rather than purely aesthetic preferences or utilitarian requirements. For example, the change from angular to more rounded forms may reflect a switch of emphasis from slab-building to coil-building techniques.

Influence on other lines of evidence

Manufacture most clearly affects the use of pottery as dating evidence. Apart from its direct use for dating, chronological change in pottery may reflect something of the development of ideas through the relationship between technical and aesthetic innovations. Otherwise manufacture has an obvious influence on those stages in the life-cycle of pottery which the potter was concerned with — its distribution and its use. The extent to which these considerations affected how the pottery was designed and made is an important factor in determining how far they themselves can be analysed. Quality of firing may affect the survival of surface finish and

decoration, which have various implications as we have seen, and it may also affect breakage.

Conclusions

This consideration of the way in which the life-cycle of pottery effects its interpretation has been far from comprehensive. Nevertheless some of the complexities of the way in which different attributes of ceramic assemblages act both as primary sources of evidence and as biases on other attributes have been illustrated. The extent to which these factors need to be assessed depends very much on what is required from the analysis of pottery and the degree of refinement sought in interpreting differences in the ceramic record. It also depends on the size and quality of assemblages; where they are small, or contain few diagnostic sherds, or are subject to severe redeposition, many of the considerations outlined above are relevant even for the most basic level of analysis such as providing broad dating evidence.

Much more could be done in pottery reports to provide at least general assessments of how the evidence may have been biased by these cultural formation-processes. In many cases this may involve recording and quantifying attributes of pottery sherds which are not standard routine at present, and are certainly seldom published, and yet present no technical difficulty. The proportion of fineware in assemblages for example is seldom reported, but it is highly relevant to many of the considerations discussed above, both in terms of direct interpretation and in the assessment of bias in other lines of evidence — this failing is, alas, as evident in reports on material from the Upper Thames to date as it is anywhere else.

It is not the purpose of this paper to put forward specific proposals for how pottery should be recorded and analysed. Nor is it suggested (even if the methods were fully developed) that all analyses should involve complicated statistical measurement of all the cumulative biases inherent in the cultural formation-processes discussed. Most are not accurately quantifiable anyway. Nevertheless they should be taken more comprehensively into account if a fuller appreciation of the quality of the evidence is to be gained. Simple statistics can be used to great effect in providing the basis for judging some of these effects: figures on the proportion of finewares, the occurrence of chronologically-diagnostic sherds, the relative sizes of sherds, and varying fabric-proportions are all easily determined and are likely to be useful clues in working towards an understanding of the interaction of the processes by which pottery assemblages attain their final character.

One of the extra benefits of assessing cultural formation-processes more systematically is that further information may be obtained about the ways in which settlements operated internally and interacted with others externally, which have been relatively neglected in the past. The desirability for what has been termed an 'integrated approach' to pottery studies is increasingly recognised (e.g. Howard, 1981, 1–3), but this still tends to be viewed more as the need to integrate the results of studying different aspects of pottery than the need to integrate the study itself as discussed by Hodder (1981b). A fully-integrated approach will not only consider the complexity of the interacting processes which result in the character of pottery assemblages, but will also be more assiduous in considering what bearing the character of other artifacts and the soil-deposits themselves may have on the interpretation of the pottery.

The full integration of the results of pottery studies within the archaeological record generally is a further step which has been discussed elsewhere (Bradley and Hodder 1979; Hodder 1981a; Ellison 1981). It has only been touched upon occasionally in this paper, but it remains the ultimate objective of ceramic studies and should not be lost in the increasing maze of methodology.

Acknowledgements

I would like to thank Martin Lawler and Mrs Valerie De Hoog for their assistance in analysing refuse-characteristics and Iron Age pottery decoration respectively. I am also grateful to Tim Allen, Simon Palmer, David Miles, Richard Hingley and Duncan Wilson for allowing me to quote unpublished information. Tim Allen, Maureen Mellor, Simon Palmer and Sarah Green have provided many helpful comments and criticisms of this paper resulting in various improvements.

References

ALLEN, T. and ROBINSON, M. 1980: Hardwick with Yelford, Mingies Ditch. *CBA Group Nine Newsletter* 9, 115–7.

AVERY, M., SUTTON, J. and BANKS, J. 1967: Rainsborough, Northants., England: Excavations 1961–5. *Proc. Prehist. Soc.* 33, 207–306.

BARRETT, J. 1978: The EPRIA Prehistoric Pottery. In Hedges, J. and Buckley, D., Excavations at a Neolithic Causewayed Enclosure, Orsett, Essex, 1975. *Proc. Prehist. Soc.* 44, 219–308.

BARRETT, J. 1980: The pottery of the Later Bronze Age in Lowland England. *Proc. Prehist. Soc.* 46, 297–319.

BRADFORD, J. 1942a: An Early Iron Age Site at Allen's Pit, Dorchester. *Oxoniensia* 7, 36–60.

BRADFORD, J. 1942b: An Early Iron Age Site on Blewburton Hill, Berks. *Berks. Archaeol. Journ.* 46, 97–104.

BRADFORD, J. and GOODCHILD, R. 1939: Excavations at Frilford, Berks., 1937–8. *Oxoniensia* 4, 1–70.

BRADLEY, R. and ELLISON, A. 1975: *Ram's Hill* (Oxford BAR 19).

BRADLEY, R. and FULFORD, M. 1980: Sherd size in the Analysis of Occupation Debris. *Bull. Instit. Archaeol.* 17, 85–94.

BRADLEY, R. and HODDER, I. 1979: British Prehistory: an integrated view. *Man* NS 14, 93–104.

CASE, H., BAYNE, N., STEELE, S., AVERY, G. and SUTERMEISTER, H. 1964: Excavations at City Farm, Hanborough, Oxon. *Oxoniensia* 29/30, 1–98.

CARVER, M. (editor) 1980: Medieval Worcester an Archaeological Framework. *Trans. Worcs. Archaeol. Soc.* 3rd Ser. 7.

COLLINS, A. 1947: Excavations on Blewburton Hill, 1947. *Berks. Archaeol. Journ.* 50, 4–29.

COLLINS, A. 1953: Excavations on Blewburton Hill, 1948 and 1949. *Berks. Archaeol. Journ.* 53, 21–64.

COLLINS, A. and COLLINS, F. 1959: Excavations at Blewburton Hill, Berks., 1953. *Berks. Archaeol. Journ.* 57, 52–73.

CUNLIFFE, B.W. 1974: *Iron Age Communities in Britain* (London).

CUNLIFFE, B.W. 1981: Danebury, Hampshire. Third Interim Report on the Excavations 1976–80. *Antiq. Journ.* 51 pt 2, 238–54.

DAVIES, S. 1981: Excavations at Old Down Farm Andover, Part II: Prehistoric and Roman. *Proc. Hants. Field Club and Archaeol. Soc.* 37, 81–163.

DAWSON, G. 1961/2: Excavations at Purwell Farm, Cassington. *Oxoniensia* 26/27, 1–6.

DE ROCHE, D. 1977: *Analysis of selected groups of Early Iron Age Pottery from the Oxford Region* (Oxford, B.Litt. thesis).

DE ROCHE, D. 1978: The Iron Age Pottery. In Parrington, M., *The Excavation of an Iron Age settlement, Bronze Age ring-ditches and Roman features at Ashville Trading Estate, Abingdon (Oxfordshire) 1974–76* (London, CBA Res. Rep. 28), 40–74.

DE ROCHE, D. and LAMBRICK, G. 1980: The Iron Age Pottery. In Hinchliffe, J. and Thomas, R., Archaeological Investigations at Appleford. *Oxoniensia* 45, 9–111.

ELLISON, A. 1981: Pottery and Socio-economic exchange in British Prehistory. In Howard and Morris 1981, 45–55.

FOWLER, P. 1960: Excavations at Madmarston Camp, Swalcliffe, 1957–8. *Oxoniensia* 25, 3–48.

HAMLIN, A. 1966: Early Iron Age Sites at Stanton Harcourt. *Oxoniensia* 31, 1–28.

HALSTEAD, P., HODDER, I. and JONES, G. 1978: Behavioural Archaeology and refuse patterns: a case study. *Norwegian Archaeol. Review* 11, 118–31.

HARDING, D. 1972: *The Iron Age in the Upper Thames Basin* (Oxford).

HARDING, D. 1974: *The Iron Age in Lowland Britain* (London).

HARDING, D. 1976: Blewburton Hill, Berkshire: Re-excavation and Reappraisal. In Harding, D. (editor), *Hillforts* (London).

HINCHLIFFE, J. and THOMAS, R., Archaeological Investigations at Appleford. *Oxoniensia* 45, 9–111.

HINGLEY, R. 1983: Excavations by R.A. Rutland on an Iron Age site at Wittenham Clumps. *Berks. Archaeol. Journ.* 70 (for 1979–80), 21–55.

HINGLEY, R. in prep: Reports on Iron Age pottery from The Loders and Roughground Farm, Lechlade.

HODDER, I. 1981a: *Symbols in Action* (Cambridge).

HODDER, I. 1981b: Pottery, Production and Use: a Theoretical Discussion. In Howard and Morris 1981, 215–20.

HOWARD, H. 1981: In the wake of distribution: towards an integrated approach to ceramic studies in Prehistoric Britain. In Howard and Morris 1981, 1–30.

HOWARD, H. and MORRIS, E. 1981: *Production and Distribution: a Ceramic Viewpoint* (Oxford, BAR S120).

JONES, M. 1978: Sampling in a Rescue context: a case study in Oxfordshire. In Cherry, J., Gamble, C. and Shennan, S., *Sampling in Contemporary British Archaeology* (Oxford, BAR 50), 191–205.

LAMBRICK, G. 1979: The Iron Age Pottery. In Lambrick and Robinson 1979, 35–46.

LAMBRICK, G. 1980: Excavations in Park Street, Towcester. *Northants. Archaeol.* 15, 35–118.

LAMBRICK, G. in prep: Report on excavations at Mount Farm, Dorchester, Oxfordshire.

LAMBRICK, G. and ROBINSON, M. 1979: *Iron Age and Roman Riverside Settlements at Farmoor, Oxfordshire* (London, CBA Res. Rep. 32).

LEVITAN, B. 1982: *Excavations at West Uley: 1979 The Sieving and Sampling Programme* (Bristol, Western Archaeol. Trust, Occ. Paper 10).

MILES, D. and PALMER, S. 1982: Fairford/Lechlade: Claydon Pike. *CBA Group Nine Newsletter* 12, 164–70.

MORRIS, E. 1981: Ceramic Exchange in Western Britain: a preliminary view. In Howard and Morris 1981, 67–81.

MYRES, J. 1937: A Prehistoric and Roman Site on Mount Farm, Dorchester. *Oxoniensia* 2, 12–40.

OLIVER, M. and APPLIN, B. 1979: Excavation of an Iron Age and Romano-British Settlement at Ructstalls Hill, Basingstoke, Hampshire, 1972–5. *Proc. Hants. Field Club and Archaeol. Soc.* 35, 41–92.

PEACOCK, D. 1968: A Petrological Study of certain Iron Age pottery from Western England. *Proc. Prehist. Soc.* 34, 414–27.

PEACOCK, D. 1969a: A contribution to the study of Glastonbury ware from South-western Britain. *Antiq. Journ.* 49, 41–61.

PEACOCK, D. 1969b: Neolithic Pottery Production in Cornwall. *Antiquity* 43, 145–9.

PEACOCK, D. 1977: Ceramics in Roman and Medieval Archaeology. In Peacock, D. (editor), *Pottery and Early Commerce* (London), 21–33.

PLOG, S. 1980: *Stylistic variation of Prehistoric Ceramics* (Cambridge).

RENFREW, C. 1977: Production and exchange in Early State Societies, The Evidence of Pottery. In Peacock, D. (editor), *Pottery and Early Commerce* (London), 1–20.

RHODES, P. 1948: A Prehistoric and Roman Site at Wittenham Clumps, Berks. *Oxoniensia* 13, 18–31.

RICHARDSON, K. and YOUNG, A. 1951: An Iron Age 'A' Site on the Chilterns. *Antiq. Journ.* 31, 132–48.

SAVORY, H. 1937: An Early Iron Age Site at Long Wittenham, Berks. *Oxoniensia* 2, 1–11.

SCHIFFER, M. 1976: *Behavioural Archaeology* (London).

WILLIAMS, A. 1951: Excavations at Beard Mill, Stanton Harcourt, Oxon., 1944. *Oxoniensia* 16, 5–22.

WILLIAMS, D. unpublished: *Fabric Analysis of Iron Age pottery from Appleford and Ashville, Oxfordshire* (Dept. Archaeology University of Southampton).

The Deposition of La Tène Iron Age Metalwork in Watery Contexts in Southern England

Andrew P. Fitzpatrick

Louernios . . . rode in a chariot over the plains distributing gold and silver to the tens of thousands of Celts who followed him . . .

(*Athenaeus* 4. 37 152D–F)

The twin uses of treasure were in possessing it and in giving it away, paradoxical as that may appear.
(M.I. Finley *The World of Odysseus*, Cambridge 1956, 65)

Introduction[1]

Although the recovery of the majority of pieces of decorated La Tène Iron Age metalwork in Britain from watery contexts has long stimulated scholarly comment, few attempts have been made to study the circumstances, or the significance, of its deposition in such contexts.

In comparison to the attention devoted recently to Bronze Age material, where this particular aspect of the archaeological record has been regarded as a phenomenon worthy of study in its own right, Iron Age material has been relatively neglected. Instead, attention has been devoted largely to settlements, ceramics and subsistence. Where metalwork has attracted attention it has usually been in studies concerned primarily with either typological or artistic considerations, and in this field there have been a number of distinguished contributions. Nonetheless,

> 'the assumption, rather than the demonstration, that art is a readily-distinguishable category of La Tène material culture has led to a greater or lesser extent, to the abstraction of artefacts from their contexts, and patterns and motifs from the objects that they embellish, not merely for procedural reasons in analysis, but also in matters of interpretation.'
>
> (Megaw 1979, 53–4, quoting Spratling)

Metallurgical studies (cf Salter and Ehrenreich, Northover this volume), or papers exploring the potential of metalwork as indicators of archaeological groupings are less frequent (Hodder 1977a and 1977b). The potential that the material and its find-contexts offer for exploring the use of material culture by Iron Age communities, and the controls that they offer on inferences drawn from other kinds of evidence have rarely been explored in recent years. Accordingly, this paper is intended as a preliminary discussion, which it is hoped will attract attention to the subject. The paper is based primarily on the metalwork from the river Thames, but rather than being concerned primarily with the objects themselves it attempts to focus attention on the social contexts of their manufacture, use and deposition. The conclusions that it reaches are traditional and concur, not surprisingly, with those of the doyens of Iron Age studies, Professors Hawkes (1976) and Piggott (1976).

Watery contexts are taken to mean rivers, springs, marshes, bogs, wells etc. and discussion is restricted to the La Tène period of the Iron Age, that is to say in Britain the fifth century BC to the Claudian conquest. Throughout, the term La Tène is used only in a chronological sense (Champion 1982) and is preferred to other, insular, terminologies to enable the southern English material to be viewed in its proper context — as part of the prehistoric (Champion 1975) and early historic archaeology of Europe.

The Structure of the Evidence

A prerequisite for any study of metalwork of the La Tène period is a characterisation of the different types of contexts from which these finds are recorded and also a consideration of what finds are not recorded from these contexts. As such characterisations of different kinds of find-contexts, and discussions of the problems involved in assessing the finds from them, have recently been discussed elsewhere in the context of Bronze Age studies (Needham and Burgess 1980; Levy 1982), they need only be summarised and altered slightly here.

For the La Tène period, contexts may be divided provisionally into six main types:

i   Settlements
ii Burials
iii Hoards
iv Watery contexts
v   Shrines
vi Stray, single and unaccompanied finds

Although most of the categories are self-explanatory, a few further comments are necessary. Obviously not all the categories are mutually exclusive and finds deposited either accidentally or deliberately could be recovered from all of them. In considering hoards, the distinction has frequently been made between hoards deposited with the intention of recovery and those deposited without any such intention. This is an important difference, if one which is difficult to demonstrate. In particular it should be stressed that the distinction between a 'stray' find and a hoard is quantitative and not necessarily qualitative. The discovery of finds such as the later Bronze Age gold fibula in a wooden box from Killymoon Demense, County Tyrone (Raferty 1970) or the Hallstatt C hoard in a wooden container from Koppenow, Pommern in Germany demonstrate that even carefully-excavated and apparently unaccompanied finds may have been accompanied at the time of deposition. As this paper is concerned primarily with finds from watery contexts, a number of particular points must be made. Before the closing phases of the La Tène period most pieces of deliberately, or formally, deposited pieces of metalwork, excepting occasional finds by divers or in eel spearing, are chance finds collected in dredging.

The finds noticed and retrieved by the dredging operators represent only a sample of the material actually brought to the surface by dredging. In these finds there will probably be a bias towards larger or complete objects and probably also selective retention, with fragments of bone, glass or pottery being less likely to be picked out. Objects of organic materials or food are very unlikely to be recognised. How much of this material is then reported to archaeological authorities and subsequently enters museum collections and/or is published is another form of filtering. These problems have been discussed by Torbrügge (1970–71), Wegner (1976) and Ehrenberg (1980). In the absence of systematic sub-aqua survey or dredging monitored by archaeologists it is not possible to assess the representative nature of the sample.

A pertinent, but difficult question to assess is the suggestion that areas of land from which La Tène metalwork has been recovered and which are at present dry may have been watery at the time of deposition. This suggestion has been advanced for a number of recent finds from dry land such as the Thrapston sword and scabbard (Megaw 1976) and the Isleham sword and scabbard (Stead et al. 1981, noting finds from old river courses). This might be resolved by the careful examination of the areas of the findspot for archaeological and pedological features and of the condition of the objects themselves. The problem deserves particular attention in the future.

The finds of La Tène metalwork from the river Thames are summarised in Fig. 12.1.[2] In the table the finds have not been grouped chronologically. This is partly because of the desire to study the composition of the finds by functional groupings within the rather arbitrarily-defined chronological period and partly because it is not, as yet, possible to date satisfactorily the most numerous type of find, the (presumptively) La Tène Iron Age spear. The same problem is faced with many types of iron tools which could be of La Tène, Roman, medieval or later date. It would be unwise to use the swords as a chronological guide, as it is not known if their use in techniques of combat remained constant throughout the period under consideration (Jope 1961). Because of these difficulties in dating the material — a product of the contexts from which they are recorded — it is not possible to attempt the kind of detailed discussion of changes through time undertaken

by Needham and Burgess (1980). Accordingly, for the present at least, a very simple provisional analysis is presented (Fig. 12.1).

A number of observations can be made about the material. There is an emphatic bias towards weaponry, primarily of offensive rather than defensive types.[3] A similar pattern is evident in the Bronze Age material from the Thames (Ehrenberg 1980; Needham and Burgess 1980). On the assumption that the identifications are correct, there is a surprisingly large number of spears and also more coins than might have been expected. Although it might be suspected that the number of coins recorded reflects only mudlarking (insofar as is possible to assess this) a number of finds are provenanced as coming from the Thames rather than the Thames foreshore. The Thames is the only English river to have produced more than one or two finds of coins, although finds are not infrequently recorded from coastal beaches. There are seven gold coins, two of silver, four of bronze (from three findspots) and eight unaccompanied finds of potins together with three small hoards. The number of potins, while not surprising in view of their known distribution, does suggest that bronze coins may be under-represented.

In common with many of the types of artefacts, the coins display a distinct concentration in the Greater London urban area. The most striking group of finds is obviously the Hallstatt D and early La Tène daggers fully discussed by Jope (1961; see also Macdonald 1978). Particularly noteworthy is the number of La Tène I fibulae, around a dozen, also from the same area. If we turn to consider the Hallstatt D finds — the daggers, the Whittingham sword (see also Spindler 1980a) the Weybridge bucket and the other metalwork finds (Jope 1961; O'Connor 1980) — all from approximately the same area as the concentrations of Bronze Age material, and if we ignore terminologies such as this paper perpetrates, there seems to be a case for continuity in the deposition of metalwork from Llynfawr to La Tène I, although there is a decrease in the amount of material in the Iron Age. La Tène II and III finds are, however, more regularly distributed along the river. Of the seven or eight swords of this date found since Piggott's survey of British La Tène swords (1950), most have been found upstream from London: Abingdon Lock, Henley, Little Wittenham (two), Wallingford Bridge and Wargrave. From London, there are only the examples from the Thames foreshore at Wandsworth and from the river between Richmond and Hampton.[4] Findspots of plough-share/currency-bars have a similar distribution.

Prima facie there would appear to be a remarkable concentration of finds in the Greater London area but, before considering further the Thames finds, it is important to compare them to other river finds of La Tène date from Britain, river finds of other periods and finds of La Tène metalwork from other kinds of contexts.

Unfortunately there is only one comparable series of La Tène river finds, those from the river Witham; and

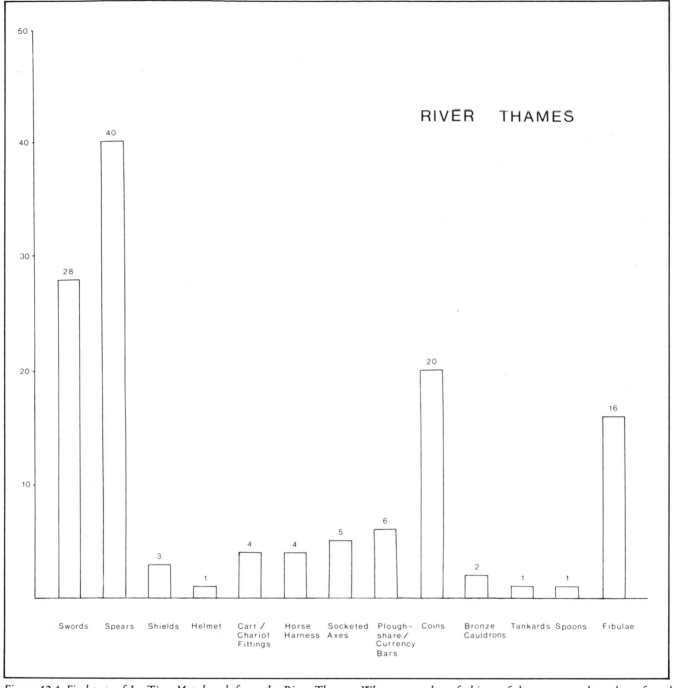

Figure 12.1 Findspots of La Tène Metalwork from the River Thames. Where a number of objects of the same type have been found together, for example coin hoards or the Maidenhead, Berks plough-share/currency bars, they have been treated as one findspot.

the number of finds concerned is much smaller (Fig. 12.2).

The martial and display nature of the finds is again noteworthy. The circumstances of the discovery of the majority of the Witham finds of all dates have been summarised by White (1979a; 1979b and 1979c) and they offer a valuable guide to the representative nature of the Thames finds. The great majority of the Witham finds were recovered in the course of the straightening, widening and scouring of the river in the late seventeenth and eighteenth centuries. How many of the finds mentioned briefly at this date, but which were not described more fully, may have been of La Tène date is a

matter for speculation. It seems likely that some of the few finds of La Tène date from the river which have been reported subsequently may have actually been discovered at this time. The only appreciable number of La Tène finds from the Witham area since then come from Naomi Field's recent excavations at the waterside site of Fiskerton. Here, in association with a causeway, four swords, three spears, pieces of horse harness and iron tools, bones and pottery were found.[5] It is tempting to compare the situation to the enigmatic Swiss sites of La Tène (NE) and Cornaux, 'Les Sauges' (NE).[6]

In contrast the Thames has been dredged frequently, although not over all of its course, and finds have been

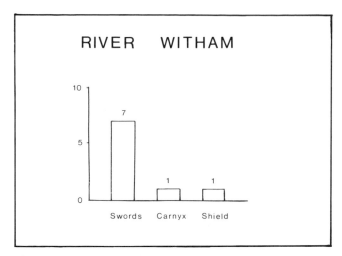

RIVER WITHAM

Figure 12.2 *Findspots of La Tène Metalwork from the River Witham. The Fiskerton finds are not included.*

recorded regularly. This subject has been discussed in detail by Ehrenberg (1980). In particular records of finds from the Thames Conservancy Board catchment area — from the Thames above Teddington to Cricklade — have been kept since 1932 and copies are available for study. Most minor rivers have not been subject to similar disturbances and have not produced substantial numbers of finds from any period.

If assessed intuitively, then piece for piece the Witham finds, which include such notable pieces as the Tattershall Ferry carnyx, the Witham shield, the Bardney swords, the Witham sword, are as impressive, if not more so, than the finds from the Thames, particularly so in view of the fact that they were all found within a short period of time. As it is also evident that there has been a disproportionate amount of post-mediaeval disturbance to the Thames in the London region and also great antiquarian interest in the area, the significance of the London finds should be considered circumspectly in view of the Witham finds and the smoothing of the distribution hinted at by the more recent finds upstream of London. Although the concentration of La Tène I finds does appear to be genuine, it would be premature to ascribe to the Thames basin as a whole a pre-eminent position during the La Tène period primarily on the evidence of metalwork, particularly in view of the small numbers of finds involved. Although analogous suggestions have been advanced for the later Bronze Age in the area, in that period access to raw metals is an important consideration; but some of the reservations advanced above could profitably be considered further in this context. This is by no means to disagree with Kent's (1978) suggestion that on the basis of the coins and the metalwork, the London area was a focus of great importance; many of the points advanced below can be held to support his suggestion. Nonetheless, for the La Tène period, at least, it is possible that the finds from the Thames may eventually prove to be quite unexceptional within southern England.

A feature common to both the Thames and Witham is

that later prehistoric finds (of the Bronze and Iron Ages) are not necessarily the most frequently-recorded ones. Not only are earlier prehistoric finds well represented from the Thames (Adkins and Jackson 1978), but there are also numerous finds of other periods such as the early mediaeval (Wilson 1965). The evidence for the Witham summarised by White (1979a; 1979b; 1979c), for the Thames by Ehrenberg (1980) and for south-west Germany by Zimmermann (1970) might suggest that archaeologists should consider whether the explanations offered by them for any given period may be valid for other periods. If they are not then, as Torbrügge (1970–71) has shown, these differences may be worthy of research in themselves. This is particularly apposite in view of the martial and elite nature of the Thames finds from the Neolithic to the early mediaeval. As has been noted, in comparison to the Bronze Age finds from the Thames there is a decline in quantity in the Iron Age. A similar decline over much of western Europe was noted by Törbrugge in his general study (1970–71) and has also been noted in studies of specific areas such as Zimmermann's (1970) of south-west Germany and Wegner's (1976) of the finds from the Main-Rhine area. The Mosel has also produced finds of Bronze Age date (Gollub 1970) but none of the Iron Age.[7] Prehistoric finds of any date from the lower Rhine are rare. Other areas are more difficult to assess, for while Bronze Age material has long been recognised from watery contexts, La Tène finds are usually thought to be extremely rare. In this context it is worth drawing attention to a number of recent finds. La Tène finds from the Netherlands and Belgium are not as infrequent as is usually thought. In particular there are a number of swords (Verwers and Ypey 1975; Van Impe and Vangeel 1981; Roymans and Ypey forthcoming a),[8] and there are also the important new finds from Pommerouel (De Boe and Hubert 1977; Hubert 1982). The well-known, if enigmatic, cave finds from the 'dry' context at Wérimont, and in particular the skeletal finds (Marien 1970), are interesting in this context. Unfortunately there is no thorough survey of the French material. Metalwork occurs regularly as grave goods, particularly in the Champagne and to the east, but dredged finds are also quite common (e.g. Ajot and Bulard 1977; Bonnamour and Bulard 1976; Patte 1977; Torbrügge 1970–71). We can confidently expect much new work of the highest quality from the tremendous recent upsurge in interest in the Iron Age, especially in northern France.

A number of minor qualifications must be set against this apparent decline in the Iron Age of the deposit of metalwork in watery contexts. Unless preserved in anaerobic conditions, ironwork is likely to be corroded and it may not be possible to assign a reliable date to corroded and/or fragmentary pieces. In general Bronze Age metalwork is less susceptible to this and, when finds of La Tène and mediaeval finds are compared, La Tène material has had perhaps a thousand years longer to disintegrate; moreover it is difficult to assign close dates to tools. Nonetheless, on the evidence at present available, the decline from the Bronze Age of the deposit of metalwork in the Thames appears to be genuine, if gradual, and forms part of a broader European pattern.

The Contexts of La Tène Metalwork

The substantial quantities of La Tène metalwork from the Thames are in sharp contrast to finds from other kinds of contexts of La Tène date. A discussion of the finds from these contexts must precede any interpretation of the river finds. Settlements rarely produce material comparable to finds from watery contexts, for, as would be expected, such material appears to have been either scrapped and re-cycled or disposed of elsewhere. Settlements in the Upper Thames Basin have rarely produced more than a few scraps of metalwork, either in older excavations (Harding 1972) or in the more recent work of the Oxfordshire Archaeological Unit. The same is true of sites in Hampshire (Champion and Champion 1981) and sites such as Tollard Royal or Gussage All Saints. The recent Danebury hoard is a rare find (Cunliffe 1981) as are the finds from the pit at Old Down Farm, which the excavator suggests might not be a hoard (Davies 1981).

In much of Britain, for a substantial part of the Iron Age, there was not a formal burial-rite which is easily discernible to the archaeologist (Whimster 1977; 1981). Even the realisation that burials — either articulated or disarticulated — within settlements are much more common than realised previously (Wilson 1981) does not, as yet at least, fill this lacuna. Accordingly, the one kind of context where the deliberate deposition of metalwork might have been expected is not available until late in the Iron Age. The effect of this is illustrated strikingly by the almost mutually-exclusive contexts of La Tène II decorated sword-scabbards in Britain and in northern France (Torbrügge 1970–71, esp Beil. 13, 2). This apparent absence of a recognisable means of disposing of the dead presents considerable difficulties in any study of La Tène metalwork in England.

Hoards of currency-bars have been studied by Allen (1967) and ironwork hoards by Manning (1972). As Saunders (1977) points out, it is not until towards the end of the Iron Age (what he terms the 'currency bar horizon') that large groups of ironwork with a variety of types of artefacts are recovered throughout western Europe. The same is true of hoards of bronzes, and the dating of these — Polden Hill and Santon for instance — is often to within decades of the Claudian conquest. Manning has suggested that the ironwork hoards may be votive deposits, as exemplified by Llyn Cerrig Bach although this find is unlikely to be a one-phase deposit. A number of European finds, although not all in watery contexts, may be cited: Dux in Czechoslovakia (Krůta 1971), Tiefenau in Switzerland (Tschumi 1929; 1948) and Kappel in Germany (Fischer 1959). Hoards of precious metals are rare, indeed apart from a few La Tène III fibulae, silver is almost entirely absent from La Tène contexts in England. Gold objects are similarly rare, apart from the well-known series of torcs which are probably to be dated to within the last two centuries BC. Whether these occur as single finds or in the East Anglian hoards, they should probably be regarded as having been deliberately deposited. In this sense both types of finds are hoards, and a similar argument can also be advanced for single finds and hoard-finds of precious-metal coins.

Single stray unaccompanied finds are recorded quite regularly. Mostly these are small objects such as fibulae which may genuinely have been accidental losses. Once again it is not until the last two centuries BC that finds, particularly cart- or chariot-fittings and pieces of horse harness, become frequent. The lack of obvious associations presents the greatest problem in the interpretation of these finds for, as mentioned above (p. 179), it is quite likely that many of them correctly belong to other kinds of find-contexts. For example the recently-discovered Little Wittenham sword and scabbard (Sherratt 1983) might derive from a dried-up watery context. It may have been an accidental loss, but in view of the foregoing evidence this must be regarded as improbable. Finally, shrines are not easily recognisable anywhere in temperate Europe until the last century BC, and even then they are not plentiful. In Britain, although a number of structures have been suggested as shrines (Drury 1980), it is only in rare cases that there is convincing structural evidence, as at Hayling Island or at Frilford,[9] or there are associated votive objects or faunal assemblages, as at Harlow, which allow confident interpretation of these sites as religious. Occasionally the number of surface finds from a site may suggest the presence of a shrine, as with the La Tène I fibulae from Woodeaton. Although the evidence for religious buildings is scanty, this should not be taken to indicate that shrines or sanctuaries did not exist; and as Ross shows (1968) these are quite likely to have been associated with watery places. In this context we may note the Dobunnic coins from the spring at Bath (Cunliffe 1980); but whether they were deposited before or after the Roman conquest of that area remains an open question.

The impression that emerges from this brief survey is that it is not until the end of the Iron Age that metalwork of all kinds, bronze, iron and of precious metals, were deposited in any quantity. This seems to be particularly true of contexts in which material was formally deposited. An important consequence of this is the difficulty in dating La Tène metalwork. Originally the metalwork as a whole was given a late dating because of its presumptive derivation from a third century BC 'Marnian' invasion. There is still a tendency to prefer late dates, usually on the basis of the decoration. As the great majority of secure associations come from towards the end of the Iron Age there is, not unnaturally, a tendency also to date decorated material which lacks recorded associations to the late Iron Age. All too often, however, this is done without reference to the objects themselves and any typological considerations that this might prompt. Much of the European dating of art styles is conditioned by their putative relations to historically attested events. To transfer these datings to supposedly derivative styles in England is a hazardous exercise, and it is here that the lack of clarity over exactly what is meant by La Tène in its multifarious, and nefarious, guises becomes most apparent. That the late British 'insular' style is distinctive from other La Tène styles is hardly surprising, for the proper body of comparanda is that of the Gallo-Roman précoce. Déchelette pointed this out long ago by distinguishing a La Tène IV for the British Isles. It is preferable to follow the evidence of the objects themselves, which appear to develop broadly parallel to the rest of the European series, rather than to lay stress on the decoration; for this course leaves southern England under-supplied in fourth-century metalwork (cf also Spratling 1978; 1979). Ultimately there may prove to be a genuine absence of finds because of the structure of the archaeological record for this period, but the absence should be demonstrated.

Interpretation

Two broad patterns seem to be distinguishable. One is the fairly consistent recovery of martial objects in rivers subject to artificial disturbance; the other is the increase in material culture entering the archaeological record in the last two centuries BC. In view of the distinctive nature of the riverine finds, and the way that they diverge from the chronological pattern of the other finds, it is difficult to avoid the conclusion that they were deposited in watery contexts for votive reasons. It is possible that the finds derive from, or are symbols for, burials; but as Torbrügge has demonstrated it seems more likely that they form part of an overall veneration in western Europe for watery places in contrast to the situation in central and eastern Europe where hoard- and grave-finds predominate (Torbrügge 1970–71; Ross 1968).

This conclusion is unsurprising; it is an interpretation long upheld by scholarly opinion. Such opinion is, however, rather less certain about what use may be made of this conclusion. Although archaeologists generally agree that the artefacts themselves will be of some value to their analyses (Champion 1975; Hodson 1980), the significance of the artefacts to the societies within which they were manufactured, used and, in this case, ultimately deposited deliberately, is an issue on which there is less consensus. As Hingley observes elsewhere in this volume there is a tendency to avoid discussing the actual societies which, most archaeologists would agree to lesser or greater extent, are the object of our study. Most recent commentators on the subject of La Tène metalwork from watery contexts have observed that the objects are likely to be votive offerings. Unfortunately they do not pursue the issue further, as if, with this conclusion, the investigation is complete. This may not be altogether unwise, particularly in the archaeological interpretation of religion, but to do so denies us the opportunity to explore how these artefacts, and the contexts in which they were deposited, were used in Iron Age societies. Arguably, it also suggests that religion is in some way a discrete institutional category passively reflecting society (Friedman 1979). Such attitudes, closely associated with the 'New Archaeology'

can be criticised on a number of points. As Barrett observes:

'Material culture in all its forms . . . is the result of actions which are at once *both* articulated through social relationships, and are also the means by which those social relationships are constructed. The social being exists through action which is formulated and reflected upon within a culturally-modified material world. Material culture is thus an active participant in the construction of the social system, and its meaning is internal to that system.'

(Barrett 1981, 206)

Artefacts are not, therefore, simply functional objects, but are also symbols (Hodder 1982). In the case of the La Tène metalwork there is clearly a deliberate selection of types. Rather than being the close of research on Iron Age societies, it is one of the starting points. At this point, however, I should like to turn to the literary evidence for Iron Age societies and in particular to those described by the classical commentators as coming from temperate Europe, the Celts. There are many difficulties in using these texts, which have been adumbrated elsewhere (Tierney 1960; Crumley 1974; Nash 1976a). These texts do not necessarily provide a window on the Iron Age so much as a mirror on the classical worlds and their concepts of ethnicity, and, in their selection of what is noteworthy, of how they perceived other societies as structured systems (Momigliano 1975; Humphreys 1983). Used uncritically by contemporary scholars they will provide only a present past, and in this sense all history is contemporary history (Hopkins 1978; Humphreys 1978). Nonetheless, with these strictures in mind, these sources provide invaluable information on Celtic society during the period with which we are concerned. The evidence that they present for a stratified society and in particular for the activities of an elite group, the aristocracy, is too well-known to need repetition here. There is a classic account in Stuart Piggott's *Ancient Europe* (1965). What is much more hazardous is the *assumption* that these texts, which relate largely to southern and central France, may be of some value in providing a social context in which to assess the relations between La Tène societies and their material culture(s) in southern England. The general similarity of the archaeological material between the areas, and Caesar's comments (*BG* 5, 12–14), might encourage this view; but it should be stressed that it is an assumption which may be disproved. In the discussion of the social contexts of the manufacture, use and deposition of La Tène metalwork which follows, this outline of Celtic society should be borne in mind.

The Organization of metalworking

Although we are relatively well-informed about technological aspects of metalworking (Salter and Ehrenreich; Northover, this volume), we know very little about the organization of it. As has been observed elsewhere, concepts such as style, workshop, artisan, artist and so forth are used with little or no discussion of what is meant by them (Spratling 1978). The classic study of the organization of English metalworking was by Fox (1958), which attempted to identify regional workshops and laid great stress on the typological development of both the objects and the decoration (if any) on them. This approach has been criticised by Spratling (1970) on two grounds: that these analyses were based on a chronology which was assumed rather than demonstrated; and that the differences which were held to be chronological could merely be contemporary variants and could be explained in a variety of ways other than by reference to the development of workshops. It is clear that while some broad regional divisions can be made, and within these groups local variations can be recognised (Hodder 1977a), it is not possible, except in exceptionally rare circumstances, to identify works which may be from the same workshop or made by the same individual. Equally, similarity of decorative motifs or zones can be explained by a variety of exchange mechanisms rather than by positing the existence of workshops or masters and their pupils. The question of whether the manufacturers of La Tène metalwork were peripatetic is a vexed one. It clearly has an important bearing on the interpretation of the material; nonetheless, we are no nearer to an understanding of this problem (Megaw 1979). Obviously one must turn to the evidence of manufacturing-sites (Wainwright and Spratling 1973); but with the exception of Gussage All Saints the evidence is poor, and even there great uncertainty exists. In the final publication of the debris of metalworking, Spratling (1979) recanted his earlier view that the detritus indicated occasional, possibly peripatetic, metalworking activity, suggesting instead that it was a regular part of the activity on the site. Spratling reached this conclusion after careful consideration of such factors as the amount of wax required for the *cire perdue* casting, and the amount of wood necessary. But in a detailed analysis of the moulds Foster (1980) supports Spratling's earlier opinion. As it is evident that not all the stages of manufacture of particular artefacts need take place in the same location (Rowlands 1971–72), the issue is complicated further. Consideration in terms of site-hierarchies of sites which have produced evidence for metalworking is of little help, for, as Harding reminds us (1980), hillforts may not have acted as central places.

Nearly all this discussion has taken place with reference to bronzeworking; ironworking has been little discussed by archaeologists. Metallurgical studies suggest that ironworking was relatively localised (Haldane 1970; Hedges and Slater 1979), and we are relatively well informed on technological aspects (Tylecote 1962; Haefner 1981). Although little is known of mining and smelting, knowledge of subsequent stages in the manufacturing process is better (Saunders 1977; Manning 1979). Material from the closing phases of the La Tène period leaves no doubt of the technical and creative ability of ironsmiths. It has been suggested by Alexander (1981) that by the first century BC there may have been two 'social levels' of ironworking in Britain: a low-prestige concern manufacturing utilitarian goods and a high-prestige activity. In this situation, he suggests, the limited supplies of good ores in many regions might provide the possibility of exercising monopoly control over them. This is a possibility that has already been advanced by Driehaus (1965) for the middle-Rhine region in the early La Tène period, and it is frequently suggested that one consideration in the development of the so-called *oppida* was the proximity of easily exploitable iron sources. Alexander does not however further discuss these suggestions, nor the possibility that, by the end of the Iron Age, smiths may have had some form of religious significance (Alexander 1981).

There are a number of areas, however, in which most students of metalworking are in agreement: in particular, the suggestions that smiths were male and that metalworking was under strict control. This latter point is especially stressed in the working of precious metals either in the sense that access to the finished products was restricted to an elite group or that access to the raw metals was only possible through an elite. The same point is made both in relation to the manufacture of bronzes, if sometimes only implicitly (Piggott 1950), and also for ironwork, particularly in relation to objects associated with feasting (Saunders 1977). The idea of peripatetic smiths is not necessarily incompatible with such strict control. Collis (1972) has drawn attention to the presence of tools in burials with weapons in England, and this might have some bearing on the status of craftsmen in society. A final important point relevant to this is the status of the craftspersons and artisans frequently suggested as resident in *oppida*. Nash's (1976b) suggestion that they manufactured luxury goods is compatible with the strict control of metalworking. Other analyses, which emphasise the development of an artisan or 'middle' class at this time (e.g. Pleiner 1979), rarely afford adequate consideration of how this could arise given the existing social context of metalworking. To ascribe it to technological determinism is hardly adequate.

It is only possible to draw attention to the great potential for further study here. Many of the problems raised by Rowlands (1970–71) and Spratling (1970; Wainwright and Spratling 1973) remain subjects for further research, and much discussion of fundamental concepts remains to be undertaken. As Saunders (1977) has pointed out, the collection and quantification of the relevant information will only come with an awareness of the problem in the field, and this conclusion cannot be over emphasised. Equally important, however, as Megaw (1982) has observed, is a detailed consideration of the social context.

The Social Context

Much of the southern English metalwork formally deposited in watery contexts before the last two centuries BC is martial in character and is usually held to have been made for and used by the Celtic elite. Any suspicion that weaponry of this sort was not owned by such a group is dispelled by consideration of the European funerary record (Lorenz 1978), and it is on such weaponry that much of the finest art of the European Iron Age is preserved. The associations have been stated eloquently by Hawkes (1976) and Piggott (1976).

The accounts that the classical commentators give of Celtic society were very probably affected by the nature of the contacts between the two communities. Although there will undoubtedly have been a variety of peaceful modes of exchanges, the Celts were often encounterd in warfare, either as mercenaries in Hellenistic armies, invaders in the Mediterranean world or, in Europe, as opponents of the Romans. The texts are by no means free of bias, ancient or modern (p. 183 supra). Nonetheless, the virtual unanimity with which they describe the Celtic pre-occupation with warfare, which approached an almost endemic scale, suggests that this topic deserves detailed consideration.

As Nash has pointed out, these sources show an elite 'overwhelmingly pre-occupied with wealth and warfare, and . . . the two were intimately connected' (Nash 1981, 13). Nash is primarily concerned with analysing the social context for the introduction, acceptance and use of precious-metal coinages, which she would see as a specialised form of wealth introduced and accepted alongside other more traditional forms such as cattle, the ownership and display of precious metals and feasting. The basis of wealth remains, however, land.

It seems unlikely that precious metal coinages were introduced or used to facilitate trade, but rather as a means of storage of wealth and means of payment. In the latter context the retention of an armed retinue, which both Polybius (2.17.2) and Caesar (BG 6.15.2) suggest was a way of assessing power, and payment for royal or state obligations seem particularly likely (Nash 1981; Fitzpatrick forthcoming a). This concern with warfare in a society articulated by relations of clientage is unsurprising. The elite are supported by the 'surplus' produce of the land which they own but which is also, in one sense, borrowed from them and cultivated for them by their clients. In this type of society ownership of land will accordingly be regarded, by the elite at least, as being of great importance. Military might or its potential use is one of the most efficaceous and important methods of ensuring the defence, retention and even expansion of land-holding. The tribute of the clients was used to support an armed retinue and, on occasion, they themselves might be called upon to serve in the armies. Success in warfare brought three main kinds of material rewards: land, captives, and booty, all of which belonged to the elite to whom, in addition, accrued the less tangible but no less important prestige of success (Garlan 1975). In this situation it can be argued that the clients appear to assume a role whereby in return for protection they are actively ensuring their continuing dependence.

As Barrett observes on the subject of clientage, these social relations are presented as natural, and, following Bourdieu (1979), he cites the (at least) threefold role of symbolism in culture, 'as allowing the formation of an objective knowledge of the world; as forming a means of communication; and as legitimising relations of power and control' (Barrett 1981, 215).

Insofar as this can be assessed from the classical commentator, the Celts appear to have what, in the context of Republican Rome, Harris has termed a 'warrior ideology' (Harris 1979). Military prowess and success were important to the stability and preservation of society. To find a system of beliefs which both sanctions and approves warfare is not surprising. As the social values governing the allocation of resources were those of an elite, and the control and gift of these resources were the prerogative of that elite, the identification of wealth and status with the appropriate goods and activities is to be expected. As Nash has pointed out, wealth and nobility were inseparable; that much of the finest decorated La Tène metalwork is associated with weaponry is seemingly natural.

We have seen that much of the metalwork is recorded from contexts in which it appears to have been deposited deliberately. Although frequently regarded as a distinct stage in analyses of the structure of the archaeological record, deposition belongs properly to the use of an object or to the stage at which it is deemed to have no further uses. It is difficult to distinguish between 'social' and 'religious' motivations for deliberate deposition if, indeed, these distinctions do have any validity (Friedman 1979; Humphreys 1978; 1983). It is not possible to pursue these issues further here. But the demonstration by Ross (1968) that throughout Celtic western Europe there appears to have been a veneration for water or watery places does pose the problem. The religious symbolism of water could probably be pursued profitably in cross-cultural studies in this respect (Humphreys and King 1981).

An obvious suggestion for La Tène metalwork is that it may have been selected for deposition because of its ambiguous roles as a symbol both of authority and wealth and of security. In order to consider this possibility it is necessary to ask how the objects were deposited. This is a subject that we can approach through archaeological evidence, at least for some contexts, as has been demonstrated by the recent excavations at Illerup (Ilkjaer and Lønstrup 1983). We must also ask in what social contexts — public or private — they were deposited. The latter issue is however, on present evidence, better approached by way of the evidence of the classical commentators. This evidence points to the public display of wealth and treasure by the elite, not solely as expended socially on feasting, gift-giving and the retention of an armed retinue, but also in ceremonial activities.

The comments of Diodorus Siculus (5. 27. 3–4), Caesar (BG 6. 17.3–5), Strabo (4. 1. 13) and Suetonius (DJ 54) all point to the public display of votive offerings, often associated with the spoils of war, and, in the case of Strabo, to the watery contexts of the aurum Tolosanum. Unfortunately we are less informed on the nature and importance of the ceremonial activities associated with the deposition and it is only possible to surmise that they were in the hands of the learned class, the Druids. Caesar comments 'when a private person or a tribe disobeys their ruling they ban them from attending sacrifices. This is their harshest penalty' (*BG* 6. 13. 6).

The roles of the Druids in Celtic society have been the subject of much, usually emotive, speculation. It is clear, however, that the learned class was intimately connected with the elite; interpreting the law, performing religious ceremonies and acting bardic roles (Nash 1976a esp 122–6). In the latter role their public approval of the elite, singing the praises of their generosity in peace (*Athenaeus* 4, 37, 152D–F) or their merit in war (6, 49, 246CD) was particularly important. Appian (*Celt.* 12) explicitly makes this point concerning Bituitus. That the elite patronized them is hardly surprising, and the association of the opening of warfare with tutelary authorities is also noteworthy (cf Garlan 1975).

The subject deserves to be explored more fully elsewhere, but it is possible to present an interpretation of the roles of the learned class as presenting (i) the structure of society, (ii) the specification by the elite of the various spheres of wealth (subsistence, luxury, prestige) and (iii) the ideology of the elite, as all being in some way 'natural'. Although the learned class have great influence over the elite, the reverse is also true through the exercise of patronage in its various forms.

In this situation we may be encouraged to view the deliberate deposition of military equipment in watery contexts, possibly accompanied by public ceremonies, as the selection of 'natural' symbols of security, status and wealth to be presented as votive offerings. The purpose of the votive offerings remains unknown; they could all be burial offerings or cenotaphs. It is possible, given the suggestions advanced above, that the deposition was exclusively the prerogative of the elite or the smiths, but this would be to assume that the objects deposited belonged to those making the deposition, which, as Humphreys (1983) observes, is a characteristically modern and western assumption. It is equally possible to suggest that they were deposited by other groups, the *plebs* or women, and that these ceremonies contributed towards making natural some of the apparent contradictions, in this analysis at least, within Celtic society. It is to the latter consideration that I should like to turn.

Gender Distinction

The literary sources leave no doubt that warfare was a male activity. In addition to the weaponry, finds of cart- or chariot-fittings and pieces of horse harness are probably also to be associated with display and warfare (Harbison 1969; Piggott 1983). If the uses of precious-metal coinages are considered — wealth-storage, payment for services, taxes, tribute, gifts and, in Celtic society, bridewealth — and if the interpretation of Celtic society outlined above is followed, it is possible that coinage may have been a male preserve.

The votive finds from a number of sanctuaries have martial characteristics. At Hayling Island numerous pieces of cart- or chariot-fittings, spears and swords and possibly also chain mail were found, and many of the objects had been deliberately bent or broken before deposition (Downey, King and Soffe 1980). A similar

pattern is discernible at Llyn Cerrig Bach (Fox 1947). The spectacular finds from the La Tène II–III sanctuary at Gournay-sur-Aronde (Oise) — 100 swords, 150 scabbards, 220 shield-umbos, 70 spearheads and 40 ferrules, 80 fibulae and 70 sword suspension-chains, nearly all deliberately damaged — follow the same pattern (Brunaux, Meniel and Rapin 1980, and, lavishly illustrated, Rapin 1982). The recent discovery in the excavations at the Gallo-Roman rural sanctuary of Ribemont-sur-Ancre (Somme) of a La Tène II–III ossuary containing between 100 and 200 individuals, but not their heads or torsos, and accompanied by three swords and scabbards, some 40 spears and 20 shield-umbos, again points to the same pattern (Cadoux 1982). The find obviously recalls the Moeuvres ossuary and suggests that the Spettisbury Rings 'massacre' (Gresham 1939) might be reconsidered.

The finds from watery contexts at Port (BE) in Switzerland — 60 swords, numerous spears, 14 daggers, knives and axes but also rhomboidal iron ingots and sickles — are part of the same pattern (Tschumi 1940). So too would appear to be the finds from La Tène (cf n. 6) — over 150 swords and scabbards, 270 spears, 22 umbos and seven virtually complete shields, 385 fibulae. As has been frequently noted of La Tène, there is virtually nothing there which was selected for deposition in contemporary female burials. These finds obviously recall the Danish moor finds, which indeed originally prompted Muller's 1898 and Raddatz's later (1952) and more influential suggestions that La Tène was a religious site. In the case of the Danish finds, however, it is likely that at least some of them represent the dedication of the arms of defeated adversaries (Ilkjaer and Lønstrup 1982).

There appears not to be any corresponding groups of artefacts which we should associate with female activities. Indeed it is noticeable that very little decorative metalwork can be associated with females. Although the British Iron Age mirror series is often held up as having belonged to females this is equivocal. Very few of the English Iron Age mirror burials have positive sexual identifications of the skeletal remains, although where this has been done it does suggest females: Birdlip (see now Staelins 1982) and, possibly, Aston (Rook *et al.* 1982). Nonetheless, the suggestion should be viewed with caution and it cannot be assumed that mirrors were exclusively owned or used by or buried with females. We may note the Scythian burials of males with mirrors and also females with apparently male symbols (Rolle 1980). In the Classical world, from which the British mirrors probably derive (Fitzpatrick, forthcoming b), mirrors were almost invariably associated with females, though Pauli (1972) has pointed out that their symbolism in one context need not be transferred to another, particularly if the objects circulate in prestige contexts.[10] To assume that they were 'female' objects is merely to impose our own ethno- and androcentric western values on to the past. Megaw has made a similar point concerning Waldalgesheim art on metalwork, where it seems to be associated most frequently with high-status males (Megaw 1982).

It is possible that a corresponding group of female offerings may exist but not be apparent in analyses which concentrate on artefacts associated with male activities. An obvious area for further research is in the faunal assemblages from sanctuaries, the composition of which when compared to those from settlements often varies quite distinctly. This has been noted for Hayling Island, Harlow and Uley, and is also evident at Gournay-sur-Aronde where, because of the recurrent indications of butchery practices, it is also possible to suggest how the animals were sacrificed (Brunaux and Meniel 1983). The composition and distribution of faunal assemblages and their relations to those from domestic sites, which themselves will reflect attitudes as to what is regarded as refuse and where it should be disposed of, may provide some insights. Nonetheless it is difficult to avoid the conclusion that archaeologists have hardly begun to consider seriously one of the most important ways that any society is structured, by gender.

Homo politicus and homo economicus

It is obvious that many of the considerations which have been used traditionally to assess social structure, power and wealth are characteristically masculine attributes. In itself this may be thought to be unremarkable, being implicit in past interpretations with their emphasis on martial activities, invasions, the construction of elaborately and possibly superfluously defended hill-forts and the manufacture and elaborate decoration of weaponry. Undoubtedly it is arguable that warfare was an important element in the structure of Celtic and, for the classical commentators, Graeco-Roman society and not the phenomenon that it has frequently been thought to be. Nonetheless these interpretations also reflect what have been characteristically male concerns in recent western thought. To see them in a Hobbesian fashion as being in some way 'natural' would be an ethnocentric assumption in the same way that Clarke's (1972) brilliant study of the Glastonbury Lake Village treats such subjects as gender and the family as being unremarkable, but which underly much of his analysis. These *are* important points, for if analysis is restricted to the public sphere the results will be asymmetrical; the public sphere is active, the private, domestic sphere is passive (Humphreys 1983) and the result is a self-perpetuating androcentric — male — view of the past. These points both underlie and belie much of the preceding arguments, for they imply that women were unimportant inthe spheres by which we traditionally assess Celtic social structure. Underlying the analysis, however, is the stress (p. 185) on domestic production as fundamental to the maintainance of society. The roles of women as a means of obtaining marriage alliances or bridewealth and ensuring demographic superiority could also be emphasised. It is evident that an important feature is the oppression of females by males, and unless we believe that there was not conflict and competition in Celtic society the question is posed how this contradiction was resolved?

One possibility lies in the presentation of society as being in some sense natural and immutable both in this world and in the other(s). In their discussion of the La Tène II–III sanctuary at Gournay-sur-Aronde, Brunaux and Meniel (1983) suggest that the sacrifices are an image of Celtic society.[11] In this the weaponry deposited by the elite symbolises both their military power and their role in the protection or enlargment of the polity. The offerings of cattle and (presumably) fruit, flowers and vegetables symbolise the domestic production of the *plebs*, consumed in the worlds of the sacred and profane. The learned class ensure the prosperity and fecundity of society and the fusion of the different groups within it, both symbolically and actually also, at the moment of sacrifice.

To these suggestions we might both add and stress the importance of such a ceremony in presenting as some way natural (Goody 1977) the structure of society, the specification of wealth in its various forms by the elite and also the ideology of the elite. In this fashion the weaponry becomes an ambiguous symbol of both power and security. It is noteworthy that cattle also appear to have been an important means by which to assess wealth in Celtic society; and the roles of the learned class in ensuring knowledge of ancestors and gods could be explored further. In this hypothesis criticism of the living world is pre-empted by its relations to the other(s), but nonetheless the contradiction remains. This is applicable both to the exploitation of women by the specification of gender roles and to clientage in its broader sense. In many ways it is an attractive hypothesis, compatible both with the interpretation of Celtic society adopted from the work of Nash and the deposition of selected, elite, artefact types in watery, probably sacred, places. Nor does it conflict with Kent's (1978) interpretation of the coinage. Indeed, if the recorded distributions of both the coins and the metalwork are not simply products of sample bias, then they may reflect an area in which warfare was important. If we are to follow these interpretations of the precious metal coinages, whatever the roles of potin, then they suggest that it was also possible to obtain wealth and kudos overseas in service as either allies or mercenaries. It is an intriguing possibility.

It is proper to conclude by emphasising some of the many difficulties. Most of what has been suggested here is not new; it is thoroughly traditional. But as Friedman (1979) points out, it necessitates much thought about the usefulness of descriptions such as social, economic or religious. Here the work of Ross (1968) and the relations between sacred and secular authority need careful consideration, as indeed do the relations between the interpretations advanced here and Hingley's studies of rural settlement elsewhere in this volume. Finally, what it does emphasise above all is the need to return to the study of material culture in its historical context. But these should not be the final words, which must surely be quoted from the judge's summing up on the claim of the Royal Irish Academy for the Broighter gold hoard (?second-first century BC) to be declared Treasure

Trove:

'The defendant's suggestion is that the articles were thrown into the sea, which they suggest covered the spot in question, as a votive offering by some Irish king or chief to some Irish sea god at some period between 300 BC and AD 100, and for this purpose they ask this court to infer the existence of the sea on the spot in question, the existence of an Irish sea god, the existence of a custom to make votive offerings in Ireland during the period suggested, and the existence of kings or chiefs who would be likely to make such offerings. The whole of their evidence (if I may so describe it) on these points is of the vaguest description.'

(R.L. Praeger *The Way that I Went*, Dublin 1939, 66)

Acknowledgements

I should like to thank Leslie Cram, Jean Macdonald, Andrew Sherratt, Ian Stead and Andrew White for their assistance during the course of my museum visits in the preparation of this article. The interpretation of Celtic society advanced here owes a great deal not only to the published work of, but also to conversations with, Daphne Nash; it is a pleasure to acknowledge my debt to her and to John Barrett, Colin Haselgrove and Victoria Pirie for thought-provoking discussions. This paper was substantially written, somewhat improbably, in Red Bay, Labrador, during July 1983. To everyone there, my thanks.

Notes

1 Most quotations from classical authors are given in translation using Tierney (1960).

2 A full gazetteer of the Iron Age finds from the Thames was collected in the preparation of this article; for reasons of space it is not included here and will be published elsewhere shortly. There are, however, two points worthy of comment. Nicholson (1980) records the possibility that the otherwise unprovenanced 'Mayer' Iron Age mirror was found in the Thames. Although a certain amount of uncertainty must surround this provenance, the analyses by Lowery and Savage (Rook *et al.* 1982) suggest that it is possible. Webster's (1978) suggestion that the Battersea Shield is a piece of Celtic work but of Roman date has not been received with any enthusiasm. The traditional Iron Age date is preferred here.

3 This may be a genuine difference or it may reflect the manufacture of helmets and shields in organic materials, as appears to be the case on the Continent.

4 An updating of Piggott's (1950) gazetteer of Iron Age swords in Britain will be included in the publication of the Thames material (cf n 2). There are in the region of 50 new finds.

5 I am grateful both to Naomi Field for discussing the site with me and generously making much information available to me in advance of her own publication, and to Andrew White for his help concerning the Witham finds.

6 This is not necessarily the view of Ms Field. It may be worthwhile summarising the recent debate over the nature of the La Tène site. The site was interpreted as a settlement of one type or another until Raddatz (1952) suggested that it was a religious site. This new interpretation was widely accepted, but was challenged by Hanni Schwab on the basis of her excavations of a very similar and apparently contemporary site at Cornaux only 5 km away (Schwab 1969; 1972; 1974). Here Schwab found the remains of a bridge comparable to those at La Tène. Sedimentological studies as well as not less than 18 bodies in the debris of the collapse of the bridge suggest that the bridge was destroyed in a flash flood. On the basis of this and of detailed studies of the hydrology and topography of the area, Schwab has suggested that La Tène was a trading post overwhelmed in the same flood as that which apparently destroyed Cornaux. This view has been received cautiously (e.g. Wyss 1974), and sediment-studies at La Tène by Berger and Joos (1977) suggest that there is no evidence for a similar flood there and that the deposits accumulated gradually, perhaps in a dead arm of the Zihl. The question must be regarded as still open, and the final publication of Schwab's excavations will have a crucial bearing not only on the interpretation of La Tène but also on the chronology of the objects found there.

7 I am grateful to Dr Alfred Haffner for discussion on this point.

8 The recent 'Denain' (Nord) sword find (Hantute and Leman-Delerive 1982) is of the type discussed by Verwers and Ypey (1975). The sword was probably a dredging find. Denain is within a few kilometres of the French-Belgian border.

9 It should be noted that at the conference Professor Harding retracted his earlier (1972) view, criticised by both Collis (1977) and Drury (1980), that the circular Iron Age structure at Frilford was a shrine.

10 Pauli's comments were made with reference to an ivory object thought to be a 'Syro-Phoenician' mirror-mount from the male burial in the 'Grafenbühl' Hallstatt D3 barrow at Asperg, Nordwürttemberg. Unfortunately, as Schindler (1980b) has pointed out, the piece belongs more probably to an Etruscan fan. Nonetheless the point still stands.

11 This is an adaptation, not an exact translation of Brunaux and Meniel 1983, 170.

References

ADKINS, R and JACKSON, R. 1978: *Neolithic Stone and Flint Axes from the River Thames* (London, Brit. Mus. Occas. Pap. 1).

AJOT, J. and BULARD, A. 1977: *L'archéologie a Chèlles* (Chèlles).

ALEXANDER, J.A. 1981: The Coming of Iron-Using to Britain. In Haefner 1981, 57–67.

ALLEN, D.F. 1967: Iron Currency Bars in Britain. *Proc. Prehist. Soc.* 33, 307–35.

BARRETT, J.C. 1981: Aspects of the Iron Age in Atlantic Scotland. A case study in the problems of archaeological interpretation. *Proc. Soc. Antiq. Scot.* 111 (1982), 205–19.

BERGER, L. and JOOS, M. 1977: Zur Wasserführung der Zihl bei der Station La Tène. In Stüber, K. and Zürcher, A. (editors), *Festschrift Walter Drack* (Zurich), 68–76.

BOE, G. DE. and HUBERT, H. 1977: Une Installation portuaire d'époque romaine à Pommeroeul. (Brussels, Archaeol. Belgica 192).

BONNAMOUR, L. and BULARD, A. 1976: Une épée celtique à fourreau décoré découverte à Montbellet (Saône-et-Loire). *Gallia* 34, 279–84.

BOURDIEU, P. 1979: Symbolic Power, *Crit. Anthrop.* 13 and 14, 77–85.

BRUNAUX, J.-L. and MENIEL, P. 1983: Le sanctuaire de Gournay-sur-Aronde (Oise): structures et rites, les animaux de sacrifice. In *Les Celtes dans le nord du bassin Parisien*, Actes du cinquieme colloque tenu a Senlis (Amiens, Rev. Archéol. Picardie. Trim 1,), 165–73.

BRUNAUX, J.-L., MENIEL, P. and RAPIN, A. 1980: Un sanctuaire gaulois à Gournay-sur-Aronde (Oise). *Gallia* 38, 1–25.

CADOUX, J.-L. 1982: L'ossuaire gauloise à Ribemont-sur-Ancre (Somme). Campagne de 1982. *Rev. Archéol. Picardie* 1, 12–13.

CHAMPION, T.C. 1975: Britain in the European Iron Age. *Archaeologia Atlantica* 1, 127–45.

CHAMPION, T.C. 1982: The Myth of Iron Age Invasions in Ireland. In Scott, B.G. (editor), *Studies on Early Ireland: Essays in Honour of M.V. Duignan* (Belfast), 39–44.

CHAMPION, T.C. and CHAMPION, S. 1981: The Iron Age in Hampshire. In Scahdla-Hall, T. and Shennan, S.J. (editors), *The Archaeology of Hampshire* (Hants. Fld. Club Monogr. 1), 37–45.

CLARKE, D.L. 1972: A provisional model of an Iron Age society. In Clarke, D.L. (editor), *Models in Archaeology* (London), 801–69.

COLLECTANEA LONDINIENSIA 1978: *Collectanea Londiniensia: Studies in London Archaeology and History presented to Ralph Merrifield* (London, London Middlesex Archaeol. Soc. Spec. Pap. 2).

COLLIS, J.R. 1973: Burials with Weapons in Iron Age Britain. *Germania* 51, 121–33.

COLLIS, J.R. 1977: Pre-Roman burial rites in north-western Europe. In Reece, R. (editor), *Burial in the Roman World* (London, CBA Res. Rep. 22), 1–13.

CRUMLEY, C.L. 1974: *Celtic Social Structure: the Generation of Archaeologically Testable Hypotheses* (Michigan, Mus. Anthrop. Michigan Pap. 54).

CUNLIFFE, B.W. 1980: The Excavation of the Roman Spring at Bath in 1979: A Preliminary Description. *Antiq. Journ.* 60, 187–206.

CUNLIFFE, B.W. 1981: Danebury, Hampshire. Third Interim Report on the excavations 1976–80. *Antiq. Journ.* 61, 238–54.

DAVIES, S.M. 1981: Excavations at Old Down Farm, Andover. Part II: prehistoric and Roman. *Proc. Hants. Field Club and Archaeol. Soc.* 37, 81–163.

DOWNEY, R., KING, A.C. and SOFFE, G. 1980: The Hayling Island Temple and Religious Connections across the Channel. In Rodwell 1980, 289–304.

DRIEHAUS, J. 1965: "Fürstengraber" und Eisenerze zwischen Mittelrhein, Mosel und Saar. *Germania* 43, 32–49.

DRURY, P. 1980: Non-Classical Religious Buildings in Iron Age and Roman Britain: A Review. In Rodwell 1980, 45–78.

DUVAL, P.-M. and HAWKES, C.F.C. (editors) 1976: *Celtic Art In Ancient Europe. Five Protohistoric Centuries* (London).

EHRENBERG, M. 1980: The occurrence of Bronze Age Metalwork in the Thames: An Investigation. *Trans. London Middlesex Archaeol. Soc.* 31, 1–15.

FISCHER, F. 1959: *Der Spätlatènezeitliche Depot-Fund von Kappel, Kr. Saulgau* (Stuttgart, Urkunden zur Vor- und Frühges aus Südwürttemberg-Hohenzollern I).

FITZPATRICK, A.P. forthcoming a: Warfare and Slavery in Later Iron Age Europe.

FITZPATRICK, A.P. forthcoming b: The British Iron Age Mirror Series: Chronology, Origins and Typology.

FOSTER, J.A. 1980: *The Iron Age Moulds from Gussage All Saints* (London, Brit. Mus. Occas. Pap. 12).

FOX, C. 1947: *A Find of the Early Iron Age from Llyn Cerrig Bach, Anglesey* (Cardiff).

FOX, C. 1958: *Pattern and Purpose* (Cardiff).

FRIEDMAN, J. 1979: *System, Structure and Contradiction. The Evolution of 'Asiatic' Social Formations* (Copenhagen, Nat. Mus. Soc. Stud. in Oceania and SE Asia 2).

GARLAN, Y. 1975: *Warfare in the Ancient World: A Social History* (London).

GOLLUB, S. 1970: Bronzezeitliche Funde aus der Mosel. *Kurtrier Jahrb.* 10, 199–203.

GOODY, J. 1977: *The Domestication of the Savage Mind* (Cambridge).

GRESHAM, C.A. 1939: Spettisbury Rings, Dorset. *Archaeol. Journ.* 96, 114–31.

HAEFNER, H. (editor) 1981: *Frühes Eisen in Europa. Festschrift Walter Guyan* (Schaffhausen).

HALDANE, W. 1970: A Study of the chemical composition of pre-Roman ironwork from Somerset. *Bull. Hist. Metallurgy Grp.* 4, 53–66.

HANTUTE, G. and LEMAN-DELERIVE, G. 1982: Une épée gauloise du musée de Denain (Nord). *Études Celtiques* 19, 83–92.

HARBISON, P. 1969: The Chariot of Celtic Funerary Tradition. In Frey, O.-H. (editor), *Marburger Beiträge zur Archäologie der Kelten. Festschrift für Wolfgang Dehn* (Fundber Hessen Beih 1), 34–58.

HARDING, D.W. 1972: *The Iron Age in the Upper Thames Basin* (Oxford).

HARDING, D.W. 1980: *Celts in Conflict. Hillfort Studies 1927–1977* (Edinburgh, Univ. Edinburgh Archaeol. Dept. Occas. Pap. 3).

HARRIS, W.V. 1979: *War and Imperialism in Republican Rome 327–70 BC* (Oxford).

HAWKES, C.F.C. 1976: Celts and Cultures; wealth, power, art. In Duval and Hawkes (editors), 1976, 1–25.

HEDGES, R.G.M. and SALTER, C.J. 1979: Source determination on Currency Bars through analysis of the slag inclusions. *Archaeometry* 21, 161–75.

HODDER, I.R. 1977a: Some New Directions in Spatial Analysis. In Clarke, D.L. (editor), *Spatial Archaeology* (London), 223–351.

HODDER, I.R. 1977b: How are we to study distributions of Iron Age material? In Collis, J.R. (editor), *The Iron Age in Britain — a review* (Sheffield), 8–16.

HODDER, I.R. (editor) 1982: *Symbolic and Structural Archaeology* (Cambridge).

HODSON, F.R. 1980: Cultures as Types? Some elements of classification Theory. *Bull. Inst. Archaeol.* 17, 1–10.

HOPKINS, K. 1978: *Conquerors and Slaves* (London).

HUBERT, F. 1982: Site portuaire de Pommeroeul. I. catalogue du matérial pré- et protohistorique. (Brussels, *Archaeol. Belgica* 248).

HUMPHREYS, S.C. 1978: *Anthropology and the Greeks* (London).

HUMPHREYS, S.C. 1983: *The Family, Women and Death* (London).

HUMPHREYS, S.C. and KING, H. (editors) 1981: *Mortality and Immortality: the Anthropology and Archaeology of Death* (London).

ILKJAER, J. and LØNSTRUP, J. 1982: Interpretation of the Great Votive Deposits of Iron Age Weapons. *Journ. Danish Archaeol.* 1, 95–103.

ILKJAER, J. and LØNSTRUP, J. 1983: Der Moorfund im Tal der Illerup — Å bei Skanderborg in Ostjütland (Dänemark). Vorbericht. *Germania* 61, 95–116.

IMPE, L. VAN. and VANGEEL, P. 1981: Een Laat La Tène zwaard uit Schulen. *Archaeol. Belgica* 238, 22–6.

JOPE, E.M. 1961: Daggers of the Early Iron Age in Britain. *Proc. Prehist. Soc.* 27, 307–43.

KENT, J.P.C. 1978: The London Area in the Late Iron Age: An interpretation of the earliest coins. In *Collectanea Londiniensia* 53–8.

KRŮTA, V. 1971: *Le trésor de Duchov dans les collections tchecoslovaques* (Ústí na Lebem).

LEVY, J.E. 1982: *Social and Religious Organization in Bronze Age Denmark. An Analysis of Ritual Hoard Finds* (Oxford, BAR Int. Ser. 124).

LORENZ, H. 1978: Totenbrauchtum: Untersuchung zur regionalen Gliederung der frühen Latènekultur. *Ber. Rom.-Germ. Komm.* 59 (1979), 1–380.

MACDONALD, J. 1978: An Iron Age Dagger in the Royal Ontario Museum. In *Collectanea Londiniensia* 1978, 44–52.

MANNING, W.H. 1972: Ironwork Hoards in Iron Age and Roman Britain. *Britannia* 3, 224–50.

MANNING, W.H. 1979: The Native and Roman contribution to the Development of Metal Industries in Britain. In Burnham, B.C. and Johnson, H.B. (editors), *Invasion and Response. The Case of Roman Britain* (Oxford, BAR Brit. Ser. 73), 111–21.

MARIEN, M. 1970: *Le Trou de l'Ambre au Bois de Wérimont, Eprave* (Brussels, Mus. Royaux Art Hist. Monogr. Archéol. Nationale 4).

MEGAW, J.V.S. 1976: An Iron Age Sword with decorated mounts of Piggott's Group V from Thrapston, Northamptonshire. *Northants. Archaeol.* 11, 165–70.

MEGAW, J.V.S. 1979: Celtic art — product of travelling craftsmen or chieftainly vassals? In Duval P.-M. and Krŭta, V. (editors), *Les mouvements celtiques du Ve au Ier siècles avant notre ère* (Paris), 49–54.

MEGAW, J.V.S. 1982: Finding Purposeful Patterns: Further notes towards a methodology of pre-Roman Celtic art. In Duval, P.-M. and Krŭta, V. (editors), *L'art celtique de la période d'expansion IVe et IIIe siècles avant notre ère* (Geneva), 213–29.

MOMIGLIANO, A.D. 1975: *Alien Wisdom* (Cambridge).

NASH, D. 1976a: Reconstructing Poseidonio's Celtic Ethnography: Some Considerations. *Britannia* 7, 111–26.

NASH, D. 1976b: The Growth of Urban Society in France. In Cunliffe, B.W. and Rowley, R.T. (editors), *Oppida: the Beginnings of Urbanisation in Barbarian Europe* (Oxford BAR Supp. Ser. 11), 95–133.

NASH, D. 1981: Coinage and State development in central Gaul. In Cunliffe, B.W. (editor), *Coinage and Society in Britain and Gaul. Some Current Problems* (London, CBA Res. Rep. 38), 10–17.

NEEDHAM, S.P. and BURGESS, C.B. 1980: The Later Bronze Age in the Lower Thames Valley: The Metalwork evidence. In Barrett, J.C. and Bradley, R.J. (editors), *Settlement and Society in the British Later Bronze Age* (Oxford, BAR Brit. Ser. 83), 437–69.

NICHOLSON, S.M. 1980: *Catalogue of the prehistoric metalwork in Merseyside County Museums* (Liverpool, Merseyside County Counc. Work Notes 2).

189

O'CONNOR, B. 1980: *Cross-Channel Relations in the Later Bronze Age* (Oxford, BAR Int. Ser. 91).

PATTE, E. 1977: Objets de La Tène des rives de l'Aisne. *Bull. Soc. Préhist. France* 74, 30–2.

PAULI, L. 1972: *Untersuchungen zur Späthallstattkultur in Nordwürttemberg. Analyse eines Kleinraumes im Grenzbereich zweier Kulturen* (Hamburg, Hamburger Beitr. Archäol. Bd. 2, Hft. 1).

PIGGOTT, S. 1950: Swords and Scabbards of the British Early Iron Age. *Proc. Prehist. Soc.* 16, 1–22.

PIGGOTT, S. 1965: *Ancient Europe* (Edinburgh).

PIGGOTT, S. 1976: Summing up of the Colloquy. In Duval and Hawkes (editors), 1976, 283–9.

PIGGOTT, S. 1983: *The Earliest Wheeled Transport* (London).

PLEINER, R. 1979: *Otázka Státu ve Staré Gallii* (Prague).

RADDATZ, K. 1952: Zur Deutung der Funde von La Tène. *Offa* 11, 24–7.

RAFERTY, J. 1970: Two Gold Hoards from Tyrone. *Journ. Royal Soc. Antiq. Ireland* 100, 169–74.

RAPIN, A. 1982: Das keltische Heiligtum von Gournay-sur-Aronde. *Antike Welt* 13, 39–60.

RODWELL, W.J. (editor) 1980: *Temples, Churches and Religion in Roman Britain* (Oxford, BAR Brit. Ser. 77).

ROLLE, R. 1980: Oiorpata. In Krüger, T. and Stephan, H.-G. (editors), *Festschirft Klaus Raddatz. Beiträge zur archäologie Nordwestdeutschlands und Mitteleuropas* (Hildesheim, Materialhft Ur- und Frühges Niedersachsens 16), 275–94.

ROOK, A.G., LOWERY, P.R., SAVAGE, R.D.A. and WILKINS, R.L. 1982: An Iron Age Bronze Mirror from Aston, Hertfordshire. *Antiq. Journ.* 62, 18–34.

ROSS, A. 1968: *Pagan Celtic Britain* (London).

ROWLANDS, M.J. 1971–72: The archaeological interpretation of prehistoric metalworking. *World Archaeol.* 3, 210–23.

ROYMANS, N. and YPEY, J. forthcoming: Spätlatènezeitliche und frührömische Flussfunde aus dem Maasgebiet bei Rossum/Lith (Niederland).

SAUNDERS, C. 1977: The Iron Firedog from Welwyn Hertfordshire, Reconsidered. *Hertfordshire Archaeol.* 5, 15–21.

SCHWAB, H. 1969: La Tène — A Late Iron Age Settlement in the light of recent excavations. *Sandoz Bull.* 15, 27–37.

SCHWAB, H. 1972: Entdeckung einer keltischen Brücke an der Zihl und ihre Bedeutung für La Tène. *Archäol. Korrespondenzbl.* 2, 289–94.

SCHWAB, H. 1974: Neue Ergebnisse zur Topographie von La Tène. *Germania* 52, 348–67.

SHERRATT, A.G. 1983: A Newly Discovered La Tène Sword and Scabbard. *Oxford Journ. Archaeol.* 2(1), 115–8.

SPINDLER, K. 1980a: Das Eisenschwert von Möhrendorf Ldkr Erlangen-Höchstadt — Ein Beitrag zu den Hallstatt-D Schwertlern. In Spindler, K. (editor), *Vorzeit zwischen Main und Donau* (Erlangen, Erlangen Forsch Reihe A, Bd 26), 206–26.

SPINDLER, K. 1980b: Zur Elfenbeinscheibe aus dem hallsattzeitlichen Fürstengrab vom Grafenbühl. *Archäol. Korrespondenzbl.* 10, 239–48.

SPRATLING, M.G. 1970: The Late Pre-Roman Iron Age Bronze Mirror from Old Warden. *Beds. Archaeol. Journ.* 5, 9–16.

SPRATLING, M.G. 1978: Review of Duval and Hawkes 1976. *Britannia* 9, 488–90.

SPRATLING, M.G. 1979: The Debris of the Metalworking. In Wainwright, G.J. *Gussage All Saints — An Iron Age Settlement in Dorset* (London, Dept. Environ. Archaeol. Rep. 10), 125–49.

STAELENS, Y.J.E. 1982: The Birdlip Cemetery. *Trans. Bristol. Gloucs. Archaeol. Soc.* 100, 19–31.

STEAD, I.M., HARTWELL, A.P., LANG, J.R.S., LA NIECE, S.C. and MEEKS, N.D. 1981: An Iron Age Sword and Scabbard from Isleham. *Proc. Cambridge Antiq. Soc.* 70, 61–74.

TIERNEY, J.J. 1960: The Celtic Ethnography of Posidonius. *Proc. Royal Irish Acad.* 60 Sec C, 189–275.

TORBRÜGGE, W. 1970–71: Vor- und frühgeschichtliche Flussfunde. Zur Ordnung und Bestimmunng einer Denkmälergruppe. *Ber. Rom.-Germ. Komm* 51–52, 1–146.

TSCHUMI, O. 1929: Der Massenfund von der Tiefenau auf der Engehalbinsel b. Bern 1849–51. *Jahrb. Schweiz Ges Urges* 21, 131–48.

TSCHUMI, O. 1940: *Die Ur- und Frühgeschichtliche Fundstelle von Port in Amt Nidau* (Bern).

TSCHUMI, O. 1948: Beiträge zur Siedlungsgeschichte des Kantons Bern Nr 25. *Jahrb. Hist. Mus. Bern* 28, 22–37.

TYLECOTE, R.F. 1962: *Metallurgy in Archaeology* (London).

VERWERS, G.J. and YPEY, J. 1975: Six Iron Age Swords from the Netherlands. *Anal. Praeh. Leid.* 8, 75–91.

WAINWRIGHT, G.J. and SPRATLING, M.G. 1973: The Iron Age settlement of Gussage All Saints. *Antiquity* 47, 109–30.

WEBSTER, G. 1978: Review of M. Macgregor 1976. *Early Celtic Art in North Britain. Britannia* 9, 490–1.

WEGNER, G. 1976: *Die vorgeschichtlichen Flussfunde aus dem Main und dem Rhein bei Mainz* (Munich, Materialhefte z Bayer Vorges Reihe A 30).

WHIMSTER, R.P. 1977: Iron Age burial in Southern Britain. *Proc. Prehist. Soc.* 43, 317–27.

WHIMSTER, R.P. 1981: *Burial Practices in Iron Age Britain. A discussion and gazetteer of the evidence c. 700 B.C.–A.D. 43* (Oxford BAR Brit. Ser. 90).

WHITE, A. 1979a: *Antiquities from the River Witham. Part 1. Prehistoric and Roman* (Lincoln, Lincs. Mus. Info. Sheet Archaeol. Ser. 12).

WHITE, A. 1979b: *Antiquities from the River Witham. Part 2. Anglo-Saxon and Viking* (Lincoln, Lincs. Mus. Info. Sheet Archaeol. Ser. 13).

WHITE, A. 1979c: *Antiquities from the River Witham. Part 3. Mediaeval* (Lincoln, Lincs. Mus. Info. Sheet Archaeol. Ser. 14).

WILSON, C.E. 1981: Burials Within Settlements in Southern Britain During the Pre-Roman Iron Age. *Bull. Inst. Archaeol.* 18, 127–69.

WILSON, D.M. 1965: Some Neglected Late Anglo-Saxon Swords. *Mediaeval Archaeol.* 9, 32–54.

WYSS, R. 1974: Grabriten, Opferplätze und weitere Belege zur geistigen Kultur der Latènezeit. In Drack, W. (editor), *Ur- und Frühgeschichtliche Archäologie der Schweiz 4, Die Eisenzeit* (Basel), 167–96.

ZIMMERMANN, W.H. 1970: Urgeschichtliche Operfunde aus Flüssen, Mooren, Quellen und Brunnen südwestdeutschlands. *Neue Ausgrabungen Forsch niedersachsen* 6, 53–92.

Tribal Boundaries Viewed from the Perspective of Numismatic Evidence

Lyn Sellwood

Introduction

The Wessex/Upper Thames area is of particular interest because it overlaps the boundaries, although not the complete territories, of three traditionally well-attested tribes: the Atrebates, with an apparent sphere of influence which includes much of Sussex and impinges upon adjacent counties, particularly those to the north and west; the Dobunni, centred upon Gloucestershire, but spreading thinly into Wales and showing a denser presence in the counties to the south and east; and the Durotriges, based in Dorset and spreading principally north and east.

It is intended here to consider only the latest phenomenon in British Celtic coinage, those issues which are frequently, but not invariably, inscribed, and which have a geographically-confined distribution which readily allows application of the epithet 'tribal'. Tribal, as used in this paper, is understood to mean a coherent grouping whose boundaries may be defined in a variety of ways, but whose structure is open to question. It is accepted that such boundaries were probably flexible and subject to change over time.

The question of absolute dates is one of the most contentious aspects of the study of British Celtic coinages. The tribal issues are generally believed to belong to the period c. 30 BC–AD 43; but it is possible that some of the people of Wessex continued to mint coins for up to two decades after this, and the coins themselves were circulated in some capacity for at least half a century after the Claudian conquest.

Coin distribution-maps have been the principal tool of scholars concerned with the definition of the tribal boundaries. There are a number of obvious reasons for this.

1 Coins are more numerous than many other Iron Age artefacts.

2 Coinage is a medium likely to be sensitive to politico/economic realities and changes; the distribution-maps may well reflect these.

3 Distributions, as mentioned above, are very coherent, at least in the later period. Relatively little interchange, in terms of the movement of coins, takes place between one coin-issuing area and another.

A useful distinction has emerged in British Celtic numismatics (Allen 1944; updated and refined in Cunliffe 1981), between the four coin-minting tribes of the south-eastern corner of Britain, the Atrebates, Cantiaci, Trinovantes and Catuvellauni and the four, again coin-issuing, who occupy a zone peripheral to this: the Durotriges, Dobunni, Coritani and Iceni. Those of the southeast mint a coinage which is more sophisticated in

every sense than that of the peripheral peoples. They produce a greater range of types and denominations, including small silver minims and bronzes. These low-value coins have sometimes been taken to indicate the existence of an incipient or actual monetary economy.

The coinages of some of the south-eastern tribes, particularly certain later issues of the Atrebates, are slavishly imitative of Roman types. The fringe-zone coinages tend only to be minted in precious metals and in large denominations, although the Durotriges are something of an aberration in these and other aspects. Fringe-zone coinages have a limited range of types and, with a few exceptions, are non-Roman in stylistic idiom.

The State of the Discipline

A brief summary of two divergent schools of approach to the problem of tribal boundaries is offered, before an attempt is made to reassess the situation. The traditional 'historical' approach is exemplified throughout the work of D.F. Allen. (A complete bibliography of Allen's work is provided in the *Numismatic Chronicle* for 1976 (Thompson 1976, 259–71), and more recently and extensively in articles by W. Rodwell (1976; 1981)). Exponents of this school identify coinage as principally a political phenomenon and are much concerned with the recognition of historical events. Opposed to this tradition is a methodology which has evolved over the last fifteen years or so, and which J. Collis (1981, 53) has dubbed 'newmismatic'. A series of publications by Collis (1971a; 1971b; 1974 and 1981), by C. Haselgrove (1976) and I. Hodder and C. Orton (1976) illustrate the principal concerns of this school, which concentrates on examining the socio-economic bases of society rather than on its political superstructure. The aim of this alternative approach is to quantify the data in order that the validity or otherwise of the basic data and of the hypotheses which seek to explain apparent patterns, can be demonstrated by the application of mathematical and statistical tests.

Followers of the traditional approach have tended to assess tribal boundaries in terms of a gross plot of all the coins minted by each group. Figure 13.1 plots the distribution of all Dobunnic, Durotrigan and Atrebatic coins. While it can be seen that each tribe has a clear home territory, boundaries fail to emerge with precision. It is generally acknowledged, within the school itself, that such maps are crude constructs and fail to reflect the subtle territorial fluctuations which may have taken place over time. This generalised, numismatic estimation of the boundaries can be supported to a limited degree

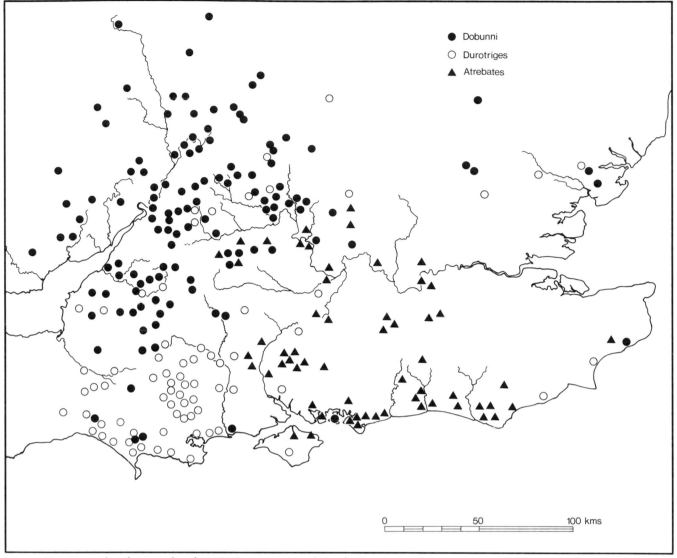

Figure 13.1 *Gross distribution of Dobunnic, Durotrigan and Atrebatic coins.*

by ancient literary and epigraphic sources. In the case of the three Wessex/Upper Thames tribes, Ptolemy's *Geography* is the most useful text. This throws little light on the boundary question, but confirms the existence of the separate entities indicated by the gross distribution-maps, and allows a name to be apportioned to each one. Ptolemy was, however, writing at a much later period (somewhere within the decade AD 140–150), although it is believed that he drew on Claudio-Neronian or at the latest early Flavian material for his account (Rivet and Smith 1979, 103). Thus, the apparent fit between the two disparate forms of evidence, artefactual and literary, separated from one another by the Roman invasion of Britain, may serve as much to illuminate the paucity of the available data as to confirm the findings.

It is generally admitted by those of the traditional school that the apparent unity of each tribal area as identified from the gross distribution-maps may well mask a more complex reality. One example of this has been identified amongst the Dobunni. Allen (1961b), was able to recognise a divide in Dobunnic territory. This was most apparent in the reign of the two latest

rulers, Corio and Bodvoc, whose coin-distributions are mutually exclusive, those of Corio occupying the territory to the south and north of the Bodvoc issues, which appear as a wedge driven into this (Fig. 13.2). A division in the Atrebatic area may be indicated by the fact that there were fairly certainly two oppida, *Calleva Atrebatum* (Silchester) whose existence is attested on the inscribed coins, and Selsey Bill. *Venta Belgarum* (Winchester) may have been a third, although evidence in support of this is ambiguous. There is a tendency amongst traditionalists to view the apparent expansions or contractions of the coin-distribution patterns as enlargements of military-based power, frequently assumed to involve the movement of peoples. At its worst, this approach can result in the construction of a pseudo-history in which 'personalities' loom large.

The aims of the new school are considerably at variance with those outlined above (for a detailed discussion of the two positions, refer to Collis (1981) and Rodwell (1981)). The questions asked of distribution-maps concern the function and usage of the artefacts. The tendency is for any recognised patterning to be interpreted in terms of spheres of social or

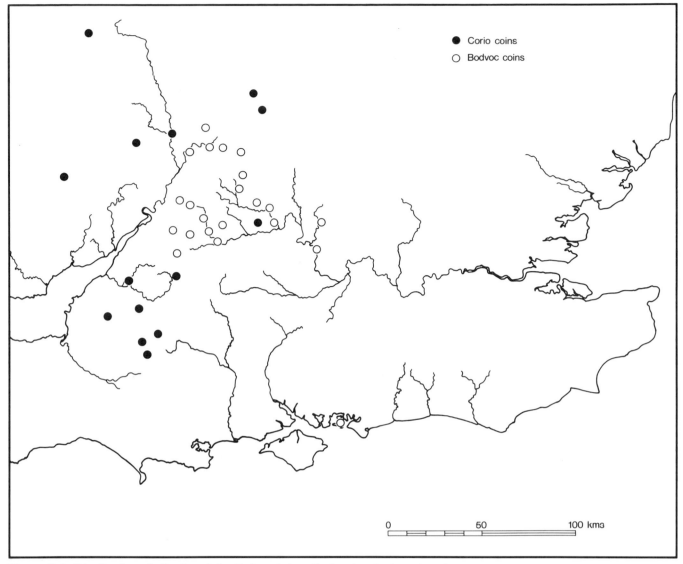

Figure 13.2 *Distribution of all coins of the Dobunnic inscribed series, Corio and Bodvoc.*

economic interest, diminishing — or even denying — the political dimension. Another fundamental characteristic is the desire to transcend an entirely subjective assessment of coin distribution-maps, and move towards a more objective, quantifiable method of examination.

The aspiration towards more objectivity is beyond reproach, but whether or not the tests applied are appropriate to the extant data-base is a contentious matter. These reservations can best be explained by providing some concrete examples. These have been taken from the book by Hodder and Orton (1976). The authors have provided (*op. cit.*, 79, fig. 4.20) a map which shows a linear, geometric boundary between Iron Age coin-distributions (the authors agree that such distributions may be indicative of tribal areas). The suggested boundaries are shown (Fig. 13.3) superimposed upon a gross plot of Dobunnic, Durotrigan and Atrebatic coins. The boundary between the respective coin-distributions (hence possibly between the tribal territories) has been obtained by placing a grid over a similar gross plot map and establishing the boundary as the grid line on either side of which the density of findspots is the same. The method appears to offer new hope; but as the

authors admit, there are considerable problems in practice.

1 The boundary-line produced depends upon the scale of grid quadrant used. This selection must involve subjective judgement.

2 The boundary-line must be subject to the vicissitudes of time. It is currently difficult to be certain to either the period over which the coins were struck or that within which they circulated.

A further bias is introduced by the differing quantities of coins produced in each area. It would appear, on current evidence, that the Durotriges minted vastly greater numbers of coins than the Dobunni or Atrebates. It should also be remembered that each of the three tribes which form the subject of this study minted a different series of denominations, which would appear to be circulated in a manner which distinguishes them one from another. This is a phenomenon recognised by Hodder (1977, 321–2) and by Collis (1971a), and is examined in more detail below.

As a final objection, it is perhaps perverse to impose divisions of this sort which ignore all landscape features.

It is admitted by Hodder and Orton (1976, 80) that

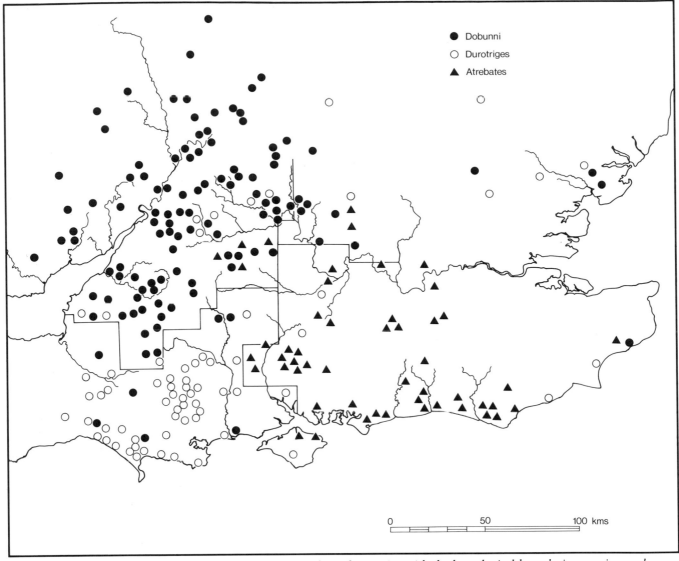

Figure 13.3 *Gross distribution of Dobunnic, Durotrigan and Atrebatic coins with the hypothetical boundaries superimposed.*

the method by which the boundary-map was produced is unsatisfactory in a number of ways; but the exercise has been examined here because there is a real danger that an assessment which offers a measure of objectivity, however small, will be accorded greater reliability than is in fact warranted.

In the same publication (1976, 196–7), a test is applied to distributions of Dobunnic and Catuvellaunian coins in the hope that it would be possible to determine whether distance emerges as the only factor affecting the progressively smaller numbers of coins found as distance from the mint site is increased; or whether fall-off is interrupted in a way which implies a bias. This bias may be physical, political, geographical or may even result from the preferences of modern collectors.

The basis for the test is a map on which the distribution of all Dobunnic coins is compared with that of the Catuvellaunian issues minted during the reign of Cunobelin at the mint of Verulamium, the nearest Catuvellaunian mint to Dobunnic territory. The density of coins is then assessed in sections along a transect drawn between Bagendon (a Dobunnic oppidum and putative mint site) and Verulamium, and the results

plotted on a graph. Fig. 13.4 shows in Section *a* the classic non-territorial pattern; the fall-off in the number of coins continuing in an uninterrupted curve both up to and beyond the point of intersection. Section *b* shows the pattern reflecting territoriality; note the sharp fall-off of coins from the point of intersection. Section *c* shows the fall in density of Dobunnic and Catuvellaunian coins as they travel further from the respective mint sites. The resultant pattern contains no suggestion of territoriality. It may be inferred from this that the concept of boundaries and, by logical extension, that of tribal entities, is inappropriate to these particular coinages.

The usefulness of the exercise is qualified. 'It is possible, however, that any sharp boundaries which did exist have been disturbed due to lack of archaeological information. Changing boundaries at different dates may have produced a blurred aggregate pattern' (Hodder and Orton 1976, 197).

The problems inherent in this application of method to data are more serious than the qualifying statement allows.

1 From a purely chronological standpoint, the test

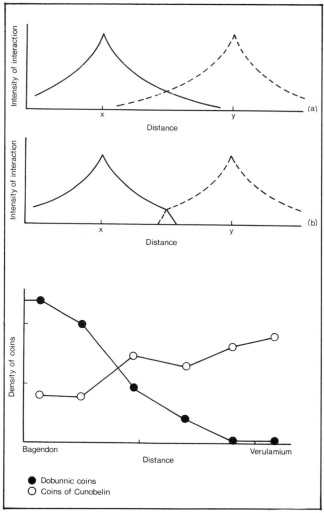

Figure 13.4 *The significance of a boundary in (a) non-territorial and (b) territorial behaviour. (c) The fall-off in density of Dobunnic and Catuvellaunian coins with distance from respective mints (Source: Hodder and Orton 1976).*

juxtaposes coins minted over perhaps seventy years by the Dobunni with those produced over perhaps half that time by the Catuvellauni.

2   The Dobunnic gold issue comprises one uninscribed and seven inscribed coinages. Their silver coins fall approximately into sixteen classes, whereas all the coins on the Catuvellaunian side of the equation were minted in the name of one ruler.

3   All of Cunobelin's gold coinage was minted at Camulodunum (Mack 1975, 70); only the bronze and silver pieces were issued from Verulamium. The test therefore considers only part of the Catuvellaunian output — the silver and bronze — as opposed to the entire Dobunnic production in both silver and gold.

In parenthesis the possibility should be noted that Dobunnic coins, too, were minted at more than one site although, since none of the issues is inscribed with the mint name, this cannot be considered certain. One possible contender as a second mint site is Camerton, Avon, and the frequent 'split' distribution seen in many of the coin-maps may be invoked in favour of this hypothesis.

A visual assessment of the distributions of Cuno-

belin's silver and bronze coins (Fig. 13.5) shows a significant number penetrating the area over which Dobunnic coins normally circulate. The gold coins, on the other hand, present an entirely different picture (Fig. 13. 6). It can be seen from this that there is a considerable concentration of coins against the angle formed by the Thames and Cherwell. These rivers may, for a number of reasons (Sellwood forthcoming), be taken to represent the eastern and southern boundaries of Dobunnic territory. Very few of the gold coins penetrate across the Thames-Cherwell line, and it may be stated that, at least in terms of a visual assessment, there is a very significant difference in the distributions of the different metal types, and the non-territorial verdict might well have been modified if these had been taken into consideration.

These two specific examples of the application of quantitative tests to numismatic data have been provided in order that some general points can be made. The aims of the school of deductive reasoning represent a healthy trend, but it is questionable whether such a methodology can be widely applied to numismatic evidence as it stands. In the first place, the actual number of coins available for study represents only a minute fraction of the total output; and this statement is quantifiable. The actual numbers of extant dies of individual Dobunnic and Atrebatic series have been fed into a computer programmed to estimate the most probable number of dies from the existing total of known dies in relation to the extant coins. For the more substantial series the results may be accorded a certain reliability. The largest class of Dobunnic silver is represented by about 70 coins, among which it has been possible to recognise 55 obverse and 45 reverse dies. The probability-estimates indicate that the series may originally have comprised 152 obverse and 118 reverse dies. This predictive method cannot be claimed to achieve complete accuracy, but it is useful in giving some indication of the order of numbers involved. Even if a series is complete in terms of dies (as is likely with some of the Atrebatic gold issues), actual numbers of coins lag well behind. It has been estimated, as a result of practical experiment (Sellwood 1963) that a pair of dies is capable of producing at least 10,000 coins. Many of the extant coins are struck from well-worn dies, and it is thus clear, even allowing for extensive re-coining, that the picture is extremely fragmentary.

The picture is not merely incomplete, it is distorted by a number of factors which introduce bias.[1] The possible nature and effect of these biases has been outlined by Rodwell (1981), and receives general, although by no means comprehensive, treatment in Appendix 1 below. A few remarks on the problem will be included here. Amongst the distorting factors which Rodwell isolates is the magnetic effect caused by the activity of collectors and museums or by the existence of a well-known site in the area. All these entities may result in a flurry of activity which throws the area into false relief relative to the distribution as a whole.

Rodwell is of the opinion that these biases, once understood, may be taken into account in the study of

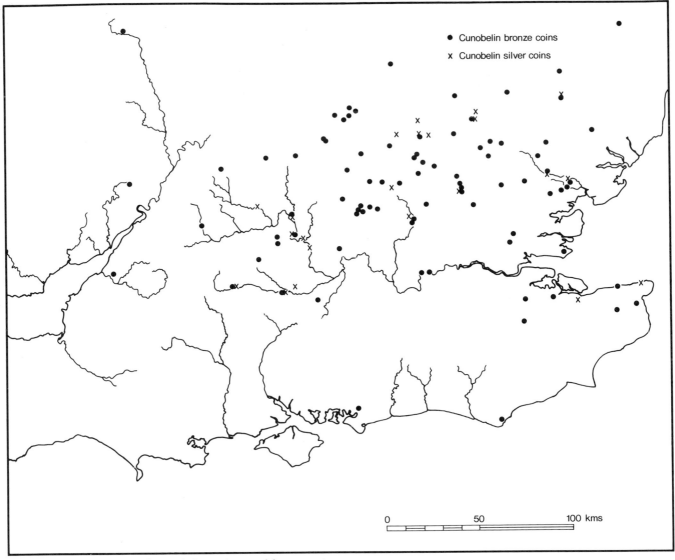

Figure 13.5 *Distribution of Cunobelin's silver and bronze coins.*

the distribution-map. This kind of aspect is, however, extremely difficult to quantify, and the richness of sites or regions may well have had a positive effect on the interest of the museum or collector. It is also true to say that this particular bias does not detract from the essential cohesion of the later coin distribution-maps.

A Reassessment of the Boundary Problem

The assumption underlying the analysis of the coin distribution-maps that follows is that visually-recognizable patterns observed on such maps reflect, at a very generalized level, behavioural trends. Given the present state of the data for much of the area under consideration, it is difficult, indeed inappropriate, to interpret these patterns very specifically. It is, however, important to question exactly what is being plotted, even if this is ultimately unanswerable. It would appear probable that the distributions of different denominations of coins represent various spheres of activity. This idea is current within British Celtic numismatics on a number of levels. Collis (1971a) extrapolates a quite detailed socio-economic hypothesis from his observations of the

phenomenon. He notes the discrepant circulations of gold and bronze coins amongst the core-territory tribes, and from this suggests a functional distinction: gold coins tend to be isolated discoveries peppered across the contemporary (Iron Age) landscape, whereas bronze coins are often concentrated on major oppida. He takes this further, and proposes that the separate denominations were in fact used by different groups of people. Hodder's (1977) conclusions from a spatial analysis of the coins in the Catuvellaunian/Trinovantian area are much more generalized (*Ibid*; 322): 'It appears that certain coin-types are more widespread than others . . . There is some suggestion that bronze coins are found less frequently in the peripheral areas of the distribution'.

Observations on this, less specific, level would seem to be appropriate to the three tribes examined in this paper. Hodder hints that low-value coins may travel less far than other denominations, and this suggestion has been examined in terms of the Dobunnic, Atrebatic and Durotrigan coinages.

The Dobunni issue gold staters, gold quarter-staters, (only six are known) and silver, some of which is quite

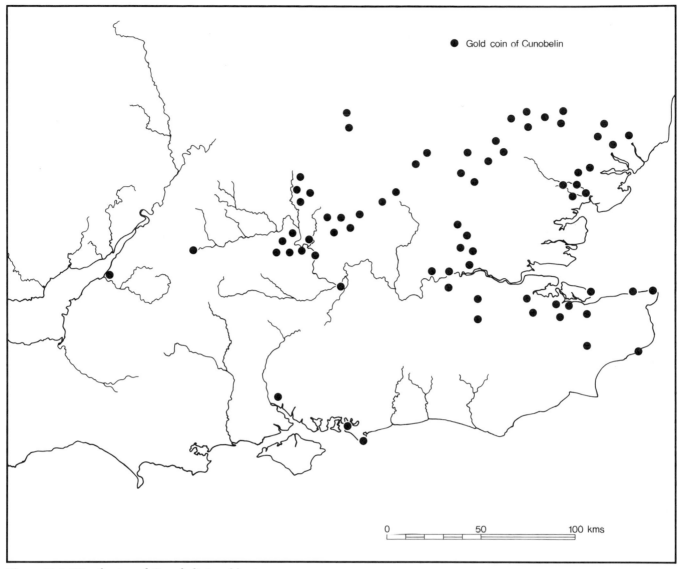

Figure 13.6 *Distribution of Cunobelin's gold coins.*

base. Figure 13.7 is a gross plot of all Dobunnic coins on which silver and gold are distinguished from one another. The area over which the two denominations circulate is essentially similar, but the few points of difference may well be significant. The boundary between the Dobunni and their non-coin-using neighbours, the Silures and Ordovices, is generally assumed to lie well west of the river Severn, demarcated by the furthest extent that Dobunnic coins penetrate into Wales. It is of interest that relatively few silver coins are found west of the river, and a high percentage of these come from Weston-under-Penyard (*Ariconium*), an entirely Roman foundation — whereas gold is present in some quantity. If it is accepted that this distribution reflects the contemporary situation with some accuracy, then a number of hypotheses can be invoked to explain the phenomenon. It is possible that Dobunnic territory proper is delineated by the circulation of gold and silver together, and that this zone in which gold predominates is peripheral to the tribal core territory, being not fully Dobunnic in the coin-using sense. It is also possible that this gold belt is actually outside Dobunnic territory, and represents Dobunnic payments of bullion for services or

as gifts to an area which is not coin-issuing. Whether Dobunnic or non-Dobunnic, this area would appear to be one in which coin is principally acceptable as bullion.

To the south and east of the Dobunnic area another phenomenon is apparent. The gold coin stays, generally, within the home territory, while the silver moves abroad. This is perhaps suggestive of the fact that Dobunnic gold is not acceptable amongst the surrounding coin-minting areas; hence the limit of circulation of the gold may, in this case, define the tribal territory. A movement of silver coins into Durotrigan territory can be observed. These may have been acceptable here because the more southerly tribe operated, for part of its existence, on a silver standard.

The distribution-maps suggest that the southern and eastern boundaries of Dobunnic territory may be defined by river systems. To the south, the boundary between Dobunnic and Durotrigan spheres of activity may be the Axe and Wylye (the Wylye has been suggested as fulfilling this function by Cunliffe (1973, 435) on a consideration primarily of numismatic material). The Cherwell/Thames angle makes a convenient boundary to the east; a supposition supported by the

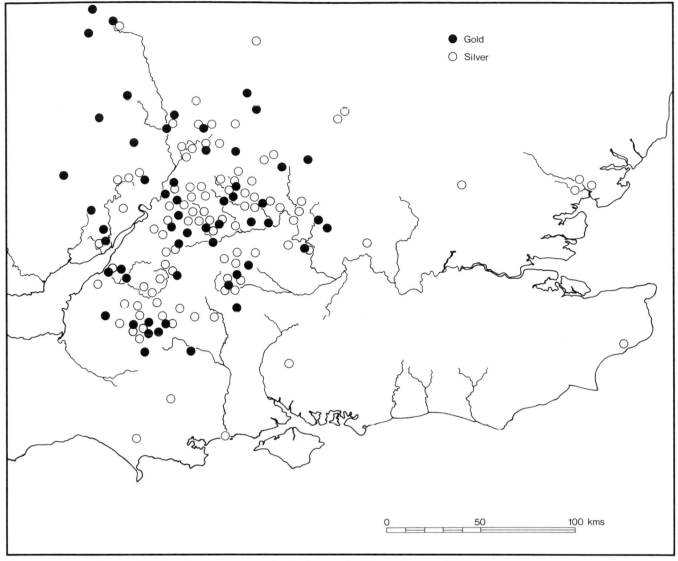

Figure 13.7 *Distribution of all Dobunnic coins in which silver and gold are distinguished.*

build-up of Catuvellaunian and other coins at this line. The small group of Dobunnic coins in central Wiltshire which is outside the postulated boundary is stylistically a separate phenomenon from regular Dobunnic issues, and will receive further attention below (p. 200).

As mentioned above, the Dobunnic silver and gold coins have a substantially similar distribution. The separate denominations behave quite otherwise amongst the Atrebates and Durotriges. Figure 13.8 shows the distribution of all gold coins during the reigns of Commius, Tincommius and Verica, and those issues of Eppillus that were minted at *Calleva*. Gold staters are distinguished from the accompanying quarters. The quarter-staters have a distribution that concentrates entirely along the coast. Each findspot is represented by a single symbol, but it should be noted that over a hundred of these coins have come from Selsey, Sussex, and that some of the additional spots on the south coast also represent more than one coin. Inland there are only two provenances, each representing a single piece. The gold full-stater coins travel over a much wider area, although they do not generally impinge upon other tribal territories. The exception to this rule occurs in the

central Wiltshire area, and in the slab of land between Hengistbury Head and Portsmouth. Evidence presented below suggests that this area is another special case. The substantial gap within the centre of the coin-distribution, if it can be accepted as real, is a further factor worth attention.

Figure 13.9 is a plot of Atrebatic coins in which the gold issues are grouped together and the silver distinguished from these. The silver is much more localized and it partially fills the lacuna in the central territory noted above. The existence of a functional distinction may be inferred from such contrasting distributions.

This is not a phenomenon peculiar to the Atrebates; it is also manifest amongst the Durotriges (and see p. 197 above). Figure 13.10 is a map showing the distribution of Durotrigan silver staters. Mack 317, and the accompanying quarter-stater coinage, Mack 319. Again, the quarter-staters have a much more confined distribution, with only a few outliers. The full staters, on the other hand, are widely scattered in a manner suggestive of a number of external contacts in adjacent territories.

Is it possible to provide a more detailed account of the boundary situation for the individual tribes than that

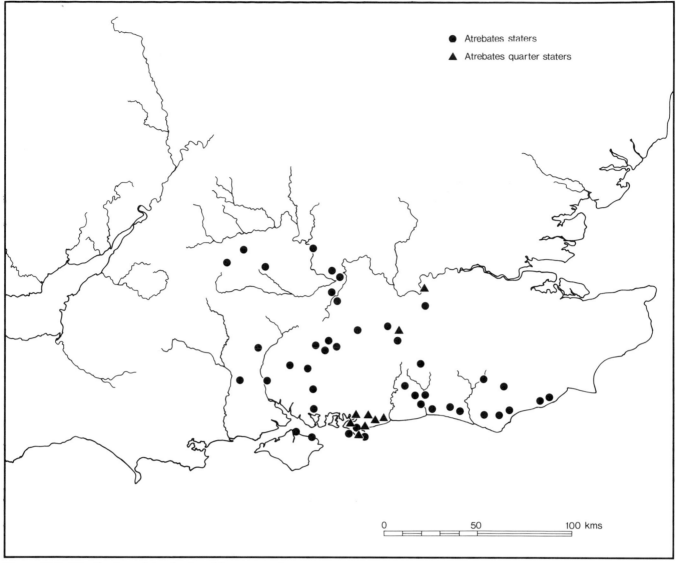

● Atrebates staters

▲ Atrebates quarter staters

0   50   100 kms

Figure 13.8 *Distribution of Atrebatic gold staters and quarter-staters.*

which has been attempted above? It is important when using distribution-maps to be aware of the level of definition that can be achieved. The numerous classes of Dobunnic silver (Allen recognised 11 regular and 6 irregular classes) superficially promise to provide information about the fluctuations of the boundary over time. Each issue has been plotted separately class by class, (Sellwood, forthcoming). The distributions expand and contract, and it would be tempting to suppose that changes in political or socio-economic organization can be inferred. Such a level of detail is, however, inappropriate. The principal impediment lies in the fact that even the earliest classes of coin are often found in post-Iron Age contexts. The chronological bracket within which early Dobunnic silver most frequently occurs on sites is between AD 50 and 100. If these coins were available to circulate in the late first century AD, then it is not unreasonable to suppose that they were still current during the period of the later Dobunnic issues. A gross plot is, therefore, all that it is safe to use at present. One of the most significant factors to emerge from such a map (e.g. Fig. 13.7 above), is the probable existence of two nuclei within the overall distribution. The northern

focus may perhaps be Bagendon, and there appears to be a southern concentration with a centre perhaps at Camerton. The dividing line between the two areas may follow the course the Bristol Avon.

A divide in Dobunnic territory was noticed by D.F. Allen, (1961b, 101–2). This division is between the coins of Corio and those of Bodvoc (Fig. 13.2), believed on stylistic and other grounds to be approximately contemporary. These two issues have almost exclusive distributions, and these were seen by Allen to divide the territory into two sectors. Hodder (1977, 322) has interpreted this division in rather different terms: 'A very clear distinction between central and peripheral zones in the area of distribution of Dobunnic coins is seen in the wider distribution of the Corio coins as opposed to the more central Bodvoc examples'. Although this analysis cannot be refuted on data available at present, the Corio coins are not scattered evenly, but have a southerly concentration, similar to that noted in the distribution of the silver. It might, therefore, be more appropriate to return to Allen's suggestion of the division within Dobunnic territory, although he did not identify the Avon as the possible frontier between them.

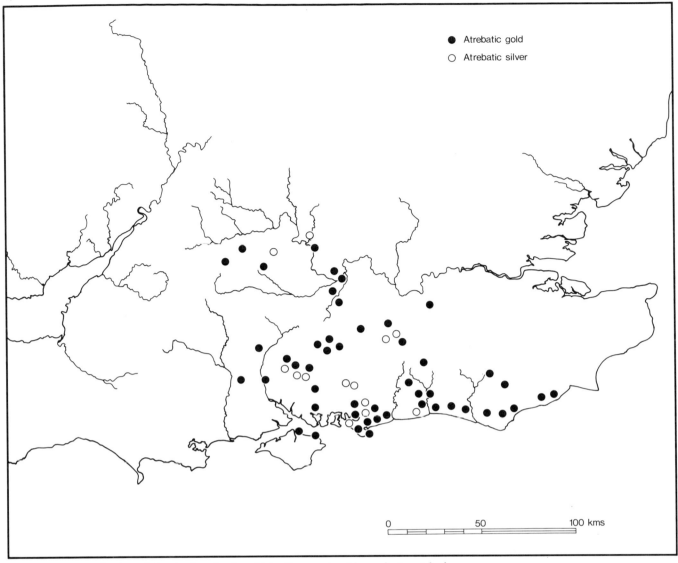

Figure 13.9 *Distribution of Atrebatic coins in which silver and gold are distinguished.*

One further region is distinct amongst the overall distribution-pattern of coins of this tribe; the central eastern Wiltshire area referred to above. This area has been shown by P. Robinson (1977) to have minted its own coinage, which while obviously akin to regular Dobunnic pieces may have different prototypes, is stylistically distinct, and does not circulate in the area in which regular Dobunnic coins are commonly found. Another point of interest is that more Atrebatic coins are found in this area than in regular Dobunnic territory.

It is perhaps possible to identify other sub-tribal groups within the Wessex/Upper Thames block. A group of coins referred to by Allen (1966) as Hampshire thin silver pieces, Mack 321, circulates within a confined area between the Atrebates and the Durotriges, effectively between Hengistbury Head and Portsmouth, extending inland as far as Winchester. Allen dated this silver issue, on the strength of its occurrence in the Le Câtillon hoard, to the mid first century BC. This date would place the coins in the period which precedes the advent of tribal coinage proper amongst the Atrebates and Durotriges. Le Câtillon is now widely regarded (Scheers, 1977, 116; Kent, 1981, 41; Mays, forthcoming)

as having a date within the thirties BC. If this more recent view is accepted, then the group of Hampshire thin silver is contemporary with and separate from at least the earliest period of coin-issuing by the two major tribes. Allen tended to regard these coins as related to the Durotrigan series. Stylistically they are closer to Armorican coins than to British issues; but because of their almost exclusive occurrence in Hampshire, they are here referred to as sub-Durotrigan.

Figure 13.11 shows a possible amendment to the traditional groupings and boundaries in the Wessex/ Upper Thames Valley area. The cohesion of the respective groups allows this sort of exercise, although it is stressed that this is only regarded as an approximation to truth. It is of interest that the principal divisions presented here are replicated on a map produced by Cunliffe (1978, 99, 7.2), Figure 13.12, which plots the distribution of selected pottery-styles in Britain in the first century BC to first century AD. The pottery groups shown here are more rigidly exclusive than any of the coin-distributions. Several points can be made from this coincidence of evidence.

1 The separateness of the southern Dobunnic area

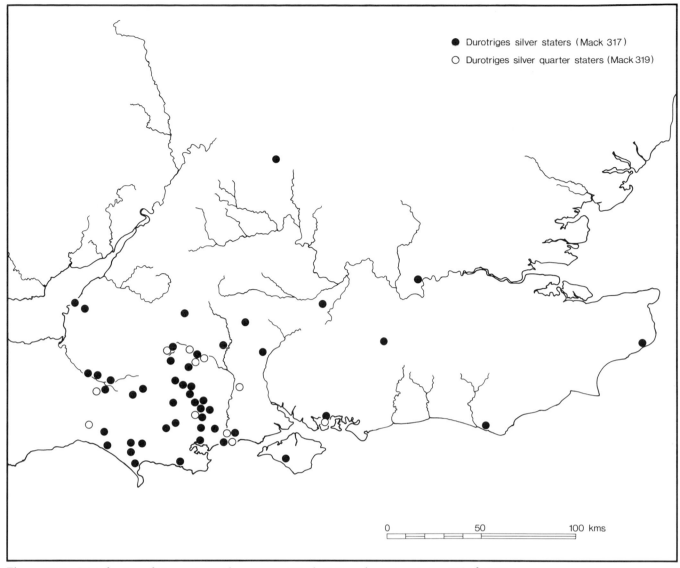

Figure 13.10 *Distribution of Durotrigan silver staters (Mack 317) and quarter-staters (Mack 319).*

from the northern, postulated from the coin-distributions, also occurs on the pottery map. Glastonbury ware of groups 2–5 extends to the valley of the Bristol Avon, with very few findspots beyond.

2 No Durotrigan ware, nor any north and south Atrebatic ware is present in the area over which the thin silver coins circulate.

3 The north and south Atrebatic wares respect the Thames as a northern boundary to their distribution.

4 Atrebatic pottery rather than Glastonbury ware circulates in the central Wiltshire sub-Dobunnic region.

It has become a commonplace that one does not expect artefacts of different types to have similar distributions. As Hodder (1977, 300) states, 'Different classes of artefacts define different levels of association'. This is perhaps too much of a blanket statement, and the key to the problem lies in whether or not artefacts can be regarded as reflecting ethnicity. It is generally accepted that the later, frequently inscribed, issues of British Celtic coins do reflect the given group's consciousness of its own identity and of its separateness from other related groups. This would explain the rigid adherance amongst the Dobunni to the triple-tailed horse reverse

and to the branched emblem on the obverse of seven of the nine issues of staters. It has been often suggested that the Atrebatic vine leaf and the Catuvellaunian wheat-ear that ornament the respective stater issues are in fact tribal insignia, and there is a possibility that some of the latest Icenian coins bear the tribal legend, inscribed in abbreviated form as ECE. The confined distributions of these artefacts is another major point in support of the argument that they are reflectors of ethnicity. Cunliffe refers to the problem of identifying ethnic groups from the archaeological record, specially in a British Iron Age (pre-coinage) situation: 'One of the ways of approach to the problem is by considering symbols which the group displayed in relation to those of adjacent groups. In reality few symbols survive in the archaeological record except in the form of preferred decoration on pottery, and there can be no assurance that pottery decoration always, or even sometimes, reflected on ethnicity'. (1984, 562: but see Cunliffe, this volume). It is suggested that the distribution of haematite-coated ware (550–450 BC) and also of decorated saucepan pottery (300–100 BC) may reflect such ethnic consciousness.

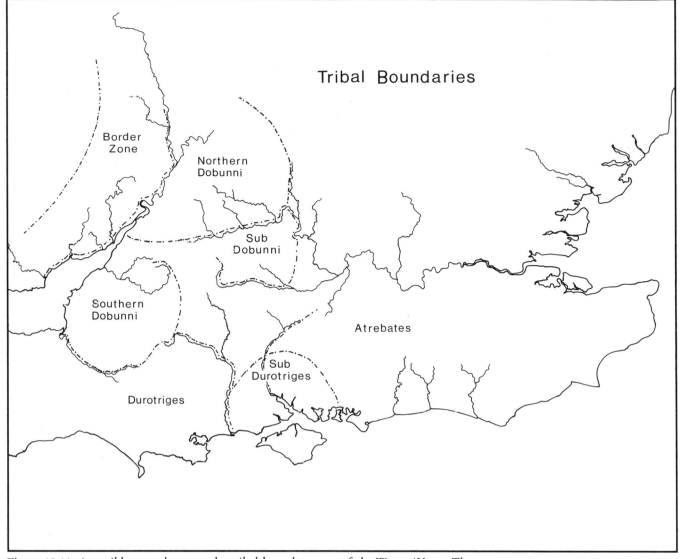

Figure 13.11 *A possible amendment to the tribal boundary map of the Wessex/Upper Thames area.*

If it is acccepted that certain pottery-types define the area of influence of coherent, possibly tribal, groups in the earlier Iron Age, it is not impossible that they do so in the later pre-Roman Iron Age. It may be that coins had completely taken over this function from the pottery, although the tight distributions of the selected ceramics and their coincidence with the proposed tribal boundaries makes this less likely.

Another maxim frequently used in an archaeological milieu is that two convergent hypotheses cannot be regarded as proof. While this is accepted, the ceramic groupings do, nevertheless, add another dimension to the purely numismatic assessment of tribal boundaries within this area.

Appendix 1

The recognition of problems concerning the usage of distribution-maps has generated an extensive literature. Articles specifically concerned with Iron Age coinage include Collis 1971a; Hogg 1971; Collis 1974; Rodwell 1976; Hodder and Orton 1976; Hodder 1977; Rodwell 1981; Collis 1981; Collis and Haselgrove, 1981.

The tenor of these articles ranges from extreme pessimism, ('the recording of Celtic coins with any hope of achieving even a modest level of efficiency, has now become an unobtainable goal' (Rodwall 1981, 50)), to equally extreme optimism ('We can observe the context of our coin finds. What sort of site do they come from — urban, religious, high-class or low-class farms — and what was their context on major sites — high-status areas, trading areas, streets or industrial zones? Is there evidence that different metal types turn up in different contexts . . ., if so what does it mean in terms of exchange systems? (Collis 1981, 53)). Neither of these statements offers a realistic reflection of the data existing at present.

Any assessment of what can fairly be said regarding coin-distributions necessitates a consideration of both statements quoted above. Rodwell's anxiety about the state of the data is based upon extensive fieldwork in Essex. He has suggested that the distribution of Celtic coins in the county is related to neither natural features nor ancient settlements. He therefore invokes modern factors as a principal determinant of the distribution-pattern. He also records that the vast majority of

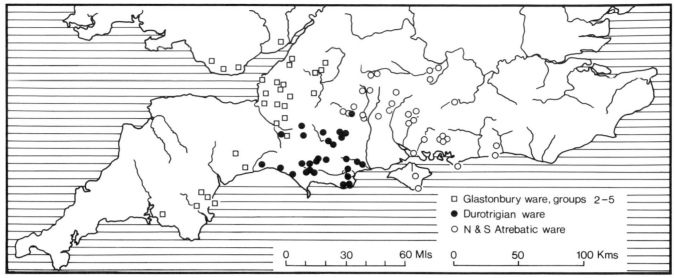

Figure 13.12 *A selection of pottery distributions in the Wessex — Upper Thames area (after Cunliffe 1978).*

Glastonbury ware, groups 2–5
Durotrigian ware
N & S Atrebatic ware

0   30   60 Mls   0   50   100 Kms

reported findspots are for the more attractive gold issues; and the reporting of casual finds is ten times more frequent for gold than other metals. Major sites, such as Camulodunum, and active collectors or archaeologists have a 'magnetic' effect in terms of the coin-finds (see above p. 193), and this has thrown a number of areas into high relief, over-representing their importance relative to the distribution as a whole.

The principal objections that Rodwell makes are countered here by data most of which relate to the Dobunni. The object is not to refute Rodwell's Essex conclusions, but to demonstrate that they cannot be accepted as of general relevance; nor is the Dobunnic evidence looked upon as representative. It will be apparent from the data presented below that Collis's questioning does not represent a practical alternative to the more traditional assessments.

None of the 475 Dobunnic coins with recorded findspots has come from an unequivocally pre-conquest context. The earliest secure date comes from the 1981 season of excavations at Bagendon, Glos. Two class I–J silver coins were found stratified in a pit with samian dated to c. AD 43 (Steve Trow pers. comm.). No coins are site/excavation finds from locations where occupation is known to be of an entirely pre-conquest date, c. 20 coins are from contexts which extend in date from the mid to the late first century AD. 7 coins are from second-century contexts and 1 coin is from a third-century context. Archaeological knowledge of the Dobunnic area is not sufficiently advanced to demonstrate with certainty whether single isolated finds are casual losses, unrelated to contemporary occupation, or not. It is therefore an exercise of limited value to seek a correlation between 'ancient' sites and the coin distribution. The scatter of coins across the distribution-maps is more or less even, although a number of concentrations are evident (discussed below) and there appears to be something of a divide, formed by the Bristol Avon, between the north and south Dobunni. This apparent divide is currently under investigation.

Amongst the Dobunni, silver coins are recovered much more frequently than gold. It might be argued that both are precious metal, but it should be remembered that many of the silver coins are very base and differ little from bronze coins in an unconserved state. A sample of coins from the Index[2] was examined in order to discover, on a more general basis, the trends of recovery. A total of 238 coins have been entered into the Index since late July 1983. In this three-month period, it was found that 73 coins (30.6%) were gold; 137 (57.6%) were silver; 4 (1.7%) were bronze; 19 (8.0%) were potin and 5 (2.1%) were bronze cores of gold-plated contemporary stater forgeries. The dominance of gold over all other metals which has been noted in Essex is not a general phenomenon on the evidence of this sample. The preponderance of silver can be better explained because the Dobunni, Iceni and Durotriges minted large silver issues than by the fact that these coins are of precious metal. Much Celtic silver is base, and when first found would appear little different to bronze. The once-common recording of gold coins at the expense of other metals has been alleviated, if this is an appropriate term, by the extensive use of metal-detectors. The current value of a small bronze or potin coin is sufficiently high to make it well worth salvaging.

The magnetic effect that Camulodunum has exercised over coin-finds since the excavations of the thirties is not a phenomenon encountered at the Dobunnic sites of Bagendon, Salmonsbury or Camerton, although it may be relevant to the Durotrigan sites of Badbury Rings, Maiden Castle and Hengistbury Head, and to the Atrebatic Silchester. The effect of local collectors and museums on coin-distribution-maps is currently under investigation.

Notes

1 The seriousness of any bias depends upon the sort of analysis which is attempted. Collis (1981, 54) observes, in reference to this problem and from the viewpoint of a committed substantivist: 'The problem of sampling-bias is, however, much more damaging to Rodwell's historical approach ... minor gaps in the material are of more

consequence to him than to me, as he relies on the total distributions for his interpretations'. The view put forward here is open to question, particularly since many of the 'gaps' are major rather than minor. In the light of the existing data-base, any analyses undertaken should be flexible and designed to refer to broad generalizations rather than to the, as yet, inestimable detail.

2 The Index of British Celtic coins, established 25 years ago by Professor S.S. Frere and D.F. Allen, and housed in the Institute of Archaeology, Oxford, aims to record every Celtic coin discovered in Britain. Each coin has a card on which is mounted a 2/1 photograph of its obverse and reverse and details of type, weight, findspot location and current owner.

Note on distribution-maps

The bases for all the distribution-maps, with the exception of those of Dobunnic coins, are Allen's gazetteer (1961, 145–285) and Haselgrove's supplementary gazetteer (1978). For the Dobunni, all findspots from the Index of a date later than 1977 have been included.

References

ALLEN, D.F. 1944: The Belgic Dynasties of Britain and their coins. *Archaeologia* 90, 1–46.

ALLEN, D.F. 1961: A study of the Dobunnic coinage. In Clifford, E.M., *Bagendon: A Belgic Oppidum a record of the excavations 1954–56* (Cambridge), 75–146.

ALLEN, D.F. 1966: Les pièces d'argent minces du comté de Hampshire: nouveau lien entre la Gaule celtique et la Grande-Bretagne. *Revue Numismatique* 7, 79–93.

CAESAR, J: *The conquest of Gaul.* (Translation by S.A. Handford. First edition 1951. Penguin books).

COLLIS, J.R. 1971a: Functional and theoretical interpretations of British coinage. *World Archaeology* 3.1, 71–83.

COLLIS, J.R. 1971b: Markets and Money. In Jesson, M. and Hill, D. (editors), *The Iron Age and its Hillforts* (Southampton), 97–103.

COLLIS, J.R. 1974: A functionalist approach to pre-Roman coinage. In Casey, P.J. and Reece, R. (editors), *Coins and the archaeologist* (Oxford, BAR 40, 1–11.

COLLIS, J.R. 1981: Coinage, Oppida and the rise of Belgic power: a reply. In Cunliffe (editor) 1981, 53–5.

COLLIS, J.R. and HASELGROVE, C. 1981: A computer-based information storage and retrieval scheme for Iron Age coin finds in Britain. In Cunliffe (editor) 1981, 57–60.

CUNLIFFE, B.W. 1973: The late pre-Roman Iron Age c. 100 BC–AD 43. In Crittal, E. (editor), *A History of Wiltshire* vol. I, part 2 (Oxford), 426–438.

CUNLIFFE, B.W. (editor) 1981: *Coinage and Society in Britain and Gaul: some current problems* (London, CBA Res. Rep. 38).

CUNLIFFE, B.W. 1981: Money and society in pre-Roman Britain. In Cunliffe (editor) 1981, 29–39.

CUNLIFFE, B.W. 1984: *Danebury: an Iron Age Hillfort in Hampshire* vol. 2 (London, CBA Res. Rep. 52).

HASELGROVE, C. 1976: External trade as a stimulus to urbanisation. In Cunliffe, B.W. and Rowley, R.T. (editors), *Oppida: the beginnings of urbanisation in Barbarian Europe* (Oxford, BAR S11), 25–49.

HASELGORVE, C. 1978: *Supplementary Gazetteer of find-spots of Celtic coins in Britain, 1977* Occasional Paper No. 11a, Institute of Archaeology, 31–34, Gordon Square, London, WC1H OPY.

HOGG, A.H.A. 1971: Some aspects of surface fieldwork. In Jesson, M. and Hill, D. (editors), *The Iron Age and its Hillforts* (Southampton), 105–25.

HODDER, I. and ORTON, C. 1976: *Spatial analysis in Archaeology* (Cambridge).

HODDER, I. 1977: Some new directions in Spatial Analysis of Archaeological data at the regional scale (macro). In Clarke, D.L. (editor), *Spatial Archaeology* (London), 223–342.

KENT, J.P.C. 1981: The origins of coinage in Britain. In Cunliffe (editor) 1981, 41–43.

MACK, R.P. 1975: *The coinage of Ancient Britain* (Third edition: London).

MAYS, M., forthcoming: *A social and economic study of the Durotriges, with particular reference to the coinage, (c. 150 BC–AD 150)* (Oxford, D.Phil. Thesis).

RIVET, A.L.F. and SMITH, C. 1979: *The Place-names of Roman Britain* (London).

ROBINSON, P. 1977: A local Iron Age coinage in silver and perhaps gold in Wiltshire. *British Numismatic Journal* 47, 5–21.

RODWELL, W. 1976: Coinage, Oppida and the rise of Belgic power in south eastern Britain. In Cunliffe, B.W. and Rowley, R.T. (editors), *Oppida: the beginnings of urbanisation in Barbarian Europe* (Oxford, BAR S11), 181–367.

RODWELL, W. 1981: Lost and found: the archaeology of find-spots of Celtic coins. In Cunliffe (editor) 1981, 43–52.

SCHEERS, S. 1977: *Traité de Numismatique Celtique II. La Gaule Belgique* (Paris).

SELLWOOD, D.G.J. 1963: Experiments in Greek minting technique. *Numismatic Chronicle* 7th series no. 3, 226–30.

SELLWOOD, L.C., forthcoming: *An archaeological and numismatic survey of the Dobunni, c. 50 BC–AD 50* (Oxford, D.Phil. Thesis).

THOMPSON, R.H. 1976: Bibliography. Published work of Derek Fortrose Allen. *Numismatic Chronicle* 136, 259–271.

Index of Subjects

houses (huts) *continued*
   floors 63, 94, 96
   gullies 63, 89
   in hillforts 27
   internal features 94, 96
   paired 63
   post-built 15, 57, 100
   'ring-groove' 91, 93
   stake-walled 93
hunting 48, 115
   dogs 114

invasion (migration) 32–3, 36, 38
iron 13, 146, 179, 182
   carburized 155, 156
   export of 132, 133, 151
   extraction sites 131
   increasing use of 153
   introduction of 130, 141
   prestige goods 130
   smithing *148*, 149, 152
   sources of ore 13, 132, 146, 147, *150*, 152
   tools 9, 135, 154, *155*

kinship 76–7, 82

lead 127, 132, 133, 134, 137
linear ditch-systems 3
livestock 30
loomweight 32, 63, 64, 107, 168

manure 112, 116
manuring 31
marginal land 4
meat
   dog 114
   production 106–7, 112, 115
metal analysis 129, 130, 131, 132, 133, 143, 158
   of brooches 134
metal imports 130, 132
metalwork 9, 131
   Carp's Tongue 127, 128, 129, 130
   contexts of discovery 178, 182
   disposal in rivers/water 142, 178–88
   effects of Roman Conquest on 143
   Ewart Park 127, 128, 129, 130, 139, 140
   in hillforts 143
   imported 143
   in settlements 142
   Wilburton 127, 128, 140
milk production 107, 109, 113, 115
mirrors 137
mode of production 75, 173
mollusca 1, 3, 6

Neolithic
   crop records 122
   monuments 1

oppida 34, 51, 143, 149, 184
   coinage in 194, 195

pastoral farming 6, 7, 9, 65, 83, 84, 85, 109, 110, 170
   camps 74
   stress from overgrazing 116
peat bog 3, 4, 8
plant remains, carbonised 120, 122, 123
ploughing 3, 110, 114, 123
ploughs 115, 120
ploughwash 6
podzols 3, 8
pollen 1, 9, 49, 120
   analysis 3, 4, 6, 28
ponds 3, 4
population
   growth 7, 9, 31, 38, 65
   level 31
pottery
   burnished 170
   decorated 13, 14, 32, 39, 170, *171, 172, 173*
   Deverel–Rimbury 13
   Early Iron Age 13, *14, 20*, 39
   and ethnicity 32
   fabric variation 174, *174*, 175
   Glastonbury ware 201
   haematite coated 18, 173
   Late Iron Age 33, 34
   life cycle of 162
   Malvernian 64, 170, 173
   Middle Iron Age 23
   recovery of 163, 164
   redeposition of 164, 165, *166*, 167
   saucepan 23, 24, *26*, 32, 36
   in Upper Thames region 64, 162–76
   uses of 169

quernstones 64

radiocarbon dating 5, 9, 13, 25, 64, 119, 122, 131, 134
ranch boundaries 30
reaping-sickles 120, 131, 141, 146, 158, 159
research programmes 12
riding
   gear 142, 186
   horses 114
ring-ditches 4
ritual complexes 4
Roman Conquest 34, 35, 51, 65, 75, 143, 178, 182

salt 13, 27, 64
sampling strategies 54, 63, 163
seasonal occupation 6, 83, 110, 116
settlement
   classification 57, 73–4
   density 46, 151
   distribution 28, 78–9
   hierarchy 30, 65, 184
shale 13, 27, 33
shellfish 48–9

shrine/temple/sanctuary 27, 182, 186, 188
   animal bones at 113, 187
slaves 33, 36
slingstones 20, 30, 31
social relations of production 76–7, 80, *82*, 85, 86
soil 1, 4
   analysis 3
   deterioration 7, 8, 31, 38, 121, 122
   erosion 3, 4, 8, 9
   loam 4
   loess 1, 4, 7
solders 137
spindle-whorl 32, 63, 107
steel 156–7
storage 64
   grain (corn) 30, 32, 34, 57
   pits 3, 6, 7, 18, 19, 20, 27, 57, 62
structures
   four-post 15, 17, 20, 27, 63, 98, 100
   rectangular 48, 96, 98
swords 65, 127, 130, 136, 141, 152, 179, 181, 188
   burial 64
   scabbard 132, 143, 182

textile production 63, 64
tin 126, 129, 130, 132, 137
   export of 131
tooth-wear 107
   cattle *108*
   pig *113*
trade 170
   in bronze 13, 31, 130, 139
   and coinage 185
   cross-Channel 31, 38, 130
   with Gaul 33
   in goats 113
   in pottery 164, 169, 170, 173
   in wine 33
transhumance 84
tribe 84–5
   boundaries 191, 192–3, *202*

urbanisation 35

valley, dry 3
valleys, drowned 1

warfare 185, 186, 187
weapons 139, 179, 184, 185, 187
weaving 64, 107
   combs 32
weeds
   acidophile 121
   of damp ground 121
welding 152
wine 33, 36
woodland 1, 3, 4, 6, 59, 65
   decline in Wessex 31
   for iron production 149
   regeneration 3, 4, 9
   secondary 4
   use by pigs 110
wool 27, 32, 107

Index of Place and Proper Names